Social Security Programs and Retirement around the World

**A National Bureau
of Economic Research
Conference Report**

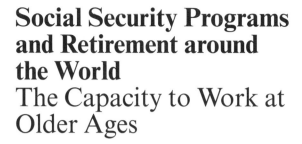

Social Security Programs and Retirement around the World
The Capacity to Work at Older Ages

Edited by **David A. Wise**

The University of Chicago Press

Chicago and London

The University of Chicago Press, Chicago 60637
The University of Chicago Press, Ltd., London
© 2017 by the National Bureau of Economic Research
All rights reserved. No part of this book may be used or reproduced
in any manner whatsoever without written permission, except in the
case of brief quotations in critical articles and reviews. For more
information, contact the University of Chicago Press, 1427 E. 60th St.,
Chicago, IL 60637.
Published 2017
Printed in the United States of America

26 25 24 23 22 21 20 19 18 17   1 2 3 4 5

ISBN-13: 978-0-226-44287-7   (cloth)
ISBN-13: 978-0-226-44290-7   (e-book)
DOI: 10.7208/chicago/9780226442907.001.0001

Library of Congress Cataloging-in-Publication Data

Names: Wise, David A., editor.
Title: Social security programs and retirement around the world : the
    capacity to work at older ages / edited by David A. Wise.
Other titles: National Bureau of Economic Research conference report.
Description: Chicago : The University of Chicago Press, 2017. | Series:
    National Bureau of Economic Research conference report | Includes
    index.
Identifiers: LCCN 2016041561 | ISBN 9780226442877 (cloth : alk.
    paper) | ISBN 9780226442907 (e-book)
Subjects: LCSH: Post-retirement employment—Health aspects—
    Econometric models. | Health expectancy—Econometric models.
    | Older people—Health and hygiene—Econometric models. |
    Older people—Employment—Econometric models. | Age and
    employment—Econometric models. | Post-retirement employment—
    Health aspects—Cross-cultural studies.
Classification: LCC RA408.A3 S64 2017 | DDC 368.3—dc23 LC
    record available at https://lccn.loc.gov/2016041561

♾ This paper meets the requirements of ANSI/NISO Z39.48–1992
(Permanence of Paper).

**Relation of the Directors to the
Work and Publications of the
National Bureau of Economic Research**

1. The object of the NBER is to ascertain and present to the economics profession, and to the public more generally, important economic facts and their interpretation in a scientific manner without policy recommendations. The Board of Directors is charged with the responsibility of ensuring that the work of the NBER is carried on in strict conformity with this object.

2. The President shall establish an internal review process to ensure that book manuscripts proposed for publication DO NOT contain policy recommendations. This shall apply both to the proceedings of conferences and to manuscripts by a single author or by one or more co-authors but shall not apply to authors of comments at NBER conferences who are not NBER affiliates.

3. No book manuscript reporting research shall be published by the NBER until the President has sent to each member of the Board a notice that a manuscript is recommended for publication and that in the President's opinion it is suitable for publication in accordance with the above principles of the NBER. Such notification will include a table of contents and an abstract or summary of the manuscript's content, a list of contributors if applicable, and a response form for use by Directors who desire a copy of the manuscript for review. Each manuscript shall contain a summary drawing attention to the nature and treatment of the problem studied and the main conclusions reached.

4. No volume shall be published until forty-five days have elapsed from the above notification of intention to publish it. During this period a copy shall be sent to any Director requesting it, and if any Director objects to publication on the grounds that the manuscript contains policy recommendations, the objection will be presented to the author(s) or editor(s). In case of dispute, all members of the Board shall be notified, and the President shall appoint an ad hoc committee of the Board to decide the matter; thirty days additional shall be granted for this purpose.

5. The President shall present annually to the Board a report describing the internal manuscript review process, any objections made by Directors before publication or by anyone after publication, any disputes about such matters, and how they were handled.

6. Publications of the NBER issued for informational purposes concerning the work of the Bureau, or issued to inform the public of the activities at the Bureau, including but not limited to the NBER Digest and Reporter, shall be consistent with the object stated in paragraph 1. They shall contain a specific disclaimer noting that they have not passed through the review procedures required in this resolution. The Executive Committee of the Board is charged with the review of all such publications from time to time.

7. NBER working papers and manuscripts distributed on the Bureau's web site are not deemed to be publications for the purpose of this resolution, but they shall be consistent with the object stated in paragraph 1. Working papers shall contain a specific disclaimer noting that they have not passed through the review procedures required in this resolution. The NBER's web site shall contain a similar disclaimer. The President shall establish an internal review process to ensure that the working papers and the web site do not contain policy recommendations, and shall report annually to the Board on this process and any concerns raised in connection with it.

8. Unless otherwise determined by the Board or exempted by the terms of paragraphs 6 and 7, a copy of this resolution shall be printed in each NBER publication as described in paragraph 2 above.

Contents

Acknowledgments   ix

Introduction   1
Courtney Coile, Kevin Milligan,
and David A. Wise

1. **Work Capacity and Longer Working Lives in Belgium**   35
Alain Jousten and Mathieu Lefebvre

2. **Health Capacity to Work at Older Ages: Evidence from Canada**   59
Kevin Milligan and Tammy Schirle

3. **Health Capacity to Work at Older Ages in Denmark**   85
Paul Bingley, Nabanita Datta Gupta,
and Peder J. Pedersen

4. **Health Capacity to Work at Older Ages in France**   111
Didier Blanchet, Eve Caroli, Corinne Prost,
and Muriel Roger

5. **Healthy, Happy, and Idle: Estimating the Health Capacity to Work at Older Ages in Germany**   149
Hendrik Jürges, Lars Thiel,
and Axel Börsch-Supan

6.   Health Capacity to Work at Older Ages:
            Evidence from Italy   181
            Agar Brugiavini, Giacomo Pasini,
            and Guglielmo Weber

7.   Health Capacity to Work at Older Ages:
            Evidence from Japan   219
            Emiko Usui, Satoshi Shimizutani,
            and Takashi Oshio

8.   Work Capacity at Older Ages in
            the Netherlands   243
            Adriaan Kalwij, Arie Kapteyn,
            and Klaas de Vos

9.   Health Capacity to Work at Older Ages:
            Evidence from Spain   269
            Pilar García-Gómez, Sergi Jiménez-Martín,
            and Judit Vall Castelló

10.   Health, Work Capacity, and Retirement
            in Sweden   301
            Per Johansson, Lisa Laun, and Mårten Palme

11.   Health Capacity to Work at Older Ages:
            Evidence from the United Kingdom   329
            James Banks, Carl Emmerson,
            and Gemma Tetlow

12.   Health Capacity to Work at Older Ages:
            Evidence from the United States   359
            Courtney Coile, Kevin Milligan,
            and David A. Wise

            Contributors   395
            Author Index   399
            Subject Index   403

Acknowledgments

Funding for this project was provided by the National Institute on Aging, grant numbers P01-AG005842 and P30-AG012810 to the National Bureau of Economic Research. We thank two anonymous reviewers for detailed and thoughtful comments. The views expressed herein are those of the authors and do not necessarily reflect the views of the National Institute on Aging, the National Institutes of Health, or the National Bureau of Economic Research.

Introduction

Courtney Coile, Kevin Milligan, and David A. Wise

Project Overview

Through the coordination of work of a team of analysts in twelve countries for nearly twenty years, the International Social Security (ISS) project has used the vast differences in social security programs across countries as a natural laboratory to study the effects of retirement program provisions on the labor force participation of older persons. This analysis is the seventh phase of the ongoing project, and it is focused on the health capacity to work at older ages.

To summarize the findings of the prior phases: The **first** phase of the project described the retirement incentives inherent in plan provisions and documented the strong relationship across countries between social security incentives to retire and the proportion of older persons out of the labor force (Gruber and Wise 1999).

The **second** phase, which was based on microeconomic analysis of the

Courtney Coile is a professor of economics at Wellesley College. She is a research associate of the National Bureau of Economic Research and an associate director of the NBER's Retirement Research Center. Kevin Milligan is professor of economics in the Vancouver School of Economics, University of British Columbia, and a research associate of the National Bureau of Economic Research. David A. Wise is the John F. Stambaugh Professor of Political Economy at the Kennedy School of Government at Harvard University. He is the area director of Health and Retirement Programs and director of the Program on the Economics of Aging at the National Bureau of Economic Research.

This chapter is part of the National Bureau of Economic Research's International Social Security (ISS) project, which is supported by the National Institute on Aging (grant P01 AG012810).The authors are indebted to Maurice Dalton for expert research assistance. We also thank the members of the other country teams in the ISS project for comments that helped to shape this chapter. For acknowledgments, sources of research support, and disclosure of the authors' material financial relationships, if any, please see http://www.nber.org/chapters /c13737.ack.

relationship between a person's decision to retire and the social security and other program incentives faced by that person, documented that incentives are a significant determinant of retirement decisions. We also considered the implications of increasing retirement program eligibility ages and showed that these changes would have large effects on employment at older ages (Gruber and Wise 2004).

The **third** phase (Gruber and Wise 2007) demonstrated the consequent fiscal implications that extending labor force participation would have on net program costs—reducing government social security benefit payments and increasing government tax revenues.

In the **fourth** phase (Gruber and Wise 2010) we focused on the concern that removing incentives to retire from social security might reduce job opportunities for youth and lead to higher youth unemployment. We found no evidence to support the "boxed economy" proposition that higher employment of older persons is associated with lower employment of youth.

The **fifth** phase (Wise 2012) shifted the focus to disability insurance (DI) and health. We found that changes in DI participation were more closely linked to DI reforms than to changes in health and that DI reforms often had a very large effect on the labor force participation of older workers.

The **sixth** phase (Wise 2016) extended the methodology used in the second phase to study the effect of DI as well as SS program incentives on retirement. We found that individuals are very responsive to retirement incentives arising from the structure of SS and DI programs and that reducing access to DI benefits would increase labor supply.

As we describe in more detail below, this **seventh** phase of the project explores the health capacity of individuals to work at older ages. Fiscal challenges facing social security and other government programs may lead to policy changes that incorporate the expectation of longer work lives, such as increases in the social security early or normal retirement ages. In this volume we ask: Are individuals healthy enough to increase their labor supply at older ages?

The results of the ongoing project are the product of analyses conducted for each country by analysts in that country. Researchers who have participated in this phase of the project are listed first below; those who have participated in prior phases are listed second in italics.

Belgium: Alain Jousten, Mathieu Lefèbvre, *Sergio Perelman, Pierre Pestieau, Raphaël Desmet, Arnaud Dellis,* and *Jean-Philippe Stijns*

Canada: Kevin Milligan, Tammy Schirle, *Michael Baker,* and *Jonathan Gruber*

Denmark: Paul Bingley, Nabanita Datta Gupta, Peder J. Pedersen, and *Michael Jørgensen*

France: Didier Blanchet, Eve Caroli, Corinne Prost, Muriel Roger, *Luc Behaghel, Melika Ben Salem, Antoine Bozio, Thierry Debrand, Ronan Mahieu, Louis-Paul Pelé,* and *Emmanuelle Walraet*

Germany: Axel Börsch-Supan, Hendrik Jürges, Lars Thiel, *Tabea Bucher-Koenen, Simone Kohnz, Giovanni Mastrobuoni, Johannes Rausch, Reinhold Schnabel,* and *Morten Schuth*
Italy: Agar Brugiavini, Giacomo Pasini, Guglielmo Weber, and *Franco Peracchi*
Japan: Takashi Oshio, Satoshi Shimizutani, Emiko Usui, *Mayu Fujii, Akiko Sato Oishi,* and *Naohiro Yashiro*
Netherlands: Adriaan Kalwij, Arie Kapteyn, and Klaas de Vos
Spain: Pilar García Gómez, Sergi Jiménez-Martín, Judit Vall-Castelló, *Michele Boldrín,* and *Franco Peracchi*
Sweden: Per Johansson, Lisa Laun, Mårten Palme, and *Ingemar Svensson*
United Kingdom: James Banks, Carl Emmerson, Gemma Tetlow, *Richard Blundell, Antonio Bozio, Paul Johnson, Costas Meghir,* and *Sarah Smith*
United States: Courtney Coile, Kevin Milligan, David Wise, *Jonathan Gruber,* and *Peter Diamond*

An important goal of the project has been to present results that are as comparable as possible across countries. Thus the chapters for each phase are prepared according to a detailed template that we developed in consultation with country participants. In this introduction, we summarize the collective results of the country analyses and borrow freely from the country chapters. In large part, however, the results presented in the introduction could only be conveyed by combined analysis of the data from each of the countries. The country chapters themselves present much more detail for each country and, in addition to the common analyses performed by all countries, often present country-specific analysis relevant to each particular country.

Introduction to the Seventh Phase

The interaction of health and work at older ages is of high policy concern. Of late, social security normal retirement ages have been raised in many developed countries, with additional increases in progress or under discussion. These reforms will not increase labor supply at older ages if it is the case that health is a strongly limiting factor in older-worker employment decisions. Moreover, on a broader policy scale the funding of retirement consumption through savings of any kind becomes more challenging when longevity is expanding rapidly. A deeper understanding of how we might split the bounty of increased longevity between work years and retirement years can assist policymakers with broad policy issues on labor market and pension regulation and incentives.

In this seventh phase of the International Social Security project, we consider the capacity to work at older ages. In particular, we consider whether the health of older persons would allow them to work longer. It is important to emphasize at the outset that the "health capacity to work" is not

intended to suggest how long people should work or what typical retirement ages should be in various countries. The age at which a person retires
is strongly influenced by early and normal legislated retirement ages in his
or her country, and also by individual health, employment opportunities,
and other circumstances. The health capacity to work, however, might be
considered in conjunction with potential increases in a country's statutory
retirement age. We will see that the health capacity to work at older ages is
typically much greater than actual employment. We begin with background
information and then explain the methods that we use to estimate the health
capacity to work at older ages.

To help to put the analysis in context, it is useful to have in mind that
employment rates in the ISS countries declined very substantially in the
decades leading up to the 1990s. As shown in table I.1, a majority of the
ISS countries saw the employment rate of men age sixty to sixty-four fall
by at least one-third, and sometimes far more, between its peak in the 1960s
or 1970s and its trough in the 1990s.[1] Thus, if peak employment rates of
men sixty to sixty-four are taken as a measure of the capacity to work, then
employment in the 1990s was much less than the capacity to work.

Indeed, employment has increased substantially in each country between
the 1990s and the present, as can be seen in the bottom row of table I.1.
Increases were greatest, in percentage terms, among those countries with
the lowest employment rates at the trough. For example, in four countries
with employment rates of 10 to 30 percent at their lowest point—Belgium,
France, Germany, and the Netherlands—employment has more than
doubled (or risen by 80 percent, in Belgium's case). Most other countries
have experienced increases of about 40 percent. In Japan, where employment
of men sixty to sixty-four never dipped below 64 percent, employment has
risen by about one-sixth; the United States has experienced a similar rise.
The trends in employment over this period are also shown in figure I.1.

The key takeaway is that employment of men ages sixty to sixty-four has
changed a great deal from the early 1960s and 1970s to 2014, with substantial decline until the mid-1990s and then substantial increases thereafter in
many countries. This decline likely reflects a variety of factors. Changes in
retirement incentives due to reforms of social security and disability insurance programs may have played an important role. Previous work in the
International Social Security project (especially Gruber and Wise 1999, 2004
and Wise 2016) has shown that differences in program incentives can explain
much of the differences in aggregate labor force participation across countries at a point in time, and also that individual-level incentives are strongly
related to retirement decisions. Many countries have raised eligibility ages

1. Note that the data series used in table I.1 starts in different years for different countries;
because employment is generally declining during this period, it is likely that the drop in employment would be larger in some countries if earlier data were available. On a related note, employment declines in the ISS countries typically began before the 1960s, so measuring the decline in
employment relative to an earlier period would show an even steeper decline.

Table 1.1 Employment rates of men ages sixty to sixty-four by country, selected years (1963–2014)

Year	Belgium (%)	Canada (%)	Denmark (%)	France (%)	Germany (%)	Italy (%)	Japan (%)	Netherlands (%)	Spain (%)	Sweden (%)	United Kingdom (%)	United States (%)
1963	—	—	—	—	—	—	—	—	—	83.1	—	77.2
1968	—	—	—	—	—	—	80.8	—	—		—	
1970	—	—	—	—	70.1	47.8		—	—		—	
1971	—	—	—	—				72.3	—		—	
1972	—	—	—	—					76.4		—	
1976	—	63.7	—	—							—	
1983	27.4		—	28.2								
1984			48.6								51.5	
1987												
1993								20.4			44.8	
1994					26.2							50.5
1995		39.9							36.7			
1996												
1998	16.0		39.7	10.4								
2002							64.0			50.0		
2005						27.6						
2008								58.8	46.8		58.4	
2013										69.6		
2014	28.5	55.4	55.7	25.3	59.4	39.2	74.3					59.0
Percent decline	−41.7	−37.2	−18.3	−63.1	−62.6	−42.3	−20.8	−71.8	−52.0	−39.8	−13.1	−34.6
Percent increase	78.7	38.7	40.4	143.2	126.5	41.9	16.0	187.9	27.6	39.2	30.3	17.0

Source: The OECD (http://stats.oecd.org/Index.aspx?QueryId=67615).

Notes: Dashes indicate years where data is not available. Years displayed on the table show the initial peak, trough, and recent peak in all countries, and are correspondingly divided into three periods. Percent decline is the percent drop in employment between the maximum value observed during the first period (1963–1984) and the minimum value in the second period (1987–2005). Because the data series starts in different years for the various countries and employment is generally declining during this period, it is likely that the percent decline would be larger for some countries if earlier years of data were available. Percent increase is the percentage rise in employment between the minimum value during the second period (1987–2005) and the maximum value in the third period (2008–2014).

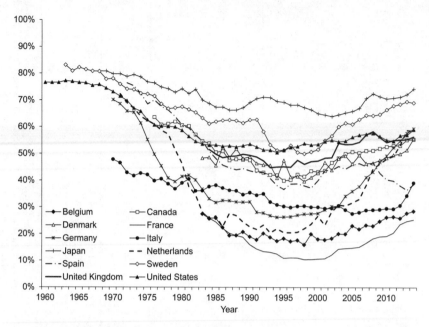

Fig. I.1   Employment rates of men ages sixty to sixty-four by country (1960–2014)
Source: The OECD (http://stats.oecd.org//Index.aspx?QueryId=67615).
Note: Each line shows the employment rate (number employed divided by population) for males between ages sixty and sixty-four.

or reduced benefit generosity for social security and tightened eligibility for disability insurance in recent years. Estimating how much of the increase in participation shown in figure I.1 can be explained by these changes is a promising area for future work. There are other explanations as well, including changes in wages, employer-provided benefits, the return to savings, and other economic factors such as swings in labor demand for older workers. Moreover, the changes might also be related to changes in health. It is this last possibility on which we focus in this phase of the project—how much the changes in employment might be explained by changes in the health capacity to work.

We use two complementary approaches to evaluate the health capacity to work. The first is based on changes in the relationship between mortality and employment over time and is referred to as the Milligan-Wise (MW) method, building on a previous study (Milligan and Wise 2015). In this approach, a decrease in mortality may be thought of as an increase in health and thus as an increase in the capacity to work. The second method is based on a comparison of the health and employment of older and slightly younger individuals and is based on the work of Cutler, Meara, and Richards-Shubik (2013); we refer to this the Cutler et al. (or CMR) method. This approach projects work capacity by first estimating the relationship between health (and other individual attributes) and employment for individuals age fifty to fifty-four, and then using those estimates along with the actual health (and other) characteristics of older individuals to predict their ability to work. Predicted employment is compared to actual employment in older age groups to estimate the additional capacity to work based on health. A third approach explores improvements in self-assessed health (SAH) over time by level of education. While this method does not yield direct estimates of the health capacity to work like the other two methods, it may be used to infer whether the ability to work at older ages is evolving differentially by socioeconomic status. We discuss the advantages, limitations, and results from each method in turn.

The Milligan-Wise Method

The Milligan-Wise method focuses on the relationship between mortality rates and employment rates. The risk of mortality in a given year at a given age is taken as a proxy for health status. This is obviously a crude proxy, but it does carry two advantages. The first is measurement. The binary nature of mortality lessens the burden of measurement compared to more subtle health measures that might vary across time, across surveys, and across countries. Moreover, because population data can be used, there is no sampling variation to contend with. The second advantage is availability. Few countries have detailed, consistent health surveys extending back to the 1970s. Using mortality, which is available for long time periods across countries, unlocks the potential of longer-run analysis.

While these advantages are clear, it is appropriate to note the limitations of this measure as well. First, the crudeness of mortality risk as a proxy for health capacity may be a concern. Our CMR analysis, described in the next section, complements the MW analysis by providing an alternative method of estimating work capacity that relies on detailed individual health data. Second, the MW approach is not well suited to estimate health capacity for women because cohorts of women reaching retirement ages in the 1970s were much less likely to have had a career than their counterparts today, making them a poor comparison group for calculating work capacity. We therefore do not report results for women using the MW approach, but do report results for women using the CMR analysis in the following section. Finally, given the population-level nature of the MW analysis, we cannot look at the within-country heterogeneity to see if the mortality-employment relationship differs by socioeconomic status. Our work on education levels and self-assessed health and mortality, highlighted in the last section of this introduction, provides some more analysis on that question of heterogeneity.

In figure I.2, we illustrate the MW method using the case of the United States. Beginning with the left-hand figure, the top dark line shows the relationship between mortality and employment that existed for men in the United States in 1977. The lower lighter line shows the relationship between

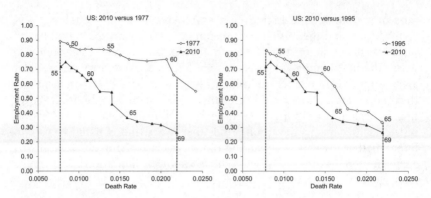

Fig. I.2   Employment versus mortality of men in the United States (selected years)
Source: Chapter 12, this volume (data from the Current Population Survey and the Human Mortality Database).

mortality and employment thirty-three years later, in 2010. In 2010, at age fifty-five, the mortality rate was 0.78 percent and the employment rate was 71.8 percent. In 1977, a mortality rate of 0.78 was experienced at age forty-nine, when the employment rate was 89.1 percent. Thus, if we ask how much more people in 2010 could work if they worked as much as those in 1977 with the same mortality rate, the answer would be 17.3 percent, the difference in the two employment rates. Repeating the calculation at age sixty-nine, in 2010 the mortality rate was 2.19 percent and the employment rate was 26.5 percent. In 1977, a mortality rate of 2.19 percent was experienced at age sixty-one, when the employment rate was 64.4 percent. This suggests that the additional work capacity at age sixty-nine is 37.9 percent.

We make similar calculations at every age and report these values in table I.2, averaging across age groups. We find additional work capacity of 15.6 percent at ages fifty-five to fifty-nine, 27.0 percent at ages sixty to sixty-four, and 41.8 percent at ages sixty-five to sixty-nine. The fact that work capacity is rising with age can be seen on the figure in the increasing divergence of the darker and lighter lines as age increases. On average, total employment of men ages fifty-five to sixty-nine was 28.1 percent lower in 2010 than it would have been if individuals worked as much as those with the same mortality worked in 1977.

The right half of figure I.2 repeats this exercise using the employment-mortality relationship that existed in 1995 rather than 1977 as the basis for comparison. Using the methodology described above, total employment of men ages fifty-five to sixty-nine in 2010 was 12.2 percent lower than it would have been if individuals worked as much as those with the same mortality in 1995. We chose 1995 for a more recent comparison year because, as shown in figure I.1, the employment rate of men ages sixty to sixty-four in the United States declined from 1960 to 1995 and then began to increase, from

Table I.2   Additional work capacity for men in the United States (MW method)

Age group	Employment rate in 2010 (%)	Employment rate in 1977 at same death rate (%)	Additional employment capacity (%)
55–59	70.5	86.0	15.6
60–64	56.2	83.2	27.0
65–69	32.3	74.1	41.8
55–69	53.0	81.1	28.1

Source: Chapter 12, this volume (authors' calculations).

51.3 percent in 1995 to 55.1 percent in 2010.[2] Our analysis suggests that even though employment rose between 1995 and 2010, people in 2010 still worked less than their counterparts in 1995 with the same mortality, as employment did not increase by enough to keep up with mortality gains.

Comparable figures for men in the remaining eleven countries are shown in figure I.3, with the earlier comparison year (1977 or similar) on the left-hand side and the more recent comparison year (1995 or similar) on the right-hand side.

A number of findings are apparent from these figures. First, all countries exhibit substantial additional capacity to work when we use the employment of those with the same mortality rate in the earlier period (1977 or similar) as a basis for comparison. To further illustrate this, we take the additional work capacity at each age (measured as the vertical distance between the darker and lighter lines) and sum these values from ages fifty-five to sixty-nine to arrive at an estimate of the total additional years of work capacity over this age range.[3] As reported in table I.3, these values range from 3.2 years for Sweden to 8.4 years for the United Kingdom, with an average of 5.5 years across all countries. These values are quite large when compared to the actual average years of work over ages fifty-five to sixty-nine in 2010—7.9 years in the United States, for example.

A second key finding is that estimated additional work capacity is much smaller when using the more recent period (1995 or similar) as a basis for comparison. The total additional years of work capacity over ages fifty-five to sixty-nine averages only 1.7 years for the countries as a group, and is one year or less in Belgium, the Netherlands, and Sweden. As shown in figure

2. These values do not match those in figure I.1 exactly because the data source is different; see chapter 12 (this volume) for details on this calculation.

3. For example, in the case of the United States, we estimate that an additional 17.3 percent of age fifty-five individuals could be working, which represents a 0.173 increase in years worked (17.3 percent of the population working one additional year). This value is 0.131 years at age fifty-six, 0.144 years at age fifty-seven, and so on, up to 0.379 years at age sixty-nine, and the total across ages fifty-five to sixty-nine is 4.22 years.

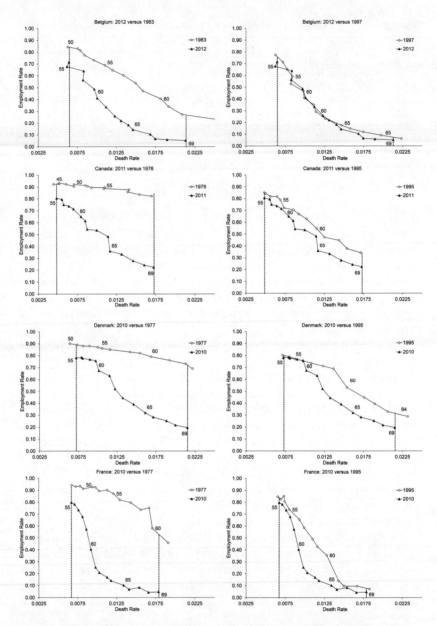

Fig. I.3   Employment versus mortality of men in eleven countries (selected years)
Source: See individual country chapters for the source data for each country.

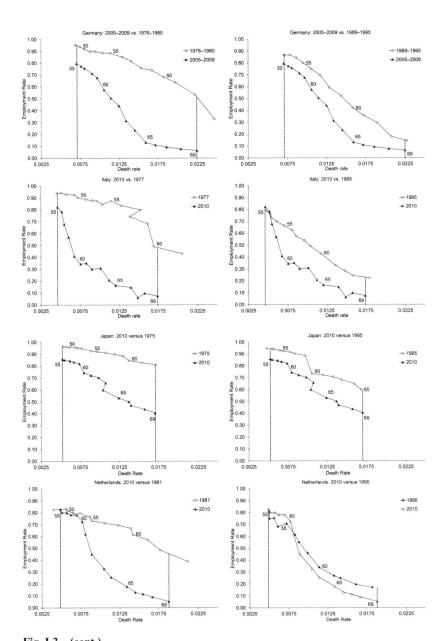

Fig. I.3 (cont.)

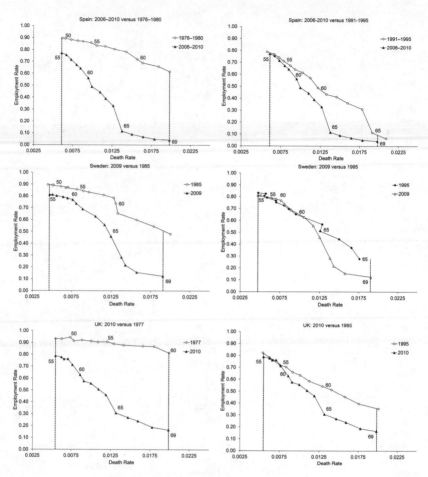

Fig. I.3   (cont.)

I.3, the two employment-mortality curves are barely distinguishable from each other in Belgium's case.

The explanation for the difference between the 1977- and 1995-based results lies in employment trends. Mortality rates fell continuously over the period 1977 to 2010, while employment rates fell between 1977 and 1995 and then rose from 1995 to 2010, as seen in figure I.1. Over the 1995 to 2010 period, increases in employment have been large enough to keep up with increases in mortality in some countries. To take sixty-one-year-olds in the Netherlands as an example, the mortality rate fell from 1.33 percent to 0.81 percent between 1995 and 2010, while the employment rate rose from 26.7 to 61.9 percent. In mortality terms, 2010's sixty-one-year-olds are like 1995's fifty-seven-year-olds, who had an employment rate of 61.2 percent. So the

Table I.3   **Years of additional work capacity for men at ages fifty-five to sixty-nine (MW method)**

Country	2010 versus 1977	2010 versus 1995
Belgium	5.0	1.0
Canada	4.9	1.3
Denmark	4.7	1.6
France	8.0	2.2
Germany	5.9	2.6
Italy	7.7	2.7
Japan	3.7	2.2
Netherlands	3.4	−0.1
Spain	7.0	2.2
Sweden	3.2	0.8
United Kingdom	8.4	1.8
United States	4.2	1.8
Average	5.5	1.7

Source: Individual country chapters.

Note: In some cases, years used differ: Belgium (1983 not 1977); Germany (2005–09 not 2010, 1989–1995 not 1995, 1976–1980 not 1977); Japan (1975 not 1977); Netherlands (1981 not 1977); and Sweden (2009 not 2010, 1985 not 1977).

estimated additional work capacity at age sixty-one, using the employment of those with the same mortality in 1995 as a basis for comparison, is close to zero. The 2010 sixty-one-year-olds are also like 1981's fifty-four-year-olds, who had an employment rate of 79.6 percent, yielding a positive estimate of work capacity (17.7 percent) when 1981 is the basis for comparison. Even though the employment of sixty-one-year-olds rose from 1981 to 2010 (from 57.3 to 61.9 percent), this is small compared with the drop in mortality (from 1.61 to 0.81 percent) and not enough to keep up with mortality gains.

To recap, in this analysis we estimate how much more older men today could work if they worked as much as those with the same level of health— as measured by mortality rates—did in the past. When we use 1977 as a basis for comparison, we estimate that there is substantial additional work capacity at ages fifty-five to sixty-nine—5.5 years on average for our sample of countries. This result can be explained by the fact that mortality rates have fallen substantially since 1977, while employment rates are either similar to or somewhat less than what they were in 1977, as evident from figure I.1. When we use 1995 as the basis for comparison, estimated work capacity shrinks substantially, to an average of 1.7 years in our sample of countries. Over the 1995 to 2010 period, employment has risen substantially in virtually all countries, as seen in figure I.1, and these employment gains have largely, if not completely, kept up with the gains in mortality.

It is not obvious whether 1995, 1977, or some other year is the "correct" comparison year to rely on in drawing inferences about additional work capacity. Using an even earlier comparison year than we have here, such as 1960 (were the data to be available), would generate even larger estimates, since both mortality and employment rates fell during these earlier decades. It is also useful to remember that our approach implicitly implies that all increases in life expectancy will translate into additional work years. If one prefers to assume that life expectancy increases would be divided between work and retirement years, one could apply some fractional factor to the estimates here. The bottom line, however, is that the Milligan-Wise approach suggests that there is significant capacity to work at older ages in all countries.

Cutler et al. Method

As discussed above, one shortcoming of the MW approach is the crudeness of using mortality as a proxy for health. We now turn to the Cutler et al. (CMR) approach to provide complementary evidence using richer and more subtle information on individual health and how it relates to employment.

Estimation

The CMR method involves two steps. The first is to estimate the relationship between employment and health (controlling for other attributes, such as education) at ages fifty to fifty-four. We choose this age range because it is before workers attain eligibility for social security and other early retirement benefits, and we wish to capture the relationship between health and employment that exists in the absence of access to retirement benefits.

For our measure of health, we employ a health index constructed using the approach described in Poterba, Venti, and Wise (2013), which we call the PVW index. The index is based on twenty-seven questions, including self-reported health diagnoses, functional limitations, medical care usage, and other health indicators. To calculate it, we first obtain the principal component of these indicators, which is the weighted average of indicators where the weights are chosen to maximize the proportion of the variance of the individual health indicators that can be explained by this weighted average. The estimated coefficients from the analysis are then used to predict a percentile score for each respondent. An individual's health index value will vary by survey wave, as updated health information is incorporated. As Poterba, Venti, and Wise (2013) demonstrate, the health index is strongly related to mortality and future health events such as stroke and diabetes onset, though not to future new cancer diagnoses. Some countries also estimate a version of the model including the individual health variables as covariates instead of the PVW index and present these results in their chapters.

To illustrate how we implement this approach, we estimate the model for those countries in our sample that are part of the Survey of Health, Ageing and Retirement in Europe (SHARE)—Belgium, Denmark, France, Germany, Italy, the Netherlands, Spain, and Sweden. We also do so for the

United States, using the Health and Retirement Study (HRS), and for the United Kingdom, using English Longitudinal Study of Ageing (ELSA), as the similarity of all of these data sets allows us to estimate a common specification for all countries.

Results are reported in table I.4. The coefficient on the PVW index is measured precisely for both men and women in each country, although the estimates vary across countries. For men, for example, the lowest estimates are in Italy and Sweden—0.0032 and 0.0027, respectively. In the eight remaining countries the estimates vary from 0.0040 in France to 0.0077 in Spain. The estimate for the United States, for example, indicates that if the health percentile (between zero and 100) increases by 10 points, the probability of employment increases by about 6 percentage points.

Prediction of the Capacity to Work

In the second step of the CMR approach, estimates similar to those in table I.4 (though obtained separately for each country by its team) are used to predict the "capacity" to work at older ages—fifty-five to fifty-nine, sixty to sixty-four, and sixty-five to sixty-nine. In essence, we combine the estimated effect of health (and other characteristics) on employment for those ages fifty to fifty-four with the actual health (and other characteristics) of those ages fifty-five to sixty-nine. This approach assumes that the relationship between health and employment will be the same for two groups, but should generate declining estimates of work capacity with age since health declines with age. We cannot test this assumption directly, but taking estimates from a similar age group makes the approach more plausible. If employment *at a given level of health* is in fact more difficult as workers age, then our estimates would tend to overstate additional work capacity; however, the magnitude of our results (presented below) suggest there is likely substantial work capacity, even allowing for this possibility. Another key assumption is that our health index is a sufficient summary measure of health and that there are no omitted dimensions of health that affect employment; as discussed above, the PVW index is quite comprehensive and strongly correlated to future health events and mortality. A final possible concern is that retirement may have a causal effect on health, although without more clarity from the literature on this point, it is difficult to hazard a guess about the effect of disregarding this pathway. Ultimately, while any empirical method will involve assumptions, to the extent that we obtain similar results using different methods, this may mitigate concerns about the limitations of any one method.

The results for men in the United States are provided in figure I.4 to illustrate the workings of this approach. For each age group, the total height of the bar represents the predicted share of individuals working, based on the estimated relationship between health and employment for those age fifty to fifty-four and the actual health of those in the older age groups. These values

Table I.4   Estimated relationship between health and employment (men and women ages fifty to fifty-four)

Dependent variable: Currently working	United Kingdom	United States	ALL SHARE	Belgium	Denmark	France	Germany	Italy	Netherlands	Spain	Sweden
					Men						
PVW health index	0.0059*	0.0062*	0.0045*	0.0052*	0.0048*	0.0040*	0.0051*	0.0032*	0.0045*	0.0077*	0.0027*
	(0.0003)	(0.0002)	(0.0003)	(0.0008)	(0.0008)	(0.0007)	(0.0009)	(0.0012)	(0.0007)	(0.0010)	(0.0010)
Education											
High school grad	-0.0215	0.0887*	0.0763*	-0.0463	0.0892	0.1729*	0.1871*	0.1348*	0.0647	0.1090*	0.1025*
	(0.0258)	(0.0157)	(0.0164)	(0.0414)	(0.0580)	(0.0400)	(0.1036)	(0.0557)	(0.0415)	(0.0587)	(0.0485)
Some college or more	0.0015	0.1285*	0.1025*	0.0526	0.0770	0.1707*	0.2239*	0.2383*	0.0781*	0.0545	0.1067*
	(0.0179)	(0.0154)	(0.0175)	(0.0402)	(0.0628)	(0.0445)	(0.1083)	(0.0609)	(0.0420)	(0.0603)	(0.0456)
Marital status											
Married	0.1360*	0.1605*	0.1121*	0.1595*	0.0953*	0.0563	0.0029	0.1266*	0.1657*	0.1437*	0.1675*
	(0.0188)	(0.0126)	(0.0169)	(0.0448)	(0.0410)	(0.0370)	(0.0480)	(0.0633)	(0.0563)	(0.0507)	(0.0568)
Occupation											
Blue collar	-0.0252	0.0417*	-0.0543*	-0.0873*	-0.0759	-0.0169	-0.1100*	0.0271	-0.0581	-0.0527	0.0465
	(0.0186)	(0.0119)	(0.0169)	(0.0436)	(0.0466)	(0.0403)	(0.0500)	(0.0688)	(0.0437)	(0.0530)	(0.0438)
Intermediate skill	-0.0074	0.0277*	-0.0064	-0.0224	0.0281	-0.0263	0.0031	0.0147	-0.0073	-0.0165	-0.0173
	(0.0205)	(0.0126)	(0.0152)	(0.0370)	(0.0400)	(0.0351)	(0.0485)	(0.0551)	(0.0420)	(0.0585)	(0.0448)
Constant	0.3461*	0.1352*	0.4027*	0.3666*	0.4301*	0.4401*	0.2999*	0.4046*	0.3995*	0.1170	0.4925*
	(0.0322)	(0.0209)	(0.0313)	(0.0741)	(0.0816)	(0.0750)	(0.1224)	(0.1360)	(0.0798)	(0.0902)	(0.1116)
Observations	2,166	6,199	3,211	563	398	523	411	283	427	282	324

					Women						
PVW health index	0.0049*	0.0048*	0.0038*	0.0042*	0.0060*	0.0028*	0.0036*	0.0006	0.0054*	0.0028*	0.0055*
	(0.0003)	(0.0002)	(0.0003)	(0.0007)	(0.0007)	(0.0007)	(0.0008)	(0.0009)	(0.0007)	(0.0008)	(0.0007)
Education											
High school grad	0.0805*	0.1326*	0.1830*	0.0253	0.1218*	0.0980*	0.2474*	0.3974*	0.1267*	0.1924*	-0.0364
	(0.0260)	(0.0135)	(0.0181)	(0.0474)	(0.0655)	(0.0447)	(0.0722)	(0.0554)	(0.0472)	(0.0648)	(0.0486)
Some college or more	0.1077*	0.2014*	0.3358*	0.1989*	0.2043*	0.2893*	0.2883*	0.5139*	0.2325*	0.4542*	-0.0214
	(0.0214)	(0.0132)	(0.0183)	(0.0531)	(0.0667)	(0.0471)	(0.0764)	(0.0630)	(0.0515)	(0.0751)	(0.0456)
Marital status											
Married	-0.0215	-0.0175*	-0.0599*	-0.0611	0.0400	-0.0757*	-0.0779*	-0.0453	-0.0983*	-0.1406*	0.0066
	(0.0172)	(0.0098)	(0.0161)	(0.0428)	(0.0392)	(0.0370)	(0.0447)	(0.0535)	(0.0517)	(0.0568)	(0.0402)
Occupation											
Blue collar	-0.0589*	0.1014*	0.0784*	-0.0769	-0.0091	0.1107*	0.0398	0.2963*	-0.0117	0.2276*	-0.2081*
	(0.0234)	(0.0132)	(0.0221)	(0.0569)	(0.0824)	(0.0555)	(0.0698)	(0.0515)	(0.0664)	(0.0507)	(0.0741)
Intermediate skill	-0.0094	0.0816*	0.1300*	0.0670	0.0706*	0.0975*	0.0145	0.3222*	-0.0059	0.2767*	-0.0624*
	(0.0224)	(0.0100)	(0.0158)	(0.0447)	(0.0389)	(0.0425)	(0.0518)	(0.0555)	(0.0444)	(0.0593)	(0.0370)
Constant	0.4288*	0.2063*	0.2275*	0.3234*	0.2335*	0.4328*	0.2902*	0.1458*	0.2896*	0.1136	0.5632*
	(0.0309)	(0.0154)	(0.0257)	(0.0711)	(0.0834)	(0.0662)	(0.0980)	(0.0702)	(0.0719)	(0.0729)	(0.0793)
Observations	**2,478**	**10,435**	**4,067**	**634**	**443**	**591**	**536**	**434**	**578**	**407**	**444**

Notes: ALL SHARE includes all countries except the United Kingdom and the United States. The pooled SHARE coefficients are similar whether or not country dummies are included. Omitted categories are less than HS education, nonmarried, and high skill or missing occupation. Standard errors are below each coefficient.

*Significant at the 10 percent level.

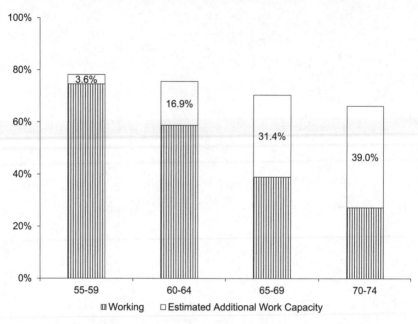

Fig. I.4   Estimated additional work capacity for men in the United States (by age)
Source: Chapter 12, this volume (authors' calculations using Health and Retirement Study).

decrease with age, as expected, reflecting the effect of declining health on employment as predicted by our model. The bar with vertical lines reflects the actual percent employed in each age group, and the white bar—predicted share working minus actual share employed—is our estimate of the additional work capacity. As the actual share employed falls more quickly with age than does the predicted share working, the estimated additional work capacity grows rapidly with age, from 3.6 percent at ages fifty-five to fifty-nine, to 16.9 percent at ages sixty to sixty-four, to 31.4 percent at ages sixty-five to sixty-nine, and 39.0 percent at ages seventy to seventy-four.

In figures I.5A, I.5B, and I.5C, we report the estimated additional work capacity for men ages fifty-five to fifty-nine, sixty to sixty-four, and sixty-five to sixty-nine, respectively, for all countries in our sample. The estimated additional work capacity at age fifty-five to fifty-nine is only 2 percent in Japan and 4 percent in the United States, but values reach 19 percent in France, 21 percent in Italy, and 22 percent in Belgium. In the sixty to sixty-four age range, estimated additional work capacity values are larger and the variance across countries is greater—values range from 14 percent in Sweden to 63 percent in France. This trend continues in the sixty-five to sixty-nine age interval, where the values range from 31 percent in the United States to 84 percent in Germany.

In the two older age groups in particular, it is evident that the differences in

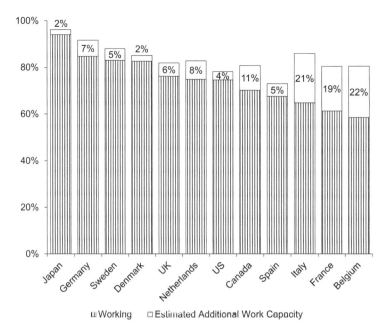

Fig. I.5A   Estimated additional work capacity by country (men ages fifty-five to fifty-nine)

Source: Individual country chapters (authors' calculations).

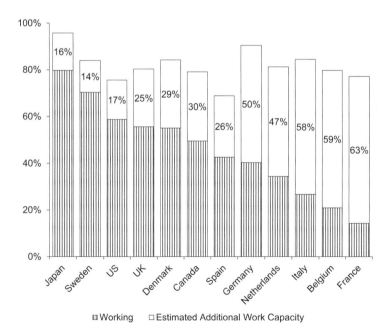

Fig. I.5B   Estimated additional work capacity by country (men ages sixty to sixty-four)

Source: Individual country chapters (authors' calculation).

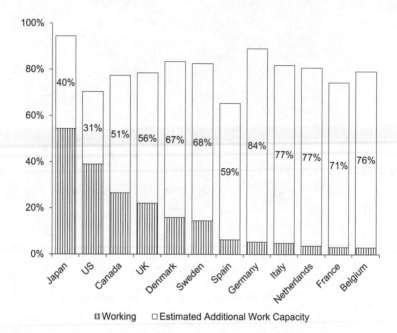

Fig. I.5C   Estimated additional work capacity by country (men ages sixty-five to sixty-nine)
Source: Individual country chapters (authors' calculations).

estimated additional work capacity across countries are not driven primarily by differences in the predicted share working. While there are some differences in predicted employment—Spain consistently has the lowest values and Japan and Germany the highest, for example—the differences in work capacity are primarily explained by differences in the actual share working across countries. For example, at ages sixty to sixty-four the predicted share working is nearly identical in the United States and France, while actual employment is much lower in France (14 percent versus 59 percent), and consequently the additional work capacity is nearly four times larger in France (63 percent versus 17 percent).

Put differently, the widely varying levels of estimated work capacity across countries cannot be explained by differences in the rate at which health declines, which would be reflected in how the predicted share working evolves with age. Rather, they are primarily due to differences in the age at which workers retire, a decision that is strongly influenced by social security incentives, as Gruber and Wise (1999) document.

These estimates of the capacity to work may seem large relative to the actual employment rate. In table I.2, however, we showed that by using the MW method for the United States we obtain estimated additional work capacity of 15.6 percent at ages fifty-five to fifty-nine, 27.0 percent at ages sixty to sixty-four, and 41.8 percent at ages sixty-five to sixty-nine, values in the range of those reported in figures I.5A, I.5B, and I.5C. The results using two very different methods are actually remarkably similar, though results from the Milligan-Wise method will depend on the base year used, as shown above.

It is possible to perform this analysis for women as well, and we report the results of this effort in figures I.6A, I.6B, and I.6C. Women's predicted employment levels (seen in the total height of the bar) are somewhat lower at every age compared to those of men, reflecting the fact that these are estimated based on the relationship between health and employment for women at ages fifty to fifty-four along with actual health of women at older ages, and women ages fifty to fifty-four are less likely to work than are men of the same age. Of greater interest, however, is the estimated additional work capacity (seen in the white bar). These values are quite similar for men and women. Across the twelve countries, for example, these values average 8.7 percent for women at ages fifty-five to fifty-nine versus 9.3 percent for men and 34.4 percent for women at ages sixty to sixty-four versus 36.1 percent for men. The difference is somewhat greater at ages sixty-five to sixty-nine, where estimated additional work capacity is 53.6 percent for women versus

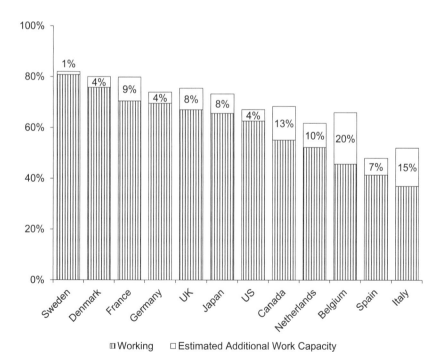

Fig. I.6A   Estimated additional work capacity by country (women ages fifty-five to fifty-nine)

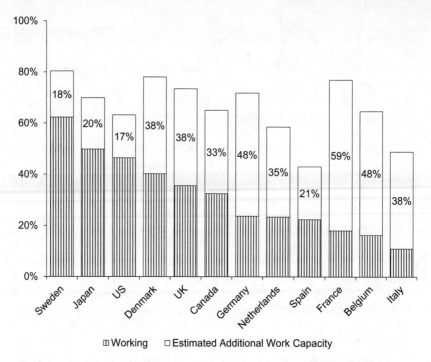

Fig. I.6B   Estimated additional work capacity by country (women ages sixty to sixty-four)

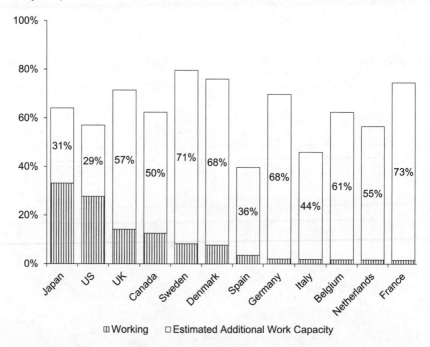

Fig. I.6C   Estimated additional work capacity by country (women ages sixty-five to sixty-nine)

63.2 percent for men. Nonetheless, the key conclusion from this analysis is that both men and women have substantial additional work capacity, as estimated using this method.

Self-Assessed Health

In the first section of the chapter, we focused on the mortality rate as a measure of changes in health over time. In this section, we explore the improvement in health over time based on self-assessed health (SAH). An important advantage of SAH is that we can look at it by level of education, as the data sets with SAH virtually always include education, while mortality records often do not. Studies such as Waldron (2007) and the National Academies of Sciences (2015) have established that gains in life expectancy over time are accruing disproportionately to individuals with higher socioeconomic status (SES). By looking at the evolution of SAH by level of SES, we wish to see if this is the case for SAH as well. Unfortunately, data limitations prevented some countries from undertaking this analysis, but we show results for several of the countries where this was possible.

To begin, we discuss trends over time in mortality and in SAH and document their similarity. Figure I.7 shows the relationship between SAH and age for five-year groups from 1972 to 2013 and between mortality and age for five-year groups from 1970 to 2009 for men in the United States. As

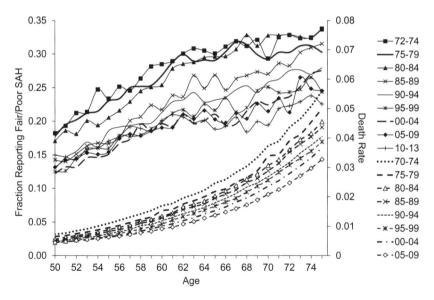

Fig. I.7   SAH and mortality by age for men in the United States (1972 to 2013)

Source: National Health Interview Survey and Human Mortality Database.

Note: Solid lines (graphed against left-hand axis) show self-assessed health for groups of years. Dashed lines (graphed against right-hand axis) show death rates for groups of years.

expected, both mortality rates and the share of men reporting themselves to be in fair or poor health (SAH) rise with age, although this is perhaps less evident for SAH in the sixties in the more recent year groups. The mortality relationships are smooth and show continuous improvement from one group of years to the next. The SAH relationships are more variable due to smaller sample sizes; while improvements over time are sometimes difficult to discern from adjacent year groups, there are large improvements when contrasting the early 1970s with late in the first decade of the twenty-first century.

Of particular interest is the fact that changes in the two series over time are relatively similar. For example, mortality at age fifty declined by 39.3 percent between 1970–74 and 2005–09, while the share reporting fair or poor health at age fifty decreased by 32.8 percent between 1972–74 and 2005–09. Over the same period, mortality at age seventy-five declined by 41.5 percent, while the share in fair or poor health at age seventy-five decreased by 33.2 percent. Alternatively, we can compare how much later certain health benchmarks are reached in later versus earlier periods. The mortality rate experienced at age fifty in 1970–74 was experienced at age fifty-seven in 2005–09, a gain of seven years, while the share of men in fair or poor health at age fifty in 1972–74 was experienced at age fifty-seven in 2005–09, also a gain of seven years. While the correspondence is not always one-to-one as in this example, overall the changes in these two health measures over time are fairly similar.

Looking across countries, there is a fairly strong correspondence between the change in reported SAH health and the change in mortality. Milligan and Wise (2012) show a scatter plot of changes in self-assessed health and mortality across the twelve ISS countries. We reproduce this scatter plot below in figure I.8. The correspondence of the two across countries is very strong, except for the United Kingdom.

Turning our focus to SAH, figure I.9 highlights trends in SAH over time in the United States, showing the relationship between age and the share of men in fair or poor health for three groups of years combined—1972–85, 1986–95, and 1996–13. The graph shows the raw data in the solid lines and quadratic-smoothed dashed lines for each of the year groupings. The reduction in fair-poor SAH seems quite large over this time period. For example, the age at which 20 percent are in fair-poor health occurs at about age fifty-four in 1972–85 and at about age sixty-two in the years 1996–2013, a difference of eight years. The age at which 25 percent of people are in fair-poor health rises by fifteen years, from age fifty-eight to age seventy-three. An alternative comparison is based on the change in the fraction that reports fair or poor health at a given age. At age sixty-five, this value is 35 percent lower in the 1996–2013 period than in the 1972–1985 period; at age sixty the value is 26 percent lower. The overall message is that the health of the population as a whole—as measured by SAH—has improved substantially in recent decades.

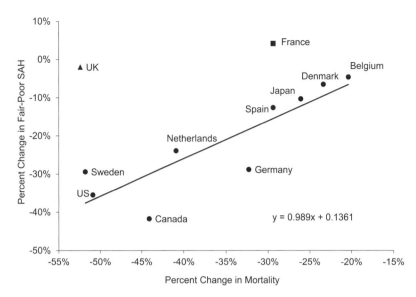

Fig. I.8   Change in SAH versus change in mortality (men ages sixty to sixty-four)
Source: Reproduced from data in Milligan and Wise (2012).
Note: Regression line includes all countries with circle marker, excluding the United Kingdom and France.

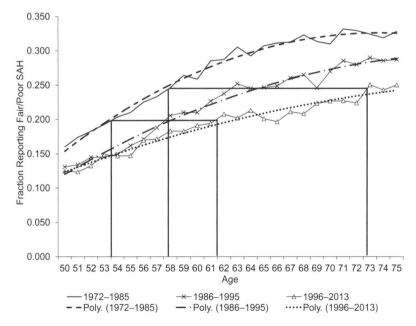

Fig. I.9   SAH by age, men in the United States (selected years)
Source: National Health Interview Survey.

To assess whether these gains in health vary by education level, we first need to define education level in a way that will yield meaningful comparisons over time. Following Bound et al. (2014), we focus on education quartiles. The use of specific categories like high school dropout can generate misleading results because the size of specific groups may be shrinking (or growing) over time, so that the group's members are increasingly negatively (or positively) selected. That is, high school dropouts today may be quite different from their counterparts of the past, making it less useful to compare how the health of people in this group has evolved over time.

Following the approach proposed by Bound et al. (2014), we begin by calculating the distribution of educational attainment for each cohort of fifty-year-olds. The top education quartile will always contain the quarter of the cohort with the highest levels of education; however, which education groups are represented in the top quartile will change over time. Figure I.10 displays these results for men in the United States. The top education quartile for the cohort reaching age fifty in 1950 includes all college graduates as well as most high school graduates; in 2012, the top quartile includes only college graduates.

Figure I.11 shows the relationship between SAH and age by education quartile ranking for men in the United States for three groups of years—

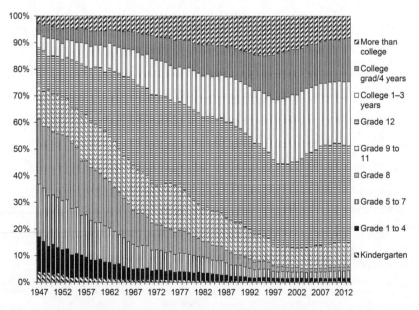

Fig. I.10   Distribution of educational attainment by cohort for men in the United States (by year cohort attained age fifty)

Source: Authors' calculations using National Health Interview Survey (accessed at www .ipums.org).

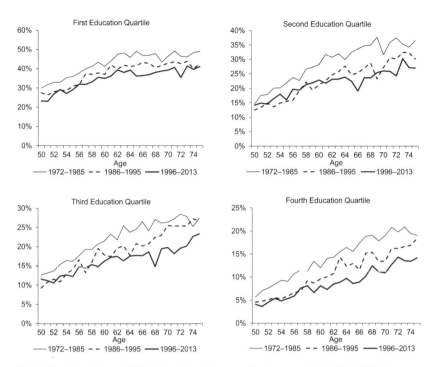

Fig. I.11   Evolution of SAH by education quartile for men in the United States
Source: National Health Interview Survey (accessed at www.ipums.org). The figure shows the share of men reporting fair or poor health.

1972 to 1985, 1986 to 1995, and 1996 to 2013. The results show that health measured by SAH improved over time in each education quartile, with the exception of a reversal in ages in the fifties in the 2nd quartile for the years 1986 to 1995. However, the percent improvement was greatest for those in the top education quartile and the lowest percent improvement was in the bottom education quartile. The percent improvements at age sixty-six, for example, are shown at the end of this section in comparison to three other countries in table I.5.

Figure I.12 is a comparable figure for France. Like the United States, the data for France show better health for higher education levels. Averaged over year intervals at age fifty, the percent in fair-poor health in the United States is about 22 percentile points greater for the 1st education quartile than for the 4th education quartile—27 for the first quartile, 14 for the second, 11 for the third, and 5 for the fourth quartile. Similarly, the difference in France between the first and fourth quartile is about 21 percentile points. But the average number of men reporting fair-poor health at age fifty is much greater in France than in the United States—38 percent in France versus 14 percent in the United States for the 2nd quartile. (This result is consistent

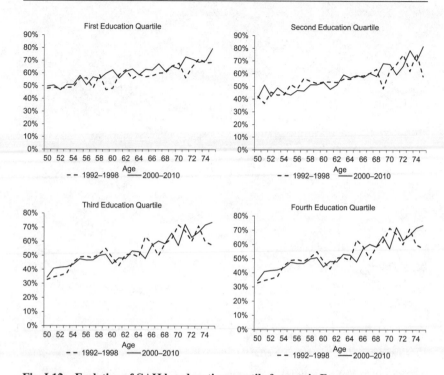

Fig. I.12   Evolution of SAH by education quartile for men in France

Source: Enquête sur la Santé et la Protection Sociale. The figure shows the share of men reporting fair or poor health.

with the well-known country-specific effects in SAH.) There is less evidence for an improvement through time for France, as the 1992–98 results are quite similar to the 2000–10 results, although the time spanned by the data is shorter here than in the United States.

We next turn to the United Kingdom in figure I.13 to see the evolution of poor health across the different education quartiles. Here, the data are pooled for men and women for greater precision and separated into two time periods: 1991 to 1999 and 2004 to 2012. As with France and the United States, those with higher education levels appear to be in better health. There is also a strong gradient with age for poor health. However, the evidence for improvements through time in the United Kingdom is weak, although there is some sign of improvement for the higher two education groups.

Finally, we look at data for Germany in figure I.14. We have data by age of the proportion who report having a chronic illness for more than one year. These data are broken down by education quartile in the manner described above, and presented for three separate years. There appear to be fewer differences across education quartiles than in other countries, with roughly the same age pattern evident in the first and fourth quartiles. However, there

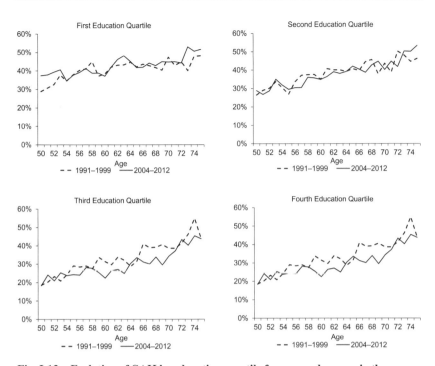

Fig. I.13   Evolution of SAH by education quartile for men and women in the United Kingdom

Source: Health Survey for England, 1991–2012. The figure shows the share of men reporting fair, bad, or very bad self-assessed general health.

does appear to be improvement over time, most noticeably in the third and fourth quartiles.

Our findings for these four countries are summarized in table I.5, taking the results at age sixty-six. Overall, for two of these four countries we highlighted, all education groups (as represented by education quartiles) have experienced gains in health over time. In addition, for three of the countries, gains have been largest for the more highly educated groups, but for France there is no education pattern for the improvements. While the results of this analysis are not directly comparable to the Milligan-Wise and Cutler-Meara results presented above, they are nonethless useful in our assessment of the health capacity to work at older ages, as they suggest that gains in health capacity to work may be biggest for higher socioeconomic status individuals.

Summary

This volume is the seventh phase of our ongoing project on retirement programs around the world. In many countries, normal retirement ages have been increasing and further increases are in progress or under consideration.

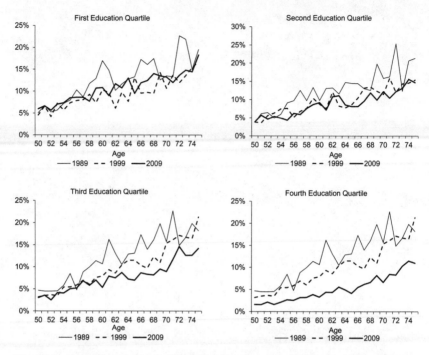

Fig. I.14   Evolution of chronic illness by education quartile for men in Germany
Source: German microcensus data. The figure shows the share of men reporting experiencing a chronic illness lasting more than one year.

Table I.5   Percent improvement in health at age sixty-six by education quintile

	1st (%)	2nd (%)	3rd (%)	4th (%)
United States	22.3	43.4	33.2	48.7
France	−7.8	1.9	2.5	0.3
United Kingdom	3.8	−1.9	23.9	19.2
Germany	30.9	43.4	50.1	42.5

Note: For each country using the results from figures I.10 to I.13, we compare the first group of years to the latest group of years. For the United States: 1972–1985 versus 1996–2013. For France: 1992–1998 versus 2000–2010. For the United Kingdom: 1991–1999 versus 2004–2012. For Germany: 1989 versus 2009.

In this phase of the project, we consider the capacity to work at older ages, particularly whether the health of older persons would allow them to work longer.

We use three approaches to evaluate the capacity to work. The first, which we refer to as the Milligan-Wise method, is based on the reduction in mortality over time. We suggest that a decrease in mortality may be thought of as an increase in health, and thus as an increase in the capacity to work. We find, however, that mortality declines since the late 1970s have not been met with equivalent increases in employment. That is, at any mortality rate, employment is lower now than it was three to four decades ago. In the United States, for example, we estimate that the additional employment capacity of men ages sixty-five to sixty-nine in 2010 is 42 percent (that is, that the employment rate could be 74 rather than 32 percent), using 1977 as the base year in the calculation and assuming a constant relationship between employment and mortality over time. In most of the ISS countries, the actual employment of men age sixty to sixty-four has been increasing since the mid-1990s, but not by enough to keep up with mortality gains, so we estimate significant additional employment capacity even when we use a base year with low employment, such as 1995. On average across all countries, our estimates suggest that men could work an additional 5.5 years with 1977 as the base of comparison or 1.7 years with 1995 as the base year.

The second method, which we refer to as the CMR method, is based on using the estimated relationship between health and employment of persons age fifty to fifty-four and the actual health of individuals age fifty-five to sixty-nine to predict the work capacity of the latter group. This method also yields predictions of the capacity to work at older ages that substantially exceed the actual proportion of people working at older ages. Based on this method, the share of the male population with the health capacity to work at ages sixty to sixty-four in the United States, for example, is about 17 percent greater than the actual percent working; between sixty-five and sixty-nine, the difference is about 31 percent. The average values for the twelve countries in our sample are 36 and 63 percent, respectively.

A third method is based on improvements in self-assessed health (SAH) over time. This method, however, was possible to implement only in certain countries. The results were mixed across countries. For most, there was a strong education gradient in the incidence of poor health. Only some countries showed improvements in health as measured by self-assessed health through time, though there was some indication that these gains were larger for the higher education quartiles.

In short, all three methods suggest that older men have substantial additional capacity to work beyond their current employment levels. We find similar results for older women using the CMR method. It is important to emphasize again that our concept of the health capacity to work is not intended to suggest how long people should work, nor to suggest what typical retirement ages should be in various countries. As people live longer and healthier lives, it may be appropriate for policymakers to consider how these gains in life expectancy should be divided between years of work and retirement. It is also important to recall that there may be other impediments to longer work lives, such as weak labor demand for older workers. Studies documenting age discrimination in hiring against older women (Neumark, Burn, and Button 2015; Lahey 2008) and higher rates of retirement during recessions (Coile and Levine 2007) suggest that this is not a trivial issue. The concept of health capacity to work, however, can be important in considering whether continued incremental increases in retirement ages, such as those that have been common in many countries over the past two or three decades, might be constrained by the health of older workers going forward. The results of this phase of the International Social Security project suggest that this is not the case.

References

Bound, John, Arline Geronimus, Javier Rodriguez, and Timothy A. Waidmann. 2014. "The Implications of Differential Trends in Mortality for Social Security Policy." Working Paper no. 2014-314, Michigan Retirement Research Center, University of Michigan.

Coile, Courtney C., and Phillip B. Levine. 2007. "Labor Market Shocks and Retirement: Do Government Programs Matter?" *Journal of Public Economics* 91 (10): 1902–19.

Cutler, David M., Ellen Meara, and Seth Richards-Shubik. 2013. "Health and Work Capacity of Older Adults: Estimates and Implications for Social Security Policy." Unpublished Manuscript. Available at SSRN: http://ssrn.com/abstract=2577858.

Gruber, Jonathan, and David A. Wise, eds. 1999. *Social Security and Retirement around the World.* Chicago: University of Chicago Press.

———. 2004. *Social Security Programs and Retirement around the World: Micro-Estimation.* Chicago: University of Chicago Press.

———. 2007. *Social Security Programs and Retirement around the World: Fiscal Implications of Reform.* Chicago: University of Chicago Press.

———. 2010. *Social Security Programs and Retirement around the World: The Relationship to Youth Unemployment.* Chicago: University of Chicago Press.

Lahey, Joanna N. 2008. "Age, Women, and Hiring: An Experimental Study." *Journal of Human Resources* 43 (1): 30–56.

Milligan, Kevin, and David A. Wise. 2012. "Introduction." In *Social Security Programs and Retirement around the World: Historical Trends in Mortality and Health, Employment, and Disability Insurance Participation and Reforms,* edited by David A. Wise. Chicago: University of Chicago Press.

———. 2015. "Health and Work at Older Ages: Using Mortality to Assess the Capacity to Work across Countries." *Journal of Population Ageing* 8 (1–2): 27–50.

National Academies of Sciences, Engineering, and Medicine. 2015. *The Growing Gap in Life Expectancy by Income: Implications for Federal Programs and Policy Responses.* Report of the Committee on the Long-Run Macroeconomic Effects of the Aging US Population-Phase II. Washington, DC: The National Academies Press.

Neumark, David, Ian Burn, and Patrick Button. 2015. "Is It Harder for Older Workers to Find Jobs? New and Improved Evidence from a Field Experiment." NBER Working Paper no. 21669, Cambridge, MA.

Poterba, James, Steve Venti, and David A. Wise. 2013. "Health, Education, and the Post-Retirement Evolution of Household Assets." NBER Working Paper no. 18695, Cambridge, MA.

Waldron, Hilary. 2007. "Trends in Mortality Differentials and Life Expectancy for

Male Social Security-Covered Workers, by Socioeconomic Status." *Social Security Bulletin* 67 (3). https://www.ssa.gov/policy/docs/ssb/v67n3/v67n3p1.html.

Wise, David A., ed. 2012. *Social Security Programs and Retirement around the World: Historical Trends in Mortality and Health, Employment, and Disability Insurance Participation and Reforms.* Chicago: University of Chicago Press.

———. 2016. *Social Security Programs and Retirement around the World: Disability Insurance Programs and Retirement.* Chicago: University of Chicago Press.

Work Capacity and Longer Working Lives in Belgium

Alain Jousten and Mathieu Lefebvre

1.1 Introduction

Previous waves of this project studied the effect of financial incentives created by formal and de facto (early) retirement programs on an individual's decision to retire, the fiscal impact of such behavior, and reforms' impact thereon. Furthermore, the impact of (early) exits on youth employment and the respective roles of health and program rules as determinants of disability program enrollment have been studied (Dellis et al. 2004; Desmet et al. 2007; Jousten et al. 2010; Jousten, Lefebvre, and Perelman 2012, 2016).

Alain Jousten is a professor at the University of Liège, Law Faculty, Tax Institute and HEC-Liège and a research fellow of the IZA and of NETSPAR. Mathieu Lefebvre is assistant professor of economics at the University of Strasbourg.

The authors acknowledge financial support from the Belspo project EMPOV (TA/00/45). This chapter uses data from the European Union Labour Force Survey (Eurostat, European Union). Eurostat has no responsibility for the results and conclusions, which are the authors' only. It also uses data from SHARE wave 5 release 1.0.0, as of March 31st 2015 (DOI: 10.6103/ SHARE.w5.100) or SHARE wave 4 release 1.1.1, as of March 28th 2013 (DOI: 10.6103/ SHARE.w4.111) or SHARE waves 1 and 2 release 2.6.0, as of November 29th 2013 (DOI: 10.6103/SHARE.w1.260 and 10.6103/SHARE.w2.260) or SHARELIFE release 1.0.0, as of November 24th 2010 (DOI: 10.6103/SHARE.w3.100). The SHARE data collection has been primarily funded by the European Commission through the 5th Framework Programme (project QLK6-CT-2001–00360 in the thematic programme Quality of Life), through the 6th Framework Programme (projects SHARE-I3, RII-CT-2006–062193, COMPARE, CIT5- CT-2005–028857, and SHARELIFE, CIT4-CT-2006–028812), and through the 7th Framework Programme (SHARE-PREP, No. 211909, SHARE-LEAP, No. 227822 and SHARE M4, No. 261982). Additional funding from the US National Institute on Aging (U01 AG09740–13S2, P01 AG005842, P01 AG08291, P30 AG12815, R21 AG025169, Y1-AG-4553–01, IAG BSR06–11, and OGHA 04–064) and the German Ministry of Education and Research, as well as from various national sources, is gratefully acknowledged (see www.share-project.org for a full list of funding institutions). Comments welcome at ajousten@ulg.ac.be. For acknowledgments, sources of research support, and disclosure of the author's or authors' material financial relationships, if any, please see http://www.nber.org/chapters/c13738.ack.

One aspect that most of these papers have essentially bypassed is work-capacity issues. This neglect is all the more striking in a country like Belgium where the public-sphere pension reform debate is to a large degree dominated by such aspects. For example, one often-voiced concern in the debate on prolonging the working life of Belgian workers is that numerous workers do not have the capacity to work longer (even if they wanted or were pushed to) because of physical or mental health and exhaustion problems, or because psychological or material limitations render continued work impossible.

The most extreme incarnation of this concern is the so-called "arduous jobs" discussion that has been raging with particular emphasis since the current coalition government—in power since the middle of 2014—has embarked on a broader pension-reform project targeting longer effective working lives. This is achieved by closing or delaying early retirement options and working toward a convergence between the various public pension schemes for wage earners, civil servants, and the self-employed. While the government strategy's main thrust mirrors recommendations of a report published by an Expert Committee on Pension Reform 2020–2040 (Expert Committee 2014), individual policy measures show differences between the expert committee and the government proposals.

The broader literature provides some evidence on the link between health and work capacity.[1] For example, relying on indicators of self-assessed health, Van Looy et al. (2014) note that subjective health levels are not any different between those who reduced their working time and those who did not. In contrast, Desmette and Vendramin (2014, 79) find that "positive evaluations on 'general health,' 'physical health' (backache, muscular pain in the upper body, muscular pan in the lower body), and 'psychological health' (depression or anxiety, fatigue and insomnia) are at the highest levels for those who think their current job is sustainable." Similarly, Jousten and Lefebvre (2013) estimate a retirement model for Belgium including health as an explanatory variable and find that it plays a statistically significant role in the individual retirement decision.

The literature, however, also cautions that work ability is only one—though very important—step in the process of keeping individuals at work. Schreurs et al. (2011) argue that "good health may be a necessary but not sufficient condition for retaining older workers," and hence "creating and sustaining a healthy workforce by no means guarantees that older employees will continue working until their official retirement age" as workplace, domestic, or other factors may also influence individuals' effective labor market attachment.

The present chapter focuses on the "necessary condition": good work ability as a precondition for higher employment. In our approach, we focus on the outcome indicator "employment rate" (see figures 1.1 and 1.2) and link it

1. See Jousten and Salanauskaite (2015) for a survey of work determinants including motivation, finances, and legislation, as well as domestic, workplace, and work ability factors.

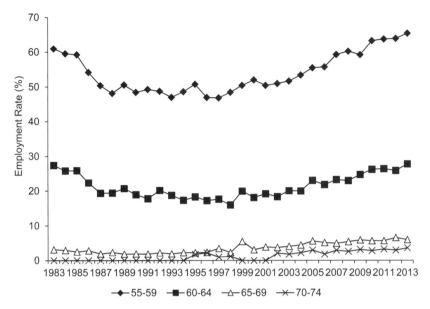

Fig. 1.1   Men's employment rate (ages fifty-five to fifty-nine to seventy to seventy-four)

Source: EU-LFS.

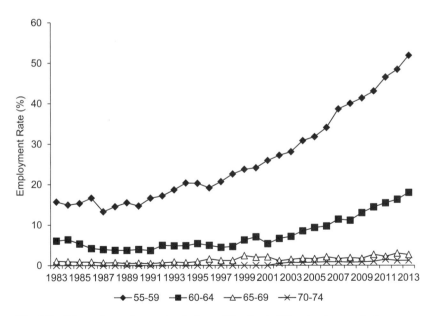

Fig. 1.2   Women's employment rate (ages fifty-five to fifty-nine to seventy to seventy-four)

Source: EU-LFS.

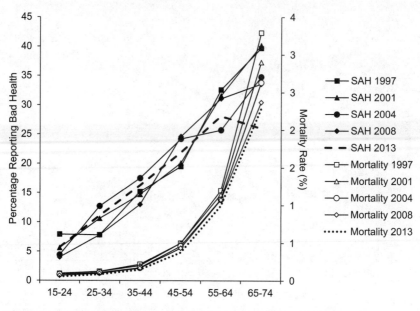

Fig. 1.3   SAH and mortality for men by age group (1997 to 2013)
Source: Human Mortality Database and Belgian Health Survey.

to general indicators of the healthiness of the older population as measured by the mortality and self-assessed health (SAH) of figure 1.3. These figures demonstrate that as we move up across age cohorts at any given point in time, employment rates fall substantially for both sexes—and this despite a generalized upward trend since the mid-1990s. While this decline is part age and part cohort effect, the question remains as to what the impact of health on these trends is.

Section 1.2 proposes an analysis using the Milligan and Wise (2015) methodology, essentially linking mortality and employment across time for those age fifty-five and older. Section 1.3 replaces mortality by a series of health conditions and explores the link between these factors and employment rate at younger ages (fifty to fifty-four) in a first step. In a second step, it proposes a simulation of employment potential at higher ages based on these first-step parameters. Section 1.4 concludes.

1.2   Milligan-Wise Method

Figure 1.4 is a good starting point both for exploring the facts about mortality across time in Belgium, as well as the methodology of Milligan and Wise (2015). The figure plots the instantaneous mortality rate of the Belgian male population as extracted from the Human Mortality Database against the male employment rate in the country as extracted from the EU Labour

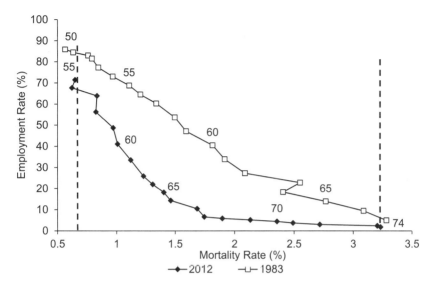

Fig. 1.4   Employment versus mortality rates for men (2012 versus 1983)
Source: Mortality rates from the Human Mortality Database; employment rate from EU-LFS.
Note: Employment rates correspond to linear interpolation as data are only available for five-year age groups.

Force Survey (EU-LFS). We focus on the male population, as Belgian females have experienced a seminal trend toward higher levels of employment and labor force participation over the last decades, hence rendering an isolation of the health from the structural effects hard to implement. The plot of figure 1.4 is done for two years: the recent year, 2012, and a latest possible reference year in the past, 1983.[2] The two outstanding—though unsurprising—facts are: (a) a strong negative relation between mortality and employment rate as age increases, and (b) a seminal trend in mortality rates at equal ages as represented by a leftward shift of the curve across time.

For the purpose of the present section, the focus lies on exploring work capacity for the older population (ages fifty-five to seventy-four), that is, those that are either below the normal retirement age or just a few years above. Leaving from the plot of figure 1.4 corresponding to the year 2012, we draw two vertical dotted lines at two bounds of the age interval of interest: one corresponds to the mortality rate observed at age fifty-five in the year 2012 of approximately 0.6 percent, and the other one to the mortality rate of 3.2 percent at age seventy-four in 2012.

The approach of Milligan and Wise (2015) then explores employment rates at equal mortality rates across time, rather than at equal ages. For example, the mortality rate of 0.6 percent as observed for a fifty-five-year-old

2. No EU-LFS data available before that date.

in 2012 corresponds to an employment level of 71 percent, while in 1983 the same mortality rate was observed for a fifty-year-old with a corresponding employment rate of 89 percent. Thus, if men had the same employment rate as their equal-mortality peers in 1983, this would lead to an 18 percentage points larger employment rate in 2012. Expressed differently, 18 percent of men age fifty-five could have worked one more year, corresponding to an average gap of 0.18 years of work for that specific age group.[3]

Similar calculations were done for all ages in the relevant range of fifty-five to seventy-four in 2012 and the results are reported in table 1.1. They indicate that if employment rates at equal mortality would have stayed constant, then the sum of the age-specific average gains of working years would add up to an additional employment capacity for the male population under study of 4.3 "years of work." This number is derived as the simple arithmetic sum of average year-of-work gains for each age cohort.

To understand the meaning and significance of this result of an extra 4.8 potential "years of work," three important elements need to be considered. First of all, the equivalence between extra employment potential (e.g., the 18 percentage points for a fifty-five-year-old in 2012) and "years of work" implicitly assumes that these extra workers would work the same hours/days/months than those that actually work. If this were to be different—either because those that currently work or those that could join work significantly less or more than the others—the equivalence would no longer hold.

Second, the total gain in years of work is a theoretical construct and has to be understood as such. For example, as the above number of 4.8 is the simple sum of potential years of work gains by age in the relevant range from fifty-five to seventy-four, it ignores any size and compositional differences between the various age cohorts. Also, and more substantially, the number is hard to interpret in a meaningful way unless one compares it to the theoretical maximum and/or currently observed years of work. As the maximum work potential by age is 100 percent (corresponding to an average year of work for that age group of 1), the total maximum years of work for the entire fifty-five to seventy-four cohort is twenty years. Expressed differently, the extra potential work capacity represents approximately 25 percent of total employment capacity, and is slightly less than the currently observed years of work of 5.1 that one can derive from the age-specific employment rates using the same methodology. In sum, results controlling for mortality improvements indicate that there is unused work capacity that could be activated to achieve almost a doubling of current levels of employment.

Third, the structure of employment and mortality rates of the chosen reference year has a strong impact on the outcome of the simulation. For

3. Notice that results would be substantially different when merely comparing employment rates for the same age group across time but ignoring mortality improvements: for fifty-five-year-olds, the employment rate actually increased from 1983 to 2012 from 69 percent to 71 percent, with mortality, however, strongly decreasing from 1.1 percent to 0.6 percent.

Table 1.1   **Additional employment capacity in 2012 using the 1983 employment-mortality relationship**

Age	Mortality rate in 2012 (%)	Employment rate in 2012 (%)	Employment rate in 1983 at same mortality rate (%)	Additional employment capacity (%)
55	0.65	71.4	84.2	12.8
56	0.62	67.7	84.6	17.0
57	0.83	63.9	78.2	14.3
58	0.82	56.3	78.9	22.6
59	0.97	48.7	72.9	24.2
60	1.01	41.1	71.8	30.7
61	1.12	33.5	68.2	34.7
62	1.23	25.9	63.7	37.8
63	1.31	22.0	61.3	39.2
64	1.40	18.2	57.6	39.5
65	1.46	14.3	55.2	40.9
66	1.69	10.5	44.4	33.9
67	1.75	6.6	42.6	36.0
68	1.90	5.9	35.3	29.4
69	2.13	5.2	26.9	21.7
70	2.36	4.4	24.7	20.3
71	2.49	3.7	17.3	13.6
72	2.72	3.0	14.5	11.5
73	3.21	2.4	6.8	4.4
74	3.23	1.8	6.1	4.3
Total years		5.1		4.8

Source: Authors' calculations using Human Mortality Database and EU-LFS.

example, no fundamental mechanism ensures a systematic leftward shift of the employment-mortality relation when moving across time. Furthermore, even a lack of a visible leftward shift does not mean that there was no change—in fact, situations may arise where negative extra employment capacity is derived, that is, where workers work more in 2012 than in the reference year considered, be it for a specific age or for the whole fifty-five to seventy-four cohort.

Figure 1.5 illustrates this point. It provides the same information as figure 1.4, but this time for the different baseline year of 1997—chosen because it corresponds to the year where the employment rate for the age cohort considered was historically at a low point before increasing again since then. Even though the curve barely moved in the employment-mortality rate space, there is a shift of the corresponding points for any given age up "along the curve" toward the northwest. Expressed differently, at any given age the mortality rate in 2012 is lower than in 1997, and the corresponding employment rate higher.

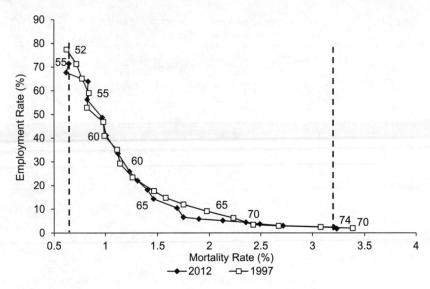

Fig. 1.5   Employment versus mortality rates (2012 versus 1997)
Source: Mortality rates from Human Mortality Database; employment rate from EU-LFS.
Note: Employment rates correspond to linear interpolation as data are only available for five-year age groups.

Figure 1.6 summarizes the findings in terms of extra years of work for the entire fifty-five to seventy-four age cohort for all possible reference years from 1983 to 2011. The graph shows that the additional employment capacity is close to zero when referencing across the last ten years, given increases in employment and decreases in mortality essentially canceling each other out. The sharpest changes could be derived if we take as reference the years farthest in the past, where both factors compound.

1.3   Cutler, Meara, and Richards-Shubik Method

The second method we employ for exploring the potential for additional employment of the older population age fifty-five to seventy-four is the method pioneered by Cutler, Meara, and Richards-Shubik (2012). The basic idea of this approach is to estimate a labor force participation model at a lower age (e.g., those age fifty to fifty-four) that includes demographic, health, and other socioeconomic variables as explanatory variables. The coefficients thus obtained are then applied to the realizations of these very same variables for the older cohort fifty-five to seventy-four to "predict" their labor force participation, in this way controlling for the effect of health or other controlled-for differences between older and younger cohorts.

Our technical approach slightly deviates from Cutler, Meara, and

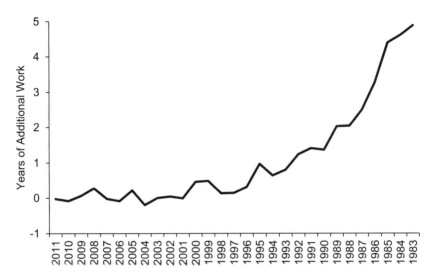

Fig. 1.6   Estimated additional employment capacity in 2012 by reference year
Note: Authors' calculations using Human Mortality Database and EU-LFS.

Richards-Shubik (2012) in that we focus on employment as the key dependent variable instead of labor force participation. The slightly different angle can be rationalized by the fact that in countries like Belgium, where early retirement by means of unemployment benefits is prevalent (be it technically as an early retiree or an unemployed), employment likely is the better outcome indicator.

We use (and pool) data from the Survey on Health, Ageing and Retirement in Europe (SHARE), waves 1, 2, 4, and 5, collected between 2004 and 2013. The survey is a cross-national panel database of micro data on health, socioeconomic status, and social and family networks of European individuals age fifty and older conducted since 2004–05. It covers a broad range of variables of special interest for this study, such as objective information of health, self-assessed health, and occupational status.

Our empirical approach is to estimate (ordinary least squares [OLS] regression) the employment model for the "young" age group (fifty to fifty-four) of men and women separately, and then apply its predictions to the older cohorts (fifty-five to seventy-four). We have a sample of 1,226 male and 1,558 female observations between age fifty and fifty-four that we rely upon for the regressions, and apply the simulations to almost 9,000 observations at older ages. Summary statistics of the survey population are provided in tables 1.2 and 1.3 for the various five-year age cohorts and by sex.

In the regressions reported in table 1.4, we use a single health measure: the PVW health index, as introduced and defined in Poterba, Venti, and

Table 1.2   **Summary statistics SHARE waves 1, 2, 4, and 5 (men)**

	Age group				
	50–54	55–59	60–64	65–69	70–74
In labor force	0.872	0.666	0.265	0.033	0.007
Subjective health					
Excellent	0.112	0.101	0.105	0.090	0.082
Very good	0.303	0.246	0.233	0.232	0.199
Good	0.399	0.430	0.428	0.439	0.433
Fair	0.150	0.171	0.188	0.192	0.223
Poor	0.036	0.052	0.045	0.047	0.062
Objective health					
ADL any	0.063	0.092	0.091	0.117	0.130
IADL any	0.071	0.096	0.102	0.108	0.160
One physical limit	0.130	0.165	0.177	0.184	0.184
More than one physical limit	0.153	0.200	0.212	0.235	0.300
Heart disease	0.065	0.078	0.100	0.158	0.186
Lung disease	0.036	0.046	0.062	0.078	0.094
Stroke	0.015	0.021	0.035	0.035	0.036
Cancer	0.018	0.038	0.050	0.057	0.085
Hypertension	0.250	0.276	0.333	0.329	0.362
Arthritis	0.089	0.123	0.130	0.165	0.176
Diabetes	0.077	0.077	0.112	0.114	0.127
Back problems	0.469	0.497	0.478	0.428	0.419
Depression	2.104	1.994	1.865	1.831	1.975
Psychological disorder	0.053	0.054	0.060	0.039	0.041
Smoking currently	0.304	0.264	0.198	0.155	0.122
Smoking formerly	0.632	0.716	0.727	0.699	0.724
Underweight	0.009	0.003	0.003	0.002	0.007
Overweight	0.423	0.317	0.333	0.342	0.337
Obese	0.174	0.167	0.157	0.173	0.127
Education					
Primary education	0.076	0.100	0.094	0.135	0.164
Secondary education	0.487	0.327	0.267	0.251	0.257
Tertiary education	0.437	0.573	0.639	0.613	0.579
Marital status					
Married	0.687	0.749	0.742	0.770	0.777
Scheme					
Wage earners	0.759	0.741	0.771	0.783	0.808
Self-employed	0.095	0.089	0.101	0.102	0.097
Civil servants	0.146	0.171	0.129	0.119	0.095
Skill					
Low skill	0.074	0.038	0.033	0.032	0.022
Medium skill	0.268	0.161	0.137	0.125	0.087
High skill	0.162	0.093	0.085	0.085	0.074
No. obs.	*1,226*	*1,442*	*1,282*	*1,049*	*795*

Source: Authors' calculations using SHARE data.

Table 1.3   Summary statistics SHARE waves 1, 2, 4, and 5 (women)

	Age group				
	50–54	55–59	60–64	65–69	70–74
In labor force	0.746	0.564	0.242	0.022	0.006
Subjective health					
Excellent	0.134	0.084	0.078	0.062	0.035
Very good	0.258	0.249	0.238	0.186	0.167
Good	0.394	0.449	0.425	0.474	0.434
Fair	0.158	0.166	0.204	0.230	0.286
Poor	0.055	0.052	0.055	0.048	0.078
Objective health					
ADL any	0.069	0.085	0.113	0.113	0.207
IADL any	0.128	0.141	0.172	0.162	0.249
One physical limit	0.163	0.170	0.194	0.176	0.171
More than one physical limit	0.247	0.315	0.349	0.406	0.511
Heart disease	0.032	0.052	0.064	0.083	0.127
Lung disease	0.044	0.042	0.057	0.064	0.055
Stroke	0.018	0.018	0.017	0.028	0.042
Cancer	0.043	0.050	0.052	0.074	0.068
Hypertension	0.229	0.268	0.330	0.394	0.439
Arthritis	0.170	0.177	0.229	0.251	0.313
Diabetes	0.045	0.077	0.090	0.115	0.122
Back problems	0.524	0.531	0.551	0.548	0.596
Depression	2.923	2.866	2.614	2.762	2.887
Psychological disorder	0.109	0.106	0.109	0.082	0.089
Smoking currently	0.247	0.210	0.142	0.085	0.077
Smoking formerly	0.476	0.529	0.515	0.428	0.391
Underweight	0.023	0.023	0.013	0.013	0.016
Overweight	0.267	0.240	0.238	0.291	0.279
Obese	0.142	0.139	0.152	0.142	0.149
Education					
Primary education	0.080	0.082	0.121	0.153	0.174
Secondary education	0.441	0.336	0.263	0.265	0.276
Tertiary education	0.478	0.582	0.615	0.582	0.550
Marital status					
Married	0.688	0.692	0.653	0.639	0.583
Scheme					
Wage earners	0.786	0.802	0.825	0.853	0.887
Self-employed	0.062	0.061	0.064	0.061	0.059
Civil servants	0.153	0.137	0.111	0.086	0.055
Skill					
Low skill	0.068	0.051	0.038	0.026	0.038
Medium skill	0.306	0.182	0.131	0.122	0.094
High skill	0.110	0.056	0.061	0.039	0.035
No. obs.	*1,558*	*1,565*	*1,325*	*1,118*	*962*

Source: Authors' calculations using SHARE data.

Table 1.4   Employment regressions, PVW health index (age group fifty to fifty-four)

| | Men | | Women | |
Variable	Coefficient	Std. error	Coefficient	Std. error
PVW index	0.004***	0.000	0.004***	0.000
Education				
Primary	Ref.	Ref.	Ref.	Ref.
Secondary	0.077*	0.041	0.099**	0.044
Tertiary	0.096**	0.043	0.186***	0.045
Marital status				
Married	0.112***	0.022	−0.063***	0.024
Scheme				
Salaried	Ref.	Ref.	Ref.	Ref.
Self-employed	0.018	0.035	0.113**	0.047
Civil servant	0.095***	0.030	0.179***	0.032
Skill				
Medium skill	Ref.	Ref.	Ref.	Ref.
Low skill	−0.211***	0.041	0.027	0.046
High skill	0.102***	0.030	0.092**	0.038
Constant	0.377***	0.045	0.306***	0.047
No. obs.	*1,226*		*1,558*	

Note: OLS regression based on SHARE data waves 1, 2, 4, and 5.
***Significant at the 1 percent level.
**Significant at the 5 percent level.
*Significant at the 10 percent level.

Wise (2013). The idea behind the PVW is simple: apply the principal components technique to the twenty-four objective and subjective health measures reported in tables 1.2 and 1.3. These include self-assessed health and various health conditions, as well as the prevalence of physical limitations, and so forth. In a second step, use the first principal component to predict a health score of the individual. Finally, the individual's score is positioned in a given percentile of the overall population used in the estimation. The score of an individual thus generally varies for across-survey waves because the health outcomes and perceptions likely vary across time. Poterba, Venti, and Wise (2013) show that the indicator traces mortality trends rather well at the individual level.

The results of table 1.4 suggest that the PVW index plays a substantial and positive role; that is, a better health score leads to more employment. Marital status plays a substantial role for men and women, though in the opposite direction—likely the result of the primary versus secondary earner status. The higher educated, as well as civil servants, are more likely to be employed for both sexes, while the required skill level for a job only seems to play significantly differently for men and women in high-qualifying jobs,

Table 1.5   Simulations of work capacity (PVW health index)

Age group	No. obs.	Actual % working	Predicted % working	Additional work capacity (%)
		Men		
55–59	1,442	58.5	80.5	22.0
60–64	1,282	20.9	79.7	58.8
65–69	1,049	3.0	79.2	76.2
70–74	795	0.7	77.5	76.8
		Women		
55–59	1,565	45.6	65.9	20.3
60–64	1,325	16.3	64.7	48.4
65–69	1,118	1.8	62.5	60.7
70–74	962	0.6	58.8	58.2

Note: Simulations based on estimates of table 1.4.

whereas a significant difference can only be observed for their male low-educated counterparts.[4]

Table 1.5 uses the estimates of table 1.4 and applies them to the older cohorts to predict work capacity based on the exogenous variables of the regressions. The table indicates that when controlling for health, work capacity clearly decreases with age, but in a rather unspectacular manner. Predicted work capacity at age seventy to seventy-four is simulated to be around 77 percent for men and 58 percent for women. These numbers are orders of magnitude larger than the ones corresponding to the actual observed employment rate in the country.[5] Figures 1.7A and 1.7B display the same information in a more visual manner, essentially showing the large potential for extra employment that one would predict using this method. To compare these results to the ones from table 1.1, we again apply a simple "synthetic" indicator of gains in years of work derived by adding up the additional work capacity across the entire age range of fifty-five to seventy-four. We obtain indicators of 11.6 and 9.3 years of extra work for men and women, respectively, hinting at a much stronger projected potential for this forward-looking method rather than the "backward-looking" Milligan-Wise methodology.

Given the generally large differences in employment outcomes observed in Belgium, we also applied the same approach by splitting the population

4. The appendix table 1A.1 provides the regression results where we replace the synthetic PVW index by the explicit battery of subjective and objective health (and physical limitation) indicators. The results are overall broadly similar, though individual parameter estimates for some of the health conditions may be influenced by underlying issues of covariation. Robustness checks excluding the scheme dummies further confirmed the results and are available upon request from the authors.

5. Appendix table 1A.2 provides simulation results when the initial estimation is obtained for the full set of health and limitation variables. The results are similar.

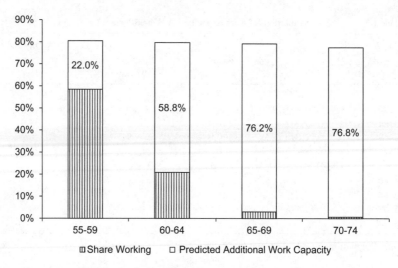

Fig. 1.7A   Share of SHARE men working and additional work capacity by age (PVW health index)
Note: Simulations based on estimates of table 1.4.

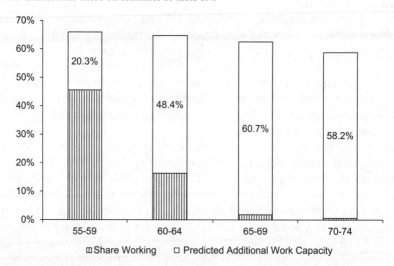

Fig. 1.7B   Share of SHARE women working and additional work capacity by age (PVW health index)
Note: Simulations based on estimates of table 1.4.

along the education dimension.[6] Results of the regressions are reported in table 1.6. They reveal some interesting differences with those presented in table 1.5. First, the positive and significant (surprising) coefficient for male civil servants disappears. While table 1.5 might have been interpreted that

6. Similar splits can be performed by scheme or skill level.

Table 1.6   Employment regressions by education—PVW health index (age group fifty to fifty-four)

| | Men | | | | | | Women | | | | | |
| | Primary | | Secondary | | Tertiary | | Primary | | Secondary | | Tertiary | |
Variable	Coefficient	Std. error	Coefficient	Std. error	Coefficient	Std. error	Coefficient	Std. error	Coefficient	Std. error	Coefficient	Std. error
PVW index	0.004**	0.002	0.005***	0.001	0.003***	0.001	0.002	0.002	0.005***	0.001	0.004***	0.001
Marital status												
Married	0.134	0.108	0.136***	0.034	0.083***	0.030	0.166*	0.098	-0.132***	0.039	-0.037	0.032
Scheme												
Salaried												
Self-employed	0.218	0.256	0.032	0.057	-0.004	0.043	-0.044	0.351	0.083	0.079	0.132**	0.057
Civil servant	0.552	0.487	0.058	0.047	0.113***	0.036	0.649**	0.300	0.243***	0.059	0.144***	0.037
Skill												
Medium skill												
Low skill	-0.176	0.116	-0.219***	0.053	-0.232**	0.107	0.174	0.109	-0.016	0.058	-0.033	0.168
High skill	-0.013	0.290	0.124**	0.062	0.102***	0.031	-0.009	0.260	0.321***	0.107	0.062	0.038
Constant	0.359***	0.119	0.402***	0.044	0.541***	0.044	0.212**	0.099	0.412***	0.048	0.500***	0.043
No. obs.	93		596		537		123		688		747	

Note: OLS regression based on SHARE data waves 1, 2, 4, and 5.

***Significant at the 1 percent level.

**Significant at the 5 percent level.

*Significant at the 10 percent level.

Table 1.7   Simulations of work capacity by education group and sex (PVW health index)

Education	Men			Women		
	Actual % working	Predicted % working	Additional work capacity (%)	Actual % working	Predicted % working	Additional work capacity (%)
			Age 55–59			
Primary	36.9	64.5	27.6	17.8	43.4	25.6
Secondary	55.4	77.9	22.5	37.3	59.2	21.9
Tertiary	63.9	84.9	21.0	54.3	72.7	18.4
			Age 60–64			
Primary	9.8	68.8	59.0	8.0	43.3	35.3
Secondary	19.1	76.8	57.7	11.1	61.2	50.1
Tertiary	23.2	83.1	59.9	20.1	71.2	51.1
			Age 65–69			
Primary	0.9	67.8	66.9	0.0	41.3	41.3
Secondary	1.1	78.5	77.4	2.0	59.8	57.8
Tertiary	4.3	82.6	78.3	2.1	69.3	67.2
			Age 70–74			
Primary	0.6	69.9	69.3	0.0	39.7	39.7
Secondary	0.4	78.7	78.3	0.0	56.5	56.5
Tertiary	1.1	80.8	79.7	1.1	65.7	64.6

Note: Simulations based on estimates of table 1.6.

civil servants' behavior actually differs, be it because of the completely different social protection environment than their salaried counterparts or for some other reason, table 1.6 indicates that this specific finding was more likely the result of interactions between the different explanatory variables education, scheme, and skill.[7]

Health, by means of the PVW index, has no significant effect for low-educated people, a distinguishing feature as compared to their better-educated counterparts. Different interpretations are again possible, two of which are the following: (a) low-educated people might have less flexibility in determining their retirement from the labor force; and (b) the health indicators contained in the PVW index (or the full set of health indicators of appendix tables 1A.1 and 1A.2) do not necessarily contain employment-determining conditions, particularly for workers with lower education who are already less likely to work to start with.

Table 1.7, as well as the accompanying figures 1.8A and 1.8B show the

---

7. The similarly surprising lack of a distinctly positive effect of self-employment subsists when running regressions by education. Given that the self-employed are excluded from many early exit routes and given that they have a substantially higher effective retirement age, one would expect the contrary. However, one has to keep in mind that the regression is done on a relatively young cohort age fifty to fifty-four, and that it is well before the main early retirement options of wage earners open up during the survey period.

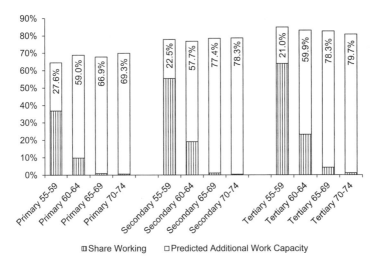

Fig. 1.8A   Share of SHARE men working and additional work capacity by age and education (PVW health index)
Note: Simulations based on estimates of table 1.6.

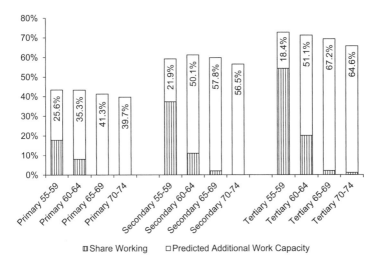

Fig. 1.8B   Share of SHARE women working and additional work capacity by age and education (PVW health index)
Note: Simulations based on estimates of table 1.6.

results of simulations based on the OLS coefficients by education of table 1.6. It reveals a picture broadly consistent with the pooled simulation results of table 1.5—namely, one of substantial additional work capacity in the population. However, it also allows extra insights beyond the pooled approach. First, it shows that the share of the population currently working at the age of fifty-five to fifty-nine has a strong education gradient—with an employment rate close to 75 percent higher for men with tertiary education than those with primary education, and a whopping 200 percent higher for women of the same age group. These findings are in line with those of Aliaj et al. (2016), who show that it is less educated Belgian females that stand out as having an unusually low employment rate, both when comparing within the country and with the neighboring countries of France, Germany, and the Netherlands. Second, as of age sixty to sixty-four, these employment rates drop dramatically for all education groups for both sexes. Almost insignificant levels are attained as of age sixty-five, where employment is more anecdotal than systematic—if only because of the strong focus of numerous social protection programs on sixty-five as a pivotal age.[8]

Though the results indicate that predicted work capacity is substantially lower for those with primary education only at all ages considered, their additional work capacity is actually the highest of all education levels at age fifty-five to fifty-nine, indicating large employment potential when considering the health, education, scheme, and skill characteristics as in our analysis.

Similar exercises can be performed by splitting the population along the "scheme" dimension, rather than education.[9] Tables 1.8 and 1.9 summarize the results of these regressions, as well as the corresponding simulated effects. They show substantial differences between the three main schemes. Table 1.9 indicates that the self-employed have a much higher actual employment level than both wage earners and civil servants, for women and men alike. Also, the simulations reveal that the age gradient of extra employment capacity is steepest for self-employed women and men. In terms of the prediction of people working, civil servants stand out as the most able to work when controlling for the health and sociodemographic variables of table 1.8. Expressed differently, while their level of actual employment is the lowest of all three schemes, their additional employment potential is by far the largest, and this for all but one of the age-sex groups considered.

All these results have to be read with a sufficient caution, keeping in mind the fact that this is only a partial analysis of health and socioeconomic determinants on an individual's ability to work. Clearly, it would be highly premature to claim that such higher employment ability should immediately

8. While retirement at a maximum age sixty-five is by and large history, workers continue to face discontinuities at sixty-five. For example, they lose their layoff protection and also continue to be rolled over from other social protection programs into the pension system at this very age.

9. We deterministically allocate people to the three schemes based on a decision tree reflecting the Belgian social security environment. For those in employment in SHARE waves 1, 2, 4, and 5, we directly observe the scheme they belong to. For those who have worked in the past, the survey provides the same information. For example, a retired civil servant would thus be classified as belonging to the civil servant scheme. All individuals where no such employment information is available are classified into the wage-earner scheme—which corresponds to the effective default option in the real world. We validate our classification using SHARELIFE. The data show that 75 percent of individuals declare a pure career in one of the three systems, with the residual dominated by people with partial wage-earner careers—a group with little end-of-working-life incentives and/or options for changing scheme.

Table 1.8　　Employment regressions by scheme, PVW health index (age group fifty to fifty-four)

| | Men | | | | | | Women | | | | | |
| | Wage earners | | Civil servant | | Self-employed | | Wage earners | | Civil servant | | Self-employed | |
Variable	Coefficient	Std. error	Coefficient	Std. error	Coefficient	Std. error	Coefficient	Std. error	Coefficient	Std. error	Coefficient	Std. error
PVW index	0.005***	0.000	0.001	0.001	0.005***	0.001	0.005***	0.000	0.004***	0.001	0.002	0.002
Marital status												
Married	0.116***	0.027	0.058	0.040	0.112*	0.062	−0.087***	0.029	0.019	0.045	−0.107	0.097
Skill												
Medium skill	Ref.	Ref.	Ref.	Ref.	Ref.	Ref.	Ref.	Ref.	Ref.	Ref.	Ref.	Ref.
Low skill	−0.208***	0.043	−0.620***	0.133	−1.141***	0.318	−0.005	0.048	−0.185	0.236	−0.737*	0.418
High skill	0.138***	0.039	0.037	0.037	0.139**	0.065	0.194***	0.052	0.069	0.048	−0.098	0.104
Constant	0.413***	0.035	0.839***	0.057	0.409***	0.090	0.416***	0.035	0.599***	0.059	0.764***	0.123
No. obs.	932		178		116		1,222		239		97	

Note: OLS regression based on SHARE data waves 1, 2, 4, and 5.

***Significant at the 1 percent level.

**Significant at the 5 percent level.

*Significant at the 10 percent level.

Table 1.9   Simulations of work capacity by scheme and sex (PVW health index)

Education	Men (PVW model)			Women (PVW model)		
	Actual % working	Predicted % working	Additional work capacity (%)	Actual % working	Predicted % working	Additional work capacity (%)
Age 55–59						
Wage earners	51.4	77.1	25.7	38.8	60.3	21.5
Civil servants	75.2	92.9	17.7	73.6	83.3	9.7
Self-employed	83.8	83.6	–0.2	72.2	78.8	6.6
Age 60–64						
Wage earners	14.0	76.4	62.4	12.5	59.4	46.9
Civil servants	33.5	92.4	58.9	25.7	84.6	58.9
Self-employed	56.4	80.6	24.2	47.7	78.5	30.8
Age 65–69						
Wage earners	1.2	76.1	74.9	0.9	58.6	57.7
Civil servants	0.4	93.5	93.1	1.0	81.2	80.2
Self-employed	15.7	81.1	65.4	14.5	77.5	63.0
Age 70–74						
Wage earners	0.2	75.2	75.0	0.0	55.5	55.5
Civil servants	0	91.5	91.5	0.0	78.3	78.3
Self-employed	6.4	80.8	74.4	10.5	74.1	63.6

Note: Simulations based on estimates of table 1.8.

lead to more employment as a policy strategy. As already indicated in the introduction, this analysis ignores many factors: household characteristics beyond marital status and workplace or system characteristics beyond the simple dummies for scheme and skill.

In sum, the analysis should be seen as a first step into the direction of a better understanding of what employment potential there is, in light of an ever-increasing need for financial resources to sustain our pension systems, and social protection more generally.

1.4   Conclusion

This chapter explores a dimension that has often been bypassed in the Belgian retirement literature, namely, the one of an individual's work ability. However, work ability is increasingly recognized as a key determinant of retirement, as discussed in Jousten and Salanauskaite (2015). We employ two methodologies to explore the link between changes in the health characteristics of the population and their work ability. To be more specific, the chapter uses employment as a proxy for work ability, hence focusing exclusively on the extensive margin of the link between improved health and work capacity.

Using the Milligan and Wise (2015) methodology linking mortality improvements to employment, we establish a significant employment potential in the Belgian population—corresponding to potential doubling of employment rates. Similarly, using a richer set of health indicators instead of mortality, the Cutler, Meara, and Richards-Shubik (2012) methodology identifies even more substantial employment potential. When separating the analysis by education level and employment scheme, we derive substantial differences in the population, highlighting the importance of institutional and workplace characteristics.

Clearly, both results should be seen as indicative rather than conclusive, in the sense that they show that improvements in health across time have left the country with a healthier population, hence harboring some degree of unused employment potential. We expressly warrant against a shortcut logic that would claim that the results are evidence of a need of massive activation. Our reading is more prudent: while substantial employment potential seems to exist, other factors such as system, workplace, and household factors are equally important determinants of the ultimate desirability of increased employment. Furthermore, our study of employment as a proxy for work ability can only be seen as a useful first step into a richer investigation of the topic—including the intensive margin of the impact on hours of work—leading us to conclude in the need for further scientific investigation of the subject.

Appendix

Table 1A.1   Employment regressions, all health variables

Variable	Men		Women	
	Coefficient	Std. error	Coefficient	Std. error
Subjective health				
Excellent	Ref.	Ref.	Ref.	Ref.
Very good	0.048	0.034	−0.017	0.037
Good	0.048	0.034	−0.024	0.036
Fair	−0.121***	0.044	−0.150***	0.047
Poor	−0.275***	0.072	−0.336***	0.067
Objective health				
ADL any	0.101**	0.047	−0.051	0.052
IADL any	−0.115**	0.045	−0.096**	0.040
One physical limit	0.043	0.031	0.001	0.032
More than one physical limit	−0.102***	0.035	−0.080**	0.034
Heart disease	−0.048	0.042	−0.036	0.066
Lung disease	−0.082	0.055	−0.108*	0.056
Stroke	−0.132	0.081	−0.186**	0.085
Cancer	−0.173**	0.079	−0.041	0.055
Hypertension	0.015	0.024	0.036	0.028
Arthritis	0.012	0.038	−0.123**	0.055

(*continued*)

Table 1A.1 (continued)

Variable	Men Coefficient	Men Std. error	Women Coefficient	Women Std. error
Diabetes	0.058	0.049	−0.094	0.065
Back problems	−0.009	0.026	−0.027	0.030
Depression	−0.020***	0.005	−0.004	0.005
Psychological disorder	−0.048	0.045	−0.043	0.038
Smoking currently	−0.029	0.025	0.009	0.032
Smoking formerly	−0.024	0.024	0.001	0.027
Underweight	−0.265**	0.106	−0.010	0.076
Overweight	0.002	0.022	−0.032	0.026
Obese	−0.019	0.030	−0.009	0.035
Education				
Primary	Ref.	Ref.	Ref.	Ref.
Secondary	0.060	0.039	0.060	0.043
Tertiary	0.071*	0.041	0.143***	0.045
Marital status				
Married	0.090***	0.022	−0.074***	0.024
Scheme				
Wage earners	Ref.	Ref.	Ref.	Ref.
Self-employed	0.026	0.034	0.107**	0.046
Civil servants	0.075***	0.029	0.174***	0.032
Skill				
Low	Ref.	Ref.	Ref.	Ref.
Medium	−0.188***	0.039	0.046	0.046
High	0.080***	0.029	0.098***	0.037
Constant	0.758***	0.055	0.701***	0.057
No. obs.	1,226		1,558	

Note: OLS regression based on SHARE data waves 1, 2, 4, and 5.
***Significant at the 1 percent level.
**Significant at the 5 percent level.
*Significant at the 10 percent level.

Table 1A.2   Simulations of work capacity, all health variables

Age group	No. obs.	Actual % working	Predicted % working	Additional work capacity (%)
		Men		
55–59	1,442	58.5	80.2	21.7
60–64	1,282	20.9	79.6	58.7
65–69	1,049	3.0	79.3	76.3
70–74	795	0.7	75.9	75.2
		Women		
55–59	1,565	45.6	65.8	20.2
60–64	1,325	16.3	64.4	28.1
65–69	1,118	1.7	62.0	60.3
70–74	962	0.6	57.3	56.7

Note: Simulations based on estimates of table 1A.1.

References

Aliaj, A., X. Flawinne, A. Jousten, S. Perelman, and L. Shi. 2016. "Old-Age Employment and Hours of Work Trends: Empirical Analysis for Four European Countries." *IZA Journal of European Labor Studies* 5 (16).

Cutler, D., E. Meara, and S. Richards-Shubik. 2012. "Health and Work Capacity of Older Adults: Estimates and Implications for Social Security Policy." Unpublished Manuscript. Available at SSRN: http://ssrn.com/abstract=2577858.

Dellis, A., R. Desmet, A. Jousten, and S. Perelman. 2004. "Micro-Modeling of Retirement in Belgium." In *Social Security Programs and Retirement around the World: Micro-Estimation*, edited by J. Gruber and D. Wise. Chicago: University Chicago Press.

Desmet, R., A. Jousten, S. Perelman, and P. Pestieau. 2007. "Micro-Simulation of Social Security in Belgium." In *Social Security Programs and Retirement around the World: Fiscal Implications of Reform*, edited by J. Gruber and D. Wise. Chicago: University Chicago Press.

Desmette, D., and P. Vendramin. 2014. "Bridge Employment in Belgium: Between an Early Retirement Culture and a Concern for Work Sustainability." In *Bridge Employment: A Research Handbook*, edited by C. Alcover, G. Topa, E. Parry, F. Fraccaroli, and M. Depolo. London: Routlege.

Expert Committee. 2014. "Un Contrat Social Performant et Fiable: Propositions de la Commission de Réforme des Pensions 2020–2040 pour une réforme structurelle des régimes de pension." Service Public Fédéral Sécurité Sociale, Brussels. http://hdl.handle.net/11245/1.474631.

Jousten, A., and M. Lefebvre. 2013. "Retirement Incentives in Belgium: Estimations and Simulations Using SHARE Data." *De Economist* 161:253–76.

Jousten, A., M. Lefebvre, and S. Perelman. 2012. "Disability in Belgium: There Is More Than Meets the Eye." In *Social Security Programs and Retirement around the World: Historical Trends in Mortality and Health, Employment, and Disability Insurance Participation and Reforms*, edited by D. Wise. Chicago: University Chicago Press.

———. 2016. "Health Status, Disability and Retirement Incentives in Belgium." In *Social Security Programs and Retirement around the World: Disability Insurance Programs and Retirement*, edited by D. Wise. Chicago: University of Chicago Press.

Jousten, A., M. Lefebvre, S. Perelman, and P. Pestieau. 2010. "The Effects of Early Retirement on Youth Unemployment: The Case of Belgium." In *Social Security Programs and Retirement around the World: The Relationship to Youth Employment*, edited by J. Gruber and D. Wise. Chicago: University Chicago Press.

Jousten A., and L. Salanauskaite. 2015. "Understanding Employment Participation of Older Workers—National Report: Belgium." In *Understanding Employment Participation of Older Workers: Creating a Knowledge Base for Future Labour Market Challenges*, edited by H.-M. Hasselhorn and W. Apt. Berlin: Federal Ministry of Labour and Social Affairs.

Milligan, K., and D. Wise. 2015. "Health and Work at Older Ages: Using Mortality to Assess the Capacity to Work across Countries." *Journal of Population Aging* 8 (1–2): 27–50.

Poterba, James, Steven Venti, and David A. Wise. 2013. "Health, Education, and the Post-Retirement Evolution of Household Assets." *Journal of Human Capital* 7 (4): 297–339.

Schreurs, B., H. Van Emmerik, N. De Cuyper, G. Notelaers, and H. De Witte. 2011. "Job Demands-Resources and Early Retirement Intention: Differences between

Blue- and White-Collar Workers." *Economic and Industrial Democracy* 32 (1): 47–68.

Van Looy, D., M. Kovalenko, D. Mortelmans, and H. De Preter. 2014. *Working Hour-Reduction in the Move to Full Retirement: How Does This Affect Retirement Preferences of 50+ Individuals in Flanders?* Leuven: Steunpunt Werk en Sociale Economie. Antwerpen: CELLO, Universiteit Antwerpen.

Health Capacity to Work at Older Ages
Evidence from Canada

Kevin Milligan and Tammy Schirle

2.1 Introduction

Health and longevity have improved substantially and continuously in Canada since the 1970s. Public pensions in Canada have not kept pace with these changes up to now.[1] In the 1980s, for example, the earnings-related Canada and Quebec Pension Plans facilitated earlier retirement by introducing an early retirement option as young as age sixty so that Canadians no longer had to wait until age sixty-five to take up benefits. More recently, the federal government had announced that the age of eligibility for Canada's public pensions delivered in the form of demogrants (Old Age Security) and related income-tested senior benefits (the Guaranteed Income Supplement) would increase from age sixty-five to age sixty-seven, affecting people born in 1958 and later. This policy change was canceled in 2016, before it was implemented.

But to what extent are older individuals able to work longer? In this study we are concerned with measuring individuals' health capacity for work. As health improves and people live longer, to what extent are they able to work

Kevin Milligan is professor of economics in the Vancouver School of Economics, University of British Columbia, and a research associate of the National Bureau of Economic Research. Tammy Schirle is associate professor of economics at Wilfrid Laurier University.

This chapter is part of the National Bureau of Economic Research's International Social Security project, which is supported by the National Institute on Aging. The authors thank members of other country teams in the ISS project for comments and suggestions. Some data used in this article was accessed at the British Columbia and South Western Ontario Research Data Centres. This chapter represents the views of the authors and does not necessarily reflect the views of Statistics Canada. For acknowledgments, sources of research support, and disclosure of the authors' material financial relationships, if any, please see http://www.nber.org/chapters/c13739.ack.

1. See Milligan and Schirle (2008) for an overview of Canada's retirement income system.

more? Of course, one's capacity to work is not directly measurable. We take two separate and distinct approaches to measuring health capacity for work among older men and women in this study.

First, we use mortality as a rough proxy for health. We relate the age-specific employment rates of men and women to their mortality rates at each age fifty-five to sixty-nine in 2011, and then construct a simple counterfactual: for a given level of mortality, how much more did people work in 1976? The difference between our observed employment rates at each age and these counterfactual employment rates suggests the extent to which individuals may be capable of working more. Our analysis does not recommend that people necessarily should work more, recognizing that increasing leisure time among older individuals is expected as income rises and will greatly improve well-being. Furthermore, we emphasize the limitations of using mortality as a proxy for health. Most importantly, mortality does not account for the incidence of chronic diseases, disability, or other activity limitations, and the relationship between mortality and these conditions may have changed over time.

Second, we relate the employment status of men and women at ages fifty to fifty-four to the employment status of men and women at older ages reporting the same health conditions. Our methods follow Cutler, Meara, and Richards-Shubik (2012), which measures the relationship between employment and health among those in the younger age group and applies that same relationship to the older age group to predict employment. We then compare the predicted to the observed employment levels of the older age group to obtain a measure of the additional employment capacity among older individuals. Again, we emphasize that this exercise is not meant to suggest that individuals should be working more at older ages, only whether the potential to work more exists.

Third, we consider whether the health capacity of older individuals to work varies by education group. We begin by offering estimates following the Cutler, Meara, and Richards-Shubik (2012) methods above, but estimating the employment rates separately for each education group. We then explore recent trends in self-assessed measures of health by education group. One challenge (pointed out in Bound et al. [2014]) in examining trends by education over time is that the average level of education in the Canadian population has increased over time. As such, the portion of the population in each education category has also changed over time. To overcome this challenge, we create education quartiles and explore health trends within each quartile.

We find that there is substantial unused work capacity among seniors in Canada. The expansion of health and longevity has not been matched by increased work by any of our measures. The chapter proceeds as follows. First, we describe the basic time trends in health and labor force participation for older Canadians. We then present the results focused on mortality as a proxy for health and how it relates to employment. Next, we explore the health and employment comparison of slightly younger and slightly older workers. Finally, we show the analysis by education groups and then conclude.

2.2   Trends in Labor Force Participation and Health

In Canada the labor force participation rates of older men and women display very different trends, presented in figures 2.1 and 2.2. For older men, there was a general decline in participation rates until the mid-1990s. For men age fifty-five to sixty-four, participation fell from 76 percent in 1976 to only 58 percent in 1995. For men age sixty-five and older, participation fell from 15 percent in 1976 and reached an historical low a bit later, at 9.4 percent in 2001. Thereafter, older men's participation rates have increased steadily, reaching 70 percent for men age fifty-five to sixty-four and 18 percent for men age sixty-five and older by 2014. The trends in male labor force participation changed despite no significant contemporaneous changes to pension policy in Canada.

Schirle (2008) has suggested a large part of the recent increase in older men's participation rates directly relates to increases in the participation rates of older women, as there may exist some complementarities in husbands' and wives' preferences for leisure time. The participation rates of older women age fifty-five to sixty-four have increased substantially over the 1976–2014 period (from 32 to 59 percent), with the largest increases occurring in the mid-1990s. For older women age sixty-five and older, rates

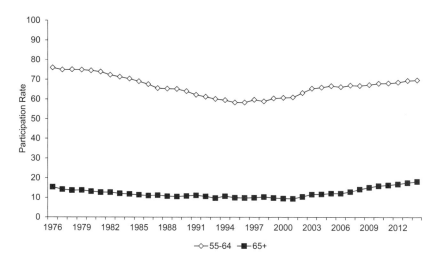

Fig. 2.1   Men's labor force participation, ages fifty-five to sixty-four and sixty-five and older (1976–2014)

Source: Statistics Canada Cansim Table 282–0002.

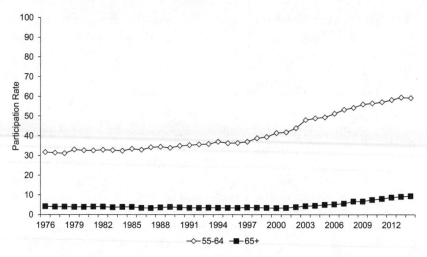

Fig. 2.2   Women's labor force participation, ages fifty-five to sixty-four and sixty-five and older (1976–2014)

Source: Statistics Canada Cansim Table 282–0002.

nearly tripled after 2000, moving from 3.3 percent in 2000 to 9.4 percent in 2014. Other Canadian research (including Au, Crossley, and Schellhorn 2005; Schirle 2010), has suggested that health is also an important factor affecting the decision to retire.

With respect to health measures, the data are more limited in measuring changes over extended periods of time. In figure 2.3, we present trends in the mortality rates of men from the ages of fifty to seventy-five for select years.[2] At all ages, the mortality rates of men have declined over time. In 1976, men age fifty-five had a mortality rate of 1.1 percent. By 2009, their mortality rate had fallen by more than half, to only 0.52 percent. In 2009, the mortality rate of 1.1 percent is not reached until age sixty-four. In figure 2.3 we also present the portion of men who report their health as fair or poor, in 1997–2001 and in 2007–2011. While this measure of health demonstrates a clear age gradient, we do not see the clear improvements in self-reported health that we could see in mortality over this shorter time period.

Similar to the experience of other countries, we see that the participation rates of older men fell until the last part of the century and then began to increase. At the same time, the participation rates of older women started to increase substantially at the end of the century. The age-specific mortality rates of men have steadily fallen over this time period. In the sections that follow, we explore the extent to which the trends in labor supply and health have moved together.

---

2. For the analysis of self-assessed health, we are constrained to the years available in the Survey of Labour and Income Dynamics.

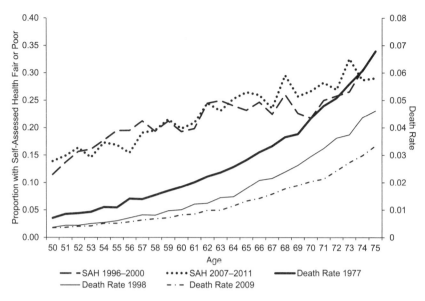

Fig. 2.3   SAH and mortality for men age fifty to seventy-five
Source: Survey of Labour and Income Dynamics and Human Mortality Database.

2.3   Estimating Health Capacity to Work Using the Milligan-Wise Method

We implement the methodology developed in Milligan and Wise (2015). We examine the relationship between employment and mortality at different points in time to characterize individuals' ability to work at older ages. In particular, we examine the extent to which individuals in 2011 were working given their mortality rates in 2011, and then compare the employment rates at comparable levels of mortality in previous years. By observing the historical patterns of employment and mortality across all available years, we create a consistent and comparable measure of the additional employment capacity that goes unused in the 2011 labor market.

It is important to recognize that mortality is a limited measure of health that does not account for the incidence of chronic diseases, disability, or other activity limitations. While improvements in mortality rates appear to align well with other indicators of health at older ages, it cannot offer a transparent measure of health capacity to work.[3] Focusing on mortality in this study, however, brings two benefits. First, using mortality allows us to produce results that are comparable across countries. Self-assessed measures

---

3. For example, health-adjusted life expectancy has improved at approximately the same rate as life expectancy in recent years (Statistics Canada 2012). Furthermore, the likelihood of seniors to be living in collective dwellings (primary health care and related facilities such as nursing homes) declined substantially over the 1981–2011 period (Milan, Wong, and Vézina 2014).

of health may lack comparability due to differences in language or culture (see, for example, Jürges 2007). Second, using mortality extends the time period available for analysis. Across time, more complete health data is only available in more recent years. In particular, Canadian data sources that can be used to create consistent national health measures over time only go back to 2001.[4] In contrast, mortality is available for Canada back to 1921.

The mortality data used in this analysis has been retrieved from the Human Mortality Database. Our employment data is from the Canadian Labour Force Survey (LFS).[5] The period we consider is 1976 through 2011, as these are the years for which we have both employment and mortality data available.

We conduct the analysis for men only, as the large increases in women's labor force participation over the entire time period make it difficult to interpret the results for women. While we expect the underlying relationship between women's health and women's capacity to work at older ages to be similar in nature to the relationship for men, differences in the propensity to work over one's lifetime across cohorts of women (see Schirle 2008) make historical health-work relationships more complex to analyze among women.

We begin by mapping the employment-mortality curves for 2011 and 1976 in figure 2.4, noting that 2011 will be used as the point of comparison in our analysis. Consider first the 2011 mortality-employment curve. In 2011, the mortality rate for fifty-five-year-old males was 0.005 (0.5 percent) and the employment rate for fifty-five-year-old males was 80.5 percent. Following the curve, as one ages the mortality rates are higher and the employment rates are lower. In 2011, the mortality rate for sixty-five-year-old men was 0.012 (1.2 percent) and the employment rate of sixty-five-year-old men was 36 percent.

In figure 2.4, the 1976 employment-mortality curve clearly lies above the 2011 curve. This tells us that for each possible mortality rate, the employment rates of men in 1976 were higher than the employment rates of men in 2011. The differences are quite large. In 2011, the employment rate of men with a mortality rate of 1.2 percent (at age sixty-five) was 36 percent. In 1976, the employment rate of men with a comparable mortality rate (at age fifty-five and a half) was 88 percent. This suggests that in 2011 the employment rates of men at age sixty-five could be substantially higher if employment had increased with improvements in mortality—by 52 percentage points. Similar comparisons between 2011 (as the reference point) and 1976 can be made for each mortality rate.

When aggregated across all mortality levels from ages fifty-five to sixty-

4. The CCHS is available since 2001, as described in the following section. Earlier surveys do not offer comparable measures over time.
5. Confidential microdata files made available through the Statistics Canada Research Data Centres program are used to construct age-gender-specific employment rates.

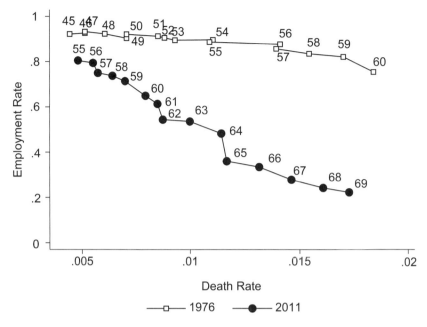

Fig. 2.4   Employment and mortality in 2011 and 1976
Source: Labour Force Survey and Human Mortality Database.

nine, we can calculate the total additional employment capacity between the two years. We present these results in table 2.1. Using 2011 as the reference year, we determine the extent to which men at each age from fifty-five to sixty-nine could be working more when compared to 1976. For example, given their mortality rate in 2011, an additional 12 percent of men age fifty-five could have worked, which implies an average 0.12 additional work years (one additional year for 12 percent of fifty-five-year-olds). Repeating this for each age and accumulating the amounts, we obtain the total potential additional employment capacity for older men in 2011, 5.31 years. This is a 65 percent increase over the 8.06 years that were actually worked between ages fifty-five and sixty-nine in 2011.

An important issue in implementing this method to measure additional employment capacity is that the choice of year to use for comparison to 2011 will matter. In figure 2.5, we present the employment-mortality curves for 2011 and 1995, the year in which the employment rates of older men in Canada reached an historic low. Since 1995, Canadian men have seen increases in employment and further reductions in mortality rates. The two employment-mortality curves are clearly not as distant as the 2011 and 1976 curves were in figure 2.4. As such, a measure of the potential additional employment capacity will be less when using 1995 rather than 1976 as the comparison.

Table 2.1　　　　　**Additional employment capacity (men)**

Age	Death rate in 2011 (%)	Employment rate in 2011 (%)	Employment rate in 1976 at same death rate (%)	Additional employment capacity (%)
55	0.48	80.50	92.46	11.96
56	0.55	79.41	92.90	13.49
57	0.57	75.00	92.68	17.68
58	0.64	73.76	91.68	17.93
59	0.70	71.41	90.58	19.16
60	0.79	64.96	91.64	26.68
61	0.85	61.37	91.31	29.94
62	0.87	54.34	90.79	36.45
63	1.00	53.54	89.58	36.04
64	1.14	48.22	88.53	40.31
65	1.17	36.01	88.45	52.45
66	1.32	33.44	87.98	54.54
67	1.46	27.79	84.67	56.88
68	1.61	24.17	82.93	58.77
69	1.73	22.24	80.85	58.61
Total years		8.0		5.3

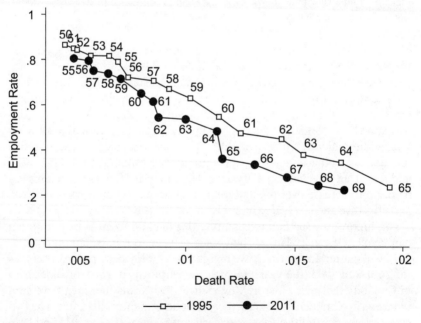

Fig. 2.5　Employment and mortality 2011 and 1995
Source: Labour Force Survey and Human Mortality Database.

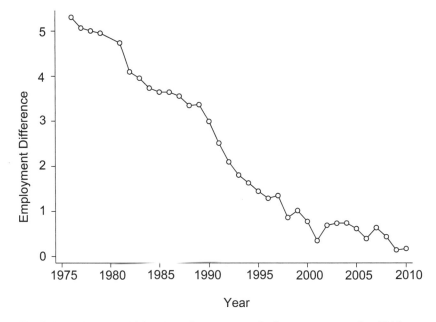

Fig. 2.6   Estimated additional employment capacity by year, compared to 2011
Source: Authors' calculations based on Labour Force Survey and Human Mortality Database.

To make this clearer, we present the total potential additional employment capacity for older men in 2011 as it depends on each comparison year 1976–2010 in figure 2.6. For each year, the graph shows on the y-axis the number of extra years of work if those in 2011 were to work at the employment rates prevalent in the year presented on the x-axis. So, the 1976 data point is set at 5.31 as explained above.

Throughout the first twenty years of the graph, employment was falling and mortality was improving. Both of these factors were therefore expanding unused work capacity; pushing in the same direction. This accounts for the steady change in work capacity from 1976 to 1995. In 1995, the work capacity relative to 2011 was 1.44 years, which is a change of 3.87 years of work from 1976.

After 1995, the employment rate of men at these ages started to increase. Mortality, on the other hand, continued its decline. So, the two factors are pushing against each other for work capacity—were men working enough to take up the new work capacity afforded through mortality improvements? The answer shown in the graph is that mortality improvements still outpaced employment in the 1995 to 2011 era, but the change was much slower than the 1976 to 1995 era. Between 1995 and 2011, work capacity expanded by 1.44 years.

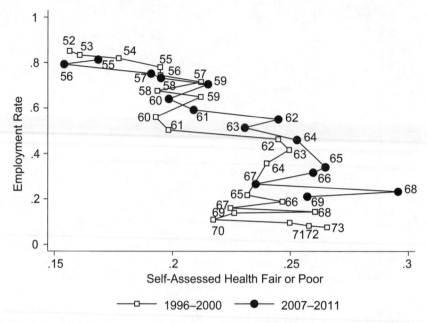

Fig. 2.7   Employment versus self-assessed health 1996–2000 versus 2007–2011
Source: Authors' calculations based on Labour Force Survey and Survey of Labour and Income Dynamics.

In figure 2.7, we repeat this exercise using the share of male respondents reporting their health to be "fair" or "poor" in place of mortality. These data are drawn from the Survey of Labour and Income Dyamics. Because of data availability, we can only start this in the late 1990s. Furthermore, because of sampling variation inherent to small sample sizes, we need to pool together several years in order to get a smooth curve. So, the figure shows two sets of years: 1996 to 2000 and 2007 to 2011. There appears to be little difference between the lines in figure 2.7. This is perhaps similar to what is seen in figure 2.5, since over this time period employment was growing at the same time as self-assessed health did not move much.

This section has explored the use of mortality to measure work capacity. By comparing the employment rates across years at a given level of mortality, we calculate an employment difference. By summing these employment differences across ages we arrive at a single measure of work capacity—the number of extra years that would be worked if employment matched the mortality-employment pattern of another year. We find that work capacity continued to improve over the entire period, but the pace of growth of the work capacity slowed substantially after 1995, as male employment started to grow.

This analysis does not suggest that older men necessarily should work more, or that all gains in mortality necessarily translate into work capacity.

Instead, we take this measure as an upper bound on the expansion of work capacity through time. This measure should be interpreted in the context of our other analysis below, which incorporates more subtle elements of health to measure work capacity.

2.4   Estimating Health Capacity to Work Using the Cutler et al. Method

Our second method of measuring health capacity to work follows the method developed by Cutler, Meara, and Richards-Shubik (2012), relating individuals' employment status to their health conditions. To begin, we estimate the following equation (for men and women separately) using samples of individuals age fifty to fifty-four:

$$\text{Employed}_i = \beta_0 + \beta_1 X_i + \beta_0 Z_i + \varepsilon_i,$$

where Employed is a dummy variable equal to one if person i is employed and zero otherwise. The set of covariates X_i includes various measures of health including self-assessed health (poor-excellent), reports of heart disease, stroke, cancer, diabetes, arthritis, obesity, back pain, and high blood pressure, and whether the person is a daily or occasional smoker. The set of covariates Z_i controls for demographic characteristics, including marital status, education, and cultural/racial origin (white or not white). A linear probability model is used to estimate the equation.

We also estimate a second version of the regression model where the covariates included in X_i are replaced with a single health index value. The index (referred to hereafter as the PVW health index) is constructed using the approach of Poterba, Venti, and Wise (2013). We construct a health index based on various indicators of health, including indicators for self-assessed fair or poor health, arthritis, back pain, heart disease, high blood pressure, diabetes, and cancer, and measures of body mass index ([BMI], based on self-reports of height and weight), the number of overnight visits to hospital, the number of doctor visits (general practitioner or other medical doctor), and the number of nurse visits.[6] To construct the indicator, we follow the work of Coile, Milligan, and Wise (chapter 12, this volume) and first obtain the first principal component of these indicators, which is the "weighted average of indicators where the weights are chosen to maximize the proportion of the variance of the individual health indicators that can be explained by this weighted average." The estimated coefficients are used to predict a percentile score for the health of each respondent, and this percentile score is used as the PVW health index.

The estimates of the regression are then used to predict the probability of employment conditional on health and demographic characteristics among those age fifty-five to seventy-four. The difference between observed

---

6. Note that US data allow for a more complete list of health indicators, including activity limitations, that we are unable to account for.

employment rates and predicted employment rates is then used to describe the potential additional employment capacity among older workers. It is important to recognize the assumptions underlying this analysis. First, we do not account for any unmeasured or omitted dimensions of health. If health declines more rapidly with age than what is reflected in our measures, then we will overestimate the additional employment capacity of those age fifty-five to seventy-four. For example, while we have indicators for heart disease as a covariate in the regression, the severity of heart disease is not measured and we expect this to become a more severe condition as individuals age. While the PVW index of health is used in an effort to address this concern, we cannot speak directly to the extent to which we may be overstating employment capacity. Second, the approach assumes that the relationship between health and employment among those age fifty-five to seventy-four is the same as among those age fifty to fifty-four. Third, discretionary retirement at ages fifty to fifty-four in Canada is not unheard of. In 2014, 7 percent of men and women age fifty to fifty-four who were separated from their jobs report that the reason for job separation was retirement.[7] To the extent that nonemployment among fifty- to fifty-five-year-olds represents retirement for nonhealth reasons, our estimates will understate the potential employment capacity at older ages.

We use a sample of men and women from the Canadian Community Health Survey from 2001 to 2012. The survey was conducted biannually from 2001 to 2005 and then annually from 2007 to 2012. Each year a new sample of individuals are interviewed. Labor market information is quite limited in the survey, but we are able to measure whether one is employed (in the previous week), some basic demographics, and the health conditions listed above.[8] Several pieces of health information are only collected periodically or for specific geographic regions as part of the CCHS's optional modules.[9] For the analysis that follows we pool together all available observations over this time period, leaving us with 21,051 male and 23,853 female observations age fifty to fifty-four for estimating our employment regression.[10]

7. Only those not holding a job at the time of the survey or were separated from a job in the previous year respond to this question. Respondents can only choose one reason for job separation and options include quits, business conditions, own illness or disability, and family responsibilities as possible responses.
8. The resulting employment rates closely match those estimated using a comparable sample in the Canadian Labour Force Survey when the previous week is used as the reference time period. Also available in the CCHS are indicators for employment in the previous three months or past year, which tends to overstate employment rates. Occupation information is only collected for those currently employed.
9. For example, in the 2012 CCHS information on activity limitations is collected only for Newfoundland and Ontario, and depression information was an optional module used in the Atlantic, Saskatchewan, and Alberta.
10. We exclude all observations with incomplete health information for the regressions and the PVW index construction. Note that in 2001, only those age fifty to sixty-four reported the information necessary for the BMI. As such, summary statistics for older groups (sixty-five to sixty-nine and seventy to seventy-four) will not include observations from 2001.

Table 2.2A   **Summary statistics (men)**

	50–54	55–59	60–64	65–69	70–74
Employed	0.821	0.702	0.495	0.266	0.134
Self-assessed health					
Excellent	0.211	0.199	0.181	0.161	0.132
Very good	0.352	0.333	0.311	0.305	0.290
Good	0.309	0.307	0.322	0.344	0.349
Fair	0.092	0.114	0.136	0.141	0.171
Poor	0.037	0.047	0.049	0.050	0.058
Health conditions					
Heart	0.050	0.093	0.123	0.167	0.212
Stroke	0.008	0.012	0.022	0.030	0.045
Cancer	0.015	0.021	0.040	0.055	0.070
High blood pressure	0.199	0.264	0.332	0.393	0.408
Arthritis	0.154	0.207	0.261	0.296	0.345
Diabetes	0.069	0.111	0.136	0.179	0.181
Back pain	0.244	0.250	0.248	0.238	0.222
Underweight	0.011	0.008	0.009	0.008	0.010
Normal weight	0.326	0.321	0.331	0.324	0.373
Overweight	0.401	0.403	0.408	0.460	0.454
Obese	0.262	0.267	0.253	0.207	0.162
Smoker-daily	0.227	0.201	0.166	0.131	0.095
Smoker-occasional	0.038	0.033	0.027	0.024	0.019
BMI	27.2	27.3	27.1	27.1	26.5
No. nights hospital	0.537	0.674	1.042	1.354	1.575
No. doctor visits	3.365	4.004	4.482	4.506	5.040
No. nurse visits	0.488	0.737	0.732	1.012	1.104
Education					
Less than HS grad.	0.153	0.184	0.247	0.303	0.375
HS graduate	0.171	0.155	0.143	0.129	0.119
Postsecondary (< BA)	0.430	0.412	0.387	0.361	0.324
University (BA +)	0.236	0.240	0.214	0.198	0.168
Married	0.794	0.818	0.820	0.830	0.814
White	0.764	0.770	0.784	0.762	0.756
No. observations	21,051	20,571	18,394	12,691	10,338

Source: CCHS.

The samples of older individuals by age group are described in tables 2.2A (men) and 2.2B (women). The likelihood of being employed rapidly falls with age, particularly after age fifty-five to fifty-nine. At ages fifty to fifty-four, 82.1 percent of men are employed in our sample; at ages fifty-five to fifty-nine 70.2 percent are employed, but at ages sixty to sixty-four only 49.5 percent are employed. For women, 71 percent are employed at ages fifty to fifty-four, and 32.5 percent by ages sixty to sixty-four.

The summary statistics in tables 2.2A and 2.2B also indicate the extent to which health deteriorates with age. Among men age fifty to fifty-four, 13 percent rated their health as fair or poor. At ages sixty-five to sixty-nine,

Table 2.2B   Summary statistics (women)

	50–54	55–59	60–64	65–69	70–74
Employed	0.710	0.551	0.325	0.126	0.049
Self-assessed health					
Excellent	0.222	0.201	0.170	0.150	0.120
Very good	0.361	0.344	0.325	0.315	0.285
Good	0.286	0.298	0.320	0.352	0.361
Fair	0.096	0.112	0.136	0.141	0.175
Poor	0.035	0.045	0.049	0.042	0.059
Health conditions					
Heart	0.028	0.046	0.074	0.100	0.145
Stroke	0.007	0.012	0.017	0.022	0.028
Cancer	0.021	0.033	0.037	0.042	0.050
High blood pressure	0.185	0.262	0.344	0.427	0.499
Arthritis	0.244	0.327	0.400	0.468	0.513
Diabetes	0.050	0.076	0.097	0.119	0.131
Back pain	0.239	0.254	0.271	0.258	0.259
Underweight	0.028	0.026	0.027	0.021	0.030
Normal weight	0.472	0.427	0.408	0.417	0.411
Overweight	0.273	0.313	0.322	0.363	0.366
Obese	0.227	0.234	0.244	0.200	0.193
Smoker-daily	0.190	0.170	0.138	0.116	0.092
Smoker-occasional	0.035	0.028	0.025	0.020	0.020
BMI	26.1	26.4	26.6	26.4	26.2
No. nights hospital	0.518	0.633	0.877	0.999	1.305
No. doctor visits	4.799	4.822	4.980	4.794	5.047
No. nurse visits	0.619	0.782	0.716	0.704	1.153
Education					
Less than HS grad.	0.143	0.199	0.276	0.338	0.412
HS graduate	0.211	0.189	0.188	0.177	0.174
Postsecondary (< BA)	0.428	0.420	0.377	0.364	0.318
University (BA +)	0.209	0.185	0.152	0.110	0.084
Married	0.745	0.733	0.703	0.647	0.560
White	0.775	0.774	0.791	0.770	0.786
No. observations	23,853	23,971	21,590	15,336	13,695

Source: CCHS.

19 percent rate their health as fair or poor. Among women, 13 percent of those age fifty to fifty-four reported fair or poor health while 18 percent of those age sixty-five to sixty-nine reported fair or poor health. Most health conditions, including heart disease, arthritis, and diabetes are more common as one ages. However some conditions, such as back pain, are not increasing with age. With respect to weight, the age patterns are not clear. On one hand, men and women appear more likely overweight as they age. On the other hand, they are less likely obese with age. Notably, the likelihood of being a smoker tends to fall with age in our samples, in part reflecting the fact that those in worst health at younger ages are not likely to survive.

Table 2.3A   **Employment regressions, all health variables**

	Men 50–54		Women 50–54	
	Coef.	Std. err.	Coef.	Std. err.
SAH				
Very good	−0.0090	0.0069	0.0081	0.0076
Good	−0.0431	0.0073	−0.0321	0.0083
Fair	−0.1821	0.0107	−0.2015	0.0117
Poor	−0.4171	0.0152	−0.4940	0.0172
Heart	−0.0299	0.0119	−0.0161	0.0174
Stroke	−0.1094	0.0290	−0.2162	0.0332
Cancer	−0.0967	0.0204	−0.0139	0.0196
High blood pressure	0.0012	0.0066	−0.0096	0.0076
Arthritis	−0.0399	0.0072	−0.0231	0.0069
Diabetes	−0.0159	0.0103	−0.0046	0.0134
Back pain	−0.0176	0.0060	−0.0197	0.0068
Underweight	0.0034	0.0242	−0.0573	0.0171
Overweight	0.0026	0.0060	0.0142	0.0067
Obese	0.0065	0.0069	−0.0041	0.0076
Smoker-daily	−0.0310	0.0062	−0.0199	0.0074
Smoker-occasional	−0.0505	0.0132	−0.0035	0.0153
Less than HS grad.	−0.0545	0.0087	−0.1337	0.0095
Postsecondary (< BA)	0.0122	0.0070	0.0642	0.0073
University (BA +)	0.0380	0.0079	0.0963	0.0086
Married	0.1183	0.0063	−0.0196	0.0064
White	0.0539	0.0060	0.0535	0.0067
Constant	0.7500	0.0109	0.7151	0.0112

Table 2.3B   **Employment regressions, PVW health index**

	Men 50–54		Women 50–54	
	Coef.	Std. err.	Coef.	Std. err.
Health index	0.0025	0.0001	0.0027	0.0001
Less than HS grad.	−0.0670	0.0089	−0.1506	0.0097
Postsecondary (< BA)	0.0158	0.0071	0.0687	0.0074
University (BA +)	0.0506	0.0080	0.1031	0.0087
Married	0.1425	0.0063	−0.0034	0.0065
White	0.0657	0.0060	0.0604	0.0068
Constant	0.5038	0.0107	0.4768	0.0110

The results of estimating our regression are presented in tables 2.3A and 2.3B. In table 2.3A, we present the results for our employment equation that includes all health variables. The results show that most of the health conditions accounted for have large and statistically significant effects on employment. Men indicating poor health are 42 percentage points less likely employed than men indicating excellent health, and the effect of poor health on women's employment is even larger (49 percentage points). Heart disease, stroke, cancer, arthritis, and back pain also have substantial and significant effects on the likelihood of men's employment. However, high blood pressure, diabetes, and weight conditions do not appear to affect men's employment. For women, a slightly different set of health conditions appears important for employment—stroke, arthritis, back pain, and weight conditions have a significant effect on the likelihood of women's employment at ages fifty to fifty-four. However, and perhaps counterintuitively, being overweight appears to increase a woman's likelihood of being employed. Being a daily smoker negatively affects men's and women's likelihood of employment.

In table 2.3B, the effect of an increase in the health index is positive and significant. For example, a 10 percentage point increase in the index raises the likelihood of being employed by 2.5 percentage points for men and 2.7 percentage points for women. This aligns well with the estimates presented in table 2.3A and we suggest the index functions well as an overall indicator of one's health. With respect to other demographic characteristics, the estimated effects do not heavily depend on whether the health variables or the index is used in the regression. In what follows, we tend to focus on the results in table 2.3B as they are most comparable with respect to interpretation of results with other countries presented in this volume.

In table 2.4 we report the results of imposing our regression estimates in tables 2.3A and 2.3B (based on a sample of fifty- to fifty-four-year-olds) on men and women age fifty-five to seventy-four and predicting their work status conditional on their health and demographics. The first set of columns in table 2.4 uses the regression estimates in table 2.3A in the simulation exercise (with all health variables included in the regression) and the second set of columns uses the regression estimates presented in table 2.3B (using the PVW health index).

Table 2.4   Simulations of work capacity

Age group	No. obs.	Use all health variables			Use PVW health index		
		Actual % working	Predicted % working	Estimated work capacity (%)	Actual % working	Predicted % working	Estimated work capacity (%)
		Men					
55–59	20,571	70.2	81.0	10.8	70.2	80.8	10.6
60–64	18,394	49.5	79.6	30.1	49.5	79.1	29.6
65–69	12,691	26.6	78.5	51.8	26.6	77.4	50.8
70–74	10,338	13.4	76.1	62.6	13.4	75.4	62.0
		Women					
55–59	23,971	55.1	68.8	13.7	55.1	68.3	13.2
60–64	21,590	32.5	66.1	33.6	32.5	65.1	32.6
65–69	15,336	12.6	64.6	51.9	12.6	62.4	49.8
70–74	13,695	4.9	61.3	56.4	4.9	59.6	54.6

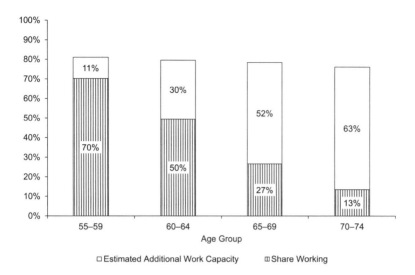

Fig. 2.8   Share of men working and additional work capacity by age
Note: Based on CCHS, regression uses PVW index, matches table 2.4 results.

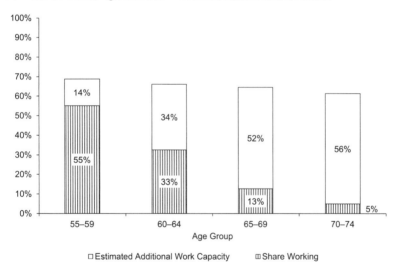

Fig. 2.9   Share of women working and additional work capacity by age
Note: Based on CCHS, regression uses PVW index, matches table 2.4 results.

The estimates in table 2.4 (also presented in figure 2.8 for men and figure 2.9 for women) indicate a substantial unused work capacity at older ages, for both men and women. At age fifty-five to fifty-nine, we observe 70 percent of men employed. The predicted percent of men working (when using the PVW health index), however, is much higher at 81 percent, implying there is an additional 11 percent of men age fifty-five to fifty-nine that could be working given their health status. These estimates are not out of line with the suggested capacity in the previous section using mortality, which suggested an additional 17.7 percent of men could be working at age fifty-seven given the mortality rate differences from 1976 to 2011. The estimates for older groups also suggest large unused work capacity. For example, for men at ages sixty-five to sixty-nine, the estimates in table 2.4 suggest employment rates could be 50.8 percentage points higher than observed. At age sixty-seven, our estimates based on mortality suggested a 56.9 percentage point additional employment capacity. If we use methods similar to those in the previous section (specifically table 2.1), the simulations imply an additional employment capacity of 4.6 years between the ages of fifty-five and sixty-nine.

Estimates for women's work capacity are slightly larger than the estimates for men at younger, but not older, ages. At ages fifty-five to fifty-nine, we estimate an additional employment capacity among women of 13 percentage points. At ages seventy to seventy-four, our estimates indicate an additional 55 percent of women could be employed, representing a slightly lower unused work capacity than among men.

In tables 2.5A and 2.5B (and graphically in figures 2.10 and 2.11), we present results based on regressions that allow the effects of health on employment to vary by education group, with an expectation that the capacity to work at older ages will vary across education groups. While it is clearly the case that more educated individuals are more likely employed at each age than less educated individuals, an education gradient for additional work capacity is not as clear.

Among men, it appears the lowest educated (with less than high school graduation in table 2.5A and figure 2.10) have the lowest employment rates and the smallest potential for additional work capacity. The notable exception here is among university-educated men at ages sixty-five to sixty-nine, who appear to have the same work capacity as those with less than high school graduation at ages sixty-five to sixty-nine. Otherwise, men with higher education—high school graduates and those with postsecondary education (university or college)—appear to have roughly the same estimated work capacity.

Among women, there is modest evidence that potential additional work capacity may have a clearer relationship with education. Similar to men, women in the lowest education group have the lowest employment rates and the lowest estimated work capacity. Among sixty- to sixty-four-year-olds and seventy- to seventy-four-year-olds there appears some evidence that additional capacity increases with education beyond high school graduation. For example, among sixty- to sixty-four-year-old women our estimates indicate 34 percent more women with high school graduation could be employed. Among those with a university degree, 38 percent more women could be employed at ages sixty to sixty-four. However, these patterns across education are not stark and are not observed for women ages fifty-five to fifty-nine and sixty-five to sixty-nine.

Table 2.5A   **Simulations of work capacity (regressions by education group)**

	Men, all health variables			Men, PVW health index		
	Actual % working	Predicted % working	Estimated work capacity (%)	Actual % working	Predicted % working	Estimated work capacity (%)
Age 55–59						
< HS grad	62.2	70.3	8.0	62.2	70.7	8.5
HS grad	70.8	83.1	12.3	70.8	82.8	12.0
PS (< BA)	71.5	82.6	11.1	71.5	81.9	10.3
University (BA +)	75.5	87.3	11.8	75.5	87.2	11.7
Age 60–64						
< HS grad	45.2	70.0	24.8	45.2	69.5	24.3
HS grad	50.2	81.5	31.3	50.2	81.4	31.2
PS (< BA)	48.4	82.1	33.8	48.4	81.0	32.6
University (BA +)	57.6	86.4	28.8	57.6	86.5	28.8
Age 65–69						
< HS grad	20.3	70.0	49.6	20.3	67.9	47.5
HS grad	27.3	81.9	54.6	27.3	81.1	53.8
PS (< BA)	25.5	81.6	56.0	25.5	79.9	54.4
University (BA +)	38.8	86.2	47.4	38.8	85.7	46.8
Age 70–74						
< HS grad	10.3	69.3	59.0	10.3	67.1	56.8
HS grad	13.3	79.5	66.2	13.3	79.7	66.4
PS (< BA)	14.1	81.0	66.9	14.1	79.3	65.2
University (BA +)	19.8	83.1	63.3	19.8	84.1	64.4

Table 2.5B   **Simulations of work capacity (regressions by education group)**

	Women, all health variables			Women, PVW health index		
	Actual % working	Predicted % working	Estimated work capacity (%)	Actual % working	Predicted % working	Estimated work capacity (%)
Age 55–59						
< HS grad	39.2	49.2	10.0	39.2	48.6	9.4
HS grad	53.0	69.3	16.3	53.0	68.2	15.3
PS (< BA)	60.2	74.0	13.8	60.2	73.5	13.3
University (BA +)	63.8	79.7	15.9	63.8	79.4	15.6
Age 60–64						
< HS grad	21.6	48.5	27.0	21.6	47.2	25.6
HS grad	33.5	68.3	34.7	33.5	67.3	33.7
PS (< BA)	37.1	73.5	36.5	37.1	72.2	35.1
University (BA +)	41.2	79.6	38.5	41.2	78.9	37.8
Age 65–69						
< HS grad	7.2	48.8	41.6	7.2	45.9	38.7
HS grad	12.0	69.6	57.6	12.0	66.9	54.9
PS (< BA)	15.4	73.4	58.0	15.4	71.3	55.9
University (BA +)	22.3	79.0	56.7	22.3	78.0	55.8
Age 70–74						
< HS grad	2.2	47.5	45.3	2.2	44.3	42.1
HS grad	5.4	68.1	62.6	5.4	65.8	60.3
PS (< BA)	6.9	71.5	64.7	6.9	70.0	63.2
University (BA +)	10.5	78.0	67.5	10.5	77.7	67.2

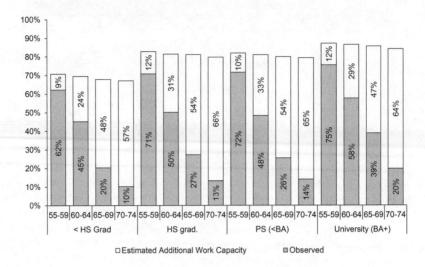

Fig. 2.10   Share of men working and estimated work capacity
Note: CCHS, regressions by education group, using PVW index. Results correspond to table 2.5A.

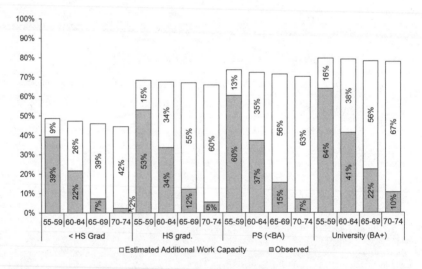

Fig. 2.11   Share of women working and estimated work capacity
Note: CCHS, regressions by education group, using PVW index. Results correspond to table 2.5B.

In this section we have employed the method of Cutler et al. to estimate the work capacity of older workers in the fifty-five to sixty-nine age range using the observed health-employment relationship among fifty- to fifty-four-year-olds. We find results that are quite similar to the mortality results, showing a substantial unused capacity to work at older ages.

2.5   Changes in Self-Assessed Health by Education Level over Time

In this section we explore further the potential for heterogeneity in health capacity and its evolution over time. Past Canadian research has demonstrated clear heterogeneity in life expectancy. Carriere and Galarneau (2012) have found that life expectancy tends to be shorter for those with less education. According to their estimates, life expectancy at age fifty was 32.4 years for people with less than a high school diploma, but thirty-six years for those with postsecondary education. Wolfson et al. (1993) used the CPP administrative data up to 1989 to relate earnings histories of men to their mortality at ages sixty-five to seventy-four. They find significant earnings-mortality gradients across earnings quintiles while accounting for various demographic characteristics. While there have been studies in other countries (including Waldron 2007; Bosworth and Burke 2014) finding that life expectancy has been growing more rapidly over time for high-income than low-income groups, there is not yet Canadian evidence to suggest a similar divergence in life expectancy among Canadians.

Here we want to more closely examine self-assessed health as reported in the Survey of Labour and Income Dynamics (SLID), 1996–2011, along the lines of socioeconomic status. We lack the information necessary for a careful measure of socioeconomic status, and turn to education as a key indicator. Using education, however, is problematic since education levels increased quite dramatically over time and failing to account for this can generate misleading results. Bound et al. (2014) suggest constructing education quartiles as an alternative to using education groups defined by levels of education attainment.

In figure 2.12, we provide estimates of the distribution of education for each year of birth among men. Pooling all available years from SLID 1993 to 2011, we find the portion of men that belong to each education category by year of birth.[11] Those born in 1921 are age seventy-five when we first observe their self-assessed health reports in 1996. Among men born in the 1920s, it was quite common to leave school before high school graduation: the median male completed some high school and the 25th percentile male completed five to eight years of elementary school. Men born in 1961 are age fifty when we observe their health in 2011. The median male born in 1961 has completed a nonuniversity postsecondary degree or certificate and the 25th percentile male has graduated from high school.

We use the information presented in figure 2.12 to construct education quartiles for each birth cohort. When assigning individuals to a quartile, we need to account for the extent to which an education category extends across quartiles. For example, for the men born in 1961, the first quartile

11. Using SLID, we are likely overstating the education levels of the earliest cohorts: for example, the 1921 cohort is observed from ages seventy-two to ninety (1993–2011) to derive the education distribution and those most educated are most likely to survive. We likely understate the education levels of the most recent cohorts as some men will upgrade education at later ages.

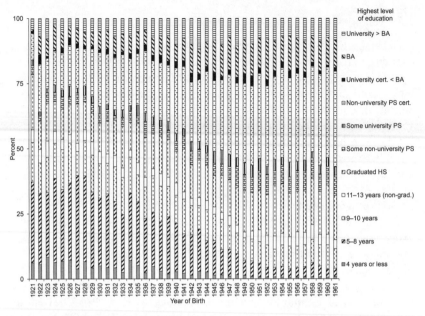

Fig. 2.12   Distribution of education completed by birth cohort (men)
Source: Based on tabulations in SLID, 1993–2011.

is represented by graduation from high school. Those reporting less than high school graduation are assigned to the first quartile. In addition, a portion of the men with high school graduation are also allocated to the first quartile. More precisely, 17 percent of men born in 1961 graduated from high school. If we could order them according to socioeconomic status, we would place 10 of the 17 percent into the first quartile. As a simpler procedure, we randomly assign 10 of the 17 percent of high school graduates to the first quartile, and place 7 of the 17 percent of high school graduates in the second quartile. The same procedure is used to allocate individuals to quartiles in each year of birth.

In figure 2.13, we present the share of men who report their health as fair or poor by age and education quartile, for the years 1996–2000 and 2007–2011. Similar to the information we provided in figure 2.3, we do not see a clear improvement in health over time for any of the education quartiles. This is despite aggregating five years of data to gain precision, and we have added smoothed polynomials to make any trends easier to recognize.

Figure 2.13 demonstrates a clear age gradient for all education quartiles. It is also clear that those with the lowest education are more likely to report poor or fair health at any age between fifty and seventy-five. Moreover, it appears the lowest educated face a steeper age gradient: for those in the first quartile, 18 percent report fair or poor health at age fifty compared to 45

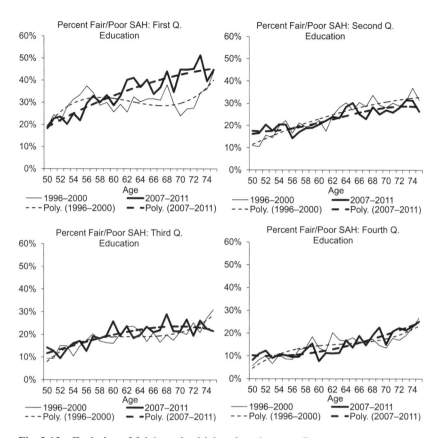

Fig. 2.13   Evolution of fair/poor health by education quartile

percent at age seventy-five. For those in the highest quartile, 8 percent report fair or poor health at age fifty compared to 25 percent at age seventy-five. Combined with evidence of shorter life expectancy among those with lower education, the heterogeneity across education groups in the evolution of their health with age remains an important consideration in the development of policy.

2.6   Discussion and Conclusion

In this chapter we study the capacity of older workers to continue working. Health has improved substantially over the decades, while employment expansion has not kept pace. The work in this chapter attempts to quantify that gap between how much work capacity has expanded and how much of it has been taken up with additional work. We do so using complementary methods that employ mortality as a simple yet comparable proxy measure for health, followed by a more subtle analysis that incorporates many observed health characteristics.

We find a substantial increase in unused work capacity of those age fifty-five to sixty-nine through time, on the order of five years of work, if workers were employed at the same rate as implied by their mortality levels or as much as workers age fifty to fifty-four with comparable health. It is not necessarily desirable for this expansion in work capacity to be filled entirely with work. Some who are elderly may have disabilities or other incapacities that do not allow continued work. Others have amassed a sufficient flow of retirement income that they prefer leisure to work. However, we consider the study of work capacity to be an important input to the ongoing discussion of how one's lifespan ought to be split between work and retirement, in the face of ever-expanding longevity and improving elderly health.

References

Au, D. W. H., T. F. Crossley, and M. Schellhorn. 2005. "The Effect of Health Changes and Long-Term Health on the Work Activity of Older Canadians." *Health Economics* 14:999–1018.

Bosworth, B. P., and K. Burke. 2014. "Differential Mortality and Retirement Benefits in the Health and Retirement Study." Working Paper, Brookings Institution. https://www.brookings.edu/research/differential-mortality-and-retirement -benefits-in-the-health-and-retirement-study/.

Bound, John, Arline Geronimus, Javier Rodriguez, and Timothy A. Waidmann. 2014. "The Implications of Differential Trends in Mortality for Social Security Policy." Working Paper no. 2014–314, Michigan Center for Retirement Research, University of Michigan.

Carriere, Yves, and Diane Galarneau. 2012. "How Many Years to Retirement?" *Insights on Canadian Society*. Statistics Canada Catalogue no. 75–006-X, December. http://www.statcan.gc.ca/pub/75-006-x/2012001/article/11750-eng.pdf.

Cutler, D. M., E. Meara, and S. Richards-Shubik. 2012. "Health and Work Capacity of Older Adults: Estimates and Implications for Social Security Policy." Unpublished Manuscript. Available at SSRN: http://ssrn.com/abstract=2577858.

Human Mortality Database. University of California, Berkeley (USA), and Max Planck Institute for Demographic Research (Germany). www.mortality.org. Accessed October 11, 2014.

Jürges, H. 2007. "True Health vs Response Styles: Exploring Cross-Country Differences in Self-Reported Health." *Health Economics* 16 (2): 163–78.

Milan, Anne, Irene Wong, and Mireille Vézina. 2014. "Emerging Trends in Living Arrangements and Conjugal Unions for Current and Future Seniors." *Insights on Canadian Society*, Statistics Canada Catalogue no. 75-006-X, February. http:// www.statcan.gc.ca/pub/75-006-x/2014001/article/11904-eng.htm.

Milligan, Kevin, and T. Schirle. 2008. "Improving the Labour Market Incentives in Canada's Public Pension System." *Canadian Public Policy* 34 (3): 281–304.

Milligan, K., and D. A. Wise. 2015. "Health and Work at Older Ages: Using Mortality to Assess the Capacity to Work across Countries." *Journal of Population Aging* 8 (1): 27–50.

Poterba, James, Steve Venti, and David A. Wise. 2013. "Health, Education, and the Post-Retirement Evolution of Household Assets." NBER Working Paper no. 18695, Cambridge, MA.

Schirle, T. 2008. "Why Have the Labour Force Participation Rates of Older Men Increased Since the Mid-1990s?" *Journal of Labor Economics* 26 (4): 549–94.

———. 2010. "Health, Pensions, and the Retirement Decision: Evidence from Canada." *Canadian Journal on Aging* 29 (4): 519–27.

Statistics Canada. 2012. Table 102–0122, Health-adjusted life expectancy, at birth and at age 65, by sex and income, Canada and provinces, occasional (years). CANSIM (database). Accessed February 9, 2015. http://www5.statcan.gc.ca/cansim /a26.

Waldron, Hilary. 2007. "Trends in Mortality Differentials and Life Expectancy for Male Social Security-Covered Workers, by Socioeconomic Status." *Social Security Bulletin* 67 (3). https://www.ssa.gov/policy/docs/ssb/v67n3/v67n3p1.html.

Wolfson, M., G. Rowe, J. F. Gentlman, and M. Tomiak. 1993. "Career Earnings and Death: A Longitudinal Analysis of Older Canadian Men." *Journal of Gerontology* 48 (4): S167–79.

3

Health Capacity to Work at Older Ages in Denmark

Paul Bingley, Nabanita Datta Gupta,
and Peder J. Pedersen

3.1 Introduction

Many countries are increasing the ages at which pension benefits are first available, and thereby reducing incentives to retire early. Moreover, with increased life expectancy, the global move from defined benefit toward defined contribution pension plans implies lower per-period consumption, all else equal, unless individuals work longer and retire later. Both of these changes push toward delayed retirement, but it remains to be shown

Paul Bingley is professor at SFI, The Danish National Centre for Social Research. Nabanita Datta Gupta is a professor in the department of economics and business economics at Aarhus University and a research fellow of IZA. Peder J. Pedersen is a research professor at SFI, The Danish National Centre for Social Research, an emeritus professor in the department of economics and business economics at Aarhus University, and a research fellow of IZA in Bonn.

This chapter is part of the National Bureau of Economic Research's International Social Security (ISS) project, which is supported by the National Institute on Aging (grant P01 AG012810). We are grateful to other ISS project team members for comments that have improved the chapter. This chapter uses data from SHARE wave 5 release 1.0.0, as of March 31st 2015 (DOI: 10.6103/SHARE.w5.100), SHARE wave 4 release 1.1.1, as of March 28th 2013 (DOI: 10.6103/SHARE.w4.111), and SHARE waves 1 and 2 release 2.6.0, as of November 29th 2013 (DOIs: 10.6103/SHARE.w1.260 and 10.6103/SHARE.w2.260). The SHARE data collection has been primarily funded by the European Commission through the 5th Framework Program (project QLK6-CT-2001-00360 in the thematic program Quality of Life), through the 6th Framework Program (projects SHARE-I3, RII-CT-2006-062193, COMPARE, CIT5-CT-2005-028857, CIT4-CT-2006-028812), and through the 7th Framework Program (SHARE-PREP, No. 211909, SHARE-LEAP, No. 227822 and SHARE M4, No. 261982). Additional funding from the US National Institute on Aging (U01 AG09740-13S2, P01 AG005842, P01 AG08291, P30 AG12815, R21 AG025169, Y1-AG-4553-01, IAG BSR06-11, and OGHA 04-064) and the German Ministry of Education and Research as well as from various national sources is gratefully acknowledged (see www.share-project.org for a full list of funding institutions). For acknowledgments, sources of research support, and disclosure of the author's or authors' material financial relationships, if any, please see http://www.nber.org/chapters /c13740.ack.

that individuals have the health capacity to sustain extended working lives. Indeed, much of the work we have done in previous stages of the International Social Security project (Wise 2015), which relates to retirement age responsiveness to pension incentives (Bingley, Datta Gupta, and Pedersen 2004), health (Bingley, Datta Gupta, and Pedersen 2012), and disability insurance (Bingley, Datta Gupta, Jorgensen, and Pedersen 2015), implicitly assumes that individuals have sufficient unused health capacity to work at older ages. In this study we will estimate how much unused health capacity to work exists.

Among the Organisation for Economic Co-operation and Development (OECD) countries, Denmark has relatively short life expectancy and late age of first eligibility to old age pension. These combined to give Danes the lowest life expectancy after pensionable age (1993–2002; 13.4 years for men and 16.6 years for women). Old age pension benefits could first be received at age sixty-seven until 2004, and this was reduced to age sixty-five by 2006 in six-month steps. In 2011 it was announced that from 2019 to 2022 the age of first eligibility will once again be raised to sixty-seven in six-month steps. Life expectancy after pensionable age jumped by three years during the first decade of the twenty-first century, the largest increase of all countries, but after the 2019–2022 reform is implemented Danes will once again have the shortest expected retirements (OECD 2011).

Denmark was the first country to automatically link pensions to life expectancy in their retirement income system (Whitehouse 2007). Beginning in 2030, Denmark will link changes in age of first eligibility to old age pension to changes in life expectancy from age sixty. The aim is to maintain life expectancy after pensionable age close to the 14.5 years observed in 2004–05, the two years before the automatic linkage reform was announced (Ministry of Integration and Social Affairs 2013). However, the rate of increase due to automatic linkage with life expectancy is capped such that pensionable age can at most increase by one year every fifth year. Projected life expectancy from age sixty in 2025 (minus 14.5 years) is rounded to the nearest half year to give the implied pensionable age in 2030. The projection to 2025 uses life expectancy from age sixty during 2013–14, and assumes a trend that adds 0.6 years. These calculations imply a pensionable age in 2030 of 69.5 years, but since pensionable age can only increase by at most one year, eligibility will be from age sixty-eight in 2030.

In several countries, gains in longevity are expected to outpace announced future delays in pensionable ages. Denmark has among the shortest life expectancies after pensionable age and has a history of policy attention to the measure. This makes Denmark an excellent case for measuring health capacity for extending the working life, since post-retirement longevity itself, regardless of health status, is a greater constraint in Denmark than anywhere else. Finding unused work capacity in Denmark ought to be a greater challenge because of the high base of work capacity used already.

In this chapter we ask to what extent older Danes have the health capacity to extend their working lives. We do this by estimating health-employment relationships in the past, or for younger cohorts today, and predicting how much work capacity there would be for older cohorts in similar health today if those estimated relationships held for today's older cohorts. Ideally, we would like to know what the health-employment relationship might be in the absence of non-health-related social security programs. We take two approaches to obtaining this counterfactual health-employment relationship, by fitting the relationship historically before the introduction of early pension benefit programs, or by fitting the relationship for younger cohorts today who have not yet reached pension benefit eligibility age.

For the first approach following Milligan and Wise (2012), we look at the historical relationship between mortality and employment rates and ask how much older people would work today, given current mortality rates, if they were to work as much as they did at a similar mortality rate in the past. Using published data from Statistics Denmark, we plot the mortality-employment relationship for several years from 1977 to 2010 and find significant unused work capacity compared to today for all baselines up until 2000. We only estimate mortality-employment relations for men for the sake of better comparison with other countries, where increasing older female labor market participation makes estimates for women difficult to interpret.

For the second approach, inspired by Cutler, Meara, and Richards-Shubik (2012), we estimate the relationship between self-assessed health (SAH) and employment for somewhat younger cohorts and ask how much older cohorts, with similar SAH, would work if the same health-employment relationship held. We use microdata from the Survey of Health and Retirement in Europe for Denmark (SHARE-Denmark) collected in 2004–13 to estimate the relationship for those age fifty to fifty-four and to predict work capacity for ages fifty-five to seventy-four. We find significant unused work capacity from age sixty and older for both men and women. Estimated unused work capacity is remarkably similar for the group; we consider using both methods—for men age fifty-five to sixty-nine—when we use a 1977 mortality-employment relationship baseline. The Cutler method implies 4.8 years and the Milligan-Wise method implies 4.6 years unused work capacity, compared to 7.6 years currently working. Women are predicted to have slightly more unused work capacity than men using the Cutler method for ages fifty-five to sixty-nine at 5.1 years, compared to 6.1 years currently working.

The remainder of the chapter is organized as follows: As background, the next section describes trends in labor force participation, health, and mortality. In section 3.3 we estimate work capacity using the historical mortality-employment relationship following Milligan and Wise (2012). In section 3.4 we describe trends in SAH, and in section 3.5 we estimate the SAH-employment relationship for younger cohorts following Cutler,

Meara, and Richards-Shubik (2012). Finally, we conclude with a discussion of the implications of our findings in section 3.6.

3.2   Trends in Labor Force Participation and Health

This section summarizes the trends in labor force participation in Denmark over the last fifty years for men and women age sixty to sixty-nine. We split the discussion for those age sixty to sixty-four and sixty-five to sixty-nine because of data availability and differences in eligibility to pension benefits between these two age groups. Figure 3.1 presents the evolution of labor force participation for sixty- to sixty-four-year-olds based on several different sources.

Until the late 1990s, trends in labor force participation by gender are very different from each other, with a 70 percentage point differential in 1960 declining to 18 percentage points by 2013. The initial decline for men in the 1960s reflects structural change with a sectoral shift of employment from agriculture, which was comprised largely of independent farmers, toward industry. The dramatic decline in labor force participation for men in 1980 is the initial impact from the introduction of a non-health-related pension benefit program, the Post Employment Wage ([PEW]; efterløn), with eligibility ages of sixty to sixty-six, depending on the sufficiently long membership

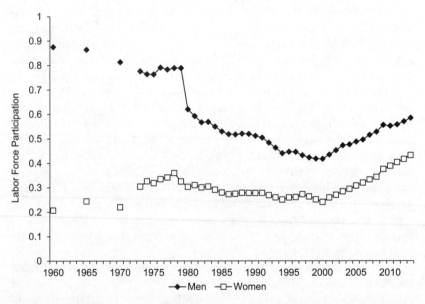

Fig. 3.1   Labor force participation rates for ages sixty to sixty-four by gender over time

Sources: Population census 1960, 1965, and 1970; annual labor force surveys 1973–1975; annual statistics based upon a 10 percent administrative sample 1976–79; and 1980–2013 administrative data on the full population.

of an unemployment insurance fund. For women, the initial impact was much smaller because of lower baseline participation and less PEW eligibility among working women due to insufficient history of Unemployment Insurance fund membership.

The strong upswing in labor force participation rates from the late 1990s, also found in many other OECD countries (see, e.g., Larsen and Pedersen 2013), is the result of several interacting factors. Since 1999 a number of policy changes have been made with the aim of discouraging early retirement. Further, average education and health has improved strongly for this group, with retirement age having a positive gradient in both factors (cf. Larsen and Pedersen 2015). Actually, sixty- to sixty-four-year-olds are the only age group to have experienced an increase in labor force participation rate since the onset of the Great Recession in 2008. For all younger age groups participation rates have fallen since 2008, especially among the young. However, in spite of improvements in health, to which we return below, labor force participation for men age sixty to sixty-four is still 20 percentage points below the level of the late 1970s. Our aim is to estimate the potential work capacity of today's older cohorts in view of reductions in mortality and SAH improvements of recent years.

In figure 3.2 we present the development of labor force participation for those age sixty-five to sixty-nine. For men, the initial level is about

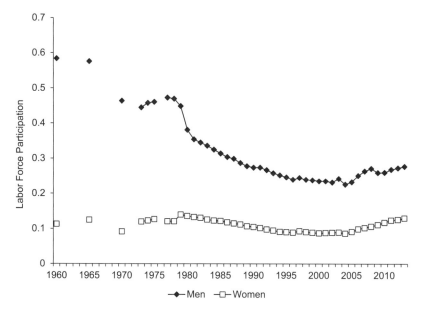

Fig. 3.2   **Labor force participation rates for ages sixty-five to sixty-nine by gender over time**

Sources: Population census 1960, 1965, and 1970; annual labor force surveys 1973–1975; annual statistics based upon a 10 percent administrative sample 1976–79; and 1980–2013 administrative data on the full population.

30 percentage points lower than for the sixty- to sixty-four-year-olds. We find the same steep decline in labor force participation in the second half of the 1960s as found for the sixty- to sixty-four-year-olds, reflecting the same switch from independent farming. Following the introduction of PEW in 1979, labor force participation falls, although less steeply than for the sixty- to sixty-four-year-olds because, of this older group, only those age sixty-five to sixty-six were eligible for PEW.

The next visible change in labor force participation rates occurs in the years immediately after 2000, which continues the increases in labor force participation for sixty- to sixty-four-year-olds in the preceding period. From 2004 to 2006, sixty-five- to sixty-six-year-olds were no longer eligible for PEW, as the age for first eligibility to Old Age Pension (folkepension) was reduced from sixty-seven to sixty-five. The modest upward trend since 2000 is somewhat diminished for men, reflecting this 2004–06 reform. Nevertheless, labor force participation for men in 2013 was half that of 1960. For women age sixty-five to sixty-nine, we see a very small increase in labor force participation after 2000. Overall, however, the level for women is stationary, around 10–12 percent, since 1960.

Summing up, for sixty- to sixty-nine-year-old men labor force participation over the last thirty to thirty-five years has declined by about 20 percentage points. As longevity has increased along with level of education, there is clearly scope for analyzing the health-related factors behind the potential for reversing this decline as part of accommodating demographic changes in the coming decades.

As an introduction to the analyses of health factors, figure 3.3 collects evidence on the development in mortality and self-assessed health for men age fifty to seventy-five over the last twenty years. Data on self-assessed health are available also for other years, but 1994 and 2013 are the most recent years where the same questions and response categories were used. The decrease in mortality is strong, despite the period being fairly short, in contrast to the years before the mid-1990s where mortality in Denmark was quite stationary at the same time as mortality was decreasing in most comparable countries. The share of men with self-assessed health in the fair-poor categories is lower in 2013 than in 1994, and the gradient with respect to age is more flat in the most recent year.

3.3   Work Capacity Estimates Based on Historical Mortality

We will use two different methods to assess the health-related capacity to work at older ages. The Cutler method is used in section 3.5. In this section we present results from applying the methods in Milligan and Wise (2012) to Danish data. The idea is to look at the relationship between mortality and employment at given ages in some earlier year. Next, we look at the employment-mortality relationship in a current year. Comparing employment at given levels of mortality in the year back in time and the current

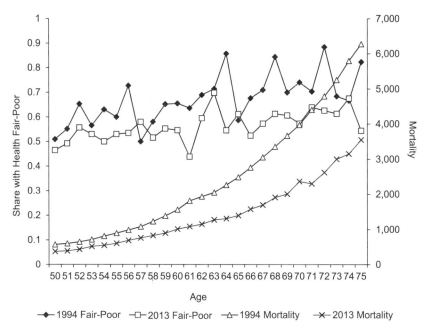

Fig. 3.3   Male self-assessed health and mortality by year over age

Sources: Mortality rates per 100,000 from Statistics Denmark. SAH from two surveys by the National Institute of Public Health of 1,100 men age fifty to seventy-five with response categories excellent, very good, good, fair, or poor.

year gives an upper-bound estimate of potential extra work capacity in the current year.

A number of conditions and reservations should be emphasized. First, it is assumed that mortality captures all health factors related to work capacity. One can argue that better measures than mortality could summarize physical and mental capacity for continued work at older ages. However, mortality has the clear advantage of being available over a very long period and being comparable between countries.

Figure 3.4 plots the relationship between mortality and employment rate for men fifty-five to sixty-nine years old in 1977 and 2010. The procedure for calculating the upper bound of the additional capacity for work is based on the lines in figure 3.4. Mortality and employment rates are plotted in figure 3.4 for each age, fifty-five to sixty-nine, in 2010. For instance, in 2010 mortality at age sixty was 1.0 percent and the employment rate was 67.4 percent. At that level of mortality, the employment rate in 1977 was 86 percent. Consequently, the upper bound of the additional work capacity in 2010 with 1977 as the base year was 18.6 percent. Running this procedure over all ages we find, not surprisingly, comparing with figure 3.1, that additional work capacity has a steep gradient in age for people in the first half of their sixties.

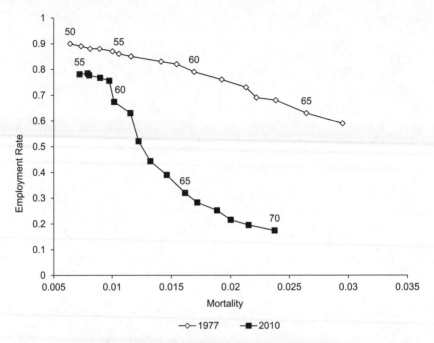

Fig. 3.4   Male employment and mortality by age in 1977 and 2010

Sources: Mortality rates from Statistics Denmark. Employment rates from Statistics Denmark based on annual information from administrative registers using a 10 percent sample in 1977 and the full population in 2010.

The results from the exercise are presented in table 3.1. In 2010, the total number of working years for men fifty-five to sixty-nine years old was 7.8. As a counterfactual, this would correspond to a situation where men fifty-five to sixty-three years old had employment rates of 100 percent and all retired when reaching age sixty-four. The accumulated additional employment capacity in 2010 with 1977 as the base year is 4.7 years, that is, a sizable 60 percent of the actual number of years worked.

In figure 3.5 the same analysis is made comparing 2010 with the much closer year, 1995. While 1977 was two years before the introduction of the PEW program, resulting in a steep decline in male employment rates from age sixty, 1995 was a low point in employment rates (cf. figure 3.1). An obvious consequence is that the two graphs in figure 3.5 are much closer to each other than the corresponding curves in figure 3.4.

Table 3.2 summarizes in the same way as table 3.1 the employment rates and mortality at each age in 2010 along with the employment rate in 1995 at the same mortality rates. A main difference compared with the case using 1977 as the base year is the lack of additional employment capacity at ages fifty-five to fifty-nine. At mortality rates above the age sixty level in 2010, we

			Employment rate	
Age	Mortality in 2010 (%)	Employment rate in 2010 (%)	in 1977 at same mortality (%)	Additional work capacity (%)

Table 3.1   Additional male work capacity in 2010 using 1977 employment-mortality relationship

Age	Mortality in 2010 (%)	Employment rate in 2010 (%)	Employment rate in 1977 at same mortality (%)	Additional work capacity (%)
55	0.72	78.1	89	10.9
56	0.79	78.4	88	9.6
57	0.80	77.7	88	10.3
58	0.90	76.7	88	11.3
59	0.98	75.6	87	11.4
60	1.02	67.4	86	18.6
61	1.15	63.1	85	21.9
62	1.22	52.1	85	32.9
63	1.32	44.4	84	39.6
64	1.46	39.0	83	44.0
65	1.61	32.0	80	48.0
66	1.72	28.3	79	50.7
67	1.88	25.2	77	51.8
68	2.00	21.6	75	53.4
69	2.15	19.5	72	52.5
Total years		7.8		4.7

Note: Own calculations based on mortality rates from Statistics Denmark and employment rates from Statistics Denmark based on annual information from administrative registers using a 10 percent sample in 1977 and the full population in 2010.

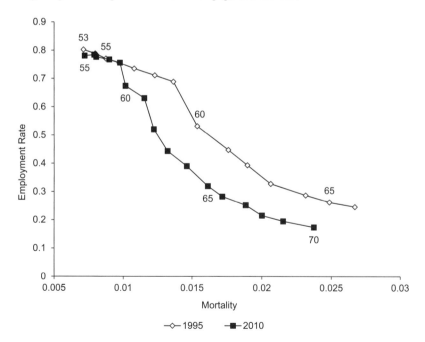

Fig. 3.5   Male employment and mortality by age in 1995 and 2010

Sources: Mortality rates from Statistics Denmark. Employment rates from Statistics Denmark based on annual information from administrative registers for the population.

Table 3.2   Additional male work capacity in 2010 using 1995 employment-mortality relationship

Age	Mortality in 2010 (%)	Employment rate in 2010 (%)	Employment rate in 1995 at same mortality (%)	Additional work capacity (%)
55	0.72	78.1	79.0	0.9
56	0.79	78.4	78.9	0.5
57	0.80	77.7	78.9	1.2
58	0.90	76.7	76.7	0.0
59	0.98	75.6	75.0	−0.6
60	1.02	67.4	74.6	7.2
61	1.15	63.1	72.4	9.3
62	1.22	52.1	71.1	19.0
63	1.32	44.4	69.7	25.3
64	1.46	39.0	60.3	21.3
65	1.61	32.0	50.4	18.4
66	1.72	28.3	46.3	18.0
67	1.88	25.2	40.0	14.8
68	2.00	21.6	35.3	13.7
69	2.15	19.5	31.4	11.9
Total years		7.8		1.6

Note: Own calculations based on mortality rates from Statistics Denmark and employment rates from Statistics Denmark based on annual information from administrative registers for the population.

find additional employment capacity, most pronounced at ages sixty-two to sixty-six. Overall, the additional employment capacity adds up to 1.6 years, or about one-third of the additional employment capacity found in table 3.1, which uses a 1977 baseline.

Figure 3.6 is a summary of the trends in the development of the relationship between mortality and employment rates by including average values for three five-year intervals: the last half of the 1970s (before the PEW program), the first half of the 1990s (when employment rates reached a minimum), and the second half of the first decade of the twenty-first century. A clear illustration of the change over the period is found looking at the pivotal age of sixty. From the late 1970s to the early 1990s, the employment rate drops by 20 percentage points with only a slight decline in mortality. Next, from the early 1990s to late in the first decade of the twenty-first century, employment goes up at age sixty along with declining mortality. From figure 3.5 we know, however, that employment for given levels of mortality is still lower late in the first decade of the twenty-first century compared with the early 1990s at age sixty and older.

Next, in figure 3.7, we have used all the years between 1977 and 2009 as base years comparing with the mortality employment relationship in 2010. As expected, the estimated additional work capacity becomes smaller as we

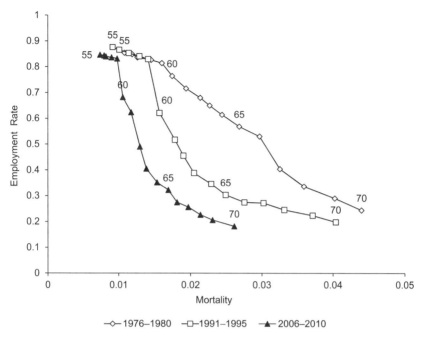

Fig. 3.6   Male employment and mortality 1976–80, 1991–95, and 2006–10

Sources: Mortality rates from Statistics Denmark. Employment rates from Statistics Denmark based on annual information from administrative registers using a 10 percent sample in 1976–79 and the full population in 1980, 1991–95, and 2006–10.

move closer to 2010; that is, differences in mortality rates become smaller and changes in employment rates also become smaller. From about the turn of the century, additional work capacity becomes stationary at a level close to zero as mortality declines faster at the same time as employment rates increase (cf. figures 3.1 and 3.2).

The additional work capacity found by using the Milligan-Wise method does not imply the normative conclusion that older people should continue working in accordance with the increase in employment capacity we find. Our finding should instead be seen as a contribution to the arguments and analyses in the so-called "healthy life debate," that is, to what extent does increasing longevity result in more healthy years with a potential for a longer working life, or is most of the gain spent in poor health and disability. There is a wide-ranging literature on this topic, of which only a few contributions are mentioned here. Mathers et al. (2001) calculate healthy life expectancy for 191 countries in 1999 using the method of Sullivan (1971), which combines surveys of SAH with life tables. They find that healthy life expectancy increases across countries at a faster rate than total life expectancy. Christensen et al. (2009) present as a conditional projection that most children born in Denmark since the turn of the century will survive until

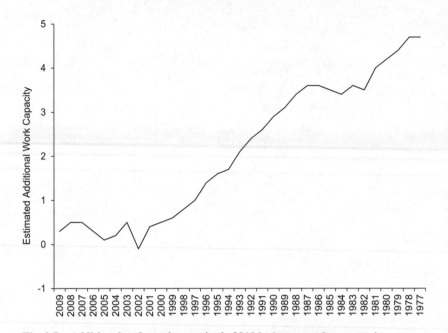

Fig. 3.7   Additional male work capacity in 2010 by base year for comparison

Source: Own calculations based on mortality rates from Statistics Denmark and employment rates from Statistics Denmark based on annual information from administrative registers using a 10 percent sample in 1977–79 and the full population in 1980–2010.

age 100 and older, but it remains to be established whether age of onset of functional limitations and disability increases in a similar way.

Using Danish data for the year 2000, Brønnum-Hansen et al. (2004) consider life expectancy and health expectancy by educational levels. They find a social gradient in both, but the gradient in health expectancy is greater than in life expectancy. Being a cross-section study, it contains only an implicit contribution to answer the question about the development over time. An attempt at an explicit answer is found in Brønnum-Hansen (2005), building on comprehensive Danish surveys from 1987 to 2000 and combined with life table data using the Sullivan (1971) method. Over this period, Brønnum-Hansen (2005) finds disability-free life time increasing more than total life expectancy, and more so for men than for women.

3.4   Self-Assessed Health and Employment by Age over Time

An alternative to the use of mortality as an overall health indicator is to rely on individuals' own evaluation and to study SAH from surveys as an indicator for health-related capacity for work. Denmark does not have a long time series of comparable SAH measures. The National Institute of

Public Health conducted a number of surveys beginning in 1987. We have access to microdata from the 1987 survey (cf. below). For other years data are available in a processed form and the results regarding SAH from two comparable surveys in 1994 and 2013 were included in figure 3.3. Besides the National Institute of Public Health surveys, we can use the European Community Household Panel (ECHP), SHARE, and other smaller surveys. For the purpose of the present study, there are issues regarding lack of comparability between surveys, coverage of only a short span of time consistently within surveys, and small sample sizes.

Below we present SAH from these surveys and relate this to the age of eligibility to the major social security programs. First, figure 3.8 presents the relationship between labor force participation rates and SAH based on a fairly small survey collected in 1977. This provides the only self-assessed health measure before the introduction of PEW. Results from the survey are described and discussed in Olsen and Hansen (1977). The SAH is measured on the horizontal axis as the share reporting their health as fair for my age group to poor. The vertical axis measures average labor force participation rate at each age. In 1977 disability insurance (DI) was the only

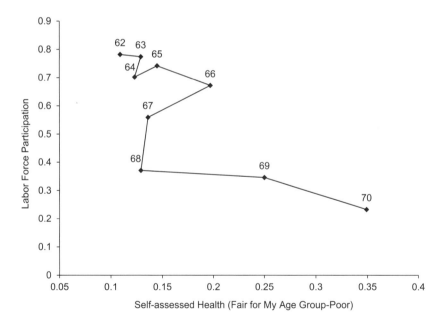

Fig. 3.8   Male SAH and labor force participation rate by age in 1977

Sources: Labor force participation rates from Statistics Denmark based upon a 10 percent administrative sample. The SAH from a survey of 600 men conducted by SFI (Olsen and Hansen 1977). Our SAH means are based on microdata from this survey retrieved from Danish Data Archive Study no. 00232. The SAH response categories are good, good for my age, fair, fair for my age, and poor.

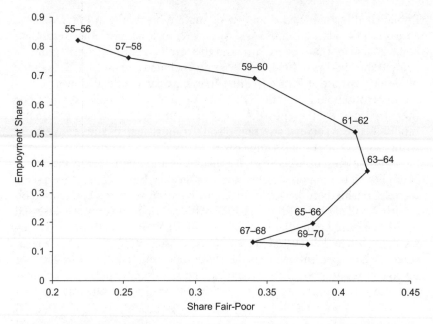

Fig. 3.9   Male SAH and labor force participation rates by age in 1986–87

Sources: Employment rates from Statistics Denmark based upon administrative data for the population. The SAH comes from a survey of 1,000 men conducted by the National Institute of Public Health. Our SAH means are based on microdata from this survey retrieved from Danish Data Archive Study, no. 01435. The SAH response categories are excellent, very good, good, fair, or poor.

early exit route from the labor market before eligibility for old age pension at age sixty-seven. The expected negative slope is found in figure 3.8, and the impact of reaching eligibility for old age pension is seen as a decline in labor force participation of about 30 percentage points without any visible deterioration of SAH—if anything, health improves for a few years right after retirement age.

There is a ten-year gap until the next available SAH measure. Results from a survey conducted by the National Institute of Public Health in 1987 are shown in figure 3.9. The horizontal axis measures the share of respondents at each age reporting health as fair-poor, while the vertical axis measures labor force participation rates. Smoothing results are shown as two-year averages. In 1987 PEW was fully phased in with eligibility from ages sixty to sixty-six, followed by OAP from age sixty-seven. The slope in figure 3.9 is clearly negative with a major deterioration of SAH from age fifty-five to the early sixties. Notice the steep decline in labor force participation from the early sixties until eligibility to old age pension followed by a moderate improvement of self-assessed health in the late sixties.

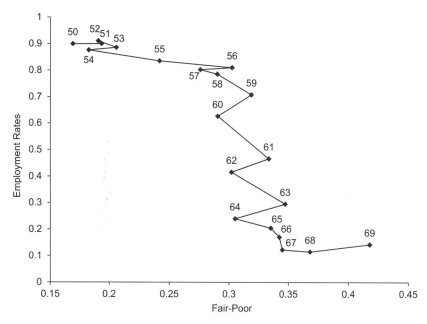

Fig. 3.10   Male SAH and employment rates by age (1994–2001)
Sources: Employment rates from Statistics Denmark based upon administrative data for the population. The SAH comes from ECHP 1994–2001 (waves 1–8) containing 4,000 Danish men age fifty to sixty-nine. The SAH response categories are very good, good, fair, bad, very bad.

Data for Denmark from the ECHP collected in the years 1994–2001 over eight waves makes it possible to construct a relationship between SAH and employment rates based on more observations by pooling over waves. The result is shown in figure 3.10 for men ages fifty to sixty-nine. The SAH deteriorates quite rapidly during the fifties, while the sixties, until age sixty-seven, are characterized by a steep drop in employment rates—more so in the PEW years than close to old age pension—at about the same level of SAH. After reaching pensionable age, SAH deteriorates again while employment rates remain around 10 percent.

In figure 3.11 we show the relationship between SAH and employment rates based on SHARE data from wave 4 collected in 2011. It appears that, after a transition from data points for single years to working with moving three-year age averages, we still have a "noisy" relationship. However, like in figure 3.10, we have a deterioration of health in the fifties followed by another phase of deterioration from the mid-sixties. In between, employment rates drop significantly, first reflecting PEW and at higher-age old age pension where the age of eligibility from 2004 to 2006 has been sixty-five years.

Once again, using Danish data from the ECHP averaged over the eight waves between 1994 and 2001, figure 3.12 shows the relationship between SAH and employment, but now separately for the three education levels classified as ISCED 0–2, ISCED 3, and ISCED 5–7. Lines for different education levels are nearly completely separated. Employment rates are initially at the same level at age fifty. The difference in employment rates has increased to 10 percentage points at age fifty-five, increasing to a difference of 25 percentage points at age sixty-five.

In summary, the general pattern of reducing labor force participation rates and worsening SAH as men age is clear throughout. However, given the infrequency with which SAH has been surveyed in Denmark, and the lack of comparability of SAH between surveys, it is not possible to speak about trends over time. Nevertheless, the relationship is steepest (greatest falls in participation for modest falls in SAH) during ages of eligibility to early pension benefits. There are striking SAH differentials by education, with the SAH deterioration from age fifty to seventy within schooling level (compulsory, high school, and college) roughly equal to mean SAH differences between schooling levels. In the next section we analyze the SAH-employment and schooling relationship in more detail.

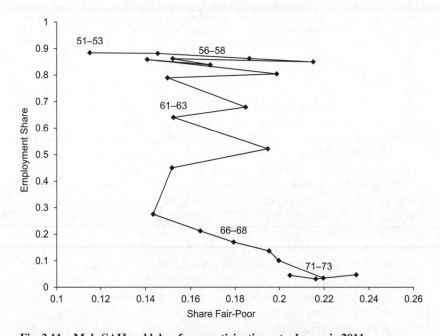

Fig. 3.11   Male SAH and labor force participation rates by age in 2011

Sources: Employment rates from Statistics Denmark based upon administrative data for the population. The SAH are from SHARE-Denmark 2011 (wave 4) containing 900 men age fifty-one to seventy-three. The SAH response categories are very good, good, fair, poor, very bad.

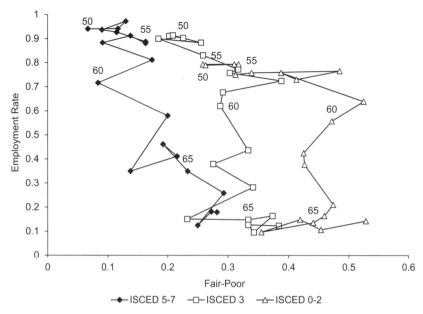

Fig. 3.12   Male SAH and employment rates by age and schooling (1994–2001)

Sources: Employment rates from Statistics Denmark based upon administrative data for the population. The SAH are from ECHP 1994–2001 (waves 1–8) containing 4,000 Danish men age fifty to sixty-nine. The SAH response categories are very good, good, fair, bad, and very bad. The ISCED codes 0–2, 3, and 5–7 correspond to compulsory schooling, high school, and college, respectively.

3.5   Work Capacity Estimates Based on Self-Assessed Health

In a second approach to estimating health capacity to work, we ask how much older cohorts would work today if they had the same relationship between SAH and employment as younger cohorts have today. This approach is inspired by Cutler, Meara, and Richards-Shubik (2012) who use HRS data to estimate the relationship between SAH, retirement, and disability insurance receipt for the near elderly and use estimates to simulate behavior of the elderly.

We use data from SHARE-Denmark, which was collected in 2004, 2006, 2011, and 2013, that is, waves 1, 2, 4, and 5. SHARE-life was conducted as wave 3 and contained retrospective questions about life histories, but not contemporaneous SAH, so we cannot use this wave for the current analysis. SHARE is a longitudinal survey that collects data across nineteen European countries on individuals age fifty or older and their spouses (Börsch-Supan et al. 2013). It has much in common with HRS, Japanese Study of Aging and Retirement (JSTAR), and English Longitudinal Study of Ageing (ELSA), making it an ideal data set for our study, which should be as comparable as possible with similar studies for other countries.

Descriptive statistics for SHARE-Denmark are presented in table 3.3 by age group and gender. Our estimations and simulations will be conducted separately by gender and these age groupings. In total we have 3,273 observations of men and 3,650 observations of women. Proportion working is always higher for men than for women, is high and fairly stable before age sixty, and then falls through age seventy, most of the reduction taking place in the late sixties for men, but evenly throughout the sixties for women. Younger age groups have more schooling, especially at the college margin, and markedly so for women. The SAH worsens with age, but levels and profiles are quite similar by gender. Men are much more likely to be overweight than women and there is a slight age gradient in obesity for men, with younger men being more obese than older. Women have more limitations than men both physically and with regard to activities of daily living. Doctor visits are common for both men and women, though somewhat less for men in their fifties. Men are more likely to have had a hospital stay than women. Nursing home stays are very uncommon. Of the eight specific health conditions considered, back problems are the most common for all ages. Arthritis doubles from the early fifties to the early seventies. Diabetes and hypertension are more common in women, and heart disease and stroke are more common in men.

In order to estimate the relationship between SAH and employment we need to characterize health in a way that allows for comparison with other countries. We calculate a single health index following Poterba, Venti, and Wise (2013), who create an index that is a reasonable predictor of mortality in HRS data. Using the health variables described in table 3.3, SAH, body mass index, types of limitations, care usage, and a set of specific health conditions, we calculate the first principal component for both genders and all age groups pooled. This principal component is used to predict a single health index and we normalize this index to percentiles, where by convention a higher percentile indicates better health. For example, (wo)men age fifty to fifty-four have a mean percentile of 58 (54), and (wo)men age seventy to seventy-four have a mean percentile of 44 (39).

The ordinary least squares (OLS) regression estimates for the dependent variable working are presented in table 3.4. The sample is age fifty to fifty-four and regressions are run separately for men and women. Better health is strongly and positively associated with employment. A move of 10 percentiles up the health distribution is associated with a 4.6 percentage point higher employment probability for women and 3.7 percentage point higher employment probability for men. High school, and especially college, is associated with higher employment probability. Married individuals are more likely to be working. Goodness-of-fit is somewhat better for women than for men.

Using the estimates from table 3.4 for the youngest of our age groups, we simulate work capacity by predicting on the basis of health and demographic characteristics for older age groups. In doing this we are assuming that the health-employment relationship is constant between age groups, so that we can meaningfully combine coefficients estimated on the younger

Table 3.3   Descriptive statistics for SHARE-Denmark estimation and simulation sample

	Men					Women				
	50–54	55–59	60–64	65–69	70–74	50–54	55–59	60–64	65–69	70–74
Working	0.862	0.826	0.551	0.159	0.037	0.827	0.758	0.402	0.078	0.019
High school	0.456	0.450	0.448	0.471	0.457	0.272	0.317	0.337	0.368	0.347
College	0.379	0.367	0.350	0.354	0.279	0.544	0.481	0.439	0.323	0.237
Married	0.700	0.684	0.728	0.699	0.659	0.728	0.670	0.666	0.624	0.582
SAH very good	0.343	0.356	0.334	0.339	0.290	0.371	0.343	0.369	0.359	0.274
SAH good	0.229	0.234	0.243	0.262	0.286	0.214	0.223	0.191	0.233	0.265
SAH fair	0.106	0.125	0.133	0.159	0.185	0.107	0.154	0.188	0.141	0.216
SAH poor	0.041	0.060	0.042	0.042	0.073	0.052	0.047	0.043	0.032	0.080
BMI underweight	0.003	0.000	0.001	0.005	0.004	0.021	0.016	0.025	0.023	0.034
BMI overweight	0.415	0.440	0.417	0.421	0.415	0.270	0.283	0.321	0.289	0.310
BMI obese	0.178	0.141	0.139	0.145	0.108	0.118	0.134	0.148	0.129	0.119
Limits any ADL	0.037	0.043	0.053	0.066	0.086	0.049	0.046	0.057	0.050	0.084
Limits any IADL	0.062	0.046	0.045	0.069	0.110	0.075	0.101	0.099	0.095	0.181
Limits physical 1	0.104	0.110	0.152	0.164	0.138	0.096	0.128	0.121	0.160	0.188
Limits physical 2+	0.099	0.116	0.117	0.130	0.213	0.161	0.196	0.257	0.213	0.338
Doctor visit	0.712	0.774	0.808	0.831	0.870	0.839	0.830	0.842	0.887	0.871
Hospital stay	0.064	0.097	0.113	0.122	0.167	0.082	0.096	0.108	0.099	0.134
Nursing home stay	0.000	0.000	0.006	0.000	0.004	0.000	0.000	0.003	0.003	0.002
Back problems	0.442	0.503	0.432	0.444	0.433	0.487	0.523	0.504	0.459	0.498
Arthritis	0.197	0.264	0.312	0.310	0.437	0.211	0.214	0.309	0.386	0.431
Diabetes	0.135	0.168	0.215	0.204	0.240	0.199	0.268	0.333	0.346	0.358
Heart disease	0.058	0.043	0.083	0.087	0.138	0.033	0.046	0.056	0.068	0.080
Lung disease	0.036	0.056	0.069	0.076	0.099	0.050	0.059	0.073	0.081	0.093
Stroke	0.033	0.033	0.032	0.043	0.084	0.021	0.023	0.020	0.023	0.039
Hypertension	0.011	0.021	0.031	0.050	0.044	0.050	0.044	0.055	0.060	0.069
Cancer	0.000	0.001	0.000	0.003	0.011	0.002	0.000	0.001	0.002	0.009
No. observations	747	766	683	622	455	878	833	766	619	464

Note: Own calculations based on SHARE-Denmark waves 1, 2, 4, and 5. Omitted groups are those with compulsory schooling, very poor SAH, normal BMI, no limitations in Activities of Daily Living (ADL), no limitations in Instrumental Activities of Daily Living (IADL), no limitations in physical activity, no doctor visits, no hospital stays, no nursing home stays, and none of the remaining health conditions.

Table 3.4   OLS regression estimates explaining employment ages fifty to fifty-four

	Women		Men	
PVW health index	0.0046	*0.0004*	0.0038	*0.0004*
High school	0.1001	*0.0356*	0.0631	*0.0350*
College	0.1826	*0.0325*	0.0884	*0.0366*
Married	0.0629	*0.0268*	0.0522	*0.0267*
2006	0.0049	*0.0351*	0.0734	*0.0335*
2011	0.0215	*0.0360*	0.0628	*0.0346*
2013	0.0215	*0.0360*	0.0628	*0.0346*
Intercept	0.8563	*0.0475*	0.8724	*0.0458*
No. observations/R-sq.	878	0.1861	747	0.1337

Note: Own calculations based on SHARE-Denmark waves 1, 2, 4, and 5. The PVW health index is calculated as first principal component from health conditions listed in table 3.3 (see Poterba, Venti, and Wise 2013). Reference category for education is compulsory schooling. The reference year is 2004.

Table 3.5   Simulations of work capacity by age

Age group	No. obs.	Actual working (%)	Predicted capacity (%)	Additional capacity (%)
Men				
55–59	766	82.6	85.4	2.4
60–64	683	55.1	84.7	29.2
65–69	622	15.9	83.7	67.5
70–74	455	3.7	80.2	76.2
Women				
55–59	833	75.8	79.9	4.3
60–64	766	40.2	77.9	37.9
65–69	619	7.8	75.8	68.3
70–74	464	1.9	70.2	68.1

Note: Own calculations based on SHARE-Denmark waves 1, 2, 4, and 5. Simulations are based on estimates presented in table3.4.

group together with observed characteristics of the older groups for simulation. One threat to the stability of this relationship might be differences in skills, occupations, and industry affiliation by age group. Jobs differ in their health demands and we need to assume the health-employment relationship is fixed across age groups for whom different types of jobs might be relevant. Furthermore, while our health index appears quite comprehensive, there may be health conditions we are unable to measure but are negatively correlated with ability to work. Such omitted health factors would bias our work capacity estimates upward—we would be overstating the amount of unused work capacity.

Results from the simulation exercise are presented in table 3.5 by age group and gender. Predicted work capacity changes only slightly with age, falling by 5 percent for men and 10 percent for women from the late fifties through till the early seventies. In order to simulate unused work capacity, we calculate the difference between predicted work capacity and observed employment. When combined with observed employment levels, which are rapidly declining with age, we simulate little unused work capacity in the late fifties, large unused capacity in the early sixties, and very large unused capacity from the late sixties. Women's unused work capacity exceeds men's until the early sixties, whereas men have more unused capacity from their seventies. Figures 3.13A and 3.13B graphically present the simulation exercise from table 3.7.

In table 3.6 we extend our simulation exercise on the basis of the same set

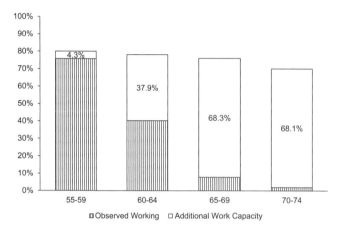

Fig. 3.13A   Employment and simulated additional work capacity by age (women)
Note: Own calculations based on SHARE-Denmark waves 1, 2, 4, and 5. Simulations are based on estimates presented in table 3.4. This is an alternative presentation of selected material from table 3.5.

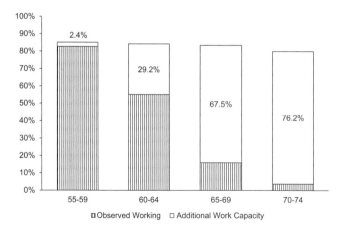

Fig. 3.13B   Employment and simulated additional work capacity by age (men)
Note: Own calculations based on SHARE-Denmark waves 1, 2, 4, and 5. Simulations are based on estimates presented in table 3.4. This is an alternative presentation of selected material from table 3.5.

Table 3.6 Simulations of work capacity by age group and schooling

	Men				Women			
Schooling	No. obs.	Actual working (%)	Predicted capacity (%)	Additional capacity (%)	No. obs.	Actual working (%)	Predicted capacity (%)	Additional capacity (%)
Age 55–59								
Primary	132	66.4	73.3	6.9	167	53.0	61.9	8.9
High school	348	83.5	85.6	2.1	262	73.9	77.0	3.1
College	286	89.7	90.3	0.6	404	86.5	89.6	3.0
Age 60–64								
Primary	128	42.0	74.1	32.1	187	25.0	63.0	38.0
High school	312	55.2	84.4	29.2	251	30.2	73.8	43.6
College	243	62.3	89.8	27.5	328	55.7	89.1	33.5
Age 65–69								
Primary	116	9.2	74.5	65.3	192	4.2	62.1	57.9
High school	291	9.2	84.3	75.1	227	6.6	77.2	70.6
College	215	28.2	86.6	58.4	200	12.5	88.0	75.5
Age 70–74								
Primary	113	0.0	73.4	73.4	187	1.6	58.9	57.3
High school	217	4.3	79.4	75.1	165	1.9	73.5	71.6
College	125	6.3	87.1	80.8	112	2.7	84.6	81.8

Note: Own calculations based on SHARE-Denmark waves 1, 2, 4, and 5. Simulations are based on estimates from data that is pooled across education groups and presented in table 3.4.

of estimates from table 3.4, but now additionally splitting the simulation by level of schooling. Once again, similar information to that contained in table 3.6 is also presented visually in figures 3.14A and 3.14B. Employment differentials by schooling exceed differences in simulated work capacity across the age range, and especially so for women. Despite the large differences in work

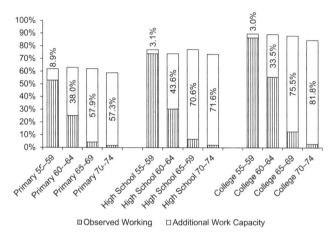

Fig. 3.14A   Employment and simulated additional work capacity by schooling and age for women

Note: Own calculations based on SHARE-Denmark waves 1, 2, 4, and 5. Simulations are based on estimates from data that is pooled across education groups and presented in table 3.4. This is an alternative presentation of selected material from table 3.6.

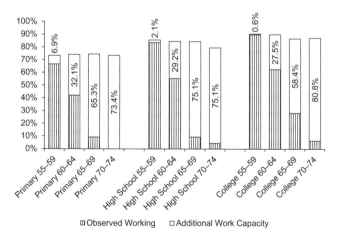

Fig. 3.14B   Employment and simulated additional work capacity by schooling and age for men

Note: Own calculations based on SHARE-Denmark waves 1, 2, 4, and 5. Simulations are based on estimates from data that is pooled across education groups and presented in table 3.4. This is an alternative presentation of selected material from table 3.6.

Table 3.7   Simulated additional years of work capacity based on SAH ages fifty-five to sixty-nine

	Men		Women	
Schooling	Actual working	Additional capacity	Actual working	Additional capacity
Primary	6.10	4.94	4.15	5.30
High school	7.34	5.35	5.60	5.85
College	8.68	4.63	7.61	5.60
All	7.60	5.03	6.16	5.55

Note: Own calculations based on SHARE-Denmark waves 1, 2, 4, and 5. Simulations are based on estimates from data that is pooled across education groups and presented in table 3.4.

capacity by schooling, simulated unused work capacity is quite similar for the late fifties and early sixties. It is in the late sixties where schooling differences in unused work capacity are most obvious, increasing by 12 percent from primary to high school and 5 percent from high school to college for women, whereas it is increasing by 10 percent from primary to high school but decreasing by 16 percent from high school to college for men. Men in their late sixties with a college degree are much more likely to be employed than men of the same age with a high school diploma, whereas health for the two groups is quite similar, leading to a similar level of simulated work capacity.

A convenient summary measure of unused work capacity that can be computed for this approach and for the previous approach is the total number of simulated years of unused work capacity over the age range fifty-five to sixty-nine. In section 3.3, figure 3.7 presented implied years of unused capacity for different baselines. Our preferred baseline is 1977, which predates the announcement of early pension benefits through the PEW program in 1978. This gives an unused work capacity for men of 4.6 years, which is consistent between methods. In table 3.7 we present simulated years of unused work capacity for our SAH-based approach. For men this is quite close at 5.0 additional years. Women have six more months unused work capacity than men. By level of schooling, women with primary or high school have three to four months more unused work capacity than men, but at the college level women have a year longer unused work capacity than men. Men and women with high school degrees have three to five months more unused work capacity than those with different schooling.

3.6   Conclusion

Already-mandated changes to future pension benefits will reduce incentives to retire early with the aim of extending the length of working lives. The implicit assumption is that older individuals actually have the health capacity to work longer. We have tested this assumption for Denmark using two methods. First, following Milligan and Wise (2012), we ask how much older people would work today, given current mortality rates, if they were to work as much as people did at a similar mortality rate in the past. Next, following Cutler, Meara, and Richards-Shubik (2012), we ask how much would older cohorts work given their SAH, if they were to work as much as younger cohorts today do with similar SAH. Both are ways of estimating health-employment relationships that we then use for predicting how much work capacity there would be for older cohorts in similar health today if those estimated relationships held for today's older cohorts.

With both methods we find substantial unused work capacity. For men we are able to compare simulations between methods and findings are very similar when we consider a 1977 baseline for the mortality-employment relationship, before introduction of an important early pension benefit program. We simulate 4.6–5.0 additional years of health capacity to work for men between ages fifty-five and sixty-nine. This compares to baseline male employment of 7.6 years from 2004 to 2013. For women we simulate 5.5 additional years of work capacity between ages fifty-five and sixty-nine, compared to baseline employment of 6.2 years. There are differences in additional work capacity by level of schooling. Those with a high school degree have the most unused work capacity. Women have more unused work capacity than men across the schooling distribution, especially at the college level, where the difference is one year.

There are several caveats that need to be applied to our simulations. Most importantly, our unused capacity numbers have no implications for how much older individuals should work. It is beyond the scope of our study to discuss whether longer working lives are desirable for society. Health has improved for the older population, whether measured by reduced mortality or better SAH, and this suggests that some additional work capacity is available. Both of the approaches we have followed assume that all health gains can be translated into longer working lives, but there are significant real world constraints on this such as labor demand, workplace discrimination and accommodation, and household and family factors. Our additional work capacity simulations are quite large and these caveats should moderate those somewhat. Nevertheless, our aim was to ask whether Danes have the health capacity to extend working lives by three years over the next fifteen, as currently announced policies assume. Our findings suggest that this additional health capacity to work does indeed exist.

References

Bingley, P., N. Datta Gupta, M. Jorgensen, and P. J. Pedersen. 2015. "Health, Disability Insurance, and Retirement in Denmark." In *Social Security Programs*

and Retirement around the World: Disability Insurance Programs and Retirement, edited by D. Wise. Chicago: University of Chicago Press.
Bingley, P., N. Datta Gupta, and P. J. Pedersen. 2004. "The Impact of Incentives on Retirement in Denmark." In *Social Security Programs and Retirement around the World: Micro-Estimation*, edited by J. Gruber and D. Wise. Chicago: University of Chicago Press.
————. 2012. "Disability Programs, Health, and Retirement in Denmark since 1960." In *Social Security Programs and Retirement around the World: Historical Trends in Mortality and Health, Employment and Disability Insurance Participation and Reforms*, edited by D. Wise. Chicago: University of Chicago Press.
Börsch-Supan, A. 2013. "SHARE Wave Four: New Countries, New Content, New Legal and Financial Framework." In *SHARE Wave 4: Innovations and Methodology*, edited by F. Malter and A. Börsch-Supan, 5–10. Munich: MEA, Max Planck Institute for Social Law and Social Policy
Brønnum-Hansen, H. 2005. "Health Monitoring. Health Expectancy in Denmark, 1987–2000." *European Journal of Public Health* 15 (1): 20–25.
Brønnum-Hansen, H., O. Andersen, M. Kjøller, and N. K. Rasmussen. 2004. "Social Gradient in Life Expectancy and Health Expectancy in Denmark." *Soz.-Präventivmed* 49:36–41.
Christensen, K., G. Doblhammer, R. Rau, and J. W. Vaupel. 2009. "Ageing Populations: The Challenges Ahead." *Lancet* 374 (9696): 1196–208.
Cutler, David M., Ellen Meara, and Seth Richards-Shubik. 2012. "Health and Work Capacity of Older Adults: Estimates and Implications for Social Security Policy." Unpublished Manuscript. Available at SSRN: http://ssrn.com/abstract=2577858.
Larsen, M., and P. J. Pedersen. 2013. "To Work, To Retire—Or Both? Labor Market Activity after 60." *IZA Journal of European Labor Studies* 2:21. DOI: 10.1186/2193-9012-2-21.
————. 2015. "Labor Force Activity after 60: Recent Trends in the Scandinavian Countries." IZA Discussion Paper no. 9393, Institute for the Study of Labor.
Mathers, C. D., R. Sadana, J. A. Salomon, C. J. L. Murray, and A. D. Lopez. 2001. "Healthy Life Expectancy in 191 countries, 1999." *Lancet* 357 (9269): 1685–91.
Milligan, K. S., and D. A. Wise. 2012. "Health and Work at Older Ages: Using Mortality to Assess the Capacity to Work across Countries." NBER Working Paper no. 18229, Cambridge, MA.
Ministry of Integration and Social Affairs. 2013. "Bekendtgørelse af lov om Social Pension." www.retsinformation.dk/Forms/R0710.aspx?id=145406.
Olsen, H., and G. Hansen. 1977. "Ældres arbejdsophør." SFI Report no. 79, Social-forskningsinstitutet, Copenhagen.
Organisation for Economic Co-operation and Development (OECD). 2011. "Pensionable Age and Life Expectancy, 1950–2050." In *Pensions at a Glance 2011: Retirement-Income Systems in OECD and G20 Countries*. Paris: OECD Publishing.
Poterba, James, Steven Venti, and David A. Wise. 2013. "Health, Education, and the Post-Retirement Evolution of Household Assets." *Journal of Human Capital* 7 (4): 297–339.
Sullivan, D. F. 1971. "A Single Index of Mortality and Morbidity." Health Services and Mental Health Administration (HSMHA). *Health Report* 86:347–54.
Whitehouse, E. R. 2007. "Life-Expectancy Risk and Pensions: Who Bears the Burden?" Social, Employment and Migration Working Paper no. 60, Paris, OECD.
Wise, David, ed. 2015. *Social Security Programs and Retirement around the World: Disability Insurance Programs and Retirement*. Chicago: University of Chicago Press.

Health Capacity to Work at Older Ages in France

Didier Blanchet, Eve Caroli, Corinne Prost,
and Muriel Roger

4.1 Introduction

Among comparable countries, France traditionally stands out as one of those where the labor force attachment of older workers is the lowest. This has been especially the case from the mid-1980s to the beginning of the twenty-first century (figure 4.1). The employment rate for the sixty to sixty-four age group was only 10 percent in 2000, 25 points below the Organisation for Economic Co-operation and Development (OECD) average, following a period of continuous decline that had started early in the 1970s. The decrease has been more limited for the fifty-five to fifty-nine age group, but nonetheless substantial. It has been concomitant with the shift of the legal retirement age from sixty-five to sixty, which took place during the first half of the 1980s and favored a phase of rapid expansion of preretirement policies targeted to this fifty-five to fifty-nine age group. This expansion was rapidly interrupted, but employment rates for male workers age fifty-five to fifty-nine then remained as low as about 60 percent throughout the 1990s and the first half of the first decade of the twenty-first century, more than 10 points below the equivalent OECD average over the period.

Yet, the long-run view provided by figure 4.1 also shows that low employment rates for those age fifty-five and older cannot be seen as a constant

Didier Blanchet belongs to the French National Statistical Institute (INSEE). Eve Caroli is professor of economics at PSL Université Paris Dauphine. Corinne Prost is a senior economist at the French National Statistical Institute (INSEE) and a research fellow at the Center for Research in Economics and Statistics (CREST). Muriel Roger is professor of economics at CES Université Paris 1 Panthéon-Sorbonne.

For acknowledgments, sources of research support, and disclosure of the authors' material financial relationships, if any, please see http://www.nber.org/chapters/c13741.ack.

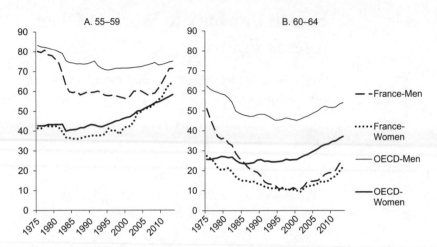

Fig. 4.1   Employment rates since 1975, fifty-five to fifty-nine and sixty to sixty-four age groups
Source: INSEE and OECD, Labour Force Surveys.

and irreversible feature of the French labor market. First of all because preexisting historical levels were not low at all: the decrease that occurred until the 1990s started from initial values that, in 1975, were close to OECD standards. And second because employment rates have entered a new ascending phase over the last fifteen years. Concerning the fifty-five to fifty-nine age group, the average employment rate for both genders has already reincreased from 50 percent in 2000 to 66 percent in 2013, above its 1975 value and in line with the OECD average. Part of this trend stems from increased labor force attachment by women of all ages, rather than from a tendency to work more at older ages. But the movement is also very significant for men, whose employment rate has increased by 10 points since 2008, despite the adverse economic conditions. Concerning the sixty to sixty-four age group, the change is more progressive but not less substantial: employment rates have regained 15 percentage points, for both men and women. This is still much below the OECD average, but the convergence is real since the trend in France is steeper than for the OECD as a whole.

A reversal is therefore undoubtedly under way, partly due to tighter preretirement policies and partly to the pension reforms that took place since 1993. According to the latest pension projections published by the Pensions Advisory Committee (*Conseil d'Orientation des Retraites* 2014), if things go on as currently expected, this upward trend in employment rates should persist over the next decades, leading by 2040 to levels close to the ones that were observed in the early 1970s.

The fact that most of the French aging process is driven by large gains in life expectancy has been particularly helpful in preparing this reversal:

allocating part of these gains to work rather than to retirement has been presented by policymakers as a natural and relatively acceptable way to contain the progression of pension expenditures.

In such a context, arguing both in favor of the possibility and the need to increase retirement ages and older workers' employment appears to be much less necessary than it used to. Yet some questions and doubts remain. An implicit hypothesis of all past reforms has been that additional years of life are years spent in good health, or at least with a health status that can be considered reasonably compatible with work. If this is not the case, the idea of sharing these additional years of life between work and retirement becomes much less self-evident.

There is even the view that pension reforms themselves could widen the gap between global and healthy life expectancies, if they induce people to work at ages where work constraints strongly deteriorate health. In other words, a question that can be asked is whether reforms have not gone "too far" in activating the retirement age variable. Are we approaching a "health barrier" to longer working lives that would have been too rapidly ignored by past reforms? This question can be asked "on average" but also, and probably more interestingly, separately by occupations or socioprofessional groups, thus questioning the adequacy of excessively uniform policies that pay too little attention to differential exposures to morbidity or mortality risks.

To tackle these issues, we rely on two different methodological approaches currently developed in the economic literature. Both methods and their variants aim at providing measures of additional work capacity. This capacity may be defined as a measure of the distance between current retirement ages and what we call the "health barrier," that is, the age at which health prevents people from working longer.

We first implement the method developed by Milligan and Wise (2012), denoted hereafter as MW, using mortality as a proxy of health. These authors compute a measure of additional work capacity for older workers (age fifty-five to sixty-nine), based on the gap in employment rates across time for given mortality rates. With the increase in longevity over time, the same mortality rate corresponds to different ages at different years. We extend the standard MW method, on the one hand, taking into account intragenerational mortality differentials and, on the other hand, using direct indicators of health status rather than the mortality proxy.

Second, as the MW method remains highly dependent on the reference period, we complete the study considering an alternative method, developed by Cutler, Meara, and Richards-Shubik (2013), denoted hereafter as CMR, which does not require any comparison over time. The approach becomes synchronic, using the work/health relationship measured at certain ages to predict the health-related work capacity of older age groups at the same period of time.

Both methods and their variants aim at providing measures of additional work capacity, that is, measures of the existing distance between current retirement ages and our suggested concept of "health barrier." However, they do not tell us by how much retirement ages *should* be increased. Individual and/or social choices concerning retirement ages need to consider many other parameters, both on the supply and the demand side of the labor market. What is at stake here is only one very specific aspect of the global optimization problem that would consider all these variables at the same time: it entails no message about how far policies should go in "exploiting" the employment reserve measured by additional work capacity. Evaluating where the health barrier is standing is one thing, making recommendations about how close to this barrier one should come is another thing, and that is clearly out of the scope of the present chapter.

Section 4.2 will present the application of the MW method in its original form, using long-run series of mortality rates as proxies of health status, with an extension taking into account intragenerational mortality differentials. This extension is made possible for France, thanks to a long tradition of production of life tables for major socioeconomic groups. Section 4.3 will explore the possibility to adapt the MW method using direct indicators of health status rather than the mortality proxy, relying on the *Enquête Santé et Protection Sociale* (ESPS) conducted by IRDES from 1992 to 2010. The CMR method will be discussed at last in section 4.4. Section 4.5 will conclude with a short discussion of the limitations to increasing retirement ages that are not covered in the present chapter.

4.2   Employment Rates and Mortality: The Milligan-Wise Approach

The Milligan-Wise methodology uses mortality as a proxy of health, and then computes a measure of additional work capacity for older workers (age fifty-five to sixty-nine) based on the gap in employment rates across time for given mortality rates. Data on mortality come from the French Statistical Institute (INSEE). We match them with employment rates by age computed using the French Labor Force Surveys (*Enquête Emploi*) from 1977 to 2012.

The main advantage of this approach is that the results are easily comparable across countries since mortality and employment are defined in a consistent way across national data. In contrast, it cannot be extended to women in a meaningful way over the period we consider because of the large shift in female labor force participation across cohorts. So, the focus of this section will be on men only.

4.2.1   Employment versus Mortality over Time

The starting point of the MW methodology is the observation that in all advanced countries, both mortality and employment rates have substantially declined over the past forty years. France is no exception to these trends

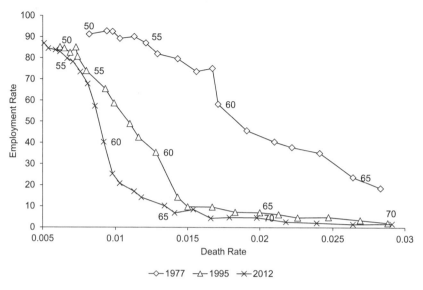

Fig. 4.2   Employment versus mortality (men)

with male death rates at fifty-five, sixty, and sixty-nine going down from 1.13 percent (1.67 percent and 3.45 percent, respectively) in 1977 to 0.62 percent (0.86 percent and 1.67 percent, respectively) in 2012. Over the same period, employment rates of men have gone down from 90.1 percent at age fifty-five (75.1 percent at sixty and 15.4 percent at sixty-nine, respectively) in 1977 to 82.9 percent at age fifty-five (57.3 percent at sixty and 4.3 percent at sixty-nine, respectively) in 2012.

A more telling way of presenting these changes is provided in figure 4.2. We graph employment rates as a function of death rates for three different years: 1977, 1995, and 2012. For given death rates, employment has strongly decreased over time. The death rate of individuals age fifty-nine in 1977 (i.e., 1.69 percent) was reached at about sixty-eight years old in 2012, while the corresponding employment rates are hugely different: 75.1 percent for the fifty-nine-year-olds in 1977 as compared to only 4.3 percent for the sixty-eight-year-olds in 2012. The changes that have taken place have generated an inward shift in the mortality-employment schedule.

This suggests that if bad health conditions—as captured by mortality—were the main obstacle to employment, older workers—age fifty-five and older—could be working much more than they actually do.

4.2.2   Measuring Mortality-Based Work Capacity

To get a precise measure of this additional work capacity, we proceed in the following way: for each level of death rate, we consider what the employment rate would be at any year t if the relationship between employment

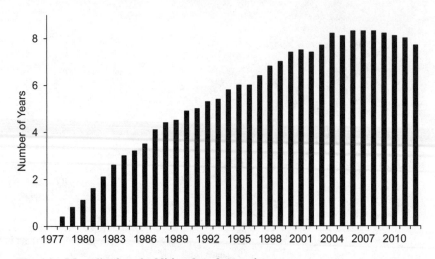

Fig. 4.3 Mortality-based additional work capacity

Note: Men age fifty-five to sixty-nine, 1978 to 2012, using 1977 as the reference year. Potential years of additional work for years 1977 to 2012, when taking 1977 as the reference.

and mortality were the same at *t* as in a reference year—taken here to be 1977. We cumulate this calculation between ages fifty-five and sixty-nine. This gives us the number of additional years French men could have worked between ages fifty-five and sixty-nine if the employment-mortality relationship had not changed since 1977 (see figure 4.3). The additional number of years of work computed in this way is referred to as "additional work capacity."

According to this calculation, the additional work capacity strongly increased from 0.4 years in 1978 to a peak of 8.3 years in the middle of the first decade of the twenty-first century. The trend started to revert in 2009, and the additional work capacity was back to 7.7 years in 2012.

Given that we compute the additional work capacity on the basis of the gap in employment rates between year *t* and a reference year, it heavily depends, by construction, on the reference year that is chosen: the higher the employment rate in the reference year, the higher the additional work capacity we obtain. Since employment rates steadily decreased in France until 2010, the additional work capacity mechanically increases with the time distance to the reference year. For year 2012, for example, it ranges from 7.3 years if the reference year is 1977 to –0.2 years if the reference year is 2010 (see figure 4.4).

4.2.3   The Limitations of the Mortality-Based Milligan-Wise Approach

The MW estimates deliver extreme upper bounds for potential increases in labor force participation rates, that is, evaluations of ages beyond which

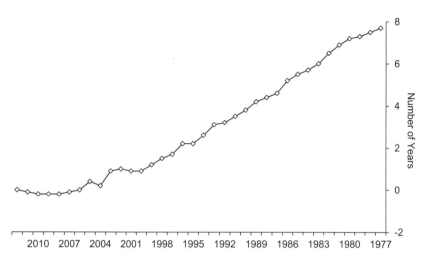

Fig. 4.4   Additional work capacity for men in 2012, using 1977 to 2011 as reference years

health limitations definitely preclude further prolongations of working lives, according to some conventional historical standards corresponding to the reference year. To interpret the results, we must bear in mind some limits of the method. The first one is that (a) it is based on a proxy of health status whose relevance is not warranted: if past declines in mortality rates have not been accompanied by equivalent declines in morbidity, the MW method will overestimate the margin that is available for increasing employment rates of older workers. A second limit (b) is the intrinsically relative character of the results: as illustrated above, they are completely dependent on the reference period used for assessing the current level of additional employment capacity. A third limit (c) is the aggregate nature of the method: it is based on average values of age-specific mortality rates, thus ignoring the strong heterogeneity of mortality risks in the population.

Limit (a) will be addressed in the next section when we examine whether the MW method can be made more to the point by using true measures of health, rather than the mortality proxy. The last section of this chapter will try to overcome limit (b): the Cutler, Meara, and Richards-Shubik (2013) method that will be used will avoid comparisons over time, replacing them by comparisons at time t across age groups. These two sections will also address limit (c), by looking at differentials in health status as observed by education level or other descriptors of socioeconomic status. But a first look at the heterogeneity issue can already be provided here, without exiting the strict MW framework, thanks to the availability, for France, of mortality data by social group.

4.2.4   Heterogeneity in Mortality-Based Work Capacity: Managers and Professionals versus Blue Collars

Disaggregating life tables according to socioeconomic status has a relatively long tradition in France, since the first systematic attempts go back to the 1960s and 1970s (Calot and Febvay 1965; Desplanques 1976). The approach combines civil registration data with information collected at successive censuses: although civil registration data provide exact age at death, they do not contain any reliable information on social status, which can be retrieved from individual census bulletins. The first studies of this kind used one-shot ad hoc confrontations of both pieces of information. Nowadays, the *Echantillon Démographique Permanent* (Permanent Demographic Sample), maintained at the French Statistical Institute (INSEE), systematically matches both kinds of information for a 1 percent representative sample of the French population. Thanks to this panel, life tables disaggregated by social group are available off-the-shelf for the following aggregate time periods: 1976–1984, 1983–1991, 1991–1998, and 2000–2008 (Blanpain and Chardon 2011).

In these data, social stratification is described on the basis of the seven-digit French socioeconomic classification. We shall focus here on managers/professionals and blue collars. In 1976–1984, life expectancies at age thirty-five were 41.7 years for the former group and 35.7 for the latter, that is, a six-year gap. In 2000–2008, the corresponding figures were 47.2 and 40.9, that is, a 6.3 year gap. At age fifty-five, values for 1976–1984 were 23.3 and 19.2, that is, a 4.1 year gap. For 2000–2008, they were, respectively, 28.4 and 23.5, that is, a 4.9 year gap. Absolute differences are, of course, smaller at age fifty-five than at thirty-five, but this is only due to the fact that life expectancy decreases with age. Reevaluated in relative terms, in 2000–2008, the gap was 14 percent at age thirty-five and close to 19 percent at age fifty-five.

How can such a feature be incorporated into the MW framework? The procedure we propose here fully respects the general spirit of the method and does not make use of socioeconomic mortality differentials for remote time periods: only data for the most recent years are sufficient. We keep the hypothesis that average mortality-employment relationships of all past periods can be used as benchmarks, and apply these successive benchmarks to mortality rates currently observed in the two social groups we consider. The counterfactual employment rates that are produced on the basis of these group-specific mortality rates are then compared to the true employment rates observed for the same groups. The period of interest is the median year of the latest time period for which differential mortality is available, that is, the year 2004. More precisely, we use mortality rates for 2000–2008 as proxies of mortality rates by social group in 2004 and, concerning employment rates, we average them over a three-year period centered around 2004, that is, 2003–2005.

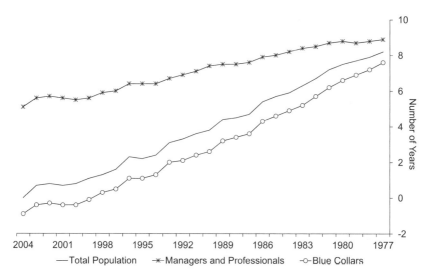

Fig. 4.5   Mortality-based additional work capacities by social group in 2004 (men age fifty-five to sixty-nine, using 1977 to 2004 as reference years)

Another option would be to compute MW additional work capacities for each of our social groups using group-specific employment/mortality relationships. Yet this would only give a measure of how much blue collars (managers/professionals, respectively) may work considering their own mortality and employment rates in the reference year, with little or no insight into the differential between them. For instance, in case of perfectly parallel changes in mortality and employment for the two groups, the result would be identical levels of additional work capacities for both, whatever the level of cross-sectional inequality between them. Put differently, this would consider that the differential gap in the reference year is also a reference and can be considered as "normal." With our methodology, we consider that the reference is the link between employment and mortality in the average population, and this sheds a better light on the situation of disadvantaged social groups.

The resulting additional work capacities of managers/professionals and blue-collar workers for the year 2004 are shown on figure 4.5 using 1977 to 2004 as successive reference years. This figure also replicates the previous computation for the general population, with 2004 rather than 2012 as the new year of interest. Understanding the results in figure 4.5 also requires looking at figure 4.6, which provides the apparent mortality-employment relationship for managers/professionals and blue collars in 2004, as well as the same relationship for the general population both in 2004 and 1977.

Results using 2004 as the reference year are instructive in that they reveal the current state of inequalities in terms of employment-mortality

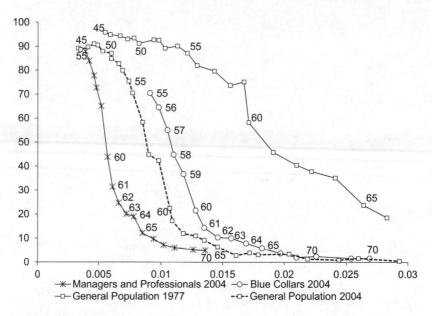

Fig. 4.6   Employment versus mortality, men (total population, managers/professionals and blue collars)

relationship. If the 2004 relationship is taken as a reference, the average additional work capacity is zero by construction, but it is as high as +5.1 years for managers and professionals whereas it is negative for blue collars, equal to –0.9 years. Managers and professionals work much less than they could do—according to the MW a priori—while blue-collar workers work slightly longer than what they should be asked to. Another way to look at these figures is to note that blue-collar workers age fifty-five had a rate of employment of 70 percent in 2003–2005, while managers and professionals the same age had a rate of employment of 87.9 percent. Over this time period the former had a mortality rate of .91 percent, while the latter reached this mortality rate at only sixty-five or sixty-six years old, that is, ages at which their employment rates were around 10 percent. This means that, if we consider 2004 managers and professionals as the reference group, blue-collar workers suffer from a 60-percentage-point *excess* work duration. Such considerations raise the question of differentiating the efforts in additional years of work that could be demanded to the different groups, in view of their current mortality levels.

In principle, the same message should remain valid when pushing the reference year backward in the past, with parallel increases of the indicators of additional employment capacity for managers/professionals and blue collars. Figure 4.5 suggests that this is not the case since the additional work capacities of both groups seem to be much closer to each other when 1977 is taken as the reference year—7.6 years and 8.9 years, respectively.

However, this paradoxical result is due to an artifact generated by the way the MW method is implemented, that is, imposing an arbitrary upper limit at age sixty-nine for the age bracket over which counterfactual employment rates are simulated. The consequence of this arbitrary limit can be understood looking at figure 4.6: as the method is applied here, the difference between the upper 1977 schedule and the bottom schedule for managers and professionals in 2004 is integrated only until about half way through the figure. Abandoning such a convention, the MW approach would reveal a considerable amount of additional work capacity for managers and professionals on the right-hand side of the graph. The impact of removing the sixty-nine-year-old age constraint is expected to be much more modest for blue-collar workers since, when integrating for them within this limit, we go up to values of mortality rates for which employment rates were already low—typically below 20 percent—in 1977. This is confirmed by figure 4.7, equivalent to figure 4.5 after removing the sixty-nine-year-old limit for computing counterfactual employment rates: an almost complete parallelism is restored between the profiles of additional work capacity for managers/professionals, blue-collar workers, and the average population.

Of course, this generates levels of additional work capacity for managers and professionals that look highly implausible—up to thirteen years with 1977 as the reference year. It incidentally highlights a limit of the MW method. The method generates estimates of additional work capacities that remain within a plausible range only thanks to the choice of an arbitrary upper-age limit until which the methodology is considered valid.

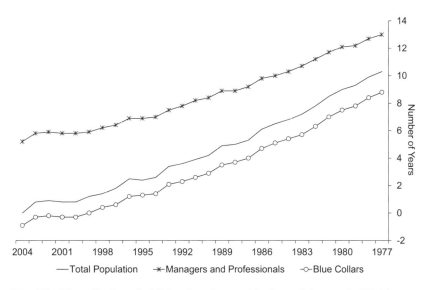

Fig. 4.7 **Mortality-based additional work capacities by social group in 2004 (men age fifty-five and older, using 1977 to 2004 as reference years)**

4.2.5   Mortality-Based Work Capacity: What Have We Learned?

The MW approach based on mortality yields very high estimates of additional work capacity. This does not mean that all this capacity should actually be used. It only suggests that, on average, health does not appear to be a major limiting factor to the increase in labor force participation of older workers. However, one has to go beyond averages and take into account the very uneven levels of mortality rates across social groups. This point is clearly supported by the analysis carried out using the data on mortality by social status available for France. Moreover, as already underlined, mortality remains a very crude proxy of health. The next sections try to overcome this drawback.

4.3   A Variant of the Milligan-Wise Approach: Replacing Mortality by Self-Assessed Health

This section addresses the concern that mortality could be a poor proxy of health by considering a more direct measure of it, that is, self-assessed health (SAH).

The data on SAH for France are provided by the ESPS (*Enquête sur la Santé et la Protection Sociale*) survey. This survey was conducted yearly from 1992 to 1997 on a rather small sample of individuals (about 1,000 per year) and every other year from 1998 to 2010 on a larger sample (about 2,000 respondents per year). SAH has been measured consistently since 1992 on a 0–10 scale, and we define poor SAH as a dummy variable equal to 1 if reported SAH scores below 8 (which corresponds to the first quartile of the distribution both for men and women in 1992) and 0 otherwise.

4.3.1   Trends in SAH over Time

Figure 4.8 (and figure 4.9, respectively) shows the relationship between poor SAH and age on the one hand, and mortality and age on the other hand for men (women, respectively). Both figures provide evidence of an age gradient in SAH and mortality, although the relationship is less smooth for SAH because of small sample size. The proportion of men reporting poor SAH in 2010 is almost three times as large at age seventy-five as at fifty—70 percent as compared to 25 percent. Age trends are less pronounced for women since the proportion reporting poor SAH is equivalent to men at age seventy-five (70 percent), but is much higher at age fifty (40 percent). This is consistent with the difference we observe across gender in the age gradient in mortality, the latter being larger for men than for women.

Yet, contrary to what we might expect—and to what is observed for mortality for men above age fifty-five and for women above age seventy—we do not see any steady improvement in SAH over time whatever the age group we consider (see figures 4.10 and 4.11). After a decline in the proportion of men and women reporting poor SAH in the first half of the 1990s, the

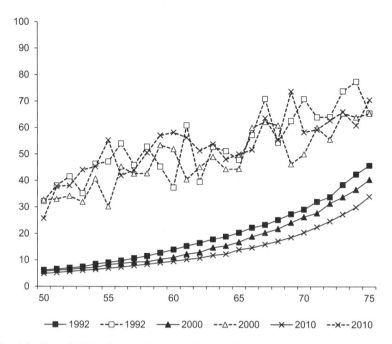

Fig. 4.8   Poor SAH and mortality, men (by age, 1992–2010)

Note: Percentage of individuals reporting SAH less than eight (dotted) and 1,000 * death rate (solid).

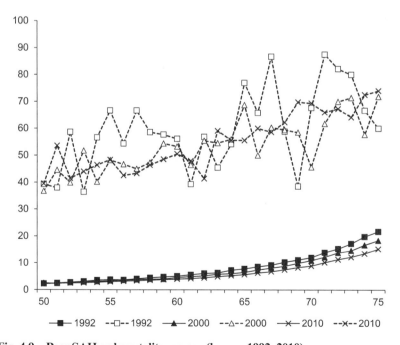

Fig. 4.9   Poor SAH and mortality, women (by age, 1992–2010)

Note: Percentage of individuals reporting SAH less than eight (dotted) and 1,000 * death rate (solid).

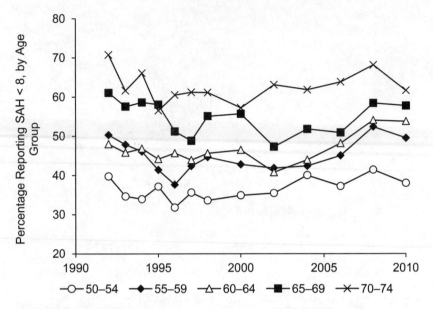

Fig. 4.10 Poor SAH by age group across time, men (1992–2010)
Note: Percentage of individuals reporting SAH less than eight, by age group. Men, all education levels.

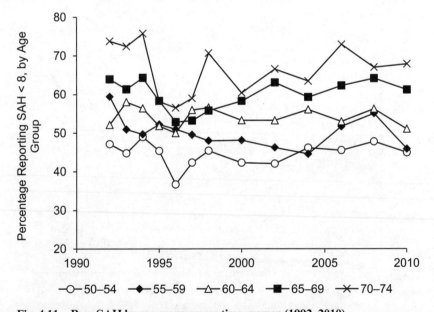

Fig. 4.11 Poor SAH by age group across time, women (1992–2010)
Note: Percentage of individuals reporting SAH less than eight, by age group. Women, all education levels.

trends revert at the beginning of the first decade of the twenty-first century, and SAH appears to deteriorate for both men and women, at least until the very last years of the decade.

The lack of clear improvement in self-assessed health over time in our data raises the issue of potential declaration biases. There is evidence in the literature that, when asked about their health, individuals in various subgroups of the population use different threshold levels to assess it, although having the same "true" health level. This gives rise to reporting heterogeneity that varies according to the type of health outcome that is considered (Tubeuf et al. 2008). Regarding SAH, low-income and low-education individuals tend to overreport it (Bago d'Uva et al. 2011; Etilé and Milcent 2006; Johnston, Propper, and Shields 2009), while women tend to underreport it as compared to men (Bago d'Uva et al. 2008). Regarding age, Lindeboom and van Doorslaer (2004) find that older adults are more inclined than younger ones to report good health for a given health status. If this happens to be the case in our data, the age-gradient evidenced in figures 4.8 and 4.9 must be considered as a lower bound since it is negatively affected by this declaration bias. However, in order for declaration biases to account for the lack of improvement in SAH over time, it would have to be the case that, within age groups, individuals tend to underreport their health status to a larger extent than they used to in the past. This may be the case if, as health systems become more efficient, individuals raise their health expectations. However, to our knowledge, there is no evidence of such trend in the literature.

A competing explanation of why time trends in poor SAH do not look more downward sloping may be that they are quite heterogeneous across social groups, with health getting better for some groups while it may have worsened for others.

4.3.2 Trends in SAH by Education

One of the most obvious social classifications to look at is the one based on education. This can be done using the ESPS Survey, which contains information on educational levels grouped into five categories until 2006 and into eight and nine groups in 2008 and 2010, respectively.

In order to compute meaningful changes in SAH by education level over time, we need to take into account the upward shift that has taken place in the educational composition of the population. One of the consequences of this shift is that low-educated workers are more selected in recent years than they were in the past. To account for this change, we first compute the distribution of years of education by cohort and gender (see figures 4.12 and 4.13 for men and women, respectively; the distribution for the whole population is shown in appendix figure 4A.1).

As can be seen in figure 4.12, the proportion of men having completed at least some higher education increased substantially between the cohorts who reached fifty in 1960 and in 2010. The same goes for the proportion

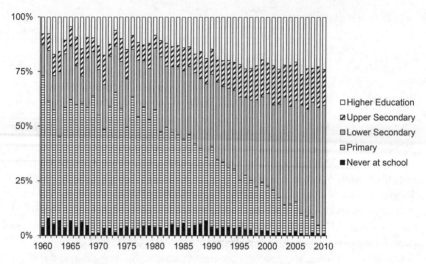

Fig. 4.12   Distribution of years of education completed by cohort, men (year each cohort attained age fifty)

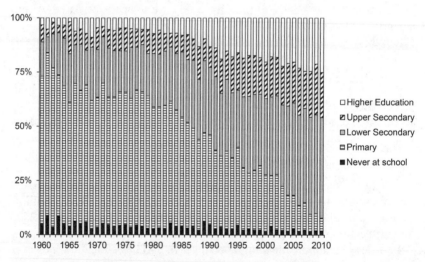

Fig. 4.13   Distribution of years of education completed by cohort, women (year each cohort attained age fifty)

with upper secondary education and for those with lower secondary education. In contrast, the share of men with only primary education has sharply declined. Those who never attended school represent a small share of the cohort who reached fifty in 2010, but it was already low for the 1960 cohort. Similar trends are observed for women (see figure 4.13), although the proportion that attains higher education in the 2010 cohort remains slightly lower than for men.

As a second step, we sort individuals by education in each age * year cell with random ordering of individuals within each level and define four education quartiles. Over the forty years considered here, the educational level of the median male and female increased from primary to lower secondary education. The first quartile did the same, while the third one moved from lower secondary education to upper secondary education.

The proportion of individuals reporting poor SAH is then computed for each single age older than fifty to seventy-five in each education quartile and eventually aggregated over two time periods: 1992–1998 and 2000–2010.

As evidenced in figures 4.14 and 4.15, higher-educated men and women are on average in better health than their low-educated counterparts. This is particularly true for both men and women in the fourth quartile of the education distribution. However, we find no evidence of a substantial improvement in SAH over time except at very old ages—for men in the upper half of the education distribution and for women in the first and third quartiles. This result has to be interpreted with caution, though, since individuals in very bad health older than seventy years old are likely to be underrepresented in the ESPS survey if they are hosted in specialized institutions, since the latter are not included in the sample. If the proportion of unhealthy older people in such institutions has increased over time, the group of older individuals in the ESPS survey is increasingly selected in terms of health, which may account for the trend observed in our data at very old ages.

Overall, we do not see very different trends in health conditions over time within age and education groups. So, the lack of steady improvement in self-assessed health observed in the French data cannot be accounted for by the fact that health conditions would improve for some groups of individuals while worsening for others, at least when these groups are defined on the basis of education.

4.3.3   Additional Work Capacity: The Milligan-Wise Approach Based on SAH

We repeat the analysis carried out for employment rates and mortality using SAH. As for mortality, we do so for men only since the strong increase in female labor force participation would generate some confusion in the interpretation of the results. To reduce the noise in the data, we average the information on SAH over two years when it is available yearly, so that what is indicated as 1992 is actually computed as the average over 1992 and 1993. In addition, we linearly adjust the age profiles of self-assessed health. The corresponding employment-health profiles are presented in figure 4.16.

We graph employment rates as a function of the proportion of individuals reporting poor SAH for three different years: 1992, 2000, and 2010. For given shares of men in poor health, employment rates decreased substantially between 1992 and 2000, before reincreasing sharply in the first decade of the twenty-first century. Whatever the share of men reporting poor SAH,

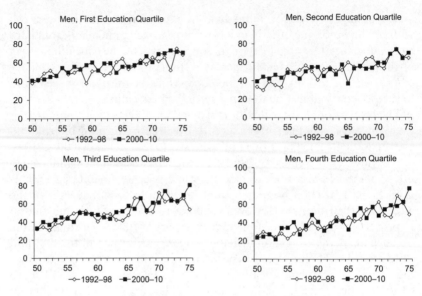

Fig. 4.14   Poor SAH by education quartile, men (1992–2010)

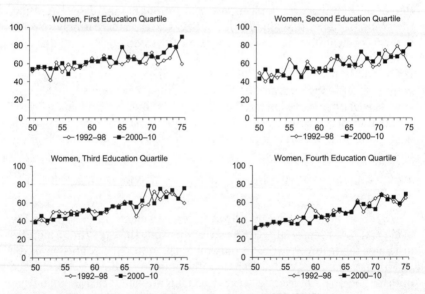

Fig. 4.15   Poor SAH by education quartile, women (1992–2010)

employment rates are higher in 2010 than in 2000, and in a number of cases, they are even higher than in 1992.

This suggests that the additional work capacity of men age fifty-five to sixty-nine as measured in 2010 is likely to be very small, if not negative, for a large number of years. This is what is evidenced in figure 4.17.

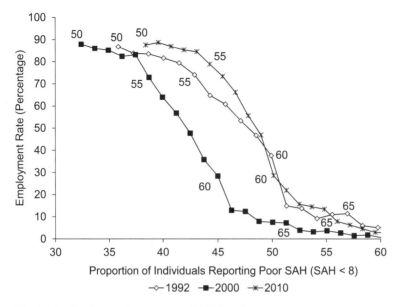

Fig. 4.16   Employment versus poor SAH (men)

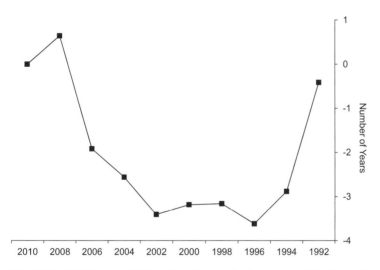

Fig. 4.17   SAH-based additional work capacity for men age fifty-five to sixty-nine in 2010, using 1992 to 2010 as reference years

According to the reference year, the additional employment capacity as measured in 2010 varies between 0 and –3.6 years. The only reference year for which it is positive is 2008 and, even in this case, it amounts to less than one year. These results are due to the fact that over the 1992–2010 period, employment rates varied very little and that the proportion of men reporting poor SAH first decreased before increasing again in the second half of the period (see figure 4.10). For some age groups, it is even higher at the end than at the beginning of the period. Given such trends, there cannot be, by construction, any positive additional work capacity as measured in 2010.

This result is in sharp contrast with what we obtained when using mortality as a proxy of health. As measured in 2012, the mortality-based additional work capacity varied between 0 and +3.2 years, according to the choice of the reference year in the 1992–2012 range. This gap in estimates with the SAH-based additional work capacity is due to the diverging trends in mortality and SAH over the period: while death rates have steadily decreased, SAH reported by men first improved before deteriorating again. One explanation for these differences in trends is that mortality and SAH do not capture the same thing. Mortality is actually a very peculiar measure of health. It captures the fact that individuals are still living, rather than dead—which is, of course, positive!—but it does not take at all into account that individuals may be living in poor health conditions. Recent work by Sieurin, Cambois, and Robine (2011) suggests that, in France, male life expectancy at age fifty increased by about 22 percent between 1999 and 2008, whereas life expectancy without functional limitations increased by only 0.6 percent over the same period. When decomposing this trend for various types of limitations, they find that, although life expectancy without physical functional limitations increased over time for men age fifty, their life expectancy without sensory and cognitive limitations actually decreased (by 3 to 8 percent). If SAH reported by men partly reflects these limitations, it is no surprise that its trend might substantially differ from that of mortality.

Overall, the results presented in sections 4.2 and 4.3 suggest that one has to be very cautious when considering our estimates of additional work capacity. Indeed, their magnitude much depends on the reference year that is chosen but, more importantly, their sign reverts when considering SAH rather than mortality as the relevant measure of health because the time trends in both variables do diverge. To overcome the problems raised by comparing different time periods, the Cutler et al. method, used in the next section, relies on comparisons across age groups rather than over time.

4.4   Simulating Employment Rates at Older Ages: The Cutler, Meara, and Richards-Shubik (2013) Approach

4.4.1   The Method

The method proposed by Cutler, Meara, and Richards-Shubik (2013) to estimate the employment capacity consists of two steps. They first estimate individual labor force participation as a function of health for individuals in a younger age group (fifty-seven to sixty-one) and then use the estimated coefficients to simulate what labor force participation would be for an older age group (sixty-two to sixty-four) if the health-participation relationship remained stable across ages. The advantage of this method is that it does not require comparing labor market outcomes and health at different points in time. The model is estimated for one age group at one period and is used to simulate the contemporaneous work capacity of another age group. The key assumption underlying the method is that the impact of health on individuals' working capacity is the same in the various age groups.

In what follows, we apply the Cutler et al. method to employment rates rather than labor force participation. We estimate employment rates separately for men and women in the fifty-one- to fifty-four-year-old group as a function of education, marital status, the type of job (employee, civil servant, self-employed), and an indicator of health. We then simulate employment rates for men and women and by education level separately in the fifty-five to fifty-nine, sixty to sixty-four, sixty-five to sixty-nine, and seventy and older age groups. Of course, the ideal methodology would require estimating separate regressions by education level. Unfortunately, we do not have enough observations in our data to do so.

4.4.2   The Data

The data we use come from the French section of the Survey of Health, Ageing and Retirement in Europe. The SHARE survey is a panel database containing individual information on health, socioeconomic status, and social and family networks for more than 85,000 individuals age fifty and older in nineteen European countries. The sample size for France is around 3,000 households per wave. The survey was carried out in 2004, 2007, 2009, 2011, and 2013. We pool all available waves except SHARELIFE (wave 3), which has data on individuals' life histories.

Our main health index is the same as in Behaghel et al. (2014). Its computation follows the methodology developed by Poterba, Venti, and Wise (2010, PVW) using the American Health and Retirement Survey data. The authors assume that latent health is revealed by responses to the long list of questions asked in the survey relative to health status and changes in health status. The PVW health index is then defined as the first principal component of these selected health measures. It is a weighted average of the health indicators with weights chosen to maximize the proportion of the variance of the individual health index that can be explained by this first principal component. This methodology has been replicated on the twenty-five health questions of the SHARE questionnaire. Details on the selected questions and the weights are provided in Behaghel et al. (2014). The index is decomposed in percentiles with percentile 1 corresponding to the worst health status and percentile 100 to the best. Unsurprisingly, the PVW index decreases with age (see figure 4.18). It is also lower for women than for men at all ages except above 93, which is consistent with widespread evidence in

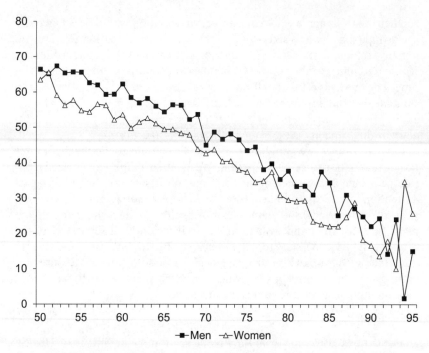

Fig. 4.18   PVW synthetic health index, by age and gender (average values over 2004, 2007, 2011, and 2013)

the literature according to which women report worse health than men do even if they have longer life expectancies (see Case and Paxson 2005).

As robustness checks, we consider alternative health measures. The first set includes self-assessed health and the subset of variables contained in the PVW index that capture the lack of personal autonomy suffered by individuals. Self-assessed health is captured by a dummy variable equal to 1 if individuals report that their health is either fair or poor and 0 if they report that it is excellent, very good, or good. We also include dummy variables for any difficulty walking, limitations in the activities of daily living,[1] and any limitation in instrumental activities of daily living.[2] On the graphs, all values are averaged over the four waves of SHARE that we use. Figures 4A.2 and 4A.3 in the appendix report age gradients for these variables.

In a third model, we include a subset of health indicators corresponding

---

1. Limitations in the activities of daily living refer to people who need the help of others to address personal care needs such as eating, bathing, dressing, or getting around inside their home.
2. Limitations in instrumental activities of daily living refer to people who need the help of other persons in handling routine needs such as everyday household chores, doing necessary business, shopping, or getting around for other purposes.

to the most severe conditions (heart problems, high blood pressure, stroke, diabetes, lung disease, and cancer), as well as arthritis, to the extent that it is highly incapacitating with respect to employment. The age gradients for these variables are provided in figures 4A.4 and 4A.5 for men and women, respectively.

4.4.3   Estimating Work Capacity

Results from linear regressions of employment rates on the PVW health index and our set of control variables are presented in table 4.1.

As expected, the PVW health index is positively correlated with employment rates for both men and women, suggesting that individuals in better health conditions have a higher probability of being in employment. Consistent with the evidence in the literature, we also find that lower-educated individuals are less likely to be in employment: the effect is significant for

Table 4.1   **Employment rates and the PVW health index (men and women age fifty-one to fifty-four)**

Dependent variable: Employment rate	Men	Women
Constant	0.567***	0.553***
	(0.052)	(0.042)
PVW synthetic health index	0.004***	0.004***
	(0.001)	(0.000)
No diploma or primary school	–0.256***	–0.109***
	(0.041)	(0.039)
Lower secondary education	–0.230***	–0.008
	(0.060)	(0.042)
Higher secondary education	–0.033	0.001
	(0.032)	(0.029)
High school diploma and above	Ref.	Ref.
	—	—
Employee	Ref.	Ref.
	—	—
Civil servant	0.092***	0.016
	(0.032)	(0.029)
Self-employed	0.061	0.056
	(0.041)	(0.044)
Married	0.033	0.092***
	(0.030)	(0.026)
Observations	713	834
R-squared	0.194	0.135

Note: Standard errors in parentheses.
***Significant at the 1 percent level.
**Significant at the 5 percent level.
*Significant at the 10 percent level.

both men and women with no diploma or only primary school, and for men with at most lower secondary education. Other control variables are found to have a differential impact on genders: civil-servant males have a higher probability to be in employment than employees, whereas the effect is not significant for females. In contrast, in the fifty-one- to fifty-four-year-old group considered here, married women are more likely to be employed than nonmarried ones, which is not the case for men.

Following the Cutler, Meara, and Richards-Shubik (2013) methodology, we use the coefficients estimated in table 4.1 to simulate employment rates for men and women in older age groups. The corresponding results are shown in table 4.2.

These estimates yield large additional work capacities on average. Considering individuals age fifty-five to fifty-nine, who are the most comparable to those on whom employment rates are estimated—who are age fifty-one to fifty-four—work capacity ranges between 9 percent and 19 percent for men. It increases with the level of education except for the most educated group—those with a high school diploma or more—whose actual employment rate is already quite high (about 80 percent). This is consistent with the fact that, although low-educated workers exit the labor force before highly educated ones, they tend to be in worse health, thus having lower predicted employment rates. Regarding women of the same age, their additional work capacity is much lower, since they work even more than men in that age group. For women with no diploma or only primary education it is about 3 percent, even slightly negative for those with lower secondary education, and no more than 12 percent for those with higher secondary education. This suggests that in the fifty-five- to fifty-nine-year-old group, there is not much room for increasing employment rates of females.

The estimated work capacities are much larger in the sixty- to sixty-four-year-old group for both men and women, ranging from 46 to 69 percent for the former and 49 to 65 percent for the latter. This is due to the fact that predicted employment rates are close to those of the fifty-five to fifty-nine age group, whereas actual employment rates precipitate: they go down to no more than 30 percent for men and 26 percent for women. This is no surprise given that, during most of the period we consider here (2004–2013), legal retirement age was sixty in France, thus generating a spike in exit rates from employment at this age. The results presented in this table suggest that if health were the only limitation to the employment of senior workers, both men and women could work much more than they actually do in the sixty to sixty-five age group.

These results are robust to using alternative health measures. The first set we consider includes poor SAH, as well as any limitation in ADL or IADL and difficulty walking. As evidenced in appendix table 4A.1, all these variables reduce the probability of being in employment with the effect being significant at least at the 5 percent level—except for IADL for women, which

Table 4.2   Work capacity by education, men and women age fifty-five to seventy and older

Percent of individuals in employment	Men			Women		
	Actual	Predicted	Estimated WC	Actual	Predicted	Estimated WC
Age 55–59						
No diploma or primary school	49.43	58.93	9.50	65.99	69.07	3.08
Lower secondary education	65.06	65.67	0.61	82.61	82.41	−0.20
Higher secondary education	65.54	84.71	19.17	70.80	82.92	12.12
High school diploma and above	79.50	92.53	13.04	75.70	85.93	10.23
Age 60–64						
No diploma or primary school	9.23	58.61	49.39	18.47	67.86	49.39
Lower secondary education	18.18	65.09	46.91	17.71	82.87	65.16
Higher secondary education	13.43	83.37	69.94	19.46	81.96	62.51
High school diploma and above	30.10	91.19	61.09	26.30	84.75	58.45
Age 65–69						
No diploma or primary school	2.42	57.47	55.06	2.05	67.67	65.62
Lower secondary education	4.26	65.33	61.07	2.00	81.08	79.08
Higher secondary education	1.39	82.30	80.92	0.87	80.60	79.73
High school diploma and above	6.33	88.11	81.78	2.69	82.24	79.55
Age 70 and older						
No diploma or primary school	0.08	51.62	51.53	0.11	61.32	61.21
Lower secondary education	0.74	54.56	53.83	0.72	72.50	71.78
Higher secondary education	0.71	77.09	76.38	1.27	74.77	73.50
High school diploma and above	0.58	83.07	82.50	1.07	77.66	76.59

is significant only at the 10 percent level. Using this specification to simulate additional work capacity, the magnitude we get is very close to that in table 4.2, although marginally larger (see table 4A.2): it ranges from 5 percent to 20 percent (52 percent to 71 percent, respectively) for men age fifty to fifty-nine (sixty to sixty-four, respectively), and from 5 percent to 12 percent (72 percent to 87 percent) for women age fifty-five to fifty-nine (sixty to sixty-four, respectively).

When using our second set of alternative health measures based on the most severe health conditions and arthritis, the impact on employment rates gets more variable across genders (see table 4A.3): women are negatively affected by strokes, diabetes, arthritis, and cancer, whereas men's employment rates are reduced by strokes, lung problems, and arthritis only. When simulating additional work capacity on this basis, the results are very similar to those in table 4.2 (see table 4A.4).

As evidenced in table 4.2—and confirmed in tables 4A.2 and 4A.4—the magnitude of the work capacity estimated with the Cutler et al. method gets substantially larger as age increases. It reaches 61 to 81 percent for men in the sixty-five to sixty-nine age group—according to their educational level—and 65 to 79 percent for women before declining slightly at older ages—but still ranging between 50 percent and 80 percent for both men and women. These figures are extremely high. Taken at face value, they suggest that health is in no way a limiting factor to increasing retirement ages for both men and women in France, whatever their educational attainment. If poorer health at old ages were the only limitation to employment, employment rates could be much higher than they actually are, even for low-skilled (low-educated) workers who have often spent a large part of their career in jobs characterized by high physical strain.

4.4.4   The Issues Raised by the Cutler et al. Approach

The very high values of work capacity generated by our estimates, in particular at old ages—seventy and older—raise a number of issues about the method. It indeed relies on two strong assumptions.

The first one is that a given health problem has exactly the same impact on the probability of being in employment (or the work capacity) at all ages. This assumption does not necessarily hold for a couple of reasons. Despite the large number of questions in SHARE, the health indicators that we have are quite crude so that we are likely to mismeasure "true health." In particular, a given reported health symptom (say arthritis) may correspond to a better or worse "true" health status according to the intensity of the pain it generates. If this intensity tends to grow over age, the same symptom will not affect the probability of being in employment in the same way across ages. A second issue has to do with the fact that the impact of a given "true" health problem may affect productivity in a different way across ages. Older workers may, in particular, be less versatile than younger ones, thereby having more difficulty developing strategies that would allow them to circumvent a temporary physical handicap. If this is the case, the direct impact of health on the probability of being in employment is not constant across ages. More specifically, if given health conditions, as we measure them, have a more negative impact on older workers than on younger ones, this will generate an upward bias in our estimates of additional work capacity, with this bias increasing as the individuals we consider get older.

Of course, the simplifying assumption according to which a given health problem has exactly the same impact on the probability of being in employment (or the work capacity) at various ages is more or less acceptable according to the age gap between the group on which the estimates are run and the group for which the simulations are made. If both groups are close enough in terms of age, the assumption may be considered reasonable. If, in contrast, they are very far apart, it is unlikely to hold. This suggests that the results we obtain for individuals age seventy and older (or even sixty-five to sixty-nine) using estimates run on individuals age fifty to fifty-four should be interpreted with great caution.

The second assumption underlying the Cutler et al. method is that there is no reverse causality from employment to health. If, in contrast, being in employment affects health and this effect varies across ages, the estimates run on the fifty- to fifty-four-year-old group are biased and the simulations carried out on the older age groups yield a biased measure of the work capacity at old ages. In particular, the latter will be overestimated if work negatively affects health at old ages. The literature on the health effects of retirement suggests that this may be the case. Indeed, most papers find a positive impact of retirement on physical health, whereas the results are more mixed for mental health, and even negative for cognitive outcomes (see Bassanini and Caroli 2014). This reverse causality effect is hard to take into account since it would require instrumenting health levels. Nonetheless, it cannot be ruled out and calls, here again, for caution in interpreting the results. The same remark applies to the MW methodology as well.

4.5 Conclusion

In the first part of this chapter, we estimated additional work capacity using the standard MW method where health is proxied by mortality. According to this approach, health does not emerge as a key limiting factor to higher employment rates in the fifty-five to sixty-nine age groups. This result comes as no surprise. As recalled in the introduction, the fact that gains in life expectancy are good news that provide a natural solution to pension problems has been regularly underlined in the French pension debate over the last two decades. It paved the way to reforms whose expected effects on retirement ages are not marginal at all. The MW method just confirms how large the window potentially opened by these gains is. Yet, this mortality-based approach already required one first qualification, that is, the need to incorporate socioeconomic mortality differentials. Accounting for these differentials did not fully revert the message that had been obtained on average: there remains some additional work capacity in the MW sense of the term for all social groups. This work capacity nevertheless displays strong variations across social groups: depending upon the reference that is chosen, the gap ranges from four to six years between the two extreme cases of blue collars and managers/professionals.

When considering SAH, which is a less crude proxy of health than mortality, our estimates of additional work capacity are substantially modified. As measured in 2010, the SAH-based capacity indeed varies between 0 and −3.6 years, thus being consistently negative. The gap in estimates between mortality and SAH-based capacity is due to the diverging trends in both variables over the period. A natural explanation for this is that mortality and SAH do not capture the same thing. As a matter of fact, the mortality proxy does not take into account that individuals may still be alive although in poor health conditions.

This result is not sufficient to invalidate the idea that the financial equilibrium of pension systems can be reached by increasing retirement ages. Its significance is indeed limited by the fact that it has been established over a relatively short time period over which employment rates have been reincreasing and SAH has had a U-shaped profile without any clear long-run trend. What would be needed is an assessment of this trend over a longer time period, typically from the mid-1970s onward. But, even if such an exercise should confirm a total lack of health improvement over the long run, the MW approach would still predict a current positive additional work capacity. This would indeed mirror the global decline of senior employment rates that has been observed since the 1970s, and this precisely corresponds to the kind of increases expected from pension reforms that have already been implemented. It would, however, mean that these reforms have come relatively close to the health barrier we try to measure here, and that there is not much scope for going further than what these reforms have already planned to do.

Comparing health (or mortality) at different time periods, as required by the MW approach, raises a number of methodological problems, in particular the dependence of the results on the reference year we choose. To circumvent such problems, the last part of the chapter uses the Cutler et al. method that relies on comparisons across age groups rather than over time. Here again, the corresponding estimates yield large additional work capacities on average, with significant variation across social groups, now identified through education levels: low-educated individuals tend to be in worse health at older ages so that their predicted employment rates are also lower.

Overall, both the mortality-based MW approach and the CMR method predict high average levels of additional work capacity. However, the picture becomes somewhat different when disaggregating the results by social groups or education. So, our results emphasize the idea that policies that would aim at activating any estimated additional work capacity should take into account, when possible, the heterogeneity of health conditions in the population.

Moreover, as mentioned in the introduction to this chapter, additional work capacity cannot be a general indicator of how much more seniors *should* work. Indeed, the methods used here leave aside many factors that may play a role in determining the "optimal" employment rate of older workers. The fact that leisure has a positive value is the first of these factors: individual and collective choices regarding retirement ages are the result of a trade-off between income and leisure. Workers that are fully employable and in perfectly good health may very rationally choose to allocate a large share of their "work capacity" to retirement rather than to work if they consider that they can afford to do so. Next and last, even if we restrict the question to the assessment of work capacity *stricto sensu*, without any message concerning how far it must be exploited, there remains the fact that health is only one of the factors that limit this work capacity. The economic literature has shown that senior workers suffer from low levels of labor demand, in particular, when they are low skilled. This may be caused by health limitations if they have spent most of their careers in high-strain jobs, but it may also be the consequence of skill obsolescence (Aubert, Caroli, and Roger 2006). Recent prospective studies have highlighted the fact that many jobs are likely to be affected by automation in the near future (Frey and Osborne 2013). Tasks that escape automation include creative intelligence, social intelligence, and perception and manipulation tasks. It is difficult to foresee the impact of age on the ability to carry out such tasks; yet it is not implausible that labor demand continues to shift toward young and middle ages, thus increasing the difficulty for older workers to stay in employment.

Appendix

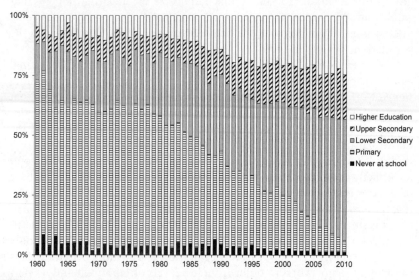

Fig. 4A.1   Distribution of years of education completed by cohort, all (year each cohort attained age fifty)

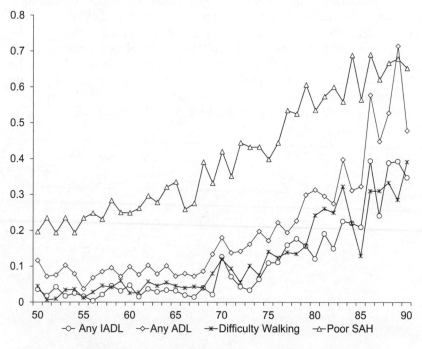

Fig. 4A.2   Poor SAH, limitations in ADL and IADL, difficulty walking, men (average values over 2004, 2007, 2011, and 2013)

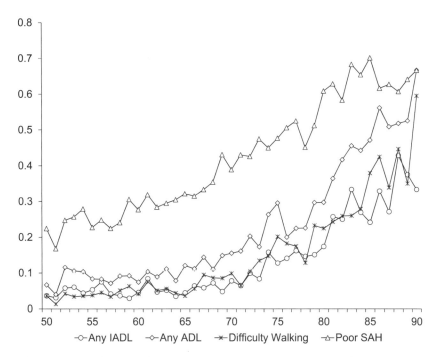

Fig. 4A.3 Poor SAH, limitations in ADL and IADL, difficulty walking, women (average values over 2004, 2007, 2011, and 2013)

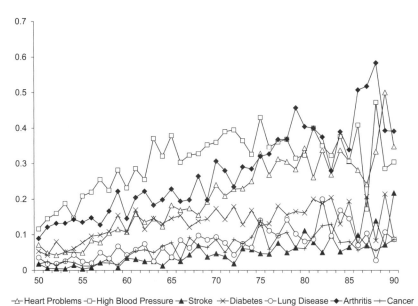

Fig. 4A.4 Most severe health conditions and arthritis, men (average values over 2004, 2007, 2011, and 2013)

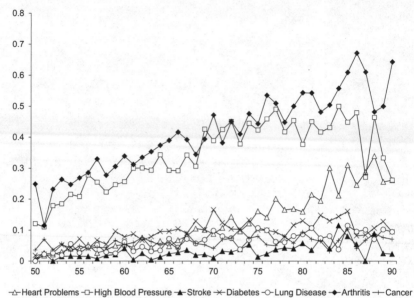

−△−Heart Problems −□−High Blood Pressure −▲−Stroke −✕−Diabetes −○−Lung Disease −◆−Arthritis −+−Cancer

Fig. 4A.5   Most severe health conditions and arthritis, women (average values over 2004, 2007, 2011, and 2013)

Table 4A.1   **Employment rates and poor SAH, ADL, IADL, and difficulty walking (men and women age fifty-one to fifty-four)**

Dependent variable: Employment rate	Men	Women
Constant	0.908***	0.851***
	(0.035)	(0.031)
Poor SAH	−0.169***	−0.115***
	(0.034)	(0.031)
Any IADL	−0.236***	−0.103*
	(0.079)	(0.057)
Any ADL	−0.163***	−0.164***
	(0.048)	(0.045)
Difficulty walking	−0.202**	−0.385***
	(0.081)	(0.070)
No diploma or primary school	−0.239***	−0.086**
	(0.040)	(0.038)
Lower secondary education	−0.211***	−0.017
	(0.058)	(0.040)
Higher secondary education	−0.033	−0.005
	(0.030)	(0.028)
High school diploma and above	Ref.	Ref.
	—	—
Employee	Ref.	Ref.
	—	—
Civil servant	0.083***	0.015
	(0.031)	(0.027)
Self-employed	0.068*	0.083**
	(0.039)	(0.042)
Married	0.034	0.086***
	(0.029)	(0.025)
Observations	726	852
R-squared	0.223	0.185

Note: Standard errors in parentheses.
***Significant at the 1 percent level.
**Significant at the 5 percent level.
*Significant at the 10 percent level.

Table 4A.2   Work capacity by education, men and women age fifty-five to seventy and older

Percent of individuals in employment	Men			Women		
	Actual	Predicted	Estimated WC	Actual	Predicted	Estimated WC
Age 55–59						
No diploma or primary school	49.43	60.20	10.77	65.99	71.90	5.90
Lower secondary education	65.06	70.32	5.26	82.61	87.21	4.61
Higher secondary education	65.54	86.39	20.85	70.80	83.64	12.84
High school diploma and above	79.50	93.79	14.29	75.70	88.63	12.93
Age 60–64						
No diploma or primary school	9.23	61.64	52.41	18.47	72.1	53.64
Lower secondary education	18.18	70.29	52.10	17.71	86.05	68.34
Higher secondary education	13.43	85.41	71.97	19.46	83.29	63.84
High school diploma and above	30.10	91.77	61.67	26.30	87.28	60.98
Age 65–69						
No diploma or primary school	2.42	61.31	58.89	2.05	71.49	69.44
Lower secondary education	4.26	69.04	64.79	2.00	80.83	78.83
Higher secondary education	1.39	85.03	83.64	0.87	82.85	81.98
High school diploma and above	6.33	90.98	84.66	2.69	84.63	81.94
Age 70 and older						
No diploma or primary school	0.08	48.82	48.74	0.11	57.50	57.38
Lower secondary education	0.74	53.44	52.70	0.72	71.19	70.48
Higher secondary education	0.71	76.98	76.27	1.27	73.10	71.82
High school diploma and above	0.58	84.45	83.87	1.07	78.76	77.69

Note: Based on estimates from table 4A.1.

Table 4A.3   Employment rates and most serious health conditions, men and women age fifty-one to fifty-four

Dependent variable: Employment rate	Men	Women
Constant	0.899***	0.849***
	(0.037)	(0.032)
Heart problem	−0.089	−0.087
	(0.065)	(0.083)
Blood pressure	−0.023	−0.051
	(0.038)	(0.034)
Stroke	−0.322**	−0.275***
	(0.128)	(0.100)
Diabetes	−0.014	−0.213***
	(0.057)	(0.069)
Lung problems	−0.233***	−0.026
	(0.088)	(0.073)
Arthritis	−0.088**	−0.066**
	(0.039)	(0.030)
Cancer	−0.152	−0.199***
	(0.098)	(0.059)
No diploma or primary school	−0.299***	−0.167***
	(0.042)	(0.039)
Lower secondary education	−0.268***	−0.044
	(0.061)	(0.042)
Higher secondary education	−0.064**	−0.019
	(0.032)	(0.029)
High school diploma and above	Ref.	Ref.
	—	—
Employee	Ref.	Ref.
	—	—
Civil servant	0.090***	0.029
	(0.033)	(0.029)
Self-employed	0.080*	0.065
	(0.041)	(0.045)
Married	0.037	0.091***
	(0.030)	(0.026)
Observations	725	852
R-squared	0.150	0.104

Note: Standard errors in parentheses.
***Significant at the 1 percent level.
**Significant at the 5 percent level.
*Significant at the 10 percent level.

Table 4.4 Work capacity by education, men and women age fifty-five to seventy and older

Percent of individuals in employment	Men			Women		
	Actual	Predicted	Estimated WC	Actual	Predicted	Estimated WC
Age 55–59						
No diploma or primary school	49.43	59.11	9.68	65.99	67.29	1.30
Lower secondary education	65.06	65.62	0.56	82.61	81.74	-0.87
Higher secondary education	65.54	84.57	19.03	70.80	83.93	13.13
High school diploma and above	79.50	94.35	14.86	75.70	87.12	11.42
Age 60–64						
No diploma or primary school	9.23	58.57	49.34	18.47	65.31	46.8
Lower secondary education	18.18	64.58	46.39	17.71	79.39	61.68
Higher secondary education	13.43	82.38	68.94	19.46	83.05	63.59
High school diploma and above	30.10	91.13	61.03	26.30	85.80	59.50
Age 65–69						
No diploma or primary school	2.42	56.12	53.71	2.05	64.01	61.97
Lower secondary education	4.26	63.10	58.84	2.00	80.10	78.10
Higher secondary education	1.39	81.18	79.80	0.87	82.12	81.25
High school diploma and above	6.33	89.16	82.83	2.69	84.17	81.48
Age 70 and older						
No diploma or primary school	0.08	53.20	53.12	0.11	60.98	60.87
Lower secondary education	0.74	55.45	54.72	0.72	74.84	74.13
Higher secondary education	0.71	78.12	77.41	1.27	77.31	76.04
High school diploma and above	0.58	85.72	85.15	1.07	81.14	80.07

Note: Based on estimates in table 4A.3.

References

Aubert, P., E. Caroli, and M. Roger. 2006. "New Technologies, Organisation and Age: Firm-Level Evidence." *Economic Journal* 116 (509): 73–93.

Bago d'Uva, T., M. Lindeboom, O. O'Donnell, and E. van Doorslaer. 2011. "Education-Related Inequity in Health Care with Heterogeneous Reporting of Health." *Journal of the Royal Statistical Society*, Series A, 174 (3): 639–64.

Bago d'Uva, T., E. van Doorslaer, M. Lindeboom, and O. O'Donnell. 2008. "Does Reporting Heterogeneity Bias the Measurement of Health Disparities?" *Health Economics* 17 (3): 351–75.

Bassanini, A., and E. Caroli. 2014. "Is Work Bad for Health? The Role of Constraint versus Choice." IZA Discussion Paper no. 7891, Institute for the Study of Labor.

Behaghel, L., D. Blanchet, and M. Roger. 2014. "Retirement, Early Retirement and Disability: Explaining Labor Force Participation after 55 in France." NBER Working Paper no. 20030, Cambridge, MA.

Blanpain, N., and O. Chardon. 2011. "Les Inégalités Sociales Face à la Mort: Tables de Mortalité par Catégorie Sociale et Indices Standardisés de Mortalité pour Quatre Périodes (1976–1984, 1983–1991, 1991–1999, 2000–2008)." WP Insee, no. F1108.

Calot, G., and M. Febvay. 1965. "La Mortalité Différentielle Suivant le Milieu Social, Période 1955–1960." *Études et Conjoncture*, no. 11, Insee.

Case, A., and C. Paxson. 2005. "Sex Differences in Morbidity and Mortality." *Demography* 42 (2): 189–214.

Conseil d'Orientation des Retraites. 2014. *Évolutions et Perspectives des Retraites en France*. Rapport annuel du COR, Juin.

Cutler, D., E. Meara, and S. Richards-Shubik. 2013. "Health and Work Capacity of Older Adults: Estimates and Implications for Social Security Policy." Unpublished Manuscript. Available at SSRN: http://ssrn.com/abstract=2577858.

Desplanques, G. 1976. *La Mortalité des Adultes Suivant le Milieu Social, Période 1955–1971*, Les Collections de l'INSEE, série D, no. 44.

Etilé, F., and C. Milcent. 2006. "Income-Related Reporting Heterogeneity in Self-Assessed Health: Evidence from France." *Health Economics* 15 (9): 965–81.

Frey, C. B., and M. A. Osborne. 2013. "The Future of Employment: How Susceptible Are Jobs to Computerization?" Working Paper, Oxford University.

Johnston, D., C. Propper, and M. Shields. 2009. "Comparing Subjective and Objective Measures of Health: Evidence from Hypertension for the Income/Health Gradient." *Journal of Health Economics* 28 (3): 540–52.

Lindeboom, M., and E. van Doorslaer. 2004. "Cut-Point Shift and Index Shift in Self-Reported Health." *Journal of Health Economics* 23 (6): 1083–99.

Milligan, K., and D. Wise. 2012. "Health and Work at Older Ages: Using Mortality to Assess the Capacity to Work across Countries." NBER Working Paper no. 18229, Cambridge, MA.

Poterba, J. M., S. F. Venti, and D. A. Wise. 2010. "The Asset Cost of Poor Health" NBER Working Paper no. 26389, Cambridge, MA.

Sieurin, A., E. Cambois, and J. M. Robine. 2011. "Les Espérances de Vie Sans Incapacité en France. Une Tendance Récente Moins Favorable que Dans le Passé." INED Working Paper no.170.

Tubeuf, S., F. Jusot, M. Devaux, and C. Sermet. 2008. "Social Heterogeneity in Self-Reported Health Status and Measurement of Inequalities in Health." IRDES Working Paper no. DT12, Institut de Recherche et Documentation en Économie de la Santé.

5

Healthy, Happy, and Idle
Estimating the Health Capacity to Work at Older Ages in Germany

Hendrik Jürges, Lars Thiel, and Axel Börsch-Supan

5.1 Introduction

In this chapter, we aim to answer a seemingly simple question for Germany: What is the proportion of older individuals who could work in the labor market if they wanted to and if they were not limited by poor health? In other words, what is the capacity to work at older ages, and after what

Hendrik Jürges is professor of health economics and management at the Schumpeter School of Business and Economics, University of Wuppertal. Lars Thiel is a researcher at the Schumpeter School of Business and Economics, University of Wuppertal. Axel Börsch-Supan is director of the Munich Center for the Economics of Aging and professor of economics at the Technical University of Munich, and a research associate of the National Bureau of Economic Research.

This chapter uses data from SHARE wave 5 release 1.0.0, as of March 31st 2015 (DOI: 10.6103/SHARE.w5.100) or SHARE wave 4 release 1.1.1, as of March 28th 2013 (DOI: 10.6103/SHARE.w4.111) or SHARE waves 1 and 2 release 2.6.0, as of November 29th 2013 (DOI: 10.6103/SHARE.w1.260 and 10.6103/SHARE.w2.260) or SHARELIFE release 1.0.0, as of November 24th 2010 (DOI: 10.6103/SHARE.w3.100). The SHARE data collection has been primarily funded by the European Commission through the 5th Framework Programme (project QLK6-CT-2001–00360 in the thematic program Quality of Life), through the 6th Framework Programme (projects SHARE-I3, RII-CT-2006–062193, COMPARE, CIT5- CT-2005–028857, and SHARELIFE, CIT4-CT-2006–028812) and through the 7th Framework Programme (SHARE-PREP, No. 211909; SHARE-LEAP, No. 227822; and SHARE M4, No. 261982). Additional funding from the US National Institute on Aging (U01 AG09740–13S2, P01 AG005842, P01 AG08291, P30 AG12815, R21 AG025169, Y1-AG-4553–01, IAG BSR06–11, and OGHA 04–064) and the German Ministry of Education and Research, as well as from various national sources is gratefully acknowledged (see www.share-project.org for a full list of funding institutions). The Microcensus data were provided by the Research Data Centers of the Federal Statistical Office and the Statistical Offices of the Länder in Düsseldorf, Germany, analyzed on site (further information: http://www.forschungsdatenzentrum.de/en/). For acknowledgments, sources of research support, and disclosure of the authors' material financial relationships, if any, please see http://www.nber.org/chapters/c13742.ack.

is currently the statutory retirement age? The answer to this question is particularly relevant for the future of the German pay-as-you-go pension system. Not everybody who is retiring from work does so because he or she is too ill, physically or mentally. Many individuals retire simply because they can, that is, they have reached the age at which they become eligible for an early retirement benefit or a regular old age pension. Employers often seem to encourage the early labor force exit of their older staff because they believe that the higher salaries paid to older workers compared to younger workers do not always reflect higher productivity. Extending working lives by raising early and normal retirement ages, therefore, is arguably the single-most effective measure to increase the sustainability of the pension system. Each additional year that is worked affects the system dependency ratio on two counts: it reduces the numerator (those receiving pension benefits) and increases the denominator (those who finance pensioners' benefits).

This simple calculus was the main reason for the German government to gradually increase in 2007 the age of retirement from sixty-five to sixty-seven, similar to many other countries. This increase, fully implemented in the year 2029, will fairly exactly extend the working life in proportion to the increase in life expectancy and therefore compensate for one important cause of population aging, namely, the increase in longevity.

While this policy is rational from a sustainability point of view, the reform was not appreciated by the populace. The government failed to win reelection and seven years later, in 2014, elements of the reform were reversed by introducing a new early retirement option at age sixty-three without any actuarial adjustment to those workers who have accumulated at least forty-five years of contributions to the public pension system. Such contributions include own contributions (payroll tax on wages earned during dependent employment) and contributions by the government during periods of education, child care, and unemployment. The policy reversal was motivated by the hypothesis that these workers have particularly poor health because they worked so long.

This motivation is in stark contrast to the substantial improvements in population health over the past half century that are reflected in continuing increases in life expectancy. Hence, lack of work capacity due to poor health should not be the major obstacle to raise retirement ages. In fact, Börsch-Supan, Coppola, and Rausch (forthcoming) showed that those employees who are eligible for the new early retirement option at age sixty-three are not more likely to have poor health at the end of their working lives when measured by the days reported as sick leave. Rather, the contrary is the case. These are surprising results that contradict the originally claimed purpose of the legislation, namely, to help the underprivileged who worked especially long and hard during their lives and consequently suffered from extra burdens. Börsch-Supan, Alt, and Bucher-Koenen (2015) confirm this finding with the SHARE data also used in this chapter. Most notably, the eligible workers self-reported a significantly lower incidence of work disability.

More generally, looking at patterns of labor force participation in Germany—in particular, the large retirement hazard rates at salient ages sixty-three or sixty-five—it should be clear that retirement timing is often not driven by bad health. For each individual, health deteriorates through a series of health shocks, that is, discontinuous changes in health. At some point, the health shock can be so large that working is no longer possible. For the population as a whole these shocks aggregate to a smooth decline in average health as people get older—so that retirement for health reasons should also follow a smooth pattern. (At the extreme we have mortality. For each individual, dying is the ultimate health shock, but survival curves are smooth.)

Even if most people do not retire for health reasons, it is not clear how far working lives could reasonably be extended. Our chapter is a first attempt to answer this question for Germany. To be sure this is a descriptive, not a normative, exercise. To estimate work capacity among the older population, we follow two different empirical approaches with a similar logic: we estimate the link between health and labor force participation in a population whose employment patterns are not or hardly affected by the current retirement and social security legislation. Using these "pure health effects" on labor force participation, we extrapolate to today's population, which is affected by today's legislation, to learn how many could not work for health reasons and how many could still work, even beyond the current normal retirement age. Independent of the method used, we get similar results. As a lower bound for today's elders, we show that, if individuals were retiring exclusively for health reasons, more than half of the population could still work until age seventy.

One possible critique of our approach is that health is not equally distributed across socioeconomic groups, with poorer or less educated individuals being in worse health. Estimating average work capacity across the entire socioeconomic spectrum thus possibly overestimates the capacity to work among those workers. Where possible, we thus add estimates separately for different education groups, with education being one important component of socioeconomic status.

The chapter is structured as follows: In section 5.2, we describe trends in health and labor force participation in Germany since the 1960s. In sections 5.3 and 5.4, we use these long-term trends to estimate the capacity to work among today's elders compared to those up to forty years in the past. Using current survey data containing detailed health information, we simulate employment among older respondents using younger individuals' behavior as reference in section 5.5. In section 5.6, we provide a more detailed analysis of trends in health across education levels. Section 5.7 summarizes our research and discusses our findings.

5.2   Pension Reforms and Long-Term Trends in Health and Employment at Older Ages

In this section we provide some background to our empirical analysis by briefly describing long-term trends in mortality, morbidity, and labor force participation at older ages in Germany. Moreover, we relate broad trends in labor force participation to historical changes in the German pension system.

Figure 5.1 shows the trend in (log) annual mortality rates in (West) Germany at ages fifty-five to fifty-nine, sixty to sixty-four, and sixty-five to sixty-nine from 1960 to 2011. The graphs clearly show that mortality rates rise with age and that mortality is higher among men than women in any given age group. Mortality rates have been fairly stable in the 1960s, especially among men, but have fallen continuously between 1970 and 2000. For instance, mortality rates among sixty- to sixty-four-year-old men have roughly halved from 2.7 percent to 1.4 percent. Since 2000, the mortality decline appears to have flattened among women. In fact, in the group of sixty-five- to sixty-nine-year-old women, there is even a slight increase in mortality rates.

Figure 5.2 shows trends in self-reported morbidity between 1989 and 2009. These numbers are based on computations from the German Microcensus (an annual survey of a 1 percent sample of the population), which asks a few broad health questions at irregular intervals. Specifically, respon-

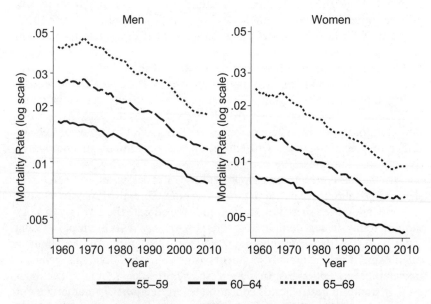

Fig. 5.1   Mortality rates at older ages, West Germany (1960 to 2011)
Source: Human Mortality Database.

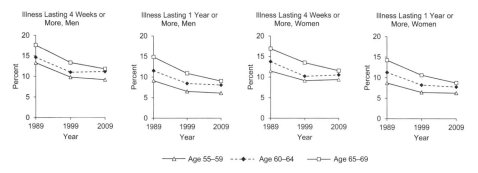

Fig. 5.2   Morbidity rates at older ages, Germany (1989–2009)
Source: Own computations from Microcensus.

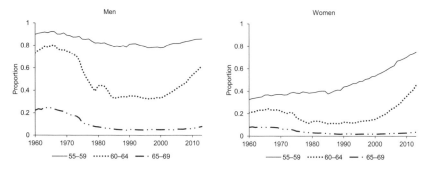

Fig. 5.3   Labor force participation rates at older ages, Germany (1960 to 2013)
Source: Microcensus.

dents are asked whether they currently suffer from any illness or condition, and if yes, how long they have suffered from this condition. We computed two summary measures of health from the answers to these questions: the prevalence of an ongoing condition that lasted at least one month, and the prevalence of long-term (> 1 year) illness (cf. Kemptner, Jürges, and Reinhold 2011). The data reveal similar prevalences among women and men and a clear age gradient. Older age groups are more likely to report suffering from long-term illness than younger age groups. Moreover, there is evidence of a steep decline in the prevalence of long-term illness between 1989 and 1999 among both sexes and all age groups. Parallel to flattening trends in mortality, the decline in the prevalence of long-term illness appears to have slowed down in the first decade of the twenty-first century.

Whereas health in terms of mortality or long-term illness has generally improved over time, the long-term trend of employment at older ages has virtually been a roller-coaster ride (see figure 5.3), especially in the group of sixty- to sixty-four-year-old men. Long-run trends in the employment of older women reflect secular changes in the role of women in the labor market, but the trend among men is clearly linked to the history of pension reforms. As explained in our previous work (e.g., Jürges et al. 2015), when the pay-as-you-go system was introduced in 1957, there was a single eligibility age for regular old age pensions: sixty-five for men and sixty for women. Earlier retirement was impossible unless one could prove a disability. In fact, in the 1960s, disability accounted for more than half of all entries into retirement among both men and women. This was the least generous period in terms of social security eligibility. About 90 percent of the fifty-five- to fifty-nine-year-old men, almost 80 percent of the sixty- to sixty-four-year-old men, and even more than 20 percent of the sixty-five- to sixty-nine-year-old men were working. Labor force participation rates among women were generally much lower, due to historical patterns of low female employment in general.

The year 1972 marked the beginning of a long phase of ever increasing generosity of the pension system that ended in the late 1980s. The 1972 reform introduced special provisions for early retirement of the long-term insured by providing old age pension benefits (without actuarially fair deductions) already at age sixty-three, given that workers had a minimum of thirty-five contribution years. Further, a special old age pension for disabled workers to be collected at age sixty-two (later at age sixty) with less stringent health requirements than disability pensions was introduced. As a result, labor force participation among sixty- to sixty-four-year-old men dropped quite dramatically from nearly 80 percent to 40 percent. The average retirement age dropped by more than two years, and the new retirement pathways substituted for the disability pathway into retirement among men age sixty and older. Further reforms that generally increased the generosity of the system followed during the 1980s. As a result, labor force participation among older workers was at a historical low throughout the 1990s.

In face of a looming demographic crisis, serious attempts to cut back on the generosity of the German pension system started in 1992. Pension benefits were anchored to net rather than to gross wages and actuarial adjustments of benefits to retirement age were introduced, albeit only gradually from 1998 onward. In 2004, the pension benefit indexation formula was modified to account for demographic developments. These reforms clearly left their mark on labor force participation among older individuals. Again, it is the sixty to sixty-four age group in which the effect was particularly salient. In this age group, participation rates have increased to more than 60 percent among men and nearly 50 percent among women in 2013.

Whether these positive trends will continue in the future is not clear, however. On the one hand, in 2007, a gradual increase in the normal retirement age from sixty-five to sixty-seven years (to be phased in between 2012 and 2029) was enacted. Retirement ages for other variants of old age pensions were increased as well (e.g., women's retirement ages were raised to match men's retirement ages). This should also give a boost to employment in the sixty-five to sixty-nine age group. On the other hand, as described in the introduction, Germany has entered yet another (transitory) phase of pension reforms. In 2014, an early retirement option at age sixty-three without actuarial adjustment was reintroduced for those with forty-five contribution years.

5.3   Estimating Work Capacity Using Long-Term Changes in Mortality

One important aim of this chapter is to provide estimates of work capacity for Germany that are comparable with those from other countries. In this section, we use age-specific mortality as an indicator of age-specific health or work capacity (Milligan and Wise 2012a). Mortality data provide information on population health that is consistently defined over time and across countries. Thus, they provide indicators of health that do not suffer from reporting bias and cross-cultural differences in response behavior that usually affect self-assessed health measures (e.g., Jürges 2007). On the downside, mortality is necessarily an imperfect indicator of health limitations relevant for work capacity as it does not reflect nonlethal conditions such as back pain or depression, which may have trends that are independent of mortality.

Bearing these limitations in mind, we estimate work capacity by looking at the relationship between mortality rates (as an age-year specific indicator of health) and employment rates at several points in time. Mortality rates increase and employment rates decrease with age, leading to a negative relationship between age-specific mortality rates and age-specific labor market participation rates in any given year. However, as shown below, the curvature of the mortality-employment relationship has changed greatly over time. General health as indicated by age-specific survival rates has generally increased, whereas the employment rates at the same ages have mostly decreased, except in recent years (see figures 5.1 and 5.3).

This implies that until recently, health and employment at any given age have moved in opposite directions over time. Given the same health status, individuals have become increasingly less likely to work. Based on these trends over time, we conduct a counterfactual analysis to estimate the potential ability of the current population to work at older ages. Specifically, we compare current employment rates with employment rates at earlier points in time, holding the mortality rate constant. In this way, we are able to assess the proportion of today's individuals whose health would allow them to work, if they worked as much as people with the same health status in the past.

We obtained age-specific mortality rates from the Human Mortality Database (HMD). We have computed average age-specific mortality rates at ages forty-five to seventy-five for four periods: 1968–1972, 1976–1980, 1989–1995, and 2005–2009. The choice of periods is motivated below. To these data we merged average age-specific employment rates for the same periods, which we computed from the (West) German Census 1970 (IPUMS database, Minnesota Population Center 2011) and selected years (1976, 1978, 1989, 1995, 2005, and 2009) of the German Microcensus. The Microcensus is the largest annually conducted household survey in Germany, and it has been carried out in West Germany since 1957 and East Germany in 1991. It covers a representative sample of 1 percent of the German population. Currently, some 370,000 households participate in the Microcensus every year. Specifically, we merged the employment rates in the 1970 census to the average 1968 to 1972 mortality rates, the average employment rates in 1976 and 1978 to the average mortality rates in 1976 to 1980, the average employment rates in 1989 to 1995 to the average mortality rates in 1989 to 1995, and the average employment rates in 2005 and 2009 to average mortality in 2005 to 2009.

Our choice of comparison periods is motivated by the history of the German pension system as described in the preceding section. We begin our analysis in 1970 as a highly relevant comparison period. It reflects the prereform phase that was also the least generous in terms of eligibility. The immediate consequences of the 1972 reform on the relationship between health (mortality) and employment are captured by the 1976–1980 period. The 1989–1995 period marks the turning point in terms of pension system generosity, and the most recent period 2005–2009 reflects the consequences of the reductions in generosity that followed. The analysis in this section exploits data that cover a fairly long time span. As we have shown in the preceding section, the employment of older women has followed long-run trends that reflect secular changes in the role of women in the labor market as much as they reflect the effect of pension reforms. Thus the following analyses are only performed for men.

Our approach is illustrated in figure 5.4. Using the most recent period (2005–2009) as the base period, we compare the mortality-employment curve in that period with the mortality-employment curve in a comparison period (here: 1970). It is instructive to compare the location of specific ages across time in this graph. Generally, data points in 2005–2009 are located south-west of those in 1970. This reflects smaller mortality rates and, simultaneously, smaller employment rates. As an example, 60 percent of men age sixty-three were working in 1970 and they had a nearly 3 percent chance of dying. In 2005–2009, only about 30 percent were working, whereas their mortality rate had also about halved to less than 1.5 percent.

We now compute the additional work capacity at some age in the base year as the vertical distance between the two curves at that age or mortality rate, respectively. For instance, in 2005–2009, the employment rate of sixty-three-year-old men was equal to 31 percent, and their mortality rate was 1.34 percent. In 1970, the employment rate of men who had the same mortality rate (and who were about fifty-six years old) was roughly 85 percent. Hence, if the same proportion of men in 2005–2009 had worked as much as men in

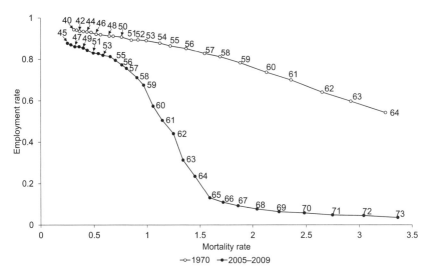

Fig. 5.4   Employment versus mortality (2005–2009 versus 1970)

Table 5.1   **Additional employment capacity in 2005–2009 using 1970 employment mortality relationship**

Age	Mortality rate in 2005–2009 (%)	Employment rate in 2005–2009 (%)	Employment rate in 1970 at same mortality rate (%)	Additional employment capacity (%)
55	0.70	79.5	91.1	11.6
56	0.76	77.3	90.7	13.5
57	0.81	75.6	90.0	14.5
58	0.91	71.1	89.4	18.3
59	0.97	67.5	89.2	21.6
60	1.06	57.	88.4	31.1
61	1.15	50.5	87.5	37.1
62	1.25	44.0	86.2	42.2
63	1.34	31.3	85.5	54.2
64	1.45	23.5	84.1	60.6
65	1.59	13.1	82.3	69.2
66	1.72	10.9	80.8	69.9
67	1.86	9.2	78.6	69.4
68	2.04	7.6	75.3	67.7
69	2.24	6.3	71.8	65.5
Total years		6.2		6.5

1970 with the same mortality rate, the employment rate of sixty-three-year-old men would have been 54 percentage points higher.

This calculation is repeated for every age from fifty-five to sixty-nine in the base period. The results are shown in table 5.1. Given the same mortality rates, we observe that employment was substantially higher in 1970 than in 2005–2009. At each mortality rate, the estimated additional employment capacity is positive and increases up to the statutory retirement age (sixty-five). We may translate these figures into additional years of work at each age. For instance, an estimated work capacity of 50 percent implies that sixty-three-year-old men in 2005–2009 would on average work 0.5 years more (at that age). Aggregating over all ages from fifty-five through sixty-nine gives the total number of additional years of work, which is equal to 6.5. Thus, if men in 2005–2009 would have worked as much as men in 1970 with the same health and if they retired at seventy, they would have worked 6.5 years more on average. Compared to actual years of employment at ages fifty-five to sixty-nine in 2005–2009 (6.2 years), this amounts to a doubling in years of work.

It is, of course, debatable whether improvements in survival rates translate fully into employment years. The question is whether the survival rates of a cohort are a good proxy for their general health. This may depend, for instance, on whether additional life years are spent in good or poor health. According to the morbidity-expansion hypothesis, increased life expectancy raises the number of unhealthy years, whereas the morbidity-compression hypothesis argues that health problems will be postponed to a shorter period at the end of life. Comparing measures of functional health collected in the German Socio-Economic Panel (SOEP) study in 1997 and 2010, Trachte, Sperlich, and Geyer (2014) find evidence for morbidity compression among the German older population. We also find that self-reported morbidity and mortality have followed similar trends over time (see section 5.2), which supports the use of mortality as proxy for morbidity. However, as we have documented in earlier research also using data from the German SOEP, secular trends in subjective health, such as health satisfaction (available since 1984) and self-reported general health (available since 1992) are more or less flat or rather inconsistent across age groups (see Börsch-Supan and Jürges 2012, figures 6 and 7). This finding is puzzling, however. First, self-rated health in the German SOEP has been shown to be predictive of future mortality, even controlling for other health measures (Jürges 2008). Thus, both measures of health are correlated on the individual level. Second, it is in contrast to findings for the United States, for instance, where self-rated health has moved in parallel to mortality over time (Milligan and Wise 2012b). We believe this evidence suggests that aggregate measures of self-rated health are not comparable over time, neither in the German SOEP (which provides the longest time series in self-rated health in Germany) nor among Germans in general. For this reason, our estimates of work capacity based on self-reported morbidity in section 5.4 should be interpreted cautiously.

Another notable point is that our estimates are sensitive to the choice of the comparison year. The year 1970 represents a peak in old age employment rates because it is unaffected by the later pension reforms that gener-

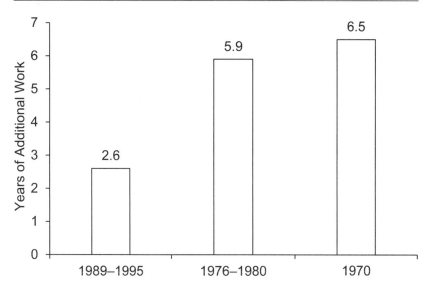

Fig. 5.5   Estimated additional employment capacity by year of comparisons

ally increased generosity and because the labor market was characterized by full employment. Later years represent employment in old age that is strongly affected by generous early retirement schemes. Therefore, employment rates in those later years do not measure the full health-related employment potential of the older population. Nevertheless, we repeated the previous calculations using the more recent comparison periods 1976–1980 and 1989–1995. We report the main results of these calculations in figure 5.5.

When 1989–1995 employment and mortality rates are used, the estimate of additional work capacity of today's workers equals only 2.6 years. This number is positive because of lower mortality/improved health, but it is driven down by the comparatively low old age employment rates in the 1990s. One can interpret these 2.6 years as the health-related gain in work capacity that could materialize even if today's pension system was as generous as the system in the 1990s. Using the late 1970s as a reference period, the estimated additional work capacity is 5.9 years, and thus much closer to our preferred estimates.

Table 5.2 summarizes our work-capacity estimates using different comparison years. It also provides an additional, yet important, interpretation of our findings. The employment rates in 1976–1980 and 1970 of men with the same mortality rates as those of men age sixty-five to sixty-nine in 2005–2009 roughly equals 65 percent and 78 percent, respectively. Thus, about two-thirds of men at these ages in 2005–2009 could work if they worked as much as men with the same health status—as measured by the probability of dying—in the past.

Table 5.2   Additional employment capacity in 2005–2009 by comparison year and
                   age group

Age group	Mortality rate in 2005–2009 (%)	Employment rate in 2005–2009 (%)	Employment rate in comparison year at same mortality rate (%)	Additional work capacity (%)
		2005–2009 vs. 1989–1995		
55–59	0.83	74.2	84.2	10.0
60–64	1.25	41.3	63.0	21.7
65–69	1.89	9.4	28.7	19.3
		2005–2009 vs. 1976–1980		
55–59	0.83	74.2	91.9	17.7
60–64	1.25	41.3	85.2	43.9
65–69	1.89	9.4	65.3	55.9
		2005–2009 vs. 1970		
55–59	0.83	74.2	90.1	15.9
60–64	1.25	41.3	86.4	45.0
65–69	1.89	9.4	77.8	68.3

5.4 Estimating Work Capacity Using Long-Term Changes in Morbidity

We now turn to the relationship between self-reported morbidity and employment at various points in time. The common five-category self-assessed health measure is unavailable in the German Microcensus, and individual health information is not collected every year. From the available information, we therefore constructed the two indicators of self-reported morbidity already described in section 5.2 for 1989, 1999, and 2009. We choose the most recent year (2009) as the base year and compare the morbidity-employment curvature with the two earlier years. To obtain more precise estimates, the original morbidity data are smoothed using a three-year moving average in age. Figure 5.6 illustrates the morbidity-employment relationship for the base year 2009 and the comparison year 1989, and the two illness measures. The x-axis now represents the share of individuals reporting their respective health problem. This graph shows that health has improved over time. At each age, the morbidity curve in 2009 lies left to the morbidity curve in 1989. That is, the prevalence of self-reported illnesses is on average lower in 2009 than in 1989. A remarkable feature of the morbidity-employment curve is the almost vertical section at ages sixty to sixty-five. Thus, whereas health does deteriorate with age before age sixty and after age sixty-five, there is no change or even a rebound in the time between. Individuals' health seems to improve while employment rates decline. One possible explanation for this finding is that retirement actually improves health, but a deeper analysis must be left to future research.

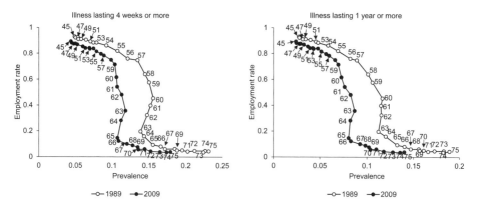

Fig. 5.6   Self-reported illness versus employment (2009 versus 1989)

Using again the vertical distance between the morbidity-employment curves in different periods, we estimated an additional work capacity, depending on the illness measure, of between 4.9 and 5.5 years. Due to the inverted S-shape of the morbidity-employment curves, there can be more than one possible employment rate at some ages/prevalences. Luckily, this applies only to very few data points at relatively high ages. In case this happened, we used the lowest employment rate so that our estimates provide some lower bound. Nevertheless, the five years of additional work capacity are substantially larger than the simulated additional 2.5 years of work calculated based on a comparable period of time (2005–2009 vs. 1989–1995) when using mortality to approximate health. Work-capacity estimates are again sensitive to the comparison year used. Whereas we obtain positive values when using 1989 as the comparison year, the estimates are practically zero when using 1999 (–0.5 and–0.2, respectively). This is not unexpected since, as we have seen in section 5.2, self-reported health has not improved as much between 1999 and 2009 as in the decade before, and labor force participation in 1999 was still largely affected by the generosity of the system and hence quite low.

5.5   Work-Capacity Estimates Using Health Changes across Age Groups

In this section, we estimate the health-related capacity to work using the approach suggested by Cutler, Meara, and Richards-Shubik (2012). The basic idea is to simulate the work capacity of older individuals based on their own health status and other characteristics using the estimated relationship between health and labor force participation of younger persons. This answers the question of how much older individuals would work if they faced the same retirement incentives as younger persons (eligible only for disability pensions), but given their own worse health level. Rather than assessing actual behavioral responses to, for example, stricter access to retirement pathways, we interpret our findings as additional work capacity above and beyond the observed employment rates.

This method basically involves two steps, a regression stage and a simulation stage. First, we estimate the relationship between employment and health, and other characteristics, of younger respondents. We choose individuals at ages fifty to fifty-four, who are not eligible for old age pensions, but can apply for disability insurance benefits. Second, we predict the labor force participation of older workers based on their actual health and characteristics using the coefficients from the regression stage. We do these calculations for individuals at ages fifty-five to fifty-nine, sixty to sixty-four, sixty-five to sixty-nine, and seventy to seventy-four.

We use the German subsample of the Survey of Health, Ageing and Retirement in Europe (SHARE) for the years 2004 to 2010 (see Börsch-Supan et al. [2013] for a description of SHARE). The SHARE data provide extensive health information at the individual level covering subjective and objective measures of physical and mental health. A major advantage of these measurements is their comparability to both the health assessments of other SHARE countries and the US Health and Retirement Study (HRS). Our estimation sample is a combined data set of the three panel waves (2004, 2006, and 2010), restricted to individuals age fifty to seventy-four. It includes approximately 1,600 men and 1,800 women, and the number of person-years roughly amounts to 2,700 and 3,000, respectively. The analysis in the regression stage is based on 399 male- and 526 female-year observations, at ages fifty to fifty-four.

The dependent variable in our regression models is a dummy variable that indicates whether a respondent currently works in the labor market, even if this is only for a few hours per week. As with any study that estimates the employment effects of health, it is important to measure the respondent's health status comprehensively. Therefore, we include a rich set of health indicators, such as self-rated health, physical limitations, limitations in activities of daily living (ADLs) and instrumental activities of daily living (IADLs), various medical conditions, weight problems, and smoking status. Furthermore, we control for the individual's marital status and a binary indicator of educational attainment, where we distinguish between low education (basic-track secondary school) and high education (intermediate or academic track secondary school).

Tables 5.3 and 5.4 report the summary statistics on dependent and independent variables for men and women, respectively. As expected, employment decreases with age, showing sharp declines in labor force participation rates particularly among individuals at ages sixty to sixty-four and sixty-five to sixty-nine. For example, the share of working men falls from 93 percent at ages fifty to fifty-four to 85 percent at ages fifty-five to fifty-nine, further

Table 5.3 **SHARE summary statistics, men**

| Variable | Age group | | | | |
	50–54	55–59	60–64	65–69	70–74
Employed	0.93	0.85	0.40	0.05	0.01
SRH excellent	0.12	0.06	0.05	0.05	0.03
SRH very good	0.31	0.22	0.19	0.14	0.11
SRH good	0.33	0.40	0.41	0.45	0.45
SRH fair	0.20	0.24	0.27	0.28	0.33
SRH good	0.05	0.07	0.08	0.08	0.07
1 physical limitation	0.14	0.18	0.19	0.18	0.25
> 1 physical limitation	0.10	0.17	0.22	0.27	0.29
Any ADL limitations	0.03	0.07	0.08	0.10	0.12
Any IADL limitations	0.03	0.03	0.04	0.05	0.05
Euro-D depression score	1.39	1.42	1.53	1.42	1.57
Heart disease	0.06	0.09	0.12	0.14	0.20
Lung disease	0.04	0.04	0.06	0.07	0.06
Stroke	0.01	0.03	0.04	0.05	0.05
Psychiatric disorder	0.17	0.17	0.12	0.11	0.11
Cancer	0.02	0.03	0.04	0.06	0.06
Hypertension	0.21	0.34	0.37	0.41	0.49
Arthritis	0.06	0.09	0.09	0.10	0.11
Diabetes	0.08	0.10	0.11	0.14	0.15
Back pain	0.45	0.51	0.52	0.52	0.55
Underweight	0.00	0.00	0.00	0.00	0.00
Overweight	0.52	0.50	0.51	0.53	0.52
Obese	0.16	0.19	0.19	0.19	0.18
Current smoker	0.34	0.30	0.27	0.19	0.11
Former smoker	0.31	0.37	0.38	0.42	0.42
High education	0.63	0.59	0.51	0.45	0.41
Married	0.77	0.84	0.83	0.85	0.89
N	399	484	580	646	448

declines to 40 percent at ages sixty to sixty-four, and eventually to 5 percent at ages sixty-five to sixty-nine. A similar pattern is observed for women, although the employment rates are generally lower than among men. Women at ages sixty to sixty-four work substantially less than men of the same age. This can partly be explained by the availability of an "old age pension for women" during the observation period, which allowed female workers to retire before age sixty-five if they met certain requirements. Regarding health, we observe that the share of individuals reporting good, fair, or poor health is increasing with age, while the proportion of those in excellent or very good health declines. The same is true for most of the remaining health measures: the probability of reporting health problems rises with age. One notable exception is psychological problems. The probability of

Table 5.4   SHARE summary statistics, women

	Age group				
Variable	50–54	55–59	60–64	65–69	70–74
Employed	0.78	0.70	0.24	0.02	0.01
SRH excellent	0.10	0.07	0.04	0.03	0.02
SRH very good	0.29	0.21	0.15	0.13	0.08
SRH good	0.42	0.43	0.47	0.44	0.45
SRH fair	0.17	0.25	0.27	0.32	0.36
SRH good	0.03	0.05	0.07	0.08	0.09
1 physical limitation	0.17	0.17	0.20	0.19	0.20
> 1 physical limitation	0.14	0.26	0.30	0.41	0.47
Any ADL limitations	0.02	0.08	0.10	0.13	0.16
Any IADL limitations	0.02	0.05	0.04	0.07	0.06
Euro-D depression score	2.01	2.21	2.15	2.38	2.34
Heart disease	0.02	0.03	0.06	0.09	0.10
Lung disease	0.02	0.05	0.06	0.06	0.06
Stroke	0.01	0.02	0.02	0.02	0.04
Psychiatric disorder	0.24	0.23	0.24	0.20	0.14
Cancer	0.04	0.06	0.06	0.06	0.08
Hypertension	0.20	0.30	0.39	0.44	0.50
Arthritis	0.07	0.15	0.14	0.18	0.16
Diabetes	0.03	0.07	0.09	0.15	0.17
Back pain	0.50	0.58	0.55	0.58	0.65
Underweight	0.01	0.01	0.01	0.01	0.01
Overweight	0.31	0.35	0.42	0.40	0.44
Obese	0.15	0.17	0.17	0.21	0.21
Current smoker	0.21	0.20	0.15	0.09	0.07
Former smoker	0.20	0.22	0.20	0.14	0.13
High education	0.62	0.57	0.44	0.34	0.25
Married	0.79	0.78	0.81	0.75	0.69
N	526	640	632	631	421

being depressed decreases as individuals are getting older. This is consistent with the observation that subjective well-being or mental health generally improves at an advanced age (Blanchflower and Oswald 2008).

As to the measurement of health, one possible approach would be to include the full set of health indicators as explanatory variables. However, this procedure is prone to interpretation problems arising from multicollinearity and measurement error. For instance, in analyses not reported here, some fairly bad health events such as suffering a stroke were actually found to increase labor force participation. We therefore follow an alternative approach that presumably mitigates these issues. Specifically, we primarily use a health index proposed by Poterba, Venti, and Wise (2013), which is based on responses to twenty-four items covering the respondents' psychological well-being, physical health, and health-care utilization. The index is

Table 5.5   **First principal component index of health based on SHARE Germany**

Health measure	Wave 1	Wave 2	Wave 4
Difficulty walking several blocks	0.29	0.27	0.28
Difficulty lifting/carrying	0.24	0.30	0.31
Difficulty pushing/pulling	0.26	0.29	0.32
Difficulty with an ADL	0.28	0.28	0.29
Difficulty climbing stairs	0.30	0.30	0.30
Difficulty stooping/kneeling/crouching	0.30	0.30	0.28
Difficulty getting up from chair	0.29	0.30	0.28
Self-reported health fair or poor	0.30	0.28	0.28
Difficulty reaching/extending arms up	0.26	0.25	0.26
Ever experience arthritis	0.16	0.15	0.19
Difficulty sitting two hours	0.22	0.23	0.18
Difficulty picking up a coin	0.14	0.18	0.17
Back problems	0.20	0.18	0.16
Ever experience heart problems	0.13	0.13	0.11
Hospital stay	0.15	0.16	0.14
Doctor visit	0.10	0.09	0.07
Ever experience psychological problem	0.11	0.09	0.11
Ever experience stroke	0.13	0.13	0.12
Ever experience high blood pressure	0.15	0.12	0.10
Ever experience lung disease	0.10	0.07	0.07
Ever experience diabetes	0.11	0.13	0.12
BMI at beginning of observation period	0.10	0.08	0.10
Nursing home stay	0.11	0.08	0.07
Ever experience cancer	0.07	0.07	0.09
N	2,966	2,478	1,487

computed as the first principal component extracted from a principal component analysis using these twenty-four items. Table 5.5 displays the factor loadings of the first principal component in the German SHARE data. All loadings are positive, implying that larger values of the first principal component represent worse health. Functional limitations and self-rated health have the greatest weight. The first principal component is then converted into individual percentiles, so that higher values reflect better health (henceforth also denoted as PVW index). Thus, we can interpret the estimated health parameters as changes in the probability of working due to a percentile increase in the health index. Figure 5.7 displays the relationship between the health-index percentiles used in the regression and simulation analyses and age. Here, higher values indicate better health status. We observe that health continuously declines with age for both men and women, although women appear to be healthier than men on average.

The PVW approach as described above implies that the same health condition has the same effect on overall health and employment among younger and older respondents. However, there are several reasons why this may

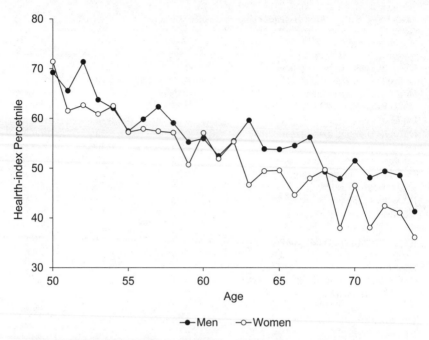

Fig. 5.7   Average health-index percentile by age and sex

not hold. Most importantly, the health indicators used here provide little information on the severity of health conditions. For instance, individuals may assess their own health relative to that of other people in the same age group (e.g., Groot 2000). Hence, a given condition of the same "objective" severity might have a stronger effect on self-perceived health and, hence, labor supply among young than among old respondents. Or, suffering from the same condition might have a stronger effect on overall health among older than among younger people. In the first case, the PVW index would underestimate the work capacity of older workers, and in the second case it would overestimate the work capacity. Furthermore, the PVW index that we use here for comparability includes self-rated health as the most important indicator. However, health might be endogenous in employment regressions. Younger workers may have financial incentives to report worse health to become eligible for disability benefits, or workers may report health problems to rationalize their work behavior (e.g., Bound et al. 1999). This could overestimate the impact of individual health on labor force participation.

To address both the measurement and endogeneity problem, we also computed for each individual an index of self-assessed health that is a linear combination of the detailed "objective" health measures mentioned above (we call this the SAH index). To be more precise, we estimated an ordered probit model of self-rated health (categories: excellent, very good, good, fair, poor) with the remaining health measures as explanatory variables (see, e.g., Jürges 2007). Each health variable is interacted with a dummy variable indicating whether the respondent belongs to one of the previously defined age groups to allow for differential effects of each health indicator on overall health. We then constructed the individual health index as the predicted linear index from the ordered probit model. Hence, we loosen the restriction that health means the same across age groups, and we reduce the endogeneity problem by instrumenting self-assessed health with arguably exogenous health variables.

To be consistent with the other chapters in this volume, our analysis primarily relies on the PVW index. We will also compare the results to the estimates obtained using both the full set of health measures and the SAH index as a robustness check. For the regression analysis of individuals age fifty to fifty-four, we estimate linear probability models of the following form:

$$(1) \qquad E_{it}^{50-54} = \alpha + \beta \cdot H_{it}^{50-54} + \gamma \cdot X_{it}^{50-54} + \varepsilon_{it},$$

where E_{it} is a binary variable indicating whether individual i is working in wave t; H_{it} represents respondent i's health status in t; X_{it} captures further control variables, and ε_{it} is a time-varying idiosyncratic error term. Equation (1) essentially represents a pooled panel regression.

In the second stage, we use the regression coefficients from equation (1) to predict the labor force participation and work capacity at older ages:

$$(2) \qquad \widehat{E_{it}}^{a} = \widehat{\alpha}^{50-54} + \widehat{\beta}^{50-54} \cdot H_{it}^{a} + \widehat{\gamma}^{50-54} \cdot X_{it}^{a},$$

where $\widehat{E_{it}}^{a}$ is the predicted employment probability of individual i who belongs to age group a; H_{it}^{a} and X_{it}^{a} are the respective health measures and control variables; $\widehat{\alpha}^{50-54}$, $\widehat{\beta}^{50-54}$, $\widehat{\gamma}^{50-54}$ are the estimated coefficients from the regression model in equation (1). Our estimation of work capacity relies on the assumption that the estimated coefficients identify the effect of poor health and other covariates on the probability of working, also for those belonging to older age groups if these older age groups faced the same (early) retirement incentives as the fifty to fifty-four age group.

Table 5.6 shows the regression results for individuals at ages fifty to fifty-four, separately for men and women. We find that the PVW health index is positively related to the probability of working. The estimated coefficient of the health index is equal 0.003 for both men and women. That is, moving up the health distribution by 1 percentile increases the probability of employment by 0.3 percentage points. Furthermore, individuals who have higher educational attainment are also more likely to work. Having completed an intermediate-track or academic-track secondary school raises the employment probability by about 6 (10) percentage points among men (women), compared to respondents with a basic-track secondary school degree. Being married is significantly and negatively related to labor force participation

Table 5.6   Employment regressions, PVW health index

	Men 50–54		Women 50–54	
Variable	Coefficient	Std. error	Coefficient	Std. error
PVW index	0.003	0.001***	0.003	0.001***
High education	0.062	0.026**	0.099	0.037***
Married	0.008	0.028	−0.117	0.044***
Wave 2	−0.011	0.025	−0.050	0.037
Wave 4	0.035	0.108	−0.068	0.130
Constant	0.706	0.042***	0.657	0.061***
N	399		526	

***Significant at the 1 percent level.
**Significant at the 5 percent level.
*Significant at the 10 percent level.

Table 5.7   Simulations of work capacity, PVW health index

Age group	No. obs.	Actual proportion working (%)	Predicted proportion working (%)	Estimated work capacity (%)
		Men		
55–59	484	84.7	91.6	6.9
60–64	580	40.3	90.4	50.1
65–69	646	5.4	89.1	83.7
70–74	448	1.1	88.2	87.1
		Women		
55–59	640	69.5	73.9	4.4
60–64	632	23.7	071.9	48.2
65–69	631	2.1	69.8	67.7
70–74	421	1.4	67.9	66.5

only among women. We obtain qualitatively and quantitatively similar results when we include the SAH index (details not shown).

Table 5.7 and figure 5.8 show the results of the simulation step, based on the PVW index. Table 5.7 shows for both men and women and each five-year age group the actual (observed) proportion working and the predicted proportion working. The estimated work capacity is calculated as the difference between the predicted and observed employment rates. The predicted employment rates for men are roughly 92 percent at ages fifty-five to fifty-nine, 90 percent at ages sixty to sixty-four, 89 percent at ages sixty-five to sixty-nine, and 88 percent at ages seventy to seventy-four. As expected, the predicted share of workers declines because health deteriorates with age and worse individual health is linked with lower employment rates. However, the decline in the projected proportion working is very small. This is also

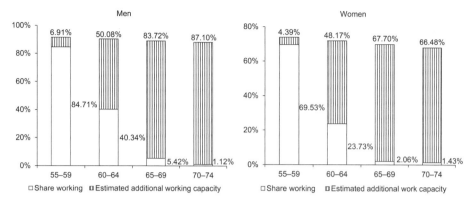

Fig. 5.8   Share of respondents working and additional work capacity by sex and age

true for women, albeit their predicted employment rates are lower at all age groups. Apparently the observed employment rates decline more rapidly with age than the predicted employment rates. This implies that the work-capacity estimates increase with age and become fairly large. For example, the additional work capacity of men is roughly 7 percent at ages fifty-five to fifty-nine (had they worked as much as men at ages fifty to fifty-four), 50 percent at ages sixty to sixty-four, 84 percent at ages sixty-five to sixty-nine, and 87 percent at ages seventy to seventy-four. Among women, the estimated additional work capacity follows the same pattern, but is somewhat smaller. When using the SAH index, which allows for larger effects of "nominal" health conditions on subjective health ratings, the estimate of additional work capacity at older ages is reduced by a few percentage points (see table 5A.1 in the appendix).

These numbers are similar to the mortality-based work-capacity estimates obtained in the previous section. Referring to table 5.2, the average additional employment for men at ages sixty to sixty-four and sixty-five to sixty-nine approximately amounts to 45 percent and 68 percent (using 1970 as the comparison year), respectively. The numbers in this section for the same age groups are equal to 50 percent and 84 percent. We think that these results are remarkably similar, despite the fact that we are using distinct methods and different measures of health status.

We conclude this section by allowing the relationship between health and employment, and health-related work capacity, to differ across socioeconomic groups. Specifically, we simulate the labor force participation of older workers separately by educational attainment (low vs. high education). There might be substantial education-related heterogeneity in the effect of health on employment, and thus work capacity. For instance, better-educated individuals are more likely to work at older ages per se, due to better health.

Furthermore, individuals with better education, or higher socioeconomic status, are more likely to recover from and survive medical conditions (e.g., Mackenbach et al. 2008). This is closely related to the observation that the better educated are also better at adhering to medical treatments (Goldman and Smith 2002), or are more likely to profit from innovations in medical technology (Glied and Lleras-Muney 2008). Generally, more schooling may improve the capacity to cope with illness. Higher-educated individuals are assumed to make better informed decisions about their health, have greater financial resources, or choose jobs that make it easier to adapt or accommodate to disabilities at the workplace (e.g., Lochner 2011).

To compute work capacity by education, we rely on the regression coefficients of the model estimated in the first step of the analysis, and compute the predicted percent working and the additional work capacity separately by education (single regression). In addition, we reestimate the regression models separately by education group (regressions by education group).

Figure 5.9 displays the simulation results by education, using the PVW index and the single-regression approach. Two patterns emerge: First, the estimated work capacity increases with age, irrespective of education and sex. Second, we find that the low educated have a higher work capacity than better-educated individuals at younger age groups (fifty-five to fifty-nine, sixty to sixty-four), whereas the high educated have higher work capacity estimates at older age groups (sixty-five to sixty-nine, seventy to seventy-four). We obtain similar relationships using the regression-by-education

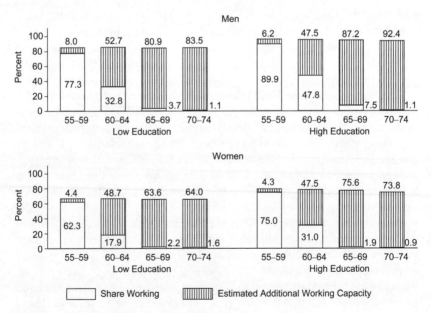

Fig. 5.9   **Work capacity by education (single regression)**

approach and alternative specifications of individual health (see tables 5A.3 and 5A.4 in the appendix). Although we find those differences across education groups, they are quite small and do not warrant dramatically different conclusions regarding work capacity.

5.6   Changes in Self-Reported Morbidity by Education Level over Time

In this section, we further assess the development of socioeconomic differences in health (and by extension, work capacity) over time. Individuals with higher socioeconomic status (SES) live longer and the social inequality in survival appears to have increased over time, also in Germany (e.g., Siegel, Vogt, and Sundmacher 2014). As discussed above, high-SES individuals may also have a higher propensity of recovering from and surviving severe medical conditions. These factors may contribute to socioeconomic differences in work capacity and other labor market outcomes at older ages.

For Germany, data on mortality by SES groups over time are unavailable. We therefore study trends in self-reported morbidity as used in the preceding sections. As an indicator of socioeconomic status, we use years of education. Direct information on years of education as such is not available in the Microcensus. But the data contain the highest secondary school degree as well as completed tertiary degrees and other occupation-related credentials. Following previous work (e.g., Jürges, Reinhold, and Salm 2011), we use this information, together with the number of years it usually takes to obtain a certain degree, to impute an individual's number of years in full-time education.

As a measure of socioeconomic status, education has some drawbacks when we study developments over time, or rather, across cohorts. As in many other countries, Germany has experienced strong improvements in educational opportunities in the past fifty years, and the proportion of workers with higher educational degrees increased substantially (Jürges, Reinhold, and Salm 2011). For instance, among men born in 1940, less than 15 percent had earned a high school diploma that would allow university entrance (*Abitur*). In contrast, among the 1980 cohort, nearly 35 percent of men earned this diploma. Obviously the Abitur must have become less selective in terms of sociodemographic background and/or ability over time, and of course this was the goal of the educational expansion in many developed countries in the second half of the last century. However, this implies that the survival rates and health outcomes by education group may not be comparable over time. As argued by Bound et al. (2014), the low educated in younger cohorts are possibly more negatively selected than their counterparts in older cohorts. In turn, this may bias the comparison of life expectancy and health across educational groups over time.

To address this problem, we use years-of-education quartiles rather than school-leaving certificates or the straight number of years of education to

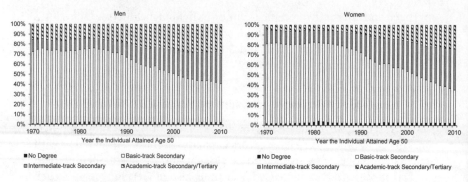

Fig. 5.10   Distribution of years of education completed by cohort (by year cohort attained age fifty)

group individuals. This approach provides consistent rankings along socioeconomic status that can be compared over time. The education quartile an individual belongs to is inferred from the individual's fractional rank in the years-of-education distribution of all individuals of the same age in the respective year. Thus, we obtain education quartiles that reflect the distribution of education years in a given cohort. As a consequence, we examine the health development in the same education quartile, although its composition in terms of degrees or years of schooling may have changed across cohorts (see figure 5.10). For instance, the highest education quartile among the older cohorts consists of university graduates as well as graduates from intermediary and high schools (academic track). Among the younger cohorts, there are almost exclusively university and high school graduates in the highest quartile.

Figures 5.11 and 5.12 show the evolution of self-reported chronic morbidity (> 1 year) by education quartile, for men and women, respectively. Since the original data are rather noisy, we also provide three-year (age) moving averages to obtain smoother estimates of the proportion of sick individuals at each age. As expected, the probability of illness rises with age. As already discussed in section 5.4, health deteriorates more slowly between age sixty and sixty-five than before or after.

More importantly, we find health improvements over time for each education quartile. That is, the prevalence of self-reported morbidity in more recent years usually lies below the 1989 figures at each age. Individuals in higher education quartiles have experienced disproportionate health improvements over time. The reduction in the probability of illness is lowest among those in the first education quartile. For example, between 1989 and 2009 the prevalence among men falls by 1.8 percentage points in the lowest education group, and by 3.1 percentage points in the highest education quartile.

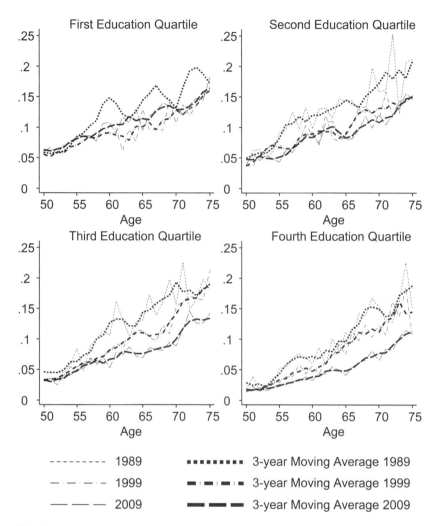

Fig. 5.11 **Evolution of self-reported chronic illness (> 1 year) by education quartile (men)**

5.7 Summary and Discussion

For half a century, mortality rates in Germany have declined at every age, and Germans today live longer on average than ever before. This seems to imply that Germans have become healthier, fitter, and increasingly capable to work in the labor market in their fifties, sixties, or even beyond, an assumption that is described by the popular quip "seventy is the new sixty." Put differently, the proportion of older workers who are limited by poor health continues to decrease, and extending working lives among those who

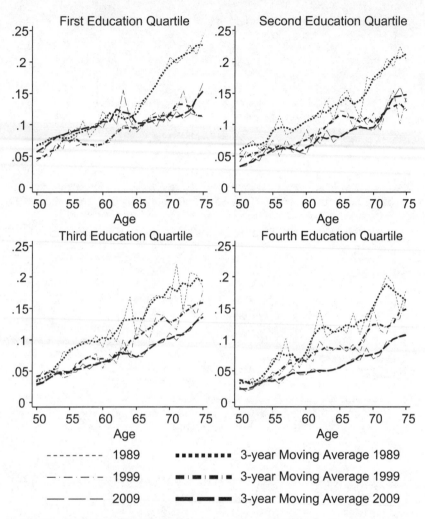

Fig. 5.12   Evolution of self-reported chronic illness (> 1 year) by education quartile (women)

have the capacity to work is arguably the best single measure to keep the German pay-as-you-go pension system financially afloat.

Obviously, extending working lives to a certain age is only sensible if a sizable proportion of the population would be able to work until that age. However, how many German workers could actually work until age sixty-seven, seventy, or even seventy-four is an open question, which to our knowledge has not yet been answered. The purpose of this chapter was to estimate the work capacity of the older population in Germany, that is, the proportion of elders who could still work in the labor market because they are not limited by poor health. For instance, we estimated the proportion of elders today who could still work by asking how many people in the past—who had the same health level (measured by the age-specific mortality rate) but who did not face the same early retirement incentives—were working. Our results show that older workers could work more than six years longer on average, and more than two-thirds of men could work until their seventieth birthday.

As an alternative approach, we used contemporary data and looked at the labor supply of individuals in their early fifties, who might have health problems that limit their ability to work but whose only early retirement option are disability pensions. Using the effect of poor health on labor force participation in this group, we simulated labor force participation in older age groups. This yields a counterfactual employment rate that would prevail if health deteriorates with age as it actually does, but under less generous retirement incentives. Here, we found even larger capacity to work among the older population. According to our calculations, more than 85 percent of men and nearly 70 percent of women could still work until they turn seventy.

To summarize, independent of the method used, we get large estimates for the capacity to work beyond the current normal retirement age. A fairly safe bet would be that today, if individuals were retiring exclusively for health reasons, more than half of the population could work until age seventy. Of course, increasing labor force participation thus far may seem unrealistic given that less than 5 percent of individuals of that age are working today. There are numerous reasons for retiring early, and poor health is certainly one of them, but the point we make in this chapter is that health is probably not the main reason, and the recent debate in Germany in which health is cited as an important reason to reduce retirement ages is not well supported by empirical evidence.

This leads us to stress an important point. We aimed at estimating the strength of the effect of poor health on retirement and wanted to know how many could work *if they wanted to*. Health, however, is not the only determinant of retirement. The large uptake of the new early retirement option at age sixty-three among healthy workers in Germany shows that the appreciation of leisure is at least an equally strong determinant of retirement as health.

Our analysis of work capacity and health is first and foremost descriptive. Turning to a normative view, we are not saying that everyone who can should work until age seventy. If workers' valuation of leisure increases as they become older, there is no economic reason to constrain their desire to retire as early or as late as they see fit as long as workers and their employers are willing to bear the financial implications. Theoretically, the German pension system already allows working past the "normal" retirement age, with a generous 6 percent increase in pension benefits per additional year worked, but very few workers make use of this option. Whether this is due to preferences for leisure, due to employer discrimination, or simply because it is the norm to retire as soon as one becomes eligible for an old age pension, is a topic for future work. In light of the results of the analysis in this chapter, it is likely not due to poor health.

Appendix

Table 5A.1   **Simulations of work capacity, alternative health measures**

		All health variables models			SAH index models		
Age group	No. obs.	Actual proportion working	Predicted proportion working	Estimated work capacity	Actual proportion working	Predicted proportion working	Estimated work capacity
			Men				
55–59	484	0.847	0.927	0.080	0.847	0.910	0.063
60–64	580	0.403	0.924	0.520	0.403	0.893	0.489
65–69	646	0.054	0.917	0.863	0.054	0.882	0.828
70–74	448	0.011	0.918	0.907	0.011	0.864	0.853
			Women				
55–59	640	0.695	0.728	0.032	0.695	0.740	0.045
60–64	632	0.237	0.701	0.464	0.237	0.720	0.483
65–69	631	0.021	0.691	0.670	0.021	0.706	0.686
70–74	421	0.014	0.664	0.649	0.014	0.688	0.674

Table 5A.2   **Work capacity by education, PVW health index**

	Men			Women		
Education	Actual proportion working	Predicted proportion working	Estimated work capacity	Actual proportion working	Predicted proportion working	Estimated work capacity
A. Single regression						
			Age 55–59			
Low	0.773	0.853	0.080	0.623	0.668	0.044
High	0.899	0.960	0.062	0.750	0.793	0.043
			Age 60–64			
Low	0.328	0.855	0.527	0.179	0.666	0.487
High	0.478	0.953	0.475	0.310	0.785	0.475
			Age 65–69			
Low	0.037	0.845	0.809	0.022	0.658	0.636
High	0.075	0.947	0.872	0.019	0.774	0.756
			Age 70–74			
Low	0.011	0.846	0.835	0.016	0.656	0.640
High	0.011	0.934	0.924	0.009	0.747	0.738
B. Regression by education						
			Age 55–59			
Low	0.773	0.910	0.138	0.623	0.695	0.072
High	0.899	0.951	0.052	0.750	0.762	0.012
			Age 60–64			
Low	0.328	0.903	0.575	0.179	0.699	0.520
High	0.478	0.947	0.469	0.310	0.745	0.435
			Age 65–69			
Low	0.037	0.890	0.853	0.022	0.695	0.673
High	0.075	0.941	0.865	0.019	0.729	0.710
			Age 70–74			
Low	0.011	0.897	0.885	0.016	0.698	0.682
High	0.011	0.935	0.924	0.009	0.709	0.699

Table 5A.3   **Work capacity by education, all health variables models**

	Men			Women		
Education	Actual proportion working	Predicted proportion working	Estimated work capacity	Actual proportion working	Predicted proportion working	Estimated work capacity
A. Single regression						
			Age 55–59			
Low	0.773	0.872	0.099	0.623	0.660	0.037
High	0.899	0.966	0.067	0.750	0.779	0.029
			Age 60–64			
Low	0.328	0.876	0.548	0.179	0.649	0.470
High	0.478	0.971	0.493	0.310	0.766	0.457
			Age 65–69			
Low	0.037	0.876	0.840	0.022	0.654	0.632
High	0.075	0.966	0.891	0.019	0.762	0.743
			Age 70–74			
Low	0.011	0.889	0.878	0.016	0.652	0.637
High	0.011	0.959	0.948	0.009	0.697	0.688
B. Regression by education						
			Age 55–59			
Low	0.773	0.922	0.149	0.623	0.668	0.044
High	0.899	0.945	0.046	0.750	0.763	0.013
			Age 60–64			
Low	0.328	0.928	0.601	0.179	0.650	0.470
High	0.478	0.941	0.463	0.310	0.754	0.444
			Age 65–69			
Low	0.037	0.919	0.882	0.022	0.683	0.661
High	0.075	0.938	0.863	0.019	0.732	0.713
			Age 70–74			
Low	0.011	0.938	0.927	0.016	0.640	0.624
High	0.011	0.943	0.932	0.009	0.718	0.709

Table 5A.4   Work capacity by education, SAH index

	Men			Women		
Education	Actual proportion working	Predicted proportion working	Estimated work capacity	Actual proportion working	Predicted proportion working	Estimated work capacity
A. Single regression						
			Age 55–59			
Low	0.773	0.844	0.072	0.623	0.671	0.048
High	0.899	0.955	0.057	0.750	0.793	0.043
			Age 60–64			
Low	0.328	0.844	0.517	0.179	0.672	0.492
High	0.478	0.940	0.463	0.310	0.781	0.472
			Age 65–69			
Low	0.037	0.838	0.801	0.022	0.670	0.648
High	0.075	0.935	0.860	0.019	0.778	0.759
			Age 70–74			
Low	0.011	0.829	0.818	0.016	0.666	0.650
High	0.011	0.914	0.903	0.009	0.753	0.743
B. Regression by education						
			Age 55–59			
Low	0.773	0.895	0.123	0.623	0.694	0.070
High	0.899	0.952	0.053	0.750	0.762	0.012
			Age 60–64			
Low	0.328	0.881	0.553	0.179	0.703	0.523
High	0.478	0.946	0.468	0.310	0.742	0.433
			Age 65–69			
Low	0.037	0.871	0.835	0.022	0.706	0.685
High	0.075	0.942	0.866	0.019	0.735	0.716
			Age 70–74			
Low	0.011	0.867	0.856	0.016	0.711	0.695
High	0.011	0.932	0.921	0.009	0.713	0.703

References

Blanchflower, D. G., and A. J. Oswald. 2008. "Is Well-Being U-Shaped over the Life Cycle?" *Social Science and Medicine* 66 (8): 1733–49.

Börsch-Supan, Axel, Benedikt Alt, and Tabea Bucher-Koenen. 2015. "Early Retirement for the Underprivileged? Using the Record-Linked SHARE-RV Data to Evaluate the Most Recent German Pension Reform." In *SHARE: A European Policy Device for Inclusive Ageing Societies*, edited by Axel Börsch-Supan, Thorsten Kneip, Howard Litwin, Michał Myck, and Guglielmo Weber. Berlin: De Gruyter.

Börsch-Supan, Axel, M. Brandt, C. Hunkler, T. Kneip, J. Korbmacher, F. Malter, B. Schaan, S. Stuck, and S. Zuber on behalf of the SHARE Central Coordination Team. 2013. "Data Resource Profile: The Survey of Health, Ageing and

Retirement in Europe (SHARE)." *International Journal of Epidemiology* 2013:1–10. doi: 10.1093/ije/dyt088.

Börsch-Supan, Axel, Michela Coppola, and Johannes Rausch. Forthcoming. "Die Rente mit 63: Wer sind die Begünstigten? Was sind die Auswirkungen auf die Gesetzliche Rentenversicherung? MEA-Discussion Paper no. 17–2014. *Perspektiven der Wirtschaftspolitik.*

Börsch-Supan, A., and H. Jürges. 2012. "Disability, Pension Reform, and Early Retirement in Germany." In *Social Security Programs and Retirement around the World: Historical Trends in Mortality and Health, Employment, and Disability Insurance Participation and Reforms,* edited by David A. Wise, 277–300. Chicago: University of Chicago Press.

Bound, J., A. T. Geronimus, J. M. Rodriguez, and T. Waidmann. 2014. "The Implications of Differential Trends in Mortality for Social Security Policy." Michigan Retirement Research Center, University of Michigan.

Bound, J., M. Schoenbaum, T. R. Stinebrickner, and T. Waidmann. 1999. "The Dynamic Effects of Health on the Labor Force Transitions of Older Workers." *Labour Economics* 6 (2): 179–202.

Cutler, D. M., E. Meara, and S. Richards-Shubik. 2012. "Health and Work Capacity of Older Adults: Estimates and Implications for Social Security Policy." Unpublished Manuscript. Available at SSRN: http://ssrn.com/abstract=2577858.

Glied, S., and A. Lleras-Muney. 2008. "Technological Innovation and Inequality in Health." *Demography* 45 (3): 741–61.

Goldman, D. P., and J. P. Smith. 2002. "Can Patient Self-Management Help Explain the SES Health Gradient?" *Proceedings of the National Academy of Sciences* 99 (16): 10929–34.

Groot, W. 2000. "Adaptation and Scale of Reference Bias in Self-Assessments of Quality of Life." *Journal of Health Economics* 19 (3): 403–20.

Human Mortality Database. University of California, Berkeley (USA), and Max Planck Institute for Demographic Research (Germany). Available at www.mortality.org.

Jürges, H. 2007. "True Health vs Response Styles: Exploring Cross-Country Differences in Self-Reported Health." *Health Economics* 16 (2): 163–78.

———. 2008. "Self-Assessed Health, Reference Levels and Mortality." *Applied Economics* 40 (5): 569–82.

Jürges, H., S. Reinhold, and M. Salm. 2011. "Does Schooling Affect Health Behavior? Evidence from the Educational Expansion in Western Germany." *Economics of Education Review* 30:862–72.

Jürges, H., L. Thiel, T. Bucher-Koenen, J. Rausch, M. Schuth, and A. Börsch-Supan. 2015. "Health, Financial Incentives, and Early Retirement: Micro-Simulation Evidence for Germany." In *Social Security Programs and Retirement around the World: Disability Insurance Programs and Retirement,* edited by David A. Wise. Chicago: University of Chicago Press.

Kemptner, D., H. Jürges, and S. Reinhold. 2011. "Changes in Compulsory Schooling and the Causal Effect of Education on Health: Evidence from Germany." *Journal of Health Economics* 30:340–54.

Lochner, L. 2011. "Nonproduction Benefits of Education: Crime, Health, and Good Citizenship." In *Handbook of the Economics of Education,* edited by E. A. Hanushek, S. Machin, and L. Wößmann, 183–282. Amsterdam: North-Holland.

Mackenbach, J. P., I. Stirbu, A.-J. R. Roskam, M. M. Schaap, G. Menvielle, M. Leinsalu, and A. E. Kunst. 2008. "Socioeconomic Inequalities in Health in 22 European Countries." *New England Journal of Medicine* 358 (23): 2468–81.

Milligan, Kevin S., and David A. Wise. 2012a. "Health and Work at Older Ages:

Using Mortality to Assess the Capacity to Work across Countries." NBER Working Paper no. 18229, Cambridge, MA.

———. 2012b. "Introduction and Summary." In *Social Security Programs and Retirement around the World: Historical Trends in Mortality and Health, Employment, and Disability Insurance Participation and Reforms*, edited by David A. Wise. Chicago: University of Chicago Press.

Minnesota Population Center. 2011. Integrated Public Use Microdata Series, International: Version 6.1 [machine-readable database], Minneapolis, University of Minnesota.

Poterba, J. M., S. F. Venti, and D. A. Wise. 2013. "Health, Education, and the Post-Retirement Evolution of Household Assets." NBER Working Paper no. 18695, Cambridge, MA.

Siegel, M., V. Vogt, and L. Sundmacher. 2014. "From a Conservative to a Liberal Welfare State: Decomposing Changes in Income-Related Health Inequalities in Germany, 1994–2011." *Social Science and Medicine* 108:10–19.

Trachte, F., S. Sperlich, and S. Geyer. 2014. "Compression or Expansion of Morbidity? Development of Health among the Older Population." *Zeitschrift für Gerontologie und Geriatrie* 1–8.

6

Health Capacity to Work at Older Ages
Evidence from Italy

Agar Brugiavini, Giacomo Pasini, and Guglielmo Weber

Population aging in Italy poses some important challenges to the public pension system for three reasons: first, Italian public debt is particularly high (over 130 percent of gross domestic product [GDP]); second, Italy has a low fertility rate, around 1.4 (its population is aging from below); third, Italians' life expectancy is among the highest in the world and rising fast (its population is aging from above). Given that the public pension system is fundamentally a pay-as-you-go (PAYG) system, this combination calls for a substantial increase in labor force participation at all ages (see Brugiavini and Peracchi 2012). Part of this increase may be obtained by encouraging female labor force participation (that is still relatively low in Italy compared to the United States, the United Kingdom, or Northern Europe), and part may be achieved by drawing in foreign workers (who compensate for aging from below). But aging from above calls for longer working lives—and the very low average effective retirement ages experienced in Italy until the end of last century suggest there are major gains to be achieved by moving in this direction.

In the light of the above it is not surprising that the public debate has focused on how to increase labor supply of workers in the age group fifty to

Agar Brugiavini is professor of economics at Ca' Foscari University of Venice. Giacomo Pasini is associate professor of economics at Ca' Foscari University of Venice and a research fellow at Netspar. Guglielmo Weber is professor of econometrics at the University of Padua.

This chapter is part of the National Bureau of Economic Research's International Social Security (ISS) project, which is supported by the National Institute on Aging (grant P01 AG012810). The authors are indebted to Raluca Elena Buia for excellent research assistance. We also thank the members of the other country teams in the ISS project for comments that helped to shape this chapter. For acknowledgments, sources of research support, and disclosure of the authors' material financial relationships, if any, please see http://www.nber.org/chapters /c13743.ack.

sixty-five both by changing the incentives to retirement and by introducing tighter conditions to be eligible for a public pension. Pension reforms have been implemented over the last three decades, including a radical reform that was introduced in 2011 to ensure sustainability of public debt.

Given that longevity is rising steadily, an issue is whether older individuals will and can indeed work. In Italy, as in many other countries, there are numerous potential obstacles to longer working lives from the labor demand side. In a country with highly unionized labor markets and seniority-based pay scales, it is common for older workers to be paid more than younger workers, even though they are not necessarily more productive. The recent reforms, which significantly postponed retirement for several workers without offering an easy transition out of the labor force, have made very clear that for older workers it can be very difficult to find work following a job loss. After the 2011 pension reform that raised the minimum retirement age for some by a wide margin, several workers who had agreed on a separation from the firm expecting to shortly retire on a public pension fell into long-term unemployment. Hence, labor demand conditions should be kept in mind when discussing the potential for extra employment related to the widely noted "unused capacity." As pointed out by Brugiavini and Peracchi (2016), obviously health conditions also need to be taken into account and measured properly before drawing any conclusions on potential labor supply.

This chapter explores whether older Italians have the health capacity to extend their working lives. As in other chapters, we use two methods to assess the capacity to work at older ages. The first method proposes a counterfactual approach where the working capacity of workers characterized by a given mortality rate today is compared with the working capacity of people with the same mortality rate looking back in the past. The relevant relationship is described by graphical evidence of the employment rate versus the mortality rate over time, using data from the Italian National Institute of Statistics (ISTAT), Eurostat, and the Human Mortality Database from 1977 to 2010 (Milligan and Wise 2012). For this analysis we focus on men, as steadily increasing rates of women's labor force participation over time make it difficult to interpret the results for women.

The second method exploits cross-sectional variability: If people with a given level of health were to work as much as their younger counterparts in similar health, how much could they work (Cutler, Meara, and Richards-Shubik 2012)? We use data from the Survey on Health, Ageing and Retirement in Europe (SHARE) to estimate the relationship between health and employment for a sample of younger males and females, age fifty to fifty-four, and use these estimates along with the actual characteristics of older individuals, age fifty-five to seventy-four, to project the latter's capacity to work conditional on health.

An important objective of this chapter is to uncover the actual determinants of the labor supply behavior of older Italians: health capacity to work may vary by education group. We first conduct the Cutler et al. analysis separately by education group and then show how self-assessed health has evolved over time by education. We take into account that average levels of education are rising over time by relying on education quartiles.

Our results suggest that there exists a "reserve" of additional health capacity to work at older ages, and depending on the methodology and the base year, this varies substantially. For the Milligan-Wise method, the amount of projected additional work capacity would be 7.4 years if we use the employment-mortality relationship that existed in 1977 as a basis for comparison and 2.6 years if we use 1995 as the base year instead. However, it should be stressed that this method implicitly assumes that all gains in life expectancy can translate into longer working lives. For the Cutler et al. method, we estimate that an additional 57 percent of men age sixty to sixty-four and 37 percent of women of the same age could be employed, relative to the share working today, based on their own health and the estimated relationship between health and employment for younger workers. Figures are even higher for older age groups, but estimates of this work gap are likely to be largely affected by the existence of a statutory retirement age at sixty-five (that has risen to sixty-six in 2015, and will rise further along with life expectancy). We find similar estimates of work capacity across education groups for men and higher work capacity for more educated women.

The chapter is organized as follows: we first provide some brief background on trends in labor force participation and health in Italy; we then outline our methodology and present the results we obtain using our two main methods; finally, we report the results of our estimation of changes in health over time by education group and discuss the findings.

6.1   Trends in Labor Force Participation and Health

The labor force participation rate for Italian men and women age fifty-five to sixty-four, though consistently lower than in United States and other developed countries, followed the same pattern in the last thirty-five years, as evident from figures 6.1 and 6.2. For men age fifty-five to sixty-four, participation fell from 60 percent in 1977 to a low of 42 percent in 2001 before rising again and reaching 56 percent by 2013. Labor force participation trends for women in the same age range look very different than those for men. Employment rates for women age fifty-five to sixty-four remained constant around 14–15 percent until 2000 when it started to increase substantially, reaching 34.7 percent in 2013, a threefold increase. Vice versa, employment rates of age sixty-five and older declined over the same period: 13.1 percent of men age sixty-five and older, and 3.5 percent of women of the same age range where employed in 1977 (the figures went down to 6.2 and 1.5, respectively, in 2013). Reforms that interested the Italian pension system since

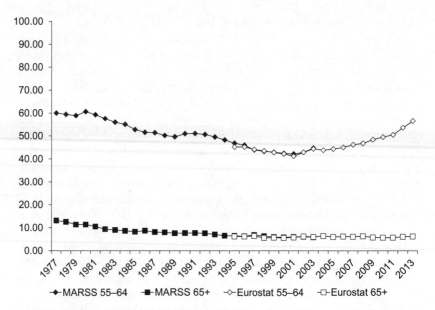

Fig. 6.1 Men's labor force participation, ages fifty-five to sixty-four and sixty-four and older (1977–2013)

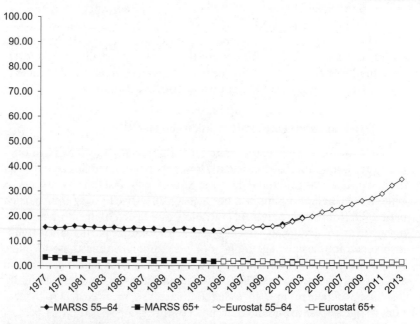

Fig. 6.2 Women's labor force participation, ages fifty-five to sixty-four and sixty-five and older (1977–2013)

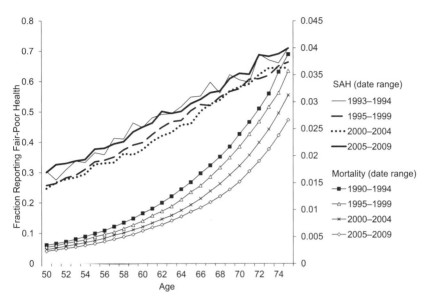

Fig. 6.3   SAH and mortality for men age fifty to seventy-five (1993 to 2013)

1993 reduced substantially the incentives to retire early that were embedded in the preexisting pension system, but this shift toward longer working life did not affect the age sixty-five and older, despite the historically high life expectancy in Italy.

Figure 6.3 presents trends in mortality and self-assessed health (SAH) for men age fifty to seventy-five over the past four decades, based on authors' calculations from the General Household Survey ([ISTAT] "Multiscopo") and the Human Mortality Database. This figure shows the well-known age gradient in mortality as well as the general trend over time toward lower mortality rates, which is quite remarkable in Italy. In 1990–94 men age sixty experienced an annual mortality rate of 1 percent, in the 2005–09 period that mortality rate is not reached until age sixty-five. Similarly, men age sixty-eight in 1990–94 had a mortality rate of 2 percent, a rate that applied to men age seventy-two in 2005–09. Improvements in SAH are not so evident from the figure, probably because the data are noisier and the time span is not long enough to appreciate such a change. Unfortunately, there are no population-wide surveys in Italy where SAH is recorded earlier than 1993. Moreover, the self-assessed health question changed from the 2008 wave: the 1 to 5 Likert scale was reversed and relabeled. As a result, the ISTAT General Household Survey reports lower average SAH in more recent cohorts. Roughly 40 percent of men age sixty report themselves to be in fair or poor health in 1995–99; in 2005–09, 40 percent of men age fifty-eight report to be in fair or poor health (at sixty, 45 percent are in fair/poor health in these later periods). Looking at yearly data rather than five-year aggregates, there is a clear shift from 2008 onward toward fair and poor health due to the question change. Improvements in SAH are therefore underestimated compared to other studies in this volume.

A first general conclusion that can be drawn from figure 6.3 is that in Italy—as in many other countries—health deteriorates with age and that health (or at least life expectancy as recorded in the Human Mortality Database) at any given age has improved over time, while figure 6.1 shows that older men's labor force participation fell until the beginning of the twenty-first century and has been rising since then. In the analysis that follows, we effectively bring together these trends in labor force participation and health as we explore how much individuals today could work based on the employment-mortality patterns experienced by previous cohorts.

6.2   Estimating Health Capacity to Work Using the Milligan-Wise Method

The first set of results builds on the methodology developed in Milligan-Wise (2012), which looks at the relationship between mortality and employment that existed at an earlier point in time along with current mortality data to generate an estimate of individuals' ability to work at older ages. The counterfactual experiment is based on the idea that, other things being equal, in principle people today could work as much as people with the same mortality rate worked in the past. While mortality is not the best health measure to relate to productivity, it has several advantages: it is defined consistently across countries, and data on mortality is available over a long period of time for the entire population at single ages for single years. Since general data limitations on health are particularly severe in Italy, the measures of health-work capacity derived from mortality experienced by the Italian population are of special interest in this volume.

The mortality data used for this analysis come from the Human Mortality Database, and the employment data is from two sources: the MARSS database provided by ISTAT for the period 1977–2003 and Eurostat from 1983 until 2012. Despite the different databases, figures 6.1 and 6.2 show how the common periods overlap almost perfectly. The reason is that both data sets are based on the Labour Force Survey, therefore linking the two series is an innocuous assumption, which allows us to consider the period 1977 through 2010, with the start year chosen to correspond to that used in Milligan and Wise (2012). The analysis is quite straightforward, as it requires mapping an employment-mortality curve, which displays the employment rate at each level of mortality for a given year, then repeating this for other years and making some calculations based on comparisons of the different

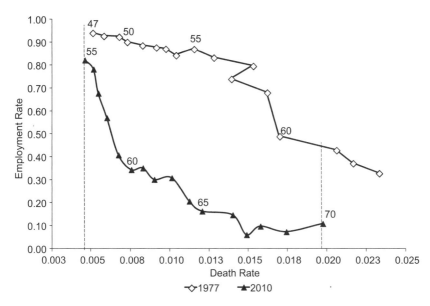

Fig. 6.4   Employment versus mortality (2010 versus 1977)

Source: Italian National Bureau of Statistics (ISTAT) MARSS data for 1977, and ISTAT data from the General Household Survey for 2010.

curves. As noted earlier, we conduct this exercise for men only, as the large increases in women's labor force participation over time make it difficult to interpret the results for women.

Our approach is illustrated in figure 6.4, which plots the employment-mortality curve for men in 2010 and in 1977. In 2010, the one-year mortality rate for fifty-five-year-old men was about 0.5 percent, and the employment rate at this age was 82 percent. In 1977, forty-seven-year-old men had a mortality rate of 0.5 percent. This reflects the mortality improvements over time discussed in the previous section. In 1977, the labor force participation for forty-seven-year-olds was 94 percent. Thus, if men in 2010 had the same employment rate as did men in 1977 with the same mortality rate, the employment rate of fifty-five-year-olds would have been 12 percentage points higher, 94 percent instead of 82 percent.

In table 6.1, we extend this exercise through age sixty-nine, asking how much more men could have worked over the age range fifty-five to sixty-nine in 2010 if they had worked as much as men with the same mortality rate worked in 1977. At age fifty-five, an additional 12 percent of men could have worked, which generates an average 0.12 additional work years. At age fifty-six, an additional 16 percent of men could have worked for an additional 0.16 work years. Repeating this analysis at each subsequent age through age sixty-nine and cumulating the amounts, we arrive at a total potential additional employment capacity of 7.4 years. This is equivalent on the graph

Table 6.1   Additional employment capacity in 2010 using 1977 employment-mortality relationship

Age	Death rate 2010	Employment rate 2010 (%)	Employment rate in 1977 corresponding to death rate of 2010 (%)	Additional employment capacity (%)
55	0.00462	82.15	93.98	11.82
56	0.00517	78.19	94.10	15.92
57	0.00548	67.73	93.51	25.78
58	0.00602	57.01	92.84	35.83
59	0.00674	40.84	92.61	51.77
60	0.00755	34.39	89.85	55.45
61	0.00829	35.19	88.70	53.52
62	0.00901	30.16	87.98	57.83
63	0.01012	30.88	85.48	54.60
64	0.01123	20.65	86.55	65.90
65	0.01204	16.32	85.57	69.25
66	0.01399	14.69	74.64	59.94
67	0.01488	6.06	78.23	72.17
68	0.01577	9.77	73.36	63.59
69	0.01742	7.38	48.35	40.97
Total years		5.31411		7.3434948

to integrating between the two curves from one vertical line to the next. As the average amount of employment between ages fifty-five and sixty-nine in 2010 is 5.3 years, an additional 7.4 years would represent a massive 139 percent increase over the baseline years of work.

It is worth noting that this method implicitly assumes that all mortality gains can translate into additional work capacity. This may not be the case if workers are living longer but are not in good health in those additional years of life. The relationship between mortality and morbidity changes over time has been the subject of a number of recent studies. As noted above in figure 6.3, we find that the share of individuals reporting themselves to be in fair or poor health at a given age has not been steadily increasing over time.

A second concern is that an additional year of life does not necessarily translate into a full additional year of work. If we use the same benchmark as in other chapters, whereby the share of life spent in work should be two-thirds of total life, one could multiply the figure above by two-thirds, arriving at an estimate of 4.9 years rather than 7.4 years (for simplicity, we do not make this conversion for the numbers reported below).

Another issue that arises in implementing this method is the choice of year to use for comparison to the present. In figure 6.5, we replicate the analysis from figure 6.4 but use 1995 as a comparison year rather than 1977. At

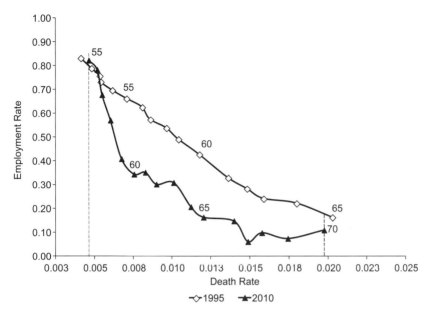

Fig. 6.5   Employment versus mortality (2010 versus 1995)
Source: Italian National Bureau of Statistics (ISTAT) MARSS data for 1977, and ISTAT data from the General Household Survey for 2010.

every age, the mortality rate is lower in 2010 than in 1995, consistent with earlier discussions. However, employment rates are higher in 2010 than in 1995—at age sixty-two, for example, the employment rate was 30 percent in 2010 versus 28 percent in 1995. Although employment at a given age has increased over time, it has not increased by enough to keep up with mortality increases, and for that reason the 1995 employment-mortality curve still lies above that for 2010, but the gap between the two curves is less than that between the 2010 and 1977 curves. Using 1995 as the comparison year, the estimated additional employment capacity from ages fifty-five to sixty-nine is 2.6 years, which is substantially smaller than the estimate of 7.4 years that we obtain when we use 1977 as the comparison year.

In figure 6.6, we show the estimated additional employment capacity as a function of the base year used. For base years close to 2010, the estimated additional employment capacity is small, as we are essentially asking if men with a given mortality rate in 2010 worked as much as men with the same mortality rate did in, say, 2008, and how much would they work. The difference between the two years is not large because neither mortality nor employment changes much over a short period of time. But as shown in the 1995 and 1977 examples, when we look back over a longer period of time, the estimated additional capacity is much larger. This is both because mortality has improved over time, as the 1995 example illustrates, and because

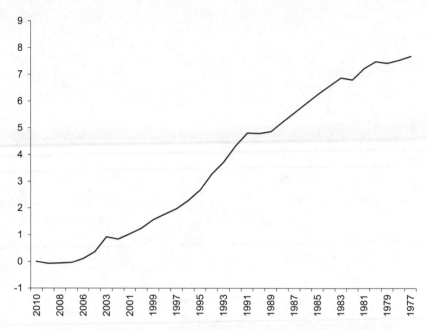

Fig. 6.6   Estimated additional employment capacity by year of comparison

employment rates today are lower than they were in the late 1970s and early 1980s (though higher than in the mid-1990s), as seen in the 1977 example.

To sum up, our estimates based on the Milligan-Wise method suggest a significant amount of additional work capacity for Italy, particularly if we take the 1970s as a benchmark. We estimate that the additional capacity from ages fifty-five to sixty-nine is 7.4 years using the 1977 employment-mortality curve as a point of comparison, or 2.6 years using 1995 as the base year. To change the assumption that an additional year of life expectancy translates into an additional year of work capacity, one can apply a fractional factor to these estimates—using the logic that the share of life spent in work and retirement should remain roughly constant, for example, would suggest multiplying these values by two-thirds.

This method is also informative about the ability of older individuals to work at specific ages. This can be seen from table 6.1, using 1977 as the comparison year. This analysis suggests that at ages sixty to sixty-four, an additional 58 percent or so of men could be employed (as the table indicates that an additional 55.4 percent could be working at age sixty, an additional 53.5 percent at age sixty-one, an additional 57.8 percent at age sixty-two, etc.); at ages sixty-five to sixty-nine, an additional 61.3 percent or so of men could be employed. These estimates can be compared to the results we generate using the next method.

6.3   Estimating Health Capacity to Work Using the Cutler et al. Method

We now turn to the second method of estimating health capacity to work, following Cutler, Meara, and Richards-Shubik (2012). In this method, we address the following question: If older individuals in a given state of health worked as much as their younger counterparts, how much would they work? Implementing this method involves a two-step process. First, we run regressions to estimate the relationship between health and employment, using a sample of workers young enough so that their employment decisions should not be affected by the availability of social security (public pension) benefits. We choose to focus on workers age fifty to fifty-four, who are still many years away from old age pension eligibility and should also be too young to qualify for early retirement schemes: the age fifty-four cutoff is chosen for comparability with the other studies in this volume, even though a small selection of workers in Italy would in the past qualify for early retirement pensions even in their early fifties. For the second step, we combine the regression coefficients along with the actual characteristics of individuals age fifty-five to seventy-four to predict the older individuals' ability to work based on health.

The data used in the analysis is the Survey of Health, Ageing and Retirement in Europe (SHARE). SHARE began in 2004 as a longitudinal study of individuals age fifty and older and their partners, with biannual interviews; in the years since, the study has been refreshed with younger cohorts in order to provide a representative survey of individuals older than age fifty. Currently, data through 2012 (wave 5) is available; we use data from waves 1–2 and 4–5 in the baseline analysis, since wave 3 is a retrospective interview and does not allow evaluating health transitions from wave 2 to wave 4. SHARE is ideally suited for a study such as this one because of the rich data on health, as well as data on employment and demographics. We use a sample of 573 male and 929 female person-year observations for the regressions; a further 4,252 male and 4,963 female person-year observations are used in our simulations of work capacity.

As in all other chapters, we estimate regressions of the following form:

$$\text{Employment}_i = \beta_0 + \beta_1 \text{health}_i + \beta_2 X_i + \varepsilon_i,$$

where Employment is a dummy equal to 1 if the individual is employed and health is a comprehensive set of health measures, including dummy variables for self-reported health status, limitations on physical activity, limitations on activities of daily living (ADLs) and instrumental activities of daily living (IADLs), individual health conditions, being over- or underweight, and being a current or former smoker. We also include variables for educational attainment and marital status. We estimate this equation as a linear probability model.

We estimate an alternative version of this regression model where the full set of health variables is replaced by a single health index value, as put forward in Poterba, Venti, and Wise (2013). The idea is to construct a health index based on twenty-four items, including self-reported health diagnoses, functional limitations, medical care usage, and other health indicators. To do so, one first obtains the first principal component of these indicators, which is the "weighted average of indicators where the weights are chosen to maximize the proportion of the variance of the individual health indicators that can be explained by this weighted average" (Poterba, Venti, and Wise 2013, 300). The estimated coefficients from the analysis are then used to predict a percentile score for each respondent, referred to as the health index. An individual's health index value typically will vary by survey wave, as updated health information is incorporated.

It is worth noting some of the key assumptions underlying our analysis. First, we assume that there are no unmeasured or omitted dimensions of health. If there were, health might be declining more rapidly with age than reflected in the health variables we have, and our estimates of ability to work at older ages could be overstated. We address this concern by including a comprehensive set of health variables, as well as by using a health index that is likely a good reflection of overall health. Second, our approach implicitly assumes that the health-employment relationship that exists for younger individuals (age fifty to fifty-four) is the same as that for older individuals (age fifty-five to seventy-four). For example, if younger workers were concentrated in white-collar jobs and older workers in blue-collar jobs, then it might be easier for a younger worker with a health problem to continue working than it would be for an older worker with the same health issue; this would lead us to overstate the ability of older individuals to work. Finally, if there is a large amount of "discretionary" (non-health-related) retirement among our sample of younger individuals, we would estimate a lower health capacity to work than what might actually exist. We have chosen a relatively young sample for the estimation to try to avoid this problem.[1] There are other assumptions underlying our analysis, which we made mainly in order to improve efficiency of the estimates, or are specific to the Italian data set. We will discuss them in detail at the end of this section.

Summary statistics for the male and female samples are shown in tables 6.2A and 6.2B. The share of employed men falls from 85 percent at ages fifty to fifty-four to 65 percent at ages fifty-five to fifty-nine, 27 percent at ages sixty to sixty-four, 5 percent at ages sixty-five to sixty-nine, and 2 percent at ages seventy to seventy-four. Employment rates for women are 56 percent at ages fifty to fifty-four, 37 percent at ages fifty-five to fifty-nine, 11 percent at ages sixty to sixty-four, 2 percent at ages sixty-five to sixty-nine,

---

1. We also acknowledge that health may be endogenous in the regressions we run if employment status has a causal effect on health.

Table 6.2A	Summary statistics, men				
	Age group				
	50–54	55–59	60–64	65–69	70–74
In labor force	0.94	0.73	0.32	0.07	0.02
Employed	0.85	0.65	0.27	0.05	0.02
Health_exc	0.16	0.11	0.09	0.09	0.06
Health_vgood	0.24	0.21	0.17	0.14	0.11
Health_good	0.44	0.46	0.43	0.39	0.38
Health_fair	0.14	0.17	0.24	0.30	0.34
Health_poor	0.02	0.04	0.06	0.09	0.11
Gali	0.15	0.22	0.27	0.38	0.44
Mobilit2	0.22	0.26	0.33	0.42	0.51
Mobilit3	0.04	0.07	0.10	0.17	0.22
ADLany	0.03	0.03	0.05	0.06	0.10
IADLany	0.02	0.03	0.05	0.08	0.12
Eurod	1.87	1.88	1.94	2.26	2.39
Heartat	0.04	0.06	0.09	0.13	0.16
Stroke	0.01	0.02	0.02	0.04	0.04
Cholester	0.13	0.17	0.19	0.24	0.24
Lungdis	0.03	0.04	0.05	0.07	0.12
Cancer	0.01	0.02	0.03	0.03	0.04
Highblpr	0.21	0.31	0.34	0.45	0.46
Arthritis	0.06	0.09	0.14	0.18	0.20
Diabetes	0.04	0.08	0.11	0.17	0.15
Osteopor	0.00	0.01	0.01	0.01	0.02
Alzheimer's	0.00	0.00	0.00	0.01	0.01
Back	0.31	0.36	0.38	0.41	0.40
Asthma	0.02	0.01	0.01	0.01	0.04
Underweight	0.00	0.00	0.00	0.00	0.00
Overweight	0.49	0.50	0.54	0.54	0.52
Obese	0.14	0.17	0.17	0.18	0.16
Smokerform	0.22	0.31	0.36	0.43	0.46
Smokecurr	0.34	0.30	0.27	0.19	0.14
Educ_lessthHS	0.54	0.56	0.63	0.71	0.79
Educ_hs	0.33	0.30	0.25	0.19	0.13
Educ_somecollege	0.02	0.03	0.03	0.03	0.02
Educ_collegemore	0.10	0.10	0.10	0.07	0.06
Married	0.81	0.89	0.90	0.88	0.86
Occ_bluecollar	0.30	0.34	0.35	0.41	0.43
Occ_lowskill	0.12	0.13	0.11	0.13	0.14
Occ_homemaker	0.00	0.00	0.00	0.00	0.00
Pencov	0.78	0.81	0.89	0.91	0.93
Obs.	582	951	1,086	1,155	1,060

Table 6.2B	Summary statistics, women				
	Age group				
	50–54	55–59	60–64	65–69	70–74
In labor force	0.60	0.41	0.12	0.02	0.00
Employed	0.56	0.37	0.11	0.02	0.00
Health_exc	0.11	0.09	0.07	0.05	0.03
Health_vgood	0.25	0.18	0.14	0.10	0.08
Health_good	0.40	0.39	0.41	0.39	0.30
Health_fair	0.20	0.27	0.30	0.35	0.42
Health_poor	0.04	0.07	0.08	0.11	0.17
Gali	0.26	0.31	0.37	0.45	0.55
Mobilit2	0.34	0.44	0.52	0.61	0.73
Mobilit3	0.13	0.18	0.25	0.33	0.46
ADLany	0.03	0.05	0.06	0.09	0.14
IADLany	0.06	0.07	0.12	0.14	0.22
Eurod	2.76	2.89	2.97	3.20	3.50
Heartat	0.03	0.03	0.05	0.08	0.10
Stroke	0.01	0.01	0.02	0.02	0.03
Cholester	0.11	0.20	0.24	0.27	0.31
Lungdis	0.02	0.04	0.03	0.05	0.08
Cancer	0.04	0.04	0.04	0.05	0.05
Highblpr	0.19	0.28	0.36	0.47	0.51
Arthritis	0.15	0.22	0.27	0.29	0.35
Diabetes	0.04	0.06	0.09	0.12	0.15
Osteopor	0.03	0.07	0.08	0.09	0.11
Alzheimer's	0.00	0.00	0.00	0.00	0.01
Back	0.39	0.46	0.53	0.54	0.60
Asthma	0.02	0.02	0.02	0.02	0.02
Underweight	0.02	0.01	0.01	0.01	0.02
Overweight	0.31	0.35	0.37	0.40	0.39
Obese	0.13	0.15	0.19	0.20	0.20
Smokerform	0.16	0.19	0.18	0.14	0.14
Smokecurr	0.23	0.21	0.15	0.13	0.08
Educ_lessthHS	0.55	0.64	0.71	0.79	0.83
Educ_hs	0.28	0.23	0.18	0.13	0.11
Educ_somecollege	0.05	0.04	0.03	0.03	0.02
Educ_collegemore	0.11	0.09	0.07	0.05	0.03
Married	0.84	0.85	0.82	0.76	0.67
Occ_bluecollar	0.13	0.15	0.20	0.21	0.24
Occ_lowskill	0.16	0.14	0.16	0.16	0.18
Occ_homemaker	0.23	0.29	0.24	0.29	0.29
Pencov	0.62	0.62	0.71	0.74	0.78
Obs.	950	1,239	1,377	1,293	1,054

and negligible at ages seventy to seventy-four. The health measures show a decline in health with age. The share of men in fair or poor health rises from 16 percent at ages fifty to fifty-four to 45 percent at ages seventy to seventy-four. Values for women are similar but slightly higher, 24 percent at ages fifty to fifty-four and 59 percent at ages seventy to seventy-four. This reflects the known result that women live longer but report themselves to be in worse health.

Turning to some of the other health measures, the share of men with more than one limitation on physical activity rises from 22 percent at ages fifty to fifty-four to 51 percent at ages seventy to seventy-four, while values for women are somewhat higher, 34 percent at ages fifty to fifty-four and 73 percent at ages seventy to seventy-four.[2] The share of individuals with limitations in ADLs rises from 3 percent to 10 percent for men across the five age categories, and from 3 to 14 percent for women; the share with limitations in IADLs shows a similar trend, rising from 2 to 12 percent for men and from 6 to 22 percent for women.[3] Finally, the share of individuals with diagnosed medical conditions also rises with age. Back pain and high blood pressure are the most common ailments, rising for men from 31 and 21 percent at ages fifty to fifty-four to 40 and 46 percent at ages seventy to seventy-four. Potentially more serious health conditions such as cancer and stroke also rise with age. The relevance of these statistics for our analysis is that they show that health deteriorates with age, so if our regressions suggest a strong relationship between health and employment, then the predicted share of individuals that are employed (estimated in the second step of our analysis) will decrease with age, as health declines.

Tables 6.3A and 6.3B display estimated regression parameters for the all health variables and health index versions of our model, respectively. Table 6.3A shows that there are statistically significant effects of some health variables on employment. For example, relative to men in excellent health, men in poor health are 39 percentage points less likely to be in employment. Some of the individual health conditions are associated with statistically significant decreases in the probability of employment of up to 32 percentage points, such as having experienced a heart attack or a stroke.

In the version of the model with the health index, Table 6.3B, the index is a statistically significant determinant of employment. Results from other chapters in this volume confirm that the index functions well as a summary statistic for health. This evidence, coupled with the lack of significance of

2. The full set of activities includes: (a) walking 100 meters; (b) sitting for about two hours; (c) getting up from a chair after sitting for long periods; (d) climbing several flights of stairs without resting; (e) climbing one flight of stairs without resting; (f) stooping, kneeling, or crouching; (g) reaching or extending your arms above shoulder level; (h) pulling or pushing large objects like a living room chair; (i) lifting or carrying weights over ten pounds/five kilos, like a heavy bag of groceries; and (j) picking up a small coin from a table.

3. ADLs include: dressing, walking across the room, bathing, eating, and getting in/out of bed; IADLs include managing meals, groceries, and medication.

Table 6.3A   Employment regressions, all health variables

	Men 50–54			Women 50–54	
Variable	Coefficient	Std. err.	Variable	Coefficient	Std. err.
Health_vgood	−0.0028	0.0450	Health_vgood	−0.0115	0.0537
Health_good	−0.0357	0.0421	Health_good	−0.0440	0.0521
Health_fair	0.0179	0.0575	Health_fair	−0.1477	0.0638*
Health_poor	−0.3956	0.1175***	Health_poor	−0.0477	0.1035
Gali	0.0062	0.0471	Gali	−0.0185	0.0414
Mobilit2	0.0345	0.0422	Mobilit2	−0.0075	0.0403
Mobilit3	−0.1197	0.0849	Mobilit3	0.0199	0.0619
ADLany	−0.1827	0.0983	ADLany	0.1826	0.0951
IADLany	0.0156	0.1292	IADLany	−0.1286	0.0706
Eurod	−0.0072	0.0085	Eurod	0.0030	0.0070
Heartat	−0.3257	0.0751***	Heartat	−0.2324	0.0967*
Stroke	−0.2502	0.1238*	Stroke	−0.1769	0.1581
Cholester	0.0650	0.0417	Cholester	0.0592	0.0495
Lungdis	−0.0552	0.0853	Lungdis	−0.0076	0.1064
Cancer	−0.2083	0.1306	Cancer	−0.0302	0.0839
Highblpr	0.0682	0.0364	Highblpr	−0.0351	0.0413
Arthritis	−0.0650	0.0624	Arthritis	−0.0317	0.0493
Diabetes	−0.1151	0.0687	Diabetes	−0.0557	0.0813
Osteopor	0.2152	0.3497	Osteopor	0.1128	0.0862
Alzheimer's	0.0000	(omitted)	Alzheimer's	0.0000	(omitted)
Back	0.0156	0.0337	Back	−0.0121	0.0364
Asthma	0.0078	0.1107	Asthma	−0.2061	0.1113
Underweight	0.1426	0.3275	Underweight	0.0454	0.0976
Overweight	0.0229	0.0308	Overweight	0.0106	0.0348
Obese	−0.0864	0.0463	Obese	−0.0051	0.0485
Smokerform	−0.0299	0.0367	Smokerform	−0.0148	0.0425
Smokecurr	0.0110	0.0321	Smokecurr	0.0028	0.0374
Educ_lessthHS	−0.0481	0.0307	Educ_lessthHS	−0.2985	0.0355***
Educ_somecollege	0.0739	0.0947	Educ_somecollege	0.1165	0.0718
Educ_collegemore	0.0968	0.0490*	Educ_collegemore	0.1404	0.0532**
Married	0.1602	0.0364***	Married	−0.1182	0.0408**
_Cons	0.7824	0.0545***	_Cons	0.8733	0.0659***
Obs.	573		Obs.	929	

***Significant at the 1 percent level.
**Significant at the 5 percent level.
*Significant at the 10 percent level.

most of the health conditions in table 6.3A, lead us to focus on the results from table 6.3B in the discussion below.

In tables 6.4A and 6.4B, we report the results of our simulation exercise. This table shows (for men and women in five-year age groups from age fifty-five to seventy-four) the actual and predicted shares employed (the latter calculated as described above by combining the coefficients from the regression analysis and the characteristics of these individuals), and the difference between these, which we term the "estimated additional work capacity." For ease of exposition, key values are also reported in figures 6.7 and 6.8.

Table 6.3B   **Employment regressions, PVW index**

	Men			Women		
Variable	Coefficient	Std. err.	Variable	Coefficient	Std. err.	
PVW	0.0023	0.0006***	PVW	0.0015	0.0006**	
Educ_lessthHS	−0.0679	0.0312*	Educ_lessthHS	−0.3138	0.0347***	
Educ_somecollege	0.0930	0.0967	Educ_somecollege	0.0954	0.0713	
Educ_collegemore	0.1060	0.0502*	Educ_collegemore	0.1581	0.0525**	
Married	0.1733	0.0362***	Married	−0.1288	0.0404**	
_Cons	0.5744	0.0611***	_Cons	0.7264	0.0587***	
Obs.	570		Obs.	919		

***Significant at the 1 percent level.
**Significant at the 5 percent level.
*Significant at the 10 percent level.

Focusing on the results obtained using the PVW health index, we predict the share of men employed to be 86 percent at ages fifty-five to fifty-nine, 84 percent at ages sixty to sixty-four, 81 percent at ages sixty-five to sixty-nine, and 80 percent at ages seventy to seventy-four. These projections decline with age because health declines with age and our regression coefficients reflect a strong association between health and employment. However, the share of men actually working declines much more quickly with age than do our predictions, from 65 percent at ages fifty-five to fifty-nine to 26 percent, 5 percent, and 2 percent in the older age groups. As a result, we estimate that the additional capacity to work is substantial and rising sharply with age, from 21 percent at ages fifty-five to fifty-nine (based on the fact that we predict that 86 percent of men will work, but only 65 percent do) to 58 percent at ages sixty to sixty-four, 77 percent at ages sixty-five to sixty-nine, and seventy to seventy-four. Results using the model including the health index instead of the full set of health variables are quite similar. In terms of the results for women, both the predicted and actual share working are substantially lower than those for men, while the estimated work capacity numbers are lower in absolute terms and fairly constant but for the lower age group: 15 percent at ages fifty-five to fifty-nine, 38 percent for ages sixty to sixty-four, and around 44 percent across the other age groups.

It is useful to compare these results to those obtained using the Milligan-Wise method, where the analysis (done for men only) suggested that employment could be about 58 percentage points higher at ages sixty to sixty-four and about 61 percentage points higher at ages sixty-five to sixty-nine if people today worked as much as people with the same mortality rate worked in 1977. These values are comparable to the 58 and 77 percent numbers found here. Given how different the two methods employed in this chapter are, it is striking that they generate results of roughly similar magnitude, at least for ages up to sixty-five.

Table 6.4A   Simulation of work capacity based on regressions with all health variables

	Men					Women				
Age group	No. obs.	Actual % working	Predicted % working	Estimated work capacity (%)	Age group	No. obs.	Actual % working	Predicted % working	Estimated work capacity (%)
55–59	934	64.78	84.93	20.15	55–59	1,220	36.80	52.00	15.19
60–64	1,046	26.48	82.55	56.07	60–64	1,340	10.90	48.25	37.35
65–69	1,114	4.85	77.43	72.58	65–69	1,266	1.98	44.59	42.61
70–74	1,016	2.37	74.14	71.78	70–74	1,020	0.29	42.14	41.85

Table 6.4B   Simulations of work capacity based on regressions with PVW index

	Men					Women			
Age group	No. obs.	Actual % working	Predicted % working	Estimated work capacity (%)	Age group	No. obs.	Actual % working	Predicted % working	Estimated work capacity (%)
55–59	927	64.72	85.91	21.18	55–59	1,206	36.90	51.90	15.00
60–64	1,036	26.64	84.41	57.77	60–64	1,328	10.93	48.90	37.98
65–69	1,111	4.86	81.82	76.96	65–69	1,257	1.99	45.98	43.99
70–74	1,010	2.38	79.87	77.49	70–74	1,009	0.30	44.00	43.71

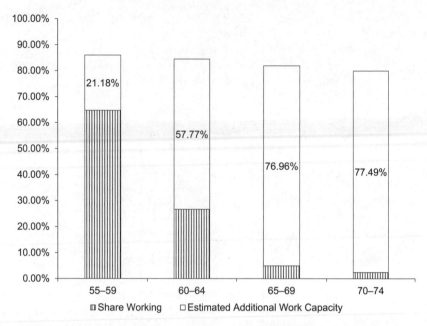

Fig. 6.7   Share of men working and additional work capacity by age

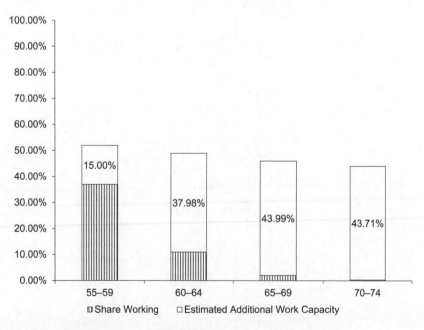

Fig. 6.8   Share of women working and additional work capacity by age

Our estimates reflect population averages, and may mask substantial heterogeneity in the ability to work longer. In particular, less educated and lower-income individuals may have less potential to extend their work lives because they are in worse health or have jobs where employment is more sensitive to health status. In the case of the Milligan-Wise analysis, it is unfortunately not possible to explore how the employment-mortality relationship has changed over time by education group or income group because Italian mortality records do not include that information. Bohacek et al. (2015) use SHARE to estimate the education gradient in mortality dividing education level into "low educated" and "high educated." Despite the low sample sizes, results for countries where mortality records are available by educational level are consistent across the different data sources. Regarding Italy, the authors find a relatively small education gradient for Italian men, and a somewhat larger premium for women.

For the present analysis, however, we can estimate work capacity separately by education. We reestimate the regression model separately by education group, which allows the relationship between employment and health to differ by education group—as might be the case, for example, if workers with less education are concentrated in blue-collar jobs where it is more difficult to continue working once one experiences a health problem than it would be in the white-collar jobs held by more highly educated workers.[4]

Our simulations of work capacity by education group are shown in table 6.5 and in figures 6.9 and 6.10. Unfortunately, data limitations force us to define only two education groups: less than high school, and high school degree or more. The actual and predicted share working varies substantially by education group—for example, the actual and predicted share working among men ages fifty-five to fifty-nine are 78 and 92 percent for those with a high school degree versus 54 and 80 percent for less than high school. These differences lead to an estimated additional work capacity for men at ages fifty-five to fifty-nine, which is 13.6 percent higher for the poorly educated. There is no difference in the additional capacity in the sixty to sixty-four age group, while the sign of the difference is inverted for the older age groups: estimated work capacity is 9 percent higher for the more educated in the sixty-five to sixty-nine age group and 11 percentage points higher for the seventy-one to seventy-five. For women, there is a 1 percentage point difference by education level in the estimated work capacity in the younger age group: the less educated women age fifty-five to sixty have an estimated work capacity of 15 percent, while the more educated of 14 percent. The difference in this age group, as in all the others, is on the level of both actual

---

4. We also generate results by education in a simpler way, continuing to use a common set of regression coefficients for all education groups but reporting the actual share working, predicted share working, and estimated additional work capacity separately by education group. The results of this exercise are qualitatively similar to those in table 6.5.

Table 6.5   Work capacity by education (regression by education group)

	Men, all health variables model			Men, PVW model		
Education	Actual % working	Predicted % working	Estimated work capacity (%)	Actual % working	Predicted % working	Estimated work capacity (%)
		Age 55–59				
Less than HS	54.18	80.08	25.9	53.93	80.99	27.1
More than HS	78.33	91.28	13.0	78.47	91.96	13.5
		Age 60–64				
Less than HS	21.65	78.24	56.6	21.88	78.95	57.1
More than HS	34.45	89.70	55.3	34.46	92.00	57.5
		Age 65–69				
Less than HS	3.41	74.21	70.8	3.43	77.08	73.6
More than HS	8.41	86.38	78.0	8.41	90.93	82.5
		Age 70–74				
Less than HS	1.50	71.07	69.6	1.51	75.31	73.8
More than HS	5.58	86.76	81.2	5.61	90.68	85.1

	Women, all health variables model			Women, PVW model		
Education	Actual % working	Predicted % working	Estimated work capacity (%)	Actual % working	Predicted % working	Estimated work capacity (%)
		Age 55–59				
Less than HS	22.32	37.08	14.8	22.76	38.31	15.6
More than HS	62.65	75.51	12.9	61.78	76.18	14.4
		Age 60–64				
Less than HS	6.91	39.90	33.0	6.86	38.45	31.6
More than HS	21.39	78.78	57.4	21.11	75.17	54.1
		Age 65–69				
Less than HS	1.07	37.15	36.1	1.01	38.24	37.2
More than HS	5.34	77.34	72.0	5.62	75.74	70.1
		Age 70–74				
Less than HS	0.25	37.00	36.7	0.24	38.16	37.9
More than HS	0.63	80.32	79.7	0.61	74.74	74.1

Note: Actual percent working in all health and PVW models vary due to differences in sample size.

and predicted employment: among the women age fifty-five to fifty-nine, 23 percent of the less educated are actually working versus 62 percent of the more educated. The predictions are 38 percent and 76 percent, respectively. As we move to older age groups, actual employment rates fall while predicted employment rates remain basically constant in both education groups. The estimated work capacity rises first at 32 percent and then stabilizes at 37 percent for the less educated, age sixty to sixty-four, sixty-five to seventy, and seventy-one to seventy-five, respectively, while it is 54 percent, 70 percent, and 74 percent among the more educated in the three age-corresponding groups.

As we mentioned earlier, the estimates we used to simulate work capacity

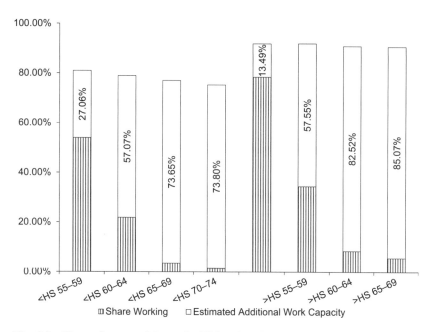

Fig. 6.9   Share of men working and additional work capacity by age and education

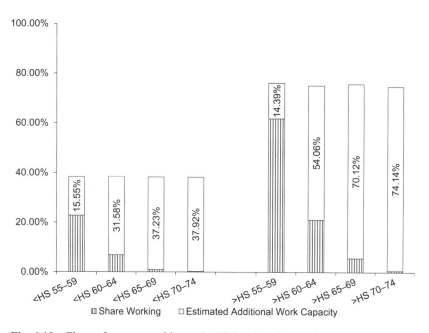

Fig. 6.10   Share of women working and additional work capacity by age and education

of older cohorts are based on assumptions common to the other contributions of this book, and some additional assumptions specific to the Italian data. First and foremost, we pooled data from 2004, 2006, 2010, and 2012 to obtain a sample large enough to compute reliable estimates. The underlying assumption is that the relation between health and retirement decision remains constant over time. A first concern relates to self-assessed health, which is included both as an explanatory variable and as a component of the health index: since the subjective evaluation of own health may vary with age, the relation between self-reported health and employment varies over time (waves). Hence, we estimated both versions of the model excluding self-assessed health from the set of regressors: work capacities are virtually unaffected compared to the reported results. Yet, a second concern related to the choice of pooling data from different waves is that the economic crisis may have changed the relation between health and retirement for individuals age fifty to fifty-four in 2010 and 2012. Therefore, we reestimated the model based only on the precrisis period (waves 1 and 2). The sample size reduces dramatically: the regressions (reported in tables 6A.1A and 6A.1B) are run with at most 262 observations for males and 413 for females. This reduction leads to a loss of significance of the PVW health index, but in the regression that includes all health conditions taken separately, most of the regressors that were significant in table 6.3A are still significant. Turning to estimated work capacity, using only waves 1 and 2 leads to flatter profiles by age: as an example, in the baseline estimations we estimated a 22 percent excess work capacity for males age fifty-five to fifty-nine using the PVW index estimations, rising to 58, 76, and 77 percent for the sixty to sixty-four, sixty-five to sixty-nine, and seventy to seventy-four ages. Using only precrisis data, the figures are 32 percent, 62 percent, 75 percent, and 77 percent, respectively. A similar picture emerges looking at women, splitting by education or moving to estimates obtained including all health variables (tables 6A.2A and 6A.2B and tables 6A.3A, 6A.3B, 6A.3C, and 6A.3D).

The difference in estimated work capacity using only the first two waves may be attributed either to the changed economic conditions or to differential labor force participation across cohorts. The surge of the economic crisis may have induced individuals to postpone retirement and stay longer in the labor market, thus the higher estimated unused capacity resulting when limiting the analysis to the precrisis sample can be the result of a lower average labor force participation. Such an effect is not separately identifiable from a cohort effect induced by the sampling scheme of SHARE: waves 4 and 5 include a refresher sample, which allows the survey to be representative of the entire age fifty and older European population in each interview year. As the panel sample ages, the new observations are mainly individuals from younger cohorts with a higher labor attachment. Again, limiting the analysis to waves 1 and 2 leads to a lower average labor force participation. Finally, a third explanation is that the difference in estimated work capacity observed restricting the sample to waves 1 and 2 may simply reflect a lack of precision due to the limited sample size. In order to rule out the latter, we pooled samples of individuals from all SHARE countries observed in waves 1 and 2, we ran the same regression including a full set of country fixed effects, and obtained simulations for Italy based on these estimates. Estimated work capacity is by and large unchanged compared to the estimates obtained using only the small Italian sample of waves 1 and 2.

A second point that may be particularly relevant for Italy is that the estimation sample includes individuals who never worked in their lives. Those individuals never faced a retirement decision, but they can define themselves as retired. The relation between health and being "retired" can be very different for this subset of individuals. While this is a negligible fraction of the surveyed population in the United States, a substantial proportion of Italian women in the relevant cohorts never participated in the labor force. Excluding these women reduces the sample from 929 to 704 observations (tables 6A.4A and 6A.4B). The difference in sample size is much more limited for males. Excluding individuals who never worked allows us to include occupational dummies in the regression. Occupational dummies turn out to be significant for women, not for men. Nevertheless, the higher education dummy loses statistical significance in this specification for women. The PVW index, though still significant, is now estimated less precisely. Looking at table 6A.5, we can observe that estimated work capacity for males is virtually unchanged, while it is substantially higher for older cohorts of women.

The overall impression is that our baseline estimates lead to conservative estimates of work capacity compared to alternative sets of results, which account for the specific characteristics of Italy.

6.4 Changes in Self-Assessed Health by Education Level over Time

In this section, we show how SAH has evolved over time for those with different levels of socioeconomic status (SES) in Italy. We follow standard practice and use education as an indicator of lifelong SES, and account for cohort differences in educational attainment by relating individual education to that of individuals born in the same year.

Figure 6.11 shows the distribution of educational attainment by birth cohort; data for men and women are aggregated in the figure because results are similar for both genders. For cohorts reaching age fifty in 1995 (born in 1945), the median individual had a middle school degree and more than 75 percent of individuals had less than a high school education. This changes rapidly over time. By 2005, the median fifty-year-old is still at the middle school level, but more than 40 percent of the individuals in the same cohort have a high school degree.

The horizontal lines on figure 6.11 show how the education quartiles are defined. For the 1995 cohort of fifty-year-olds, for example, the lowest

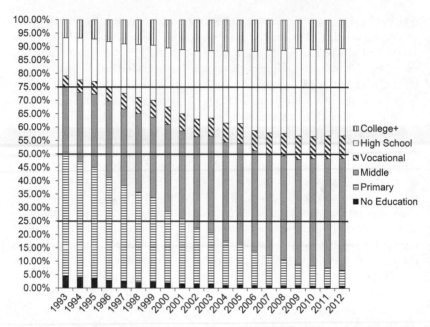

Fig. 6.11   Distribution of years of education completed by cohort (by year cohort attained age fifty)

quartile includes all of those with no or primary school education. The next quartile includes the rest of the primary school group and some of the middle school graduates. The 3rd quartile largely consists of those with a middle school degree, while the top quartile includes the remainder of high school graduates and everyone with some college or more education. In the 2005 cohort of fifty-year-olds, the lowest quartile includes some middle school graduates and everyone with primary school, while the third quartile includes only vocational training and high school graduates. The key point is that the educational composition of the population changes over time, even in a relatively short time window as the one we consider. That is why we focus on education quartiles to have a consistent measure of the less and more educated.

In figure 6.12, we plot the share of individuals who report themselves to be in fair or poor health by age for two different time periods, 1993–1999 and 2000–2007, separately, by education quartile. The data for these figures comes from the ISTAT General Household Survey, and are aggregated over seven years for greater precision. The familiar negative relationship between age and health is evident from the figures, as is the fact that health is better among the higher education quartiles. What interests us particularly is the evolution of SAH over time across education quartiles. In the case of Italy, we do not find significant improvements in health over time in any educa-

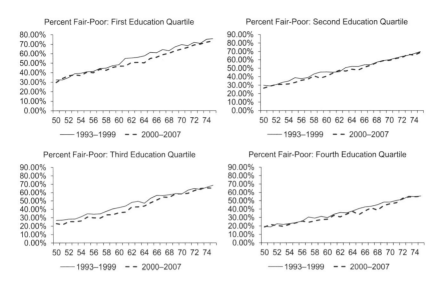

Fig. 6.12   **Percentage in fair or poor health by education quartile**

tional quartile, but for older individuals in the first education quartile. This may be due to the relatively short time period that we have data for: ISTAT General Household Survey report data on self-assessed health covering the period 1993–2012, but in the 2008 questionnaire the question changed limiting the comparable data to fourteen years in all, from 1993 until 2007.

6.5   Discussion and Conclusion

The Italian public pension system has undergone several reforms over the past quarter century aimed at increasing the effective retirement age and making the whole system of support to the older population sustainable in both the short and long run. One of the features of these reforms has been an explicit link of public pension eligibility to life expectancy, on the assumption that working lives can be extended at a similar pace as longevity increases. Critics of these reforms have claimed that work beyond a certain age is made hard or even impossible by health deterioration and other physical impediments (such as limited mobility).

In this chapter we have used data from different sources (official statistics from ISTAT, as well as the Italian component of the Survey on Health, Ageing and Retirement in Europe) to assess the validity of this widely voiced criticism to the goal of longer working lives.

First of all, we have assessed how much individuals could work now if people with a given mortality rate today worked as much as those with the same mortality rate in the past. Next we have estimated how much individuals could work, if older individuals with a given health status worked as much as their younger (fifty to fifty-four) counterparts with the same health status. Both methods suggest substantial additional work capacity, of the order of a potential employment increase of 56–58 percent of the population at ages sixty to sixty-four and of 61–69 percent at ages sixty-five to sixty-nine. We have investigated the heterogeneity of work capacity, and found greater work capacity among more educated individuals as compared to the less educated, at least for individuals age sixty or more.

Appendix

Table 6A.1A   Employment regressions, all health variables, precrisis waves

	Men 50–54			Women 50–54	
Variable	Coefficient	Std. err.	Variable	Coefficient	Std. err.
Health_vgood	−0.077	0.069	Health_vgood	−0.042	0.087
Health_good	−0.123	0.062*	Health_good	−0.092	0.082
Health_fair	0.023	0.087	Health_fair	−0.263	0.099**
Health_poor	−0.520	0.182**	Health_poor	−0.091	0.159
Gali	0.017	0.071	Gali	0.025	0.058
Mobilit2	0.106	0.063	Mobilit2	0.024	0.055
Mobilit3	−0.197	0.120	Mobilit3	0.035	0.090
ADLany	−0.045	0.160	ADLany	0.417	0.140**
IADLany	−0.323	0.186	IADLany	−0.116	0.093
Eurod	−0.008	0.014	Eurod	0.018	0.010
Heartat	−0.346	0.098***	Heartat	−0.199	0.139
Stroke	0.048	0.349	Stroke	−0.223	0.208
Cholester	0.083	0.064	Cholester	0.097	0.075
Lungdis	−0.081	0.122	Lungdis	0.003	0.122
Cancer	−0.172	0.190	Cancer	−0.022	0.126
Highblpr	0.084	0.053	Highblpr	−0.015	0.057
Arthritis	−0.022	0.079	Arthritis	0.001	0.062
Diabetes	−0.286	0.106**	Diabetes	−0.093	0.152
Osteopor	0.165	0.371	Osteopor	0.161	0.089
Alzheimer's	0.000	(omitted)	Alzheimer's	0.000	(omitted)
Back	−0.004	0.051	Back	−0.032	0.053
Asthma	0.062	0.117	Asthma	−0.202	0.112
Underweight	0.000	(omitted)	Underweight	0.012	0.200
Overweight	0.026	0.047	Overweight	0.003	0.049
Obese	−0.023	0.066	Obese	0.115	0.072
Smokerform	−0.134	0.056*	Smokerform	−0.043	0.063
Smokecurr	0.018	0.050	Smokecurr	0.040	0.056
Educ_lessthHS	−0.135	0.046**	Educ_lessthHS	−0.468	0.052***
Educ_somecollege	−0.045	0.173	Educ_somecollege	−0.051	0.103
Educ_collegemore	0.067	0.071	Educ_collegemore	0.073	0.088
Married	0.110	0.054*	Married	0.015	0.061
_Cons	0.941	0.082***	_Cons	0.789	0.099***
Obs.	262		Obs.	413	

***Significant at the 1 percent level.
**Significant at the 5 percent level.
*Significant at the 10 percent level.

Table 6A.1B   Employment regressions, PVW index, precrisis waves

	Men			Women	
Variable	Coefficient	Std. err.	Variable	Coefficient	Std. err.
PVW	0.002	0.001	PVW	0.000	0.001
Educ_lesst~S	−0.112	0.046*	Educ_lesst~S	−0.457	0.050***
Educ_somec~e	0.071	0.175	Educ_somec~e	−0.065	0.101
Educ_colle~e	0.109	0.074	Educ_colle~e	0.118	0.087
Married	0.160	0.054**	Married	−0.025	0.059
_Cons	0.655	0.088***	_Cons	0.785	0.085***
Obs.	260		Obs.	407	

***Significant at the 1 percent level.
**Significant at the 5 percent level.
*Significant at the 10 percent level.

Table 6A.2A   Simulations of work capacity, all health variables, precrisis waves

	Men					Women			
Age group	No. obs.	Actual % working	Predicted % working	Estimated work capacity (%)	Age group	No. obs.	Actual % working	Predicted % working	Estimated work capacity (%)
55–59	428	52.80	82.10	29.30	55–59	552	25.54	45.80	20.26
60–64	445	20.45	78.95	58.50	60–64	582	6.53	42.77	36.24
65–69	467	6.00	71.61	65.61	65–69	513	1.75	39.74	37.99
70–74	389	1.54	62.86	61.32	70–74	364	0.00	39.01	39.01

Table 6A.2B   Simulations of work capacity, PVW index, precrisis waves

	Men					Women			
Age group	No. obs.	Actual % working	Predicted % working	Estimated work capacity (%)	Age group	Nc. obs.	Actual % working	Predicted % working	Estimated work capacity (%)
55–59	424	52.83	84.75	31.92	55–59	545	25.50	45.30	19.79
60–64	440	20.45	82.58	62.12	60–64	578	6.57	41.52	34.94
65–69	467	6.00	81.38	75.38	65–69	507	1.78	39.75	37.97
70–74	388	1.55	78.34	76.79	70–74	360	0.00	35.95	35.95

Table 6A.3A   **Work capacity by education (single regression)**

	Men, all health variables model			Men, PVW model		
Education	Actual % working	Predicted % working	Estimated work capacity (%)	Actual % working	Predicted % working	Estimated work capacity (%)
			Age 55–59			
Less than HS	41.73	73.70	32.0	41.43	78.52	37.1
More than HS	68.79	94.06	25.3	69.19	93.68	24.5
			Age 60–64			
Less than HS	17.04	71.85	54.8	17.26	77.81	60.5
More than HS	28.36	94.69	66.3	27.82	93.47	65.6
			Age 65–69			
Less than HS	3.50	65.43	61.9	3.50	76.88	73.4
More than HS	13.01	87.03	74.0	13.01	92.80	79.8
			Age 70–74			
Less than HS	1.22	58.19	57.0	1.22	75.36	74.1
More than HS	3.33	85.00	81.7	3.39	92.63	89.2

Note: Actual percent working in all health and PVW models vary due to differences in sample size.

Table 6A.3B   **Work capacity by education (single regression)**

	Women, all health variables model			Women, PVW model		
Education	Actual % working	Predicted % working	Estimated work capacity (%)	Actual % working	Predicted % working	Estimated work capacity (%)
			Age 55–59			
Less than HS	13.39	31.77	18.4	13.33	30.58	17.2
More than HS	52.63	76.98	24.4	52.35	78.04	25.7
			Age 60–64			
Less than HS	5.11	32.45	27.3	5.16	30.84	25.7
More than HS	11.36	78.48	67.1	11.36	78.12	66.8
			Age 65–69			
Less than HS	0.96	31.22	30.3	0.98	30.97	30.0
More than HS	5.15	77.77	72.6	5.15	77.61	72.5
			Age 70–74			
Less than HS	0.00	34.39	34.4	0.00	31.23	31.2
More than HS	0.00	82.00	82.0	0.00	76.47	76.5

Note: Actual percent working in all health and PVW models vary due to differences in sample size.

Table 6A.3C   Work capacity by education (regression by education group)

	Men, all health variables model			Men, PVW model		
Education	Actual % working	Predicted % working	Estimated work capacity (%)	Actual % working	Predicted % working	Estimated work capacity (%)
			Age 55–59			
Less than HS	41.73	71.44	29.7	41.43	78.97	37.5
More than HS	68.79	92.10	23.3	69.19	92.63	23.4
			Age 60–64			
Less than HS	17.04	66.64	49.6	17.26	78.58	61.3
More than HS	28.36	91.98	63.6	27.82	92.21	64.4
			Age 65–69			
Less than HS	3.50	58.61	55.1	3.50	77.83	74.3
More than HS	13.01	87.66	74.7	13.01	90.74	77.7
			Age 70–74			
Less than HS	1.22	53.27	52.1	1.22	76.46	75.2
More than HS	3.33	88.45	85.1	3.39	90.11	86.7

Note: Actual percent working in all health and PVW models vary due to differences in sample size.

Table 6A.3D   Work capacity by education (regression by education group)

	Women, all health variables model			Women, PVW model		
Education	Actual % working	Predicted % working	Estimated work capacity (%)	Actual % working	Predicted % working	Estimated work capacity (%)
			Age 55–59			
Less than HS	13.39	32.95	19.6	13.33	31.43	18.1
More than HS	52.63	77.84	25.2	52.35	76.25	23.9
			Age 60–64			
Less than HS	5.11	32.96	27.9	5.16	31.95	26.8
More than HS	11.36	80.42	69.1	11.36	74.83	63.5
			Age 65–69			
Less than HS	0.96	32.27	31.3	0.98	32.45	31.5
More than HS	5.15	82.81	77.7	5.15	76.62	71.5
			Age 70–74			
Less than HS	0.00	34.02	34.0	0.00	33.20	33.2
More than HS	0.00	82.12	82.1	0.00	74.68	74.7

Note: Actual percent working in all health and PVW models vary due to differences in sample size.

Table 6A.4A   Employment regressions, all health variables excluding those who never worked in their lives

Men 50–54			Women 50–54		
Variable	Coefficient	Std. err.	Variable	Coefficient	Std. err.
Health_vgood	–0.0086	0.0447	Health_vgood	–0.0415	0.0532
Health_good	–0.0455	0.0417	Health_good	–0.0243	0.0522
Health_fair	–0.0062	0.0572	Health_fair	–0.0874	0.0664
Health_poor	–0.4336	0.1201***	Health_poor	–0.0914	0.1027
Gali	0.0292	0.0470	Gali	–0.0615	0.0427
Mobilit2	0.0464	0.0418	Mobilit2	–0.0062	0.0414
Mobilit3	–0.0621	0.0864	Mobilit3	0.0734	0.0662
ADLany	–0.2191	0.0974*	ADLany	0.1778	0.0985
IADLany	–0.0071	0.1310	IADLany	–0.1138	0.0776
Eurod	–0.0043	0.0084	Eurod	0.0090	0.0073
Heartat	–0.3331	0.0741***	Heartat	–0.2941	0.1110**
Stroke	–0.2579	0.1221*	Stroke	–0.3366	0.1584*
Cholester	0.0677	0.0417	Cholester	0.0171	0.0511
Lungdis	–0.0694	0.0845	Lungdis	–0.0565	0.1058
Cancer	–0.2226	0.1296	Cancer	–0.0319	0.0847
Highblpr	0.0742	0.0363*	Highblpr	–0.0700	0.0429
Arthritis	–0.0380	0.0623	Arthritis	–0.0062	0.0524
Diabetes	–0.1226	0.0678	Diabetes	0.0202	0.0942
Osteopor	0.1161	0.3457	Osteopor	0.1515	0.0915
Alzheimer's	0.0000	(omitted)	Alzheimer's	0.0000	(omitted)
Back	0.0092	0.0333	Back	–0.0202	0.0374
Asthma	–0.0003	0.1093	Asthma	–0.2663	0.1158*
Underweight	0.1045	0.3230	Underweight	–0.0216	0.0911
Overweight	0.0281	0.0306	Overweight	0.0418	0.0364
Obese	–0.0864	0.0459	Obese	0.0339	0.0519
Smokerform	–0.0236	0.0363	Smokerform	–0.0805	0.0412
Smokecurr	0.0113	0.0319	Smokecurr	0.0165	0.0385
Educ_lessthHS	–0.0202	0.0326	Educ_lessthHS	–0.0837	0.0388*
Educ_somecollege	0.0736	0.0933	Educ_somecollege	0.0636	0.0662
Educ_collegemore	0.0900	0.0486	Educ_collegemore	0.0633	0.0492
Married	0.1443	0.0364***	Married	–0.0715	0.0409
Occ_bluecollar	–0.0388	0.0340	Occ_bluecollar	–0.2651	0.0486***
Occ_lowskill	–0.0635	0.0467	Occ_lowskill	–0.2124	0.0430***
_Cons	0.7993	0.0546***	_Cons	0.9680	0.0650***
Obs.	569		Obs.	704	

***Significant at the 1 percent level.
**Significant at the 5 percent level.
*Significant at the 10 percent level.

Table 6A.4B		Employment regressions, PVW index excluding those who never worked in their lives			
Men			Women		
Variable	Coefficient	Std. err.	Variable	Coefficient	Std. err.
PVW	0.0020	0.0006**	PVW	0.0012	0.0006*
Educ_lessthHS	−0.0603	0.0310	Educ_lessthHS	−0.1942	0.0362***
Educ_somecollege	0.0951	0.0957	Educ_somecollege	0.0502	0.0678
Educ_collegemore	0.1052	0.0497*	Educ_collegemore	0.1033	0.0499*
Married	0.1571	0.0363***	Married	−0.1152	0.0420**
_Cons	0.6070	0.0614***	_Cons	0.8325	0.0616***
Obs.	566		Obs.	697	

***Significant at the 1 percent level.
**Significant at the 5 percent level.
*Significant at the 10 percent level.

Table 6A.5A Simulations of work capacity, excluding those who never worked in their lives, all health variables

		Men					Women		
Age group	No. obs.	Actual % working	Predicted % working	Estimated work capacity (%)	Age group	No. obs.	Actual % working	Predicted % working	Estimated work capacity (%)
55–59	928	65.09	85.65	20.56	55–59	851	51.59	71.37	19.79
60–64	1,028	26.65	84.03	57.38	60–64	966	14.80	68.53	53.73
65–69	1,103	4.90	79.11	74.22	65–69	842	2.85	65.48	62.63
70–74	1,003	2.30	76.09	73.79	70–74	689	0.44	61.41	60.97

Table 6A.5B   Simulations of work capacity, excluding those who never worked in their lives, PVW index

	Men					Women				
Age group	No. obs.	Actual % working	Predicted % working	Estimated work capacity (%)		Age group	Nc. obs.	Actual % working	Predicted % working	Estimated work capacity (%)
55–59	921	65.04	86.45	21.41		55–59	844	51.54	71.46	19.92
60–64	1,019	26.79	85.18	58.39		60–64	958	14.82	69.17	54.34
65–69	1,101	4.90	82.77	77.87		65–69	837	2.87	67.36	64.49
70–74	998	2.30	80.98	78.68		70–74	685	0.44	65.67	65.23

References

Bohacek, R, L. Crespo, P. Mira, and J. Pijoan-Mas. 2015. "The Educational Gradient in Life Expectancy in Europe: Preliminary Evidence from SHARE." In *First Results Book for the Fifth Wave of SHARE*, edited by A. Börsch-Supan, H. Litwin, M. Mych, and G. Weber. Berlin: De Gruyter.

Brugiavini, A., and F. Peracchi. 2012. "Health Status, Welfare Programs Participation and Labor Force Activity in Italy." In *Historical Trends in Mortality and Health, Employment, and Disability Insurance Participation and Reforms*, edited by David A. Wise, 175–216. Chicago: University of Chicago Press.

———. 2016. "Health Status, Disability Insurance, and Incentives to Exit the Labor Force in Italy. Evidence from SHARE." In *Social Security Programs and Retirement around the World: Disability Insurance Programs and Retirement*, edited by David A. Wise, 411–54. Chicago: University of Chicago Press.

Cutler, David M., Ellen Meara, and Seth Richards-Shubik. 2012. "Health and Work Capacity of Older Adults: Estimates and Implications for Social Security Policy." Unpublished Manuscript. Available at SSRN: http://ssrn.com/abstract=2577858.

Cutler, David M., Kaushik Ghosh, and Mary Beth Landrum. 2014. "Evidence for Significant Compression of Morbidity in the Elderly US Population." In *Discoveries in the Economics of Aging*, edited by David A. Wise. Chicago: University of Chicago Press.

Milligan, Kevin S., and David A. Wise. 2012. "Health and Work at Older Ages: Using Mortality to Assess the Capacity to Work across Countries." NBER Working Paper no. 18229, Cambridge, MA.

Poterba, James, Steve Venti, and David A. Wise. 2013. "Health, Education, and the Post-Retirement Evolution of Household Assets." *Journal of Human Capital* 7 (4): 297–339.

7
Health Capacity to Work at Older Ages
Evidence from Japan

Emiko Usui, Satoshi Shimizutani, and Takashi Oshio

The combination of a shrinking labor force and large fiscal deficits is an urgent and common challenge among developed countries. The main driving force for both of these serious concerns is the rapid speed of population aging: it dampens labor force participation with continuing lower fertility and expands fiscal deficits under a pay-as-you-go public pension program. A natural and simultaneous solution for these two policy challenges is to encourage older adults to continue to work for as long as possible in terms of age. Thus, the main visible target of recent pension reforms has been to raise pension eligibility ages, although pension reforms are often accompanied by revisions in a variety of other aspects such as coverage, adequacy, and sustainability, as well as work incentives (OECD 2013). Indeed, many developed countries have implemented or are planning to execute public pension reforms to extend the normal retirement (i.e., pensionable) age.

Japan is also confronted with a declining labor force and enormous fiscal deficits, both of which are the most pronounced of the Organisation for Economic Co-operation and Development (OECD) countries. Although the labor force participation rate of those age sixty-five and older in Japan is higher than in most other developed countries, there have been many policy debates on raising the normal pensionable age. In recent years, Japan has

Emiko Usui is associate professor at the Institute of Economic Research at Hitotsubashi University. Satoshi Shimizutani is senior research fellow at Ricoh Institute of Sustainability and Business. Takashi Oshio is professor at the Institute of Economic Research at Hitotsubashi University

This chapter is part of the National Bureau of Economic Research's International Social Security (ISS) project, which is supported by the National Institute on Aging. We thank the members of the other country teams in the ISS project for helpful comments and suggestions. For acknowledgments, sources of research support, and disclosure of the authors' material financial relationships, if any, please see http://www.nber.org/chapters/c13744.ack.

begun extending the eligible age for pensions. For male pensioners, since 2001, the eligible age for the flat-rate component increased from sixty by one year for every three years to reach sixty-five years in 2013. Furthermore, the eligible age for the wage-proportional component has been scheduled to rise from 2013 by one year for every three years to reach sixty-five years in 2025. For female pensioners, while maintaining a five-year lag relative to that for men, the eligible age for the flat-rate benefit started to be raised in 2006, and that for the wage-proportional benefit will start to be raised in 2018 in the same manner (Oshio, Oishi, and Shimizutani 2011).

However, there is a possibility that a simple extension of the eligible pensionable age may not extend work lives because not all older adults are necessarily able to work even if they are willing to. In particular, one major possible constraint on working is health, either physical or mental, which may also be associated with declining cognitive function. If this is the case, a simple extension of eligible pension age, which considers fiscal consolidation and ignores heterogeneity among older adults, may result in increasing inequality between healthy and unhealthy individuals and impair the overall living standard of older adults.

Keeping heterogeneity in health among older adults in mind, this chapter examines the work capacity of older Japanese—that is, the extent to which they can potentially extend their work lives—based on two analytic methods. Specifically, we first employ the Milligan-Wise method, which examines how much people with a given mortality rate today could work if they were to work as much as those with the same mortality rate worked in the past (Milligan and Wise 2012). For this analysis, we use the aggregated data from Population Census and Life Tables from 1975 to 2010, and focus on men, because the diversity of women's occupational statuses makes it difficult to interpret their association with health.

Second, we apply the Cutler et al. method, which examines how much people with a given level of health could work if they were to work as much as their younger counterparts in similar health (Cutler, Meara, and Richards-Shubik 2012). For this analysis, we use microdata from the Japanese Study on Aging and Retirement (JSTAR) to estimate the relationship between health and employment for people age fifty-one to fifty-four, and use this association, along with the actual characteristics of older people age fifty-five to seventy-four, to simulate the latter's capacity to work based on health. Further, we examine whether health capacity to work varies by education group.

Results from both of these methods underscore a large work capacity among older people in Japan. The Milligan-Wise method shows that the amount of projected additional work capacity would be 3.7 years if we use the employment-mortality relationship that existed in 1975 as a basis for comparison. This amount would be 2.2 years if we use 1995 as the base year instead. The results obtained by the Cutler et al. method suggest that roughly an additional one in five men and women age sixty to sixty-four and one in two men and women age sixty-five to sixty-nine could be employed, relative to the share working today, based on their own health profile and the estimated relationship between health and employment for younger workers. Finally, our analysis by education group finds somewhat higher work capacity for more educated individuals than less educated ones when they are at age sixty-five and above.

The remainder of this chapter is organized in the following manner. Section 7.1 provides a brief overview of trends in labor force participation and health in Japan. Sections 7.2 and 7.3 estimate health capacity to work, based on the Milligan-Wise and Cutler et al. methods, respectively. Finally, section 7.4 concludes.

7.1   Trends in Labor Force Participation and Health

Figures 7.1 and 7.2 depict the trends of labor force participation rates for Japanese men and women, respectively, between 1970 and 2014. For men age fifty-five to sixty-four, the participation rate has stayed between 80 and 90 percent with minor cyclical fluctuations. In contrast, participation for

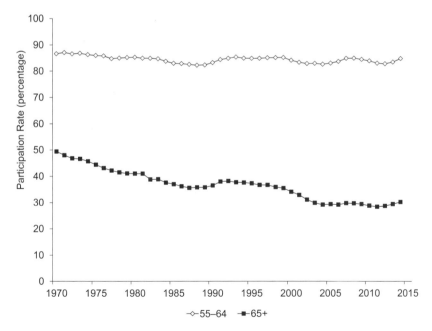

Fig. 7.1   Men's labor force participation, ages fifty-five to sixty-four and sixty-five and older (1970–2014)

Source: Statistics Bureau, Labor Force Survey.

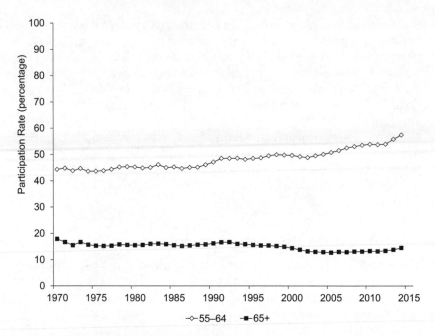

Fig. 7.2   Women's labor force participation, ages fifty-five to sixty-four and sixty-five and older (1970–2014)
Source: Statistics Bureau, Labor Force Survey.

men age sixty-five and older has been on a long-term downtrend; however, it stopped declining early in the twenty-first century, presumably reflecting a gradual increase in the eligible age for pension benefits since 2001. Oshio, Oishi, and Shimizutani (2011) showed that a series of pension reforms since the mid-1980s has reduced disincentives to work by making pension benefits less generous. During the past forty-four years, however, men's participation has still dropped remarkably: from 49 percent in 1970 to 30 percent in 2014.

Labor force participation trends for women show a different evolution. Participation among women age fifty-five to sixty-four has been steadily rising from 44 percent in 1977 to 57 percent in 2014, while for women age sixty-five and older, participation has remained almost flat during the same period, stabilizing at 13 to 14 percent in recent years.

Figure 7.3 depicts the trends in mortality and self-assessed health (SAH) for men age fifty to seventy-five over the past decades. The data on mortality and SAH are based on the Life Tables and the Comprehensive Surveys of Living Conditions, respectively, both released by the Ministry of Health, Labour and Welfare (MHLW). The figure first confirms downward shifts in age-mortality curves over time. The mortality rate was 0.8 percent for men age fifty-five in 1975–79, whereas that mortality rate is not reached until age

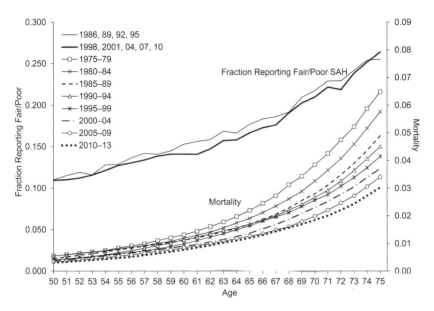

Fig. 7.3   SAH and mortality for men age fifty to seventy-five

sixty in 2010–13. Similarly, men age sixty-five in 1975–79 had a mortality rate of 2.2 percent, a rate that applied to men age seventy-two in 2010–13.

SAH, which is depicted in the upper part of the figure, also improved between 1986 and 2010. We compare the averages of the fractions reporting fair/poor SAH for 1986–95 and 1998–2010, respectively, because the original SAH data are very noisy due to small sample sizes. The curve for 1998–2010 is generally located below that for 1986–95, with the fraction reporting fair/poor SAH in 1986–95 corresponding to that for an age two or three years younger in 1998–2010.

Taken as a whole, figure 7.3 confirms that health in terms of both mortality and SAH at any given age has improved over recent decades, while figure 7.1 shows that older men's labor force participation has been stabilizing since the middle of the first decade of the twenty-first century after declining gradually. We address how much individuals today could work based on the employment-mortality relationship of the past in the following section.

7.2   Estimating Health Capacity to Work Using the
Milligan-Wise Method

Using the Milligan-Wise method, we estimate an individuals' ability to work at older ages based on the relationship between mortality and employment that existed at an earlier point in time along with current mortality

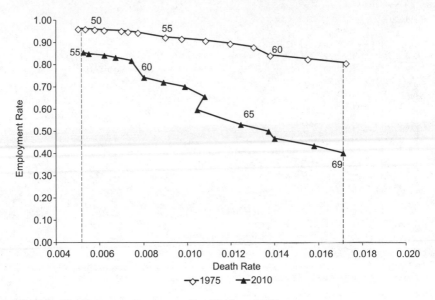

Fig. 7.4   **Employment versus mortality (2010 vs. 1975)**

data in Japan. The mortality and employment data used for this analysis
come from the Life Tables released by the MHLW and Population Censuses released by the Statistics Bureau. The Population Census is conducted
every five years, and we use the data for 1975, 1995, and 2010. We draw an
employment-mortality curve, which displays the employment rate at each
level of mortality for a given year, and repeat this for other years, making
some calculations based on comparisons of the different curves. We focus
on men only for this analysis.

Figure 7.4 compares the employment-mortality curves for men in 2010
and in 1975. In 2010, the one-year mortality rate for fifty-five-year-old men
was about 0.5 percent and the employment rate at this age was 86 percent.
In 1975, forty-nine-year-old men had a mortality rate of 0.5 percent, while
the mortality rate for fifty-five-year-olds was 0.9 percent. In 1975, the labor
force participation rate for forty-nine-year-olds was 93 percent. Thus, if men
in 2010 had the same employment rate as did men in 1975 with the same
mortality rate, the employment rate of fifty-five-year-olds would have been
7 percentage points higher.

We extend this exercise through age sixty-nine. Table 7.1 shows how much
more men in 2010 could have worked over the age range fifty-five to sixty-
nine if they had worked as much as men with the same mortality rate worked
in 1975. At age fifty-five, an additional 11 percent of men could have worked,
which generates an average 0.11 additional work years (one additional year
for 10.7 percent of fifty-five-year-olds). At age fifty-six, an additional 11.2

Table 7.1   **Additional employment capacity in 2010, using 1975 employment-mortality relationship**

Age	Death rate in 2010 (%)	Employment rate in 2010 (%)	Employment rate in 1975 at same death rate (%)	Additional employment capacity (%)
55	0.52	85.7	96.4	10.7
56	0.55	85.0	96.2	11.2
57	0.62	84.3	95.8	11.4
58	0.67	83.3	95.6	12.3
59	0.74	81.9	95.0	13.1
60	0.80	74.4	94.5	20.1
61	0.89	72.2	92.7	20.5
62	0.98	70.3	91.9	21.6
63	1.08	65.8	91.1	25.4
64	1.04	59.8	91.4	31.6
65	1.24	53.2	89.1	35.9
66	1.37	50.1	84.7	34.6
67	1.40	46.9	84.2	37.3
68	1.58	43.7	82.5	38.8
69	1.71	40.4	81.1	40.7
Total years		10.0		3.7

percent of men could have worked for an additional 0.11 work years. We repeat this calculation at each subsequent age through age sixty-nine and cumulated the amounts to obtain an estimated total amount of additional employment capacity of 3.7 years, which is equivalent to integrating between the two curves from one vertical line to the next in figure 7.4. As the average length of employment between ages fifty-five and sixty-nine in 2010 is 10.0 years, an additional 3.7 years would represent a 37 percent increase over the baseline year of work.

The results depend on the choice of year of comparison. In figure 7.5, we replace 1975 with 1995 as the base year. The mortality-employment rate curve for 1995 still lies above that for 2010, but the gap between the two curves is less than that between the 2010 and 1975 curves in figure 7.4. Using 1995 as the comparison year, the estimated additional employment capacity from ages fifty-five to sixty-nine is 2.2 years, substantially smaller than the estimate of 3.7 years that we obtain when we use 1975 as the comparison year.

We repeat this calculation using 1980, 1985, 1990, 2000, and 2005 as the comparison years. Figure 7.6 depicts the estimated additional employment capacity for each comparison year. When we look back over a longer period of time, the estimated additional capacity is much larger: from 0.4 years for 2005 to 3.7 years for 1975. This evolution reflects both improving mortality and declining employment, as seen in figures 7.1 and 7.3, respectively.

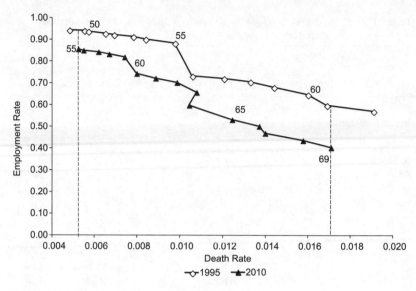

Fig. 7.5   Employment versus mortality (2010 vs. 1995)

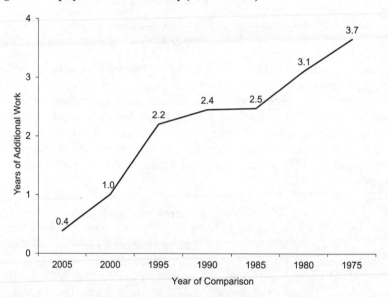

Fig. 7.6   Estimated additional employment capacity by year of comparison

It is also of great interest to estimate work capacity using other measures of health. In figures 7.7 and 7.8, we replicate the approach used in figure 7.4 with SAH and activity limitations in place of mortality. Data on SAH and activity limitations are available from the Comprehensive Surveys of Living Conditions, which has been conducted by the MHLW every three years since

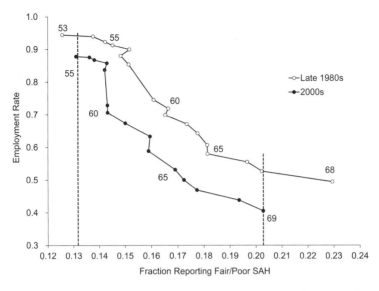

Fig. 7.7   Employment versus SAH (late 1980s and early twenty-first century)

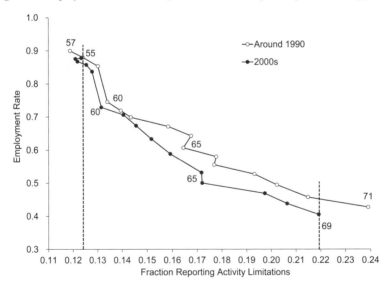

Fig. 7.8   Employment versus daily activity limitations (around 1990 and early twenty-first century)

1986. In figures 7.7 and 7.8, the horizontal axis reflects the share of individuals who report themselves to be in fair or poor health (figure 7.7) or the share of those who report that they have any activity limitations (figure 7.8). Due to limited sample sizes and data discontinuity, we average data over the late 1980s (1986 and 1989) and early twenty-first century (2001, 2004, 2007, and

2010) for SAH, and around the 1990s (1989 and 1992) and over the early twenty-first century (2001, 2004, 2007, and 2010) for activity limitations.

These two figures present the same patterns of health improvement over time as already shown for mortality in figure 7.4. For example, in the first decade of the twenty-first century, 13.2 percent of fifty-five-year-olds were in fair or poor health. The employment rate would rise to 94 percent from 88 percent in the early twenty-first century if they were to work in the late 1980s with the same SAH status. For activity limitations, there are no substantial differences among the younger individuals (age sixty-two and younger), but the older individuals worked less in the first decade of the twenty-first century than around the 1990s, even with the same degree of activity limitations.

We can estimate work capacity, basing our calculations on these employment-health curves in the same manner shown in table 7.1. We find that the additional capacity between ages fifty-five and sixty-nine is 2.0 years using SAH (comparing the late 1980s and the first decade of the twenty-first century) and 1.3 years using activity limitations (comparing around the 1990s and the early twenty-first century). These values are roughly comparable to those obtained using mortality rates as a measure of health, which are illustrated in figure 7.6.

In conclusion, estimates based on the Milligan-Wise method suggest a significant amount of additional work capacity. We estimate that the additional capacity from ages fifty-five to sixty-nine is 3.7 years using the 1975 employment-mortality curve as a point of comparison, or 2.2 years using 1995 as the base year.

7.3   Estimating Health Capacity to Work Using the Cutler et al. Method

In this section, we apply the second method of estimating health capacity to work, that is, the Cutler et al. method, to the elderly Japanese population. For this method, we first run regression models to estimate the relationship between health and employment, for workers age fifty-one to fifty-four, who are sufficiently young that their employment decisions are not affected by the availability of social security benefits. In the second step, we simulate the health capacity to work of individuals age fifty-five to seventy-four, by combining the regression coefficients with their actual characteristics.

We use the data from the Japanese Study on Aging and Retirement (JSTAR). The JSTAR is a family survey similar to those in other countries such as the Health and Retirement Study (HRS) in the United States, the English Longitudinal Survey on Ageing (ELSA) in the United Kingdom, and the Survey on Health, Aging and Retirement in Europe (SHARE) in continental Europe.

In 2007, JSTAR conducted the first wave of data collection for the baseline from five municipalities (Takikawa city in Hokkaido Prefecture, Sendai city in Miyagi Prefecture, Adachi ward in Tokyo Metropolis, Shirakawa town in Gifu Prefecture, and Kanazawa city in Ishikawa Prefecture). Then, in 2009, JSTAR conducted the second wave of data collection; this involved reinterviewing respondents in the first wave in the five municipalities and beginning to collect baseline data from two new municipalities (Naha city in Okinawa Prefecture and Tosu city in Saga Prefecture). Thereafter, JSTAR implemented the third wave to collect data from third interviews with respondents in the second round in the initial five municipalities, second interviews with respondents in the first round in two municipalities, and baseline interviews for new samples in three new municipalities (Chofu city in Tokyo Metropolis, Tondabayashi city in Osaka Prefecture, and Hiroshima city in Hiroshima Prefecture).

The sample at the baseline in each municipality is males and females age fifty to seventy-four years, who were randomly chosen from household registration. The sample size at the baseline is approximately 8,000, and the average response rate at the baseline is approximately 60 percent. We pool all the observations from first to third waves in the estimation. We have a sample of roughly 647 male and 690 female person-year observations for the regressions; a further 5,157 male and 5,194 female person-year observations are used in our simulations of work capacity.

We estimate a linear probability model to predict a binary variable of employment, which is equal to 1 if the individual is employed, by a set of health measures, including dummy variables for self-assessed health status, limitations on physical activity, limitations on activities of daily living (ADLs) and instrumental activities of daily living (IADLs), individual health conditions, being over- or underweight, and being a current or former smoker. We also include variables for educational attainment, marital status, and pension coverage as explanatory variables.

We estimate an alternative version of this regression model where the full set of health variables is replaced by a single health index value, developed using the approach described in Poterba, Venti, and Wise (2013). We construct a health index based on twenty-three questions, including self-assessed health diagnoses, functional limitations, medical care usage, and other health indicators. To this end, we obtain the first principal component of a set of health measures. The estimated coefficients from the analysis are then used to predict a percentile score for each respondent, referred to as the health index.

Tables 7.2A and 7.2B show summary statistics for the male and female samples. The share of employed men remains above 90 percent at ages fifty-five to fifty-nine, gradually declines in the sixties, and then reaches to 36 percent at ages seventy to seventy-four. Employment rates for women are 20–30 percentage points lower in each age group. The health measures tend to be stable between ages fifty to sixty-nine, but worsen after that age. The share of men in fair or poor health rises gradually from 10.8 percent at ages fifty-one to fifty-four, 12.4 percent at ages fifty-five to fifty-nine, 15.6 percent

Table 7.2A　　　　Summary statistics, men

	Age group				
	51–54	55–59	60–64	65–69	70–74
Employed	0.960	0.934	0.758	0.531	0.362
Health: Excellent	0.305	0.269	0.302	0.218	0.139
Health: Very good	0.229	0.261	0.225	0.261	0.251
Health: Good	0.358	0.346	0.318	0.344	0.326
Health: Fair	0.093	0.102	0.130	0.138	0.230
Health: Poor	0.015	0.022	0.026	0.039	0.054
Physical limits: One	0.032	0.034	0.044	0.098	0.158
Physical limits: Many	0.011	0.026	0.038	0.054	0.080
ADL: Any	0.027	0.028	0.041	0.052	0.062
IADL: Any	0.021	0.019	0.043	0.051	0.075
CESD score	12.05	11.86	11.12	10.79	11.63
Heart disease	0.087	0.119	0.130	0.181	0.229
Stroke	0.015	0.026	0.050	0.095	0.088
Psychiatric condition	0.033	0.026	0.009	0.013	0.009
Lung disease	0.015	0.015	0.026	0.030	0.026
Cancer	0.029	0.031	0.084	0.089	0.073
High blood pressure	0.367	0.429	0.484	0.458	0.495
Arthritis	0.040	0.022	0.022	0.040	0.050
Diabetes	0.167	0.207	0.186	0.238	0.204
Weight: Under	0.031	0.019	0.022	0.025	0.037
Weight: Over	0.285	0.254	0.267	0.265	0.264
Weight: Obese	0.038	0.034	0.016	0.021	0.018
Smoker: Former	0.341	0.402	0.402	0.470	0.534
Smoker: Current	0.412	0.392	0.352	0.270	0.204
Education: HS dropout	0.110	0.164	0.233	0.319	0.430
Education: HS graduate	0.370	0.465	0.441	0.438	0.375
Education: Some college	0.102	0.094	0.053	0.046	0.039
Education: College grad	0.417	0.276	0.273	0.198	0.156
Married	0.850	0.880	0.909	0.927	0.917
Employee pension insurance	0.729	0.714	0.793	0.761	0.718
National pension insurance	0.257	0.275	0.313	0.244	0.277
Chofu	0.038	0.036	0.058	0.063	0.060
Sendai	0.138	0.159	0.121	0.132	0.098
Kanazawa	0.136	0.153	0.167	0.102	0.110
Takikawa	0.040	0.071	0.104	0.101	0.110
Shirakawa	0.150	0.152	0.071	0.114	0.127
Adachi	0.119	0.116	0.105	0.139	0.133
Naha	0.138	0.127	0.090	0.088	0.125
Tosu	0.089	0.071	0.097	0.103	0.092
Hiroshima	0.097	0.079	0.125	0.108	0.089
Tondabayshi	0.055	0.035	0.061	0.048	0.056
No. obs.	528	743	702	725	663

Note: Chofu, Sendai, and others indicate the names of municipalities.

Table 7.2B   Summary statistics, women

	Age group				
	51–54	55–59	60–64	65–69	70–74
Employed	0.727	0.640	0.476	0.283	0.169
Health: Excellent	0.283	0.267	0.266	0.183	0.153
Health: Very good	0.264	0.266	0.236	0.221	0.237
Health: Good	0.330	0.342	0.338	0.375	0.332
Health: Fair	0.098	0.104	0.139	0.178	0.211
Health: Poor	0.024	0.021	0.021	0.044	0.067
Physical limits: One	0.055	0.066	0.077	0.163	0.265
Physical limits: Many	0.047	0.055	0.063	0.114	0.108
ADL: Any	0.022	0.039	0.044	0.063	0.085
IADL: Any	0.017	0.023	0.036	0.059	0.076
CESD score	12.11	11.85	11.55	11.43	11.80
Heart disease	0.068	0.108	0.104	0.140	0.188
Stroke	0.004	0.026	0.042	0.045	0.052
Psychiatric condition	0.056	0.054	0.038	0.047	0.042
Lung disease	0.015	0.008	0.022	0.019	0.014
Cancer	0.064	0.062	0.084	0.063	0.057
High blood pressure	0.293	0.365	0.420	0.453	0.509
Arthritis	0.109	0.113	0.102	0.112	0.138
Diabetes	0.060	0.087	0.106	0.140	0.129
Weight: Under	0.087	0.082	0.066	0.055	0.049
Weight: Over	0.178	0.173	0.225	0.242	0.240
Weight: Obese	0.032	0.024	0.019	0.030	0.036
Smoker: Former	0.085	0.082	0.084	0.077	0.065
Smoker: Current	0.156	0.124	0.104	0.053	0.061
Education: HS dropout	0.078	0.153	0.250	0.374	0.481
Education: HS graduate	0.430	0.481	0.508	0.459	0.382
Education: Some college	0.347	0.282	0.180	0.134	0.109
Education: College grad	0.146	0.085	0.062	0.033	0.028
Married	0.822	0.815	0.820	0.771	0.727
Employee pension insurance	0.470	0.477	0.555	0.372	0.319
National pension insurance	0.526	0.500	0.634	0.565	0.593
Chofu	0.062	0.050	0.063	0.052	0.044
Sendai	0.121	0.131	0.126	0.122	0.111
Kanazawa	0.180	0.166	0.147	0.124	0.113
Takikawa	0.033	0.075	0.068	0.078	0.102
Shirakawa	0.092	0.079	0.073	0.098	0.162
Adachi	0.105	0.116	0.122	0.137	0.121
Naha	0.145	0.174	0.098	0.127	0.141
Tosu	0.069	0.066	0.104	0.105	0.082
Hiroshima	0.133	0.094	0.141	0.110	0.068
Tondabayshi	0.060	0.050	0.058	0.048	0.056
No. obs.	579	724	778	735	733

Note: Chofu, Sendai, and others indicate the names of municipalities.

at ages sixty to sixty-four, 17.7 percent at ages sixty-five to sixty-nine, to 28.4 percent at ages seventy to seventy-four. The values for women are similar. The share of men with one or more limits on their physical activity gradually rises from 4.3 percent at ages fifty-one to fifty-four, 6.0 percent at ages fifty-five to fifty-nine, 8.2 percent at ages sixty to sixty-five, 15.2 percent at ages sixty-five to sixty-nine, to 23.8 percent at ages seventy to seventy-four. Values for women are substantially higher with a somewhat steeper gradient: from 10.2 percent at ages fifty to fifty-four to 36.7 percent at ages seventy to seventy-four. The share of individuals with limitations in ADLs gradually rises from 2.7 percent to 6.2 percent for men across the five age categories, and from 2.2 to 8.5 percent for women; the share with limitations in IADLs show a similar trend, rising from 2 to 8 percent for both men and women. The share of individuals with diagnosed medical conditions also rises with age. High blood pressure is one of the most common issues, rising from 36.7 percent at ages fifty-one to fifty-four to 49.5 percent at ages seventy to seventy-four for men and from 29.3 percent at ages fifty-one to fifty-four to 50.9 percent at ages seventy to seventy-four for women. More serious health conditions such as cancer and stroke also rise with age. Overall, the health conditions of the elderly decline gradually with no sharp deterioration between the ages of fifty and seventy-four.

Tables 7.3A and 7.3B provide the estimation results of the regression models for all health variables and for the health index versions of our model, respectively. Table 7.3A reveals that there are modestly significant effects of several health variables on employment. For example, relative to men in excellent health, men in poor health are 36 percentage points less likely to be employed; for women, the value is 31 points. The CESD (Center for Epidemiologic Studies Depression Scale) and psychiatric problems modestly reduce the probability of employment. Compared with men, health variables are more closely associated with employment for women. Having limits on physical activity and experiencing cancer reduce the probability of employment by more than 20 percentage points. Table 7.3B shows a close association between the health index and employment, consistent with the results in table 7.3A. A 10-percentage-point increase in the index raises the probability of employment by 0.9 percentage points for men and by 3.9 percentage points for women. We focus on the results from table 7.3B in what follows.

Table 7.4 summarizes the simulation results: for men and women in five-year age groups from age fifty-five to seventy-four, it shows the share employed, the predicted share employed (calculated by combining the coefficients from the regression analysis and the actual characteristics of these individuals), and the difference between these, which we term the estimated additional work capacity. On the basis of the health index results (right-hand part), we predict the share of men employed to be 96 percent at ages fifty-five to fifty-nine and sixty to sixty-four, 94 percent at ages sixty-five to sixty-nine and seventy to seventy-four. The projected share of men employed

Table 7.3A   **Employment regressions, all health variables**

Variable	Men 51–54		Women 51–54	
	Coefficient	Std. error	Coefficient	Std. error
Health: Very good	−0.0036	0.0164	−0.0446	0.0467
Health: Good	0.0021	0.0151	−0.0338	0.0446
Health: Fair	−0.0060	0.0413	−0.1384	0.0732*
Health: Poor	−0.3605	0.2017*	−0.3055	0.1370**
Physical limits: One	−0.0904	0.1300	−0.2326	0.0951**
Physical limits: Many	−0.1249	0.0990	−0.2688	0.1015***
IADL: Any	0.0079	0.0859	−0.1258	0.1589
CESD score	−0.0035	0.0018*	−0.0005	0.0024
Heart disease	−0.0153	0.0387	0.0330	0.1105
Stroke	−0.1136	0.2015	0.4090	0.0956***
Psychiatric condition	−0.2625	0.1447*	−0.1683	0.1267
Lung disease	−0.0557	0.1140	−0.0429	0.2331
Cancer	0.0894	0.0756	−0.2028	0.1232*
High blood pressure	0.0221	0.0221	0.0388	0.0543
Arthritis	0.0045	0.0811	−0.1431	0.0904
Diabetes	0.0132	0.0350	0.1878	0.1021*
Weight: Under	−0.0186	0.0533	0.1210	0.0456***
Weight: Over	0.0137	0.0169	−0.0218	0.0514
Weight: Obese	−0.0054	0.0450	−0.1374	0.1076
Smoker: Former	−0.0054	0.0174	0.0731	0.0612
Smoker: Current	−0.0153	0.0188	0.0674	0.0463
Education: HS dropout	−0.0002	0.0289	−0.1194	0.0682*
Education: Some college	−0.0127	0.0292	−0.0487	0.0424
Education: College grad	0.0243	0.0191	0.0432	0.0526
Married	0.0504	0.0328	−0.1315	0.0416***
No. obs.	631		690	

Notes: Regressions include indicators for missing variables. All regressions control for municipalities and survey years.
***Significant at the 1 percent level.
**Significant at the 5 percent level.
*Significant at the 10 percent level.

Table 7.3B   **Employment regressions, PVW health index**

Variable	Men 51–54		Women 51–54	
	Coefficient	Std. error	Coefficient	Std. error
PVW index	0.0009	0.0004**	0.0039	0.0007***
Education: HS dropout	−0.0029	0.0321	−0.2092	0.0734***
Education: Some college	−0.0051	0.0306	−0.0497	0.0415
Education: College grad	0.0343	0.0183*	0.0194	0.0526
Married	0.0570	0.0316*	−0.0954	0.0432**
No. obs.	647		685	

Note: Municipalities and survey years are controlled for.
***Significant at the 1 percent level.
**Significant at the 5 percent level.
*Significant at the 10 percent level.

Table 7.4   Simulations of work capacity

Age group	Use all health variables				Use PVW health index			
	No. obs.	Actual % working	Predicted % working	Estimated work capacity (%)	No. obs.	Actual % working	Predicted % working	Estimated work capacity (%)
Men								
55–59	1,235	93.3	94.8	1.6	1,211	94.0	96.2	2.2
60–64	1,355	79.0	94.9	15.9	1,228	79.7	95.8	16.0
65–69	1,297	53.3	93.6	40.3	1,129	54.3	94.4	40.2
70–74	1,270	36.4	91.4	55.0	1,054	37.6	93.5	56.0
Women								
55–59	1,167	65.6	74.7	9.1	1,141	65.6	73.2	7.6
60–64	1,366	50.3	73.9	23.6	1,207	49.9	69.9	20.1
65–69	1,299	32.6	68.8	36.3	1,107	33.2	64.1	30.9
70–74	1,362	19.5	65.1	45.6	1,136	18.8	60.6	41.7

declines, albeit modestly, with age, because health declines with age and employment is modestly related to health as shown in our regression results. However, the share of men actually working declines more quickly with age than do our predictions, from 94 percent at ages fifty-five to fifty-nine to 80 percent, 54 percent, and 38 percent in the older age groups. As a result, the estimated capacity to work is substantial and rises sharply with age, from 2 percent at ages fifty-five to fifty-nine to 16 percent at ages sixty to sixty-four, 40 percent at ages sixty-five to sixty-nine, and 56 percent at ages seventy to seventy-four. Results using the model including individual health variables (left-hand part) are quite similar. For women, both the predicted and actual share working are somewhat lower than those for men. Their work capacity is estimated to be 8 percent, 20 percent, 31 percent, and 42 percent across the four age groups. The numbers are somewhat higher for younger groups and lower for older ones, compared with the cases for men. The share of individuals working and additional work capacity are depicted in figures 7.9 and 7.10 for men and women, respectively.

We can compare these results with those obtained using the Milligan-Wise method. As seen in table 7.1, that method suggested that employment could be 20–32 percentage points higher at ages sixty to sixty-four and 36–41 percentage points higher at ages sixty-five to sixty-nine if people today worked as much as people with the same mortality rate worked in 1975. These values are slightly higher and are affected by the choice of base year,

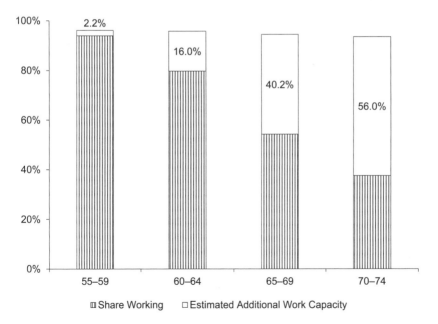

Fig. 7.9   Share of JSTAR men working and additional work capacity by age

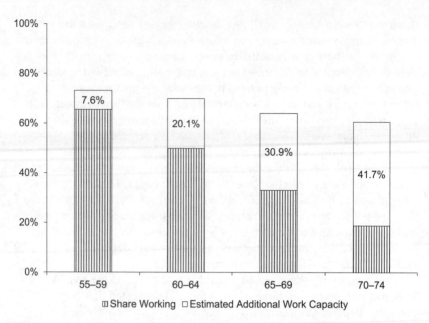

Fig. 7.10   Share of JSTAR women working and additional work capacity by age

but it is noteworthy that they are in the same ballpark as the 16 percentage points at ages sixty to sixty-four and 40 percent points at ages sixty-five to sixty-nine found here in the Cutler et al. method.

Finally, we augment our basic results with an analysis that estimates work capacity separately by education, considering the possibility that the ability to work longer depends on educational attainment. We reestimate the regression model separately by education group. It might be the case that workers with less education are concentrated in blue-collar jobs where it is more difficult to continue working once one experiences a health problem than it would be in the white-collar jobs held by more highly educated workers.

Tables 7.5A and 7.5B, along with figures 7.11 and 7.12, present our simulation results of work capacity by education group for men and women, respectively. As seen in table 7.5A, the actual and predicted share working do not vary substantially by education group except for ages sixty-five to sixty-nine. More interestingly, we observe no clear tendency for the less educated to have a smaller estimated additional work capacity from either the model using all health variables or the one using the health index. There is no clear tendency for women, either, as seen in table 7.5B. These results are confirmed by figures 7.11 and 7.12.

However, we cannot rule out the risk that estimation results are biased through limited sample sizes. We condense the four education groups into two—that is, high school or below and any college—and reestimate work

Table 7.5A **Work capacity by education (regression by education group)**

	Men, all health variables model			Men, PVW model		
Education	Actual % working	Predicted % working	Estimated work capacity (%)	Actual % working	Predicted % working	Estimated work capacity (%)
			Age 55–59			
< High school	92.2	99.9	7.7	93.7	93.5	–0.2
High school	93.1	93.7	0.5	93.1	94.8	1.8
Some college	99.2	98.1	–1.1	99.1	99.2	0.1
College grad	94.8	98.3	3.5	95.3	97.7	2.4
			Age 60–64			
< High school	81.4	101.9	20.5	79.4	89.1	9.7
High school	76.6	95.6	19.1	77.9	95.4	17.5
Some college	83.3	92.7	9.3	84.5	94.8	10.3
College grad	81.2	97.7	16.6	81.3	97.5	16.2
			Age 65–69			
< High school	60.3	97.9	37.6	60.1	87.0	27.0
High school	50.4	95.8	45.4	52.0	94.6	42.4
Some college	47.8	86.7	38.9	46.9	92.1	45.2
College grad	47.5	97.4	49.9	48.3	96.7	48.5
			Age 70–74			
< High school	38.6	97.1	58.5	38.7	84.8	46.1
High school	35.0	92.9	57.9	35.1	93.7	58.6
Some college	31.6	82.2	50.6	39.1	96.5	57.4
College grad	38.4	97.9	59.5	40.9	96.0	55.1

Note: Actual percent working in all health and PVW models vary due to differences in sample size.

Table 7.5B **Work capacity by education (regression by education group)**

	Women, all health variables model			Women, PVW model		
Education	Actual % working	Predicted % working	Estimated work capacity (%)	Actual % working	Predicted % working	Estimated work capacity (%)
			Age 55–59			
< High school	64.8	82.5	17.7	64.5	62.9	–1.6
High school	64.3	78.5	14.1	64.3	78.2	13.9
Some college	65.6	75.0	9.4	66.0	71.8	5.8
College grad	69.0	76.9	7.9	68.6	85.5	16.9
			Age 60–64			
< High school	50.5	79.5	29.0	49.8	62.1	12.3
High school	48.8	76.7	27.9	49.2	76.2	27.1
Some college	54.5	77.0	22.5	53.2	70.3	17.1
College grad	46.6	72.5	25.9	46.6	78.9	32.3
			Age 65–69			
< High school	34.1	77.7	43.6	33.9	57.3	23.4
High school	32.4	73.2	40.8	32.3	74.1	41.8
Some college	32.7	70.4	37.7	31.2	63.9	32.7
College grad	33.3	73.3	40.0	35.9	81.6	45.7
			Age 70–74			
< High school	19.1	78.4	59.2	17.7	51.7	34.0
High school	22.0	71.9	50.0	21.0	73.8	52.8
Some college	16.7	73.4	56.7	16.4	61.4	45.0
College grad	11.5	81.4	69.8	16.0	73.9	57.9

Note: Actual percent working in all health and PVW models vary due to differences in sample size.

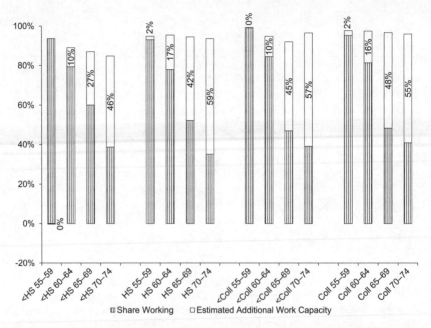

Fig. 7.11 Share of JSTAR men working and additional work capacity by age and education

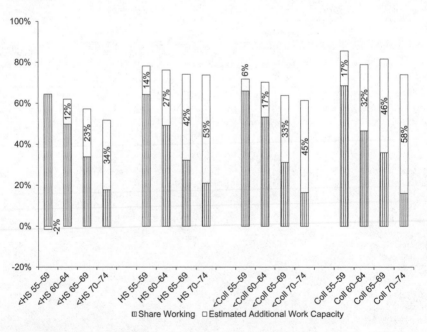

Fig. 7.12 Share of JSTAR women working and additional work capacity by age and education

Table 7.6A   **Work capacity by education (regression by education group)**

	Men, all health variables model			Men, PVW model		
Education	Actual % working	Predicted % working	Estimated work capacity (%)	Actual % working	Predicted % working	Estimated work capacity (%)
			Age 55–59			
HS or less	92.9	92.8	−0.1	93.3	94.4	1.2
Any college	96.0	97.7	1.7	96.3	97.7	1.4
			Age 60–64			
HS or less	78.2	92.9	14.7	78.4	94.1	15.7
Any college	81.6	96.8	15.2	81.9	97.9	15.9
			Age 65–69			
HS or less	54.8	89.7	34.9	55.6	93.1	37.6
Any college	47.6	97.2	49.6	48.0	96.3	48.3
			Age 70–74			
HS or less	36.9	87.0	50.1	37.0	92.2	55.1
Any college	36.5	96.0	59.5	40.4	95.7	55.2

Note: Actual percent working in all health and PVW models vary due to differences in sample size.

Table 7.6B   **Work capacity by education (regression by education group)**

	Women, all health variables model			Women, PVW model		
Education	Actual % working	Predicted % working	Estimated work capacity (%)	Actual % working	Predicted % working	Estimated work capacity (%)
			Age 55–59			
HS or less	64.4	77.3	12.9	64.4	74.6	10.3
Any college	66.4	77.5	11.1	66.7	75.5	8.8
			Age 60–64			
HS or less	49.3	76.4	27.1	49.4	71.6	22.2
Any college	53.0	77.2	24.2	51.8	72.5	20.7
			Age 65–69			
HS or less	33.2	70.7	37.5	33.0	65.6	32.6
Any college	32.9	74.3	41.4	32.2	69.2	36.9
			Age 70–74			
HS or less	20.4	66.4	46.1	19.1	62.1	43.0
Any college	15.9	75.8	60.0	16.3	66.9	50.6

Note: Actual percent working in all health and PVW models vary due to differences in sample size.

capacity. Tables 7.6A and 7.6B summarize the results. There is no substantial difference between less and more educated individuals for both men and women younger than age sixty-five. For men and women age sixty-five and older, more educated individuals tend to have more work capacity (except for the results for men age seventy to seventy-four in the model using the health index).

Emiko Usui, Satoshi Shimizutani, and Takashi Oshio

7.4 Discussion and Conclusion

In this study, we have examined the health capacity of older Japanese based on two analytic approaches: the Milligan-Wise method (using aggregated data from the Population Census and Life Tables) and the Cutler et al. method (using microdata from the JSTAR). Results from both of these methods underscore a large work capacity among older people in Japan. The Milligan-Wise findings show that the amount of projected additional work capacity would be 3.7 years if we use the employment-mortality relationship that existed in 1975 as a basis for comparison and 2.2 years if we use 1995 as the base year. The Cutler et al. method suggests that roughly an additional one in five men and women age sixty to sixty-four and one in three men and women age sixty-five to sixty-nine could be employed, relative to the share working today, based on their own health assessment and the estimated relationship between health and employment for younger workers. Finally, our analysis by education group finds somewhat higher work capacity for more educated individuals than less educated ones when they are at age sixty-five and older.

We can expand this analysis in many directions in the Japanese context. For example, we can divide work status into full- and part-time work, considering the fact that a substantial portion of Japanese employees shift to part-time work after retiring from primary full-time work, rather than completely going out of the labor force (Shimizutani 2011; Shimizutani and Oshio 2010; Usui, Shimizutani, and Oshio 2014). Second, it is of interest to compare work/retirement behavior between individuals who have been employed and self-employed (Usui, Shimizutani, and Oshio 2016). Those who have been employed are likely to experience mandatory retirement and receive relatively high public pension benefits, making them inclined to retire or move to part-time work after retiring from primary full-time work regardless of their health condition. Meanwhile, the self-employed have no mandatory retirement and receive relatively low, fixed-rate pension benefits, probably making their work/retirement more closely associated with health conditions. This difference also may lead to their having different subjective assessments of employment: as being over- or underemployed.

References

Cutler, David M., Ellen Meara, and Seth Richards-Shubik. 2012. "Health and Work Capacity of Older Adults: Estimates and Implications for Social Security Policy." Unpublished Manuscript. Available at SSRN: http://ssrn.com/abstract=2577858.
Milligan, Kevin S., and David A. Wise. 2012. "Health and Work at Older Ages: Using Mortality to Assess the Capacity to Work across Countries." NBER Working Paper no. 18229, Cambridge, MA.

Organisation for Economic Co-operation and Development (OECD). 2013. "Pensions at a Glance 2013: OECD and G20 indicators." http://www.oecd.org/pensions/public-pensions/OECDPensionsAtAGlance2013.pdf.

Oshio, Takashi, Akiko S. Oishi, and Satoshi Shimizutani. 2011. "Social Security Reforms and Labor Force Participation of the Elderly in Japan." *Japanese Economic Review* 62 (2): 248–71.

Poterba, James, Steve Venti, and David A. Wise. 2013. "Health, Education, and the Post-Retirement Evolution of Household Assets." *Journal of Human Capital* 7 (4): 297–339.

Shimizutani, Satoshi. 2011. "A New Anatomy of the Retirement Process in Japan." *Japan and the World Economy* 23 (3): 141–52.

Shimizutani, Satoshi, and Takashi Oshio. 2010. "New Evidence on the Initial Transition from Career Job to Retirement in Japan." *Industrial Relations* 49 (2): 248–74.

Usui, Emiko, Satoshi Shimizunani, and Takashi Oshio. 2014. "Work Capacity of Older Adults in Japan." CIS Discussion paper series no. 635, Center for Intergenerational Studies. http://cis.ier.hit-u.ac.jp/Common/pdf/dp/2014/dp635.pdf.

———. 2016. "Are Japanese Men of Pensionable Age Underemployed or Overemployed?" *Japanese Economic Review* 67 (2): 150–68.

Work Capacity at Older Ages in the Netherlands

Adriaan Kalwij, Arie Kapteyn, and Klaas de Vos

8.1 Introduction

Male employment rates at older ages in the Netherlands started falling in the early 1970s, reaching a historical low around the mid-1990s. Since then, the trend has reversed and male employment rates at older ages have continued to increase (OECD 2015). Pension policy is likely to have played a key role in these trends. Early retirement schemes introduced since 1980 enabled workers to retire before the normal retirement age of sixty-five. Reforms of that policy have resulted in less generous early retirement schemes from the mid-1990s onward (Euwals et al. 2009; Kapteyn and de Vos 1999). In addition, policy reforms regarding disability and unemployment insurance are likely to have played a role as well (de Vos, Kapteyn, and Kalwij 2012; Kalwij, de Vos, and Kapteyn 2015). The trends in the Netherlands are in line with developments in many other OECD countries where social security programs and pension schemes in the past two decades have been redesigned to create stronger incentives for continued work at older ages (Gruber and Wise 2004; Wise 2012).

A recent pension reform aimed at keeping people in employment at older ages in the Netherlands has been to increase the normal retirement age. Up until 2012 the normal retirement age was sixty-five. It is now projected to increase gradually to sixty-six in 2018 and sixty-seven in 2021. After that

Adriaan Kalwij is associate professor of economics at Utrecht University. Arie Kapteyn is professor of economics and director of the Center for Economic and Social Research at the University of Southern California and a research associate of the National Bureau of Economic Research. Klaas de Vos is a senior researcher at CentERdata.

For acknowledgments, sources of research support, and disclosure of the authors' material financial relationships, if any, please see http://www.nber.org/chapters/c13745.ack.

the normal retirement age will be further raised in line with increases in population life expectancy, up to age seventy and three months. The normal retirement age is the age at which one starts receiving social security benefits, so that an increase in the retirement age induces many workers to postpone retirement until they reach the normal retirement age. Another institutional factor of importance is a recent new pension law meant to tackle the problem of low funding ratios of pension funds resulting from the 2007–2008 financial crisis, a continuing increase in life expectancy, and low interest rates. In response to these low funding ratios, most pension funds have not fully adjusted their pension benefits and entitlements for price inflation, while some have applied nominal cuts. It is expected that the new pension law will reduce financial risk for the pension funds at the cost of reducing benefits of future retirees compared to current retirees. Since more than 90 percent of workers are covered by an occupational pension scheme, it is likely to affect the decision of when to stop working.

While one may argue that the institutional settings have by and large determined the above-mentioned major trends in male employment rates at older ages, the health of older workers will determine to what extent the most recent reforms can further increase employment rates at older ages. For this reason we aim to provide in this chapter an estimate for the Netherlands of the additional work capacity at older ages (fifty to seventy-four) accounting for the health of individuals in this age group. For this purpose we follow the two methodologies as outlined in the introduction of this volume. The first methodology is referred to as the Milligan and Wise method (Milligan and Wise 2012). This method groups people by gender, year, and age and uses the mortality rate as an indicator for health to answer the following question: *How much could older people of a certain age, and in a specific year, work if they worked as much as people in the past with the same mortality rate?*

To answer this question, we use data on mortality from the Human Mortality Database[1] and Statistics Netherlands,[2] and employment rates from administrative surveys.

The second methodology is referred to as the Cutler, Meara, and Richards-Shubik method (Cutler, Meara, and Richards-Shubik 2012). This method uses individual-level survey data on peoples' health status to answer the following question: *How much would older people of certain age, and in a specific year, work if they worked as much as younger people (age fifty to fifty-four) with the same health?*

To answer this question one needs a measure of health. We will return to that later. We use data from the Dutch branch of the Survey of Health, Ageing and Retirement in Europe (SHARE-NL).

In addition, we use a third method that uses the age-year specific mortality rates of the Milligan and Wise method as an additional health indica-

1. http://www.mortality.org/.
2. http://www.cbs.nl.

tor when applying the Cutler, Meara, and Richards-Shubik method. We have also considered an additional method where we would use answers to a five-point self-assessed health question (from "excellent" to "poor") to gauge increases in work capacity, using data from the CentERpanel, which has been asking health questions since 1993.[3] It turns out that, in contrast with the other health measures, the self-assessed health (SAH) variable does not show any clear trend over the past couple of decades. This may simply reflect that people's standards of what it means to be in good health have evolved over time, which would invalidate the use of SAH as a comparison yardstick across time.

The chapter proceeds as follows: Section 8.2 describes the main historical trends in employment and health during the past four decades. Section 8.3 presents results for the Milligan and Wise method, while section 8.4 presents the results for the Cutler, Meara, and Richards-Shubik method. Section 8.5 presents results of the third method in which we use age-year specific mortality rates. Section 8.6 discusses the main findings and concludes.

8.2   Historical Trends in Employment and Health

Figure 8.1 shows the decrease in male employment rates at older ages in the Netherlands from the 1970s onward. Particularly in the early eighties, generous early retirement schemes provided a strong incentive to retire at ages younger than the state pension age of sixty-five. Many of those who were not entitled to early retirement had access to slightly less generous but still attractive disability and unemployment insurance programs. Around the mid-1990s the employment rate of people age sixty to sixty-four reached its lowest point. Over time, various policy reforms were introduced to limit the number of persons taking the disability and unemployment routes to retirement. Moreover, early retirement schemes were first made more actuarially fair, and later on by and large abolished. As a result, the trend of ever-decreasing employment rates of older males has reversed since about 1995. Nowadays, the employment rate of males age sixty to sixty-four is at the same level as at the end of the seventies when the early retirement schemes were first introduced. Figure 8.2 shows that the female employment rates in the age groups fifty to fifty-four and fifty-five to fifty-nine have increased over the entire observation period. The profound societal changes underlying these trends, which gave women a more equal share in the distribution of socioeconomic responsibilities, eventually increased the employment rate of sixty- to sixty-four-year-old women in the last decade of the observation period.

One will note that the graphs for the employment rates of men and women age sixty-five to sixty-nine start in 1995. Before 1995, employment

---

3. Information on this data set can be found at http://www.centerdata.nl/en/databank/centerpanel-data-0.

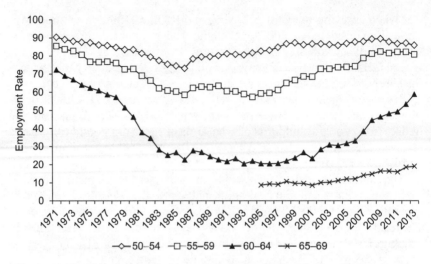

Fig. 8.1 Men's employment rates, ages fifty to fifty-four, fifty-five to fifty-nine, sixty to sixty-four, and sixty-five to sixty-nine (1971–2013)

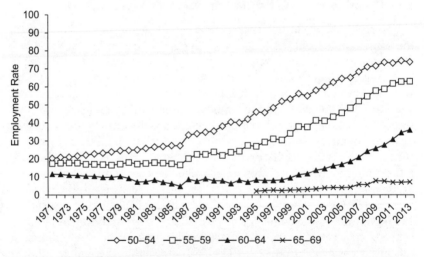

Fig. 8.2 Women's employment rates, ages fifty to fifty-four, fifty-five to fifty-nine, sixty to sixty-four, and sixty-five to sixty-nine (1971–2013)

of individuals over age sixty-five was not separately recorded, as it was felt that so few in that age bracket were working that it was not worth recording their numbers. Gradually employment rates in this age category are increasing, not as fast as in, for instance, the United States (Maestas 2010; Maestas and Zissimopoulos 2010; Coile, Milligan, and Wise, chapter 12, this volume), but nevertheless noticeable. Among males the employment rate has reached 20 percent.

Figure 8.3A shows the decrease in male mortality rates over time, which can be used to assess the increased work capacity of the older age groups. Roughly speaking, mortality at age fifty-four in the beginning of the observation period equals mortality at age sixty-four in recent years, and the mortality rate at age fifty-nine in the early 1970s was about the same as the mortality at age sixty-nine in the early 2010s. To the extent that the employment rate of sixty-nine-year-olds in 2010 is lower than the employment rate of fifty-nine-year-olds in 1970, this could imply potential extra work capacity.

While figure 8.3A implies a clear improvement in the health of older men, figure 8.3B shows a much less clear pattern for men's self-assessed health

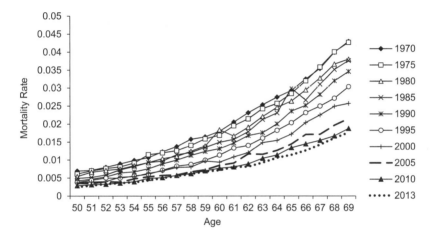

Fig. 8.3A   Men's mortality by age for selected years

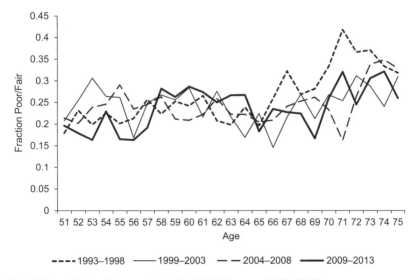

Fig. 8.3B   Men's self-assessed health (SAH) by age (1993–2013)

(SAH). One explanation for the absence of a clear age gradient up to age seventy is that people may adjust their standard of what good health means, or they may assess their own health in comparison with the health of their peers. If the health of the population increases, individual SAH therefore need not necessarily increase. As noted before, the data on SAH are taken from a different and a much smaller data set, the CentERpanel, which has information on about 2,000 individuals per year from 1993 onward.

8.3   Work Capacity: Milligan and Wise Method

We implement the Milligan and Wise method for the period 1981–2010. We use population mortality data from the Human Mortality Database and Statistics Netherlands. We compute employment rates by age, gender, and year using the Income Panel Study of the Netherlands ([IPO] Inkomens Panel Onderzoek; CBS 2009). The IPO is an administrative database of individual incomes collected by Statistics Netherlands from official records such as tax records, population registry, institutions that pay out (insurance) benefits, and the department of housing (because of rent subsidies). Data are available for the years 1981, 1985, 1989–2010. The IPO is a representative sample of the Dutch population of, on average, about 95,000 individuals per year. Most important for our study is that IPO contains data on the labor market status for each member of the household in which a sample individual lives. Statistics Netherlands assigns a labor market status to an individual based on the largest income component. An individual is defined to be in employment if the largest share of his or her income is from labor income, including income from self-employment. The IPO contains no information on levels of education, and our selected sample consists of men age fifty to sixty-nine.[4]

Figure 8.4 plots employment rates and mortality rates (by age year) for men in 1981 and 2010. It shows that for all ages male employment rates at a given mortality rate are higher in 1981 than in 2010. This suggests that people with the same health work less in 2010 than in 1981 and that from a health perspective there is unused work capacity. The difference is fairly small at younger ages and much larger in the older age groups. Thus it appears that unused work capacity is concentrated in the higher age groups.

Figure 8.5 shows that this unused work capacity in 2010 is much smaller when we compare it with the employment and mortality figures for 1995. Still, there appears some unused work capacity at higher levels of mortality if we take 1995 as a base. Interestingly, figure 8.1 shows a steep increase in men's employment rates between 1995 and 2010. Figure 8.5 implies that this increase has been barely enough to keep up with the decrease in mortality that would justify that more people work.

---

4. There are few employed men age seventy to seventy-four in the sample. Due to data confidentiality rules, we are not allowed to present these numbers.

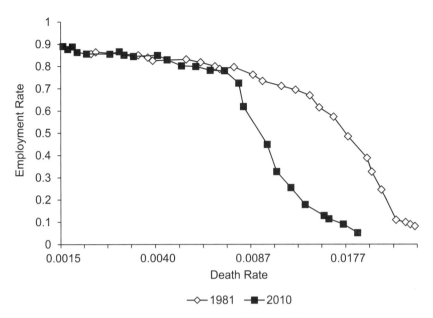

Fig. 8.4   Men's employment versus mortality (2010 vs. 1981)

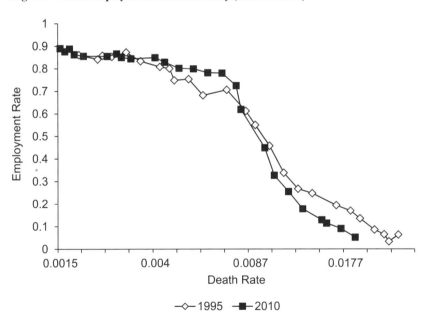

Fig. 8.5   Men's employment versus mortality (2010 vs. 1995)

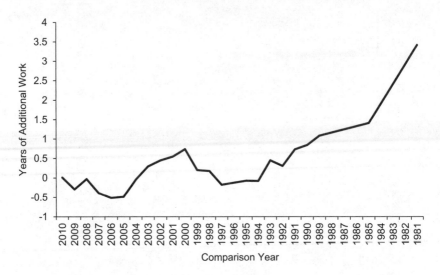

Fig. 8.6   Estimated additional employment capacity at ages fifty to sixty-nine for men by year of comparison

Figure 8.6 shows the estimated additional work capacity in 2010 for men at ages fifty to sixty-nine for different comparison years. For example, the last observation for 1981 is essentially the difference between the two lines in figure 8.4. This difference turns out to be a total of 3.5 years of work. Reading figure 8.6 from right to left, for the comparison years after 1981 the additional work capacity decreases as fewer people at a given mortality rate are employed. Obviously, for this method the year that is taken as a base is crucial. For the comparison years after about 1994 the additional work capacity in 2010 hovers around zero, and this in part is caused by employment rates keeping up with the health improvements in the population (i.e., decreasing mortality over time). By construction, the additional work capacity is zero in 2010.

Table 8.1 provides a more detailed breakdown of the calculation of additional work capacity by age, taking 1981 as a base. It shows considerable additional work capacity at older ages when comparing the years 1981 and 2010. The additional work capacity exceeds 10 percentage points for all ages above sixty and peaks at almost 50 percentage points at age sixty-five. In 2010 the employment rate of sixty-five-year-old men was 18 percent. In 1981, the employment rate of persons with the same mortality rate as sixty-five-year-old men in 2010 was 67 percent. These numbers should be interpreted as indicative rather than as exact estimators of extra work capacity. Other characteristics of the sixty-five-year-olds without employment (e.g., a possible lack of appropriate skills) in 2010 might make it difficult for them to find gainful employment.

Table 8.1   **Additional employment capacity in 2010 using the 1981 employment-mortality relationship**

Age	Death rate in 2010 (%)	Employment rate in 2010 (%)	Employment rate in 1981 at the same death rate (%)	Additional work capacity (%–points)
50	0.29	85.54	84.97	–0.56
51	0.31	86.62	84.97	–1.64
52	0.33	85.05	84.97	–0.07
53	0.36	84.44	84.97	0.53
54	0.40	84.94	83.91	–1.03
55	0.49	82.90	83.07	0.17
56	0.51	80.18	83.07	2.89
57	0.57	79.91	81.75	1.84
58	0.62	78.18	79.98	1.80
59	0.70	78.00	79.63	1.63
60	0.77	72.44	76.18	3.75
61	0.81	61.91	76.18	14.27
62	0.89	44.85	73.41	28.55
63	1.05	32.68	71.14	38.46
64	1.14	25.51	69.44	43.94
65	1.34	17.80	66.91	49.11
66	1.45	12.88	57.33	44.45
67	1.55	11.42	57.33	45.91
68	1.67	9.03	48.42	39.40
69	1.88	5.16	38.80	33.64
50–69		11.19	14.66	3.47

Note: Additional work capacity is the difference between the fourth and third columns.

8.4   Work Capacity: Cutler, Meara, and Richards-Shubik Method

Individual-level data are drawn from the Survey of Health, Ageing and Retirement in Europe (SHARE), a harmonized, multidisciplinary, and representative cross-national panel survey covering the fifty and older population in twenty European countries. We use the Dutch branch of SHARE (SHARE-NL). The Dutch waves were conducted in 2004, 2007, 2011, and 2013.[5] SHARE includes information on socioeconomic status (e.g., employment, income, and education), health (e.g., self-reported subjective health and doctor diagnosed conditions, physical and cognitive functioning, and behavioral risks), and psychological conditions (e.g., mental health, well-being, and life satisfaction).

5. These are the first, second, fourth, and fifth waves of SHARE. The third wave of SHARE is not comparable with these selected waves as it contains mainly retrospective information about respondents' lives.

Table 8.2A   Summary statistics, men

	Age group				
	51–54	55–59	60–64	65–69	70–74
Employment	0.847	0.749	0.344	0.037	0.011
Excellent health (SAH)	0.153	0.169	0.145	0.115	0.089
Very good health (SAH)	0.215	0.179	0.186	0.165	0.164
Good health (SAH)	0.460	0.450	0.418	0.453	0.406
Fair health (SAH)	0.148	0.174	0.211	0.230	0.287
Poor health (SAH)	0.024	0.029	0.039	0.037	0.055
One physical limitation	0.088	0.113	0.118	0.143	0.147
> 1 physical limitation	0.119	0.132	0.156	0.144	0.197
ADL limitations	0.037	0.042	0.054	0.046	0.047
IADL limitations	0.052	0.064	0.073	0.065	0.106
Depressed (CESD-scale > 0)	0.788	0.746	0.677	0.695	0.730
Ever experienced heart problems	0.052	0.081	0.118	0.154	0.193
Ever experienced stroke	0.018	0.034	0.029	0.022	0.053
Ever experienced lung disease	0.047	0.048	0.075	0.055	0.084
Ever experienced cancer	0.024	0.031	0.035	0.058	0.075
Ever experienced high blood pressure	0.178	0.195	0.265	0.290	0.343
Ever experienced arthritis	0.030	0.040	0.056	0.061	0.070
Ever experienced diabetes	0.049	0.066	0.093	0.138	0.134
Underweight (BMI < 18.5)	0.003	0.002	0.007	0.001	0.006
Overweight (25 < BMI < 30)	0.473	0.504	0.492	0.467	0.495
Obese (BMI > 30)	0.124	0.135	0.150	0.177	0.134
Former smoker	0.660	0.697	0.722	0.752	0.758
Current smoker	0.301	0.264	0.212	0.202	0.158
Low educated (ISCED 1 and 2)	0.390	0.404	0.452	0.484	0.548
Median educated (ISCED 3)	0.292	0.269	0.241	0.254	0.223
High educated (ISCED 4 and 5)	0.318	0.327	0.307	0.262	0.229
Born abroad	0.230	0.461	0.541	0.565	0.587
Married	0.821	0.859	0.884	0.865	0.875
Occupational pension fund participant	0.712	0.753	0.774	0.845	0.835
PVW health index	62.244	59.806	56.524	54.300	49.333
Number of observations	708	967	1,073	951	641

Notes: SAH: self-assessed health; (I)ADL: (Instrumental) Activity of Daily Living; physical limitations are related to walking several blocks, lifting or carrying something, pushing or pulling something, climbing stairs, stooping, kneeling or crouching, getting up from chair, reaching/extending arms up, sitting two hours, and picking up a coin; CESD: Center for Epidemiologic Studies Depression; BMI: Body Mass Index; ISCED: 1997 International Standard Classification of Education.

For our analysis we select individuals age fifty to seventy-four and, after removing observations with missing information on key variables (about 25 percent), our final sample consists of 2,373 men (4,340 year observations) and 2,725 women (5,178 year observations). Tables 8.2A and 8.2B present summary statistics. The level of education is defined according to the 1997 International Standard Classification of Education ([ISCED]; MEA 2011). ISCED 1–2 will be referred to as a low level of education, ISCED

Table 8.2B Summary statistics, women

	Age group				
	51–54	55–59	60–64	65–69	70–74
Employment	0.650	0.522	0.234	0.018	0.009
Excellent health (SAH)	0.168	0.140	0.142	0.124	0.093
Very good health (SAH)	0.193	0.167	0.151	0.139	0.131
Good health (SAH)	0.431	0.428	0.461	0.452	0.465
Fair health (SAH)	0.169	0.218	0.202	0.248	0.275
Poor health (SAH)	0.039	0.047	0.044	0.037	0.036
One physical limitation	0.120	0.147	0.162	0.178	0.162
> 1 physical limitation	0.234	0.248	0.261	0.271	0.338
ADL limitations	0.047	0.053	0.047	0.053	0.081
IADL Limitations	0.128	0.137	0.130	0.140	0.191
Depressed (CESD-scale > 0)	1.335	1.269	1.206	1.213	1.228
Ever experienced heart problems	0.027	0.048	0.065	0.068	0.075
Ever experienced stroke	0.011	0.021	0.019	0.028	0.051
Ever experienced lung disease	0.057	0.080	0.068	0.085	0.073
Ever experienced cancer	0.045	0.041	0.065	0.056	0.066
Ever experienced high blood pressure	0.197	0.231	0.283	0.295	0.400
Ever experienced arthritis	0.071	0.103	0.102	0.112	0.121
Ever experienced diabetes	0.055	0.066	0.082	0.085	0.098
Underweight (BMI < 18.5)	0.013	0.012	0.013	0.012	0.013
Overweight (25 < BMI < 30)	0.345	0.348	0.359	0.370	0.380
Obese (BMI > 30)	0.162	0.180	0.186	0.191	0.166
Former smoker	0.615	0.599	0.570	0.487	0.426
Current smoker	0.280	0.249	0.194	0.150	0.128
Low educated (ISCED 1 and 2)	0.438	0.527	0.604	0.648	0.741
Median educated (ISCED 3)	0.301	0.224	0.181	0.183	0.152
High educated (ISCED 4 and 5)	0.261	0.249	0.215	0.169	0.106
Born abroad	0.264	0.477	0.583	0.605	0.584
Married	0.804	0.848	0.818	0.778	0.704
Occupational pension fund participant	0.574	0.554	0.475	0.450	0.375
PVW health index	52.361	49.772	49.822	48.123	44.369
Number of observations	982	1,219	1,266	969	742

Notes: SAH: self-assessed health; (I)ADL: (Instrumental) Activity of Daily Living; Physical limitations are related to walking several blocks, lifting or carrying something, pushing or pulling something, climbing stairs, stooping, kneeling or crouching, getting up from chair, reaching/extending arms up, sitting two hours, and picking up a coin; CESD: Center for Epidemiologic Studies Depression; BMI: Body Mass Index; ISCED: 1997 International Standard Classification of Education.

3 as medium level of education, and ISCED 4–5 as a high level of education. Labor force status is self-reported by respondents. We distinguish between employment (including self-employment) and nonemployment. A health index is constructed based on self-assessed health limitations such as self-assessed limitations of activities of daily living and self-reported health status. Health has many dimensions and we follow Poterba, Venti, and Wise (2013) to construct a measure of general health using a principal

Table 8.3A   Employment regressions, all health variables

Variable	Men 50–54		Women 50–54	
	Coefficient	Std. error	Coefficient	Std. error
Very good health (SAH)	–0.0216	0.0389	0.0430	0.0448
Good health (SAH)	–0.0715	0.0350*	–0.0461	0.0401
Fair health (SAH)	–0.1810	0.0497*	–0.1404	0.0561*
Poor health (SAH)	–0.4309	0.0914*	–0.2531	0.0909*
One physical limitation	0.0012	0.0435	0.0188	0.0438
> 1 physical limitation	–0.0960	0.0451*	–0.1200	0.0423*
ADL limitations	0.0367	0.0671	–0.0852	0.0719
IADL Limitations	–0.1989	0.0574*	–0.0496	0.0473
Depressed (CESD-scale > 0)	–0.0117	0.0120	–0.0192	0.0122
Ever experienced heart problems	0.0554	0.0537	–0.0905	0.0857
Ever experienced lung disease	0.0907	0.0571	–0.0424	0.0598
Ever experienced stroke	–0.1468	0.0893	0.0457	0.1301
Ever experienced cancer	–0.0109	0.0767	0.0037	0.0656
Ever experienced high blood pressure	0.0190	0.0331	0.0137	0.0352
Ever experienced arthritis	0.0027	0.0711	–0.1004	0.0566
Ever experienced diabetes	0.0176	0.0568	–0.0946	0.0638
Underweight (BMI < 18.5)	–0.3808	0.2232	–0.1583	0.1190
Overweight (25 < BMI < 30)	0.0056	0.0259	–0.0126	0.0305
Obese (BMI > 30)	0.0150	0.0405	–0.0763	0.0414
Former smoker	–0.0499	0.0280	–0.0242	0.0323
Current smoker	–0.0407	0.0301	–0.0136	0.0356
Low educated (ISCED 1 and 2)	–0.0747	0.0292*	–0.0353	0.0327
High educated (ISCED 4 and 5)	0.0020	0.0299	0.0877	0.0365*
Born abroad	–0.0941	0.0282*	–0.0085	0.0313
Married	0.1617	0.0319*	–0.0872	0.0352*
Occupational pension fund participant	0.1406	0.0265*	0.2859	0.0279*
Constant	0.8023	0.0499*	0.7089	0.0582*
No. obs.	708		982	

Notes: SAH: self-assessed health; (I)ADL: (Instrumental) Activity of Daily Living; Physical limitations are related to walking several blocks, lifting or carrying something, pushing or pulling something, climbing stairs, stooping, kneeling or crouching, getting up from chair, reaching/extending arms up, sitting two hours, and picking up a coin; CESD: Center for Epidemiologic Studies Depression; BMI: Body Mass Index; ISCED: 1997 International Standard Classification of Education.
*Significant at the 5 percent level.

components analysis. The weights corresponding to the first principal component are used to construct a health index. The index values are next transformed into percentiles, where 0 is worst health and 100 is best health. In the tables we refer to this index as the PVW health index. Table 8.2A and 8.2B report summary statistics for the men and women in our sample. In line with what is known from the literature, these statistics show, for example, that fewer women than men are employed, women are on average unhealthier than men, and health worsens with age.

To assess work capacity we first estimate an employment equation by

Table 8.3B   **Employment regressions, PVW health index**

Variable	Men 50–54		Women 50–54	
	Coefficient	Std. error	Coefficient	Std. error
PVW health index (0–100)	0.0035	0.0005*	0.0049	0.0005*
Low educated (ISCED 1 and 2)	–0.0762	0.0297*	–0.0470	0.0325
High educated (ISCED 4 and 5)	0.0054	0.0307	0.0993	0.0365*
Born abroad	–0.1032	0.0285*	–0.0252	0.0311*
Married	0.1849	0.0317*	–0.0748	0.0350*
Occupational pension fund participant	0.1626	0.0268*	0.3002	0.0279*
Constant	0.4123	0.0467*	0.2806	0.0482*
No. obs.	708		982	

*Significant at the 5 percent level.

gender for individuals age fifty to fifty-four as outlined in Coile, Milligan, and Wise (chapter 12, this volume). At these ages employment is unlikely to be influenced by retirement incentives. The employment model is estimated using two empirical specifications. The first specification includes all health limitations as explanatory variables. The results are presented in table 8.3A. The second specification, referred to as the PVW health index in the tables with results, excludes all health limitations variables and includes the abovementioned health index. The results of the second specification are presented in table 8.3B. Apart from health variables, educational attainment, marital status, whether born abroad, whether covered by an occupational pension scheme, and survey year are controlled for. Table 8.3A shows that most health limitations have no significant effect on the employment probability. It is mainly SAH that is associated with the employment probability, and the estimated coefficients suggest that men and women who assess their health as fair or poor are less likely to be employed compared to men and women who assess their health as excellent or very good. The effects of the levels of education show that low-educated men and women are less likely to be employed than high-educated men and women. Finally, men and women who are participants in an occupational pension fund are more likely to be employed.

The estimation results of the employment equations using only individuals age fifty to fifty-four are used to predict employment at later ages. These predictions are in the columns with the heading "Predicted working" in table 8.4. The difference between the actual and predicted percentage working is our estimated additional work capacity. The differences in additional work capacity implied by the results of the model with all health variables (table 8.3A) and the results of the model with the PVW health index (table 8.3B) are minimal. Figures 8.7 and 8.8 summarize the main findings based on table 8.3B. Graphs based on table 8.3A would be virtually identical. Figure

Table 8.4   Simulations of work capacity

	Use all health variables				Use PVW health index			
Age group	No. obs.	Actual working (%)	Predicted working (%)	Estimated additional work capacity (% points)	No. obs.	Actual working (%)	Predicted working (%)	Estimated additional work capacity (% points)
Men								
55–59	967	74.9	82.9	8.0	967	74.9	82.8	7.9
60–64	1,073	34.4	81.9	47.5	1,073	34.4	81.2	46.8
65–69	951	3.7	82.3	78.6	951	3.7	80.7	77.1
70–74	641	1.1	78.8	77.7	641	1.1	78.3	77.2
Women								
55–59	1,219	52.2	61.7	9.5	1,219	52.2	61.7	9.5
60–64	1,266	23.4	59.1	35.7	1,266	23.4	58.6	35.2
65–69	969	1.8	57.5	55.7	969	1.8	56.6	54.8
70–74	742	0.9	53.7	52.7	742	0.9	52.0	51.1

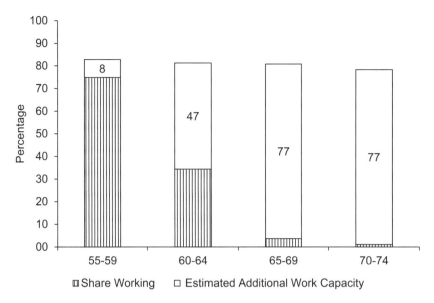

Fig. 8.7 Share of men working and additional work capacity by age

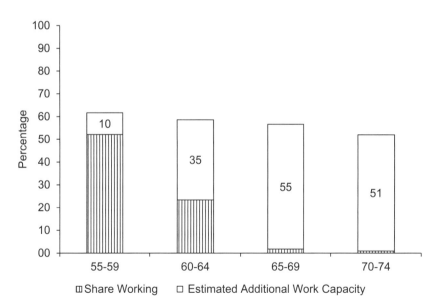

Fig. 8.8 Share of women working and additional work capacity by age

Table 8.5A   **Work capacity by education (regression by education group)**

	Men, all health variables model			Men, PVW health index model		
Education	Actual working (%)	Predicted working (%)	Estimated additional work capacity (% points)	Actual working (%)	Predicted working (%)	Estimated additional work capacity (% points)
	Age 55–59					
ISCED 1–2	66.8	73.2	6.5	66.8	73.7	7.0
ISCED 3	74.6	85.3	10.7	74.6	85.3	10.7
ISCED 4–5	85.1	94.3	9.1	85.1	92.0	6.9
	Age 60–64					
ISCED 1–2	27.6	73.6	45.9	27.6	73.8	46.2
ISCED 3	37.8	85.4	47.6	37.8	84.6	46.8
ISCED 4–5	41.6	93.1	51.5	41.6	90.7	49.0
	Age 65–69					
ISCED 1–2	3.7	74.9	71.2	3.7	74.0	70.3
ISCED 3	3.7	85.5	81.8	3.7	84.4	80.7
ISCED 4–5	3.6	95.2	91.6	3.6	90.8	87.2
	Age 70–74					
ISCED 1–2	1.1	71.0	69.9	1.1	71.7	70.5
ISCED 3	1.4	83.3	81.9	1.4	81.8	80.4
ISCED 4–5	0.7	94.3	93.6	0.7	89.1	88.4

Notes: ISCED 1–2: low level of education; ISCED 3: medium level of education; and ISCED 4–5: high level of education.

8.7 shows that the estimated additional work capacity for men is 8 percent at ages fifty-five to fifty-nine; it increases to 77 percent at ages sixty-five to sixty-nine and seventy to seventy-four. For women, figure 8.8 shows that the estimated additional work capacity is somewhat lower at older ages and about 51 percent at ages seventy to seventy-four.

Tables 8.5A and 8.5B differentiate the calculations by level of education: the employment regressions are estimated separately by education group, and the resulting additional work capacity percentages are calculated separately for persons with low, medium, and high levels of education. These results are summarized in figures 8.9 and 8.10 and show that the additional work capacity increases with the level of education, especially in the age groups older than sixty-five. Notably, the differences between the results on the basis of the employment regression using all health variables and the results using the PVW index are again only marginal.

Tables 8.6A and 8.6B present comparable results where the employment equation is estimated in a single regression, but the estimated additional work capacity is differentiated by level of education. Generally speaking, the results are comparable to those in tables 8.5A and 8.5B, although a some-

Table 8.5B   **Work capacity by education (regression by education group)**

	Women, all health variables model			Women, PVW health index model		
Education	Actual working (%)	Predicted working (%)	Estimated additional work capacity (% points)	Actual working (%)	Predicted working (%)	Estimated additional work capacity (% points)
	Age 55–59					
ISCED 1–2	41.4	55.7	14.3	41.4	55.4	14.0
ISCED 3	56.0	58.1	2.0	56.0	60.9	4.9
ISCED 4–5	71.4	77.6	6.2	71.4	76.6	5.2
	Age 60–64					
ISCED 1–2	18.4	55.4	37.0	18.4	53.4	35.0
ISCED 3	29.7	57.5	27.8	29.7	61.1	31.4
ISCED 4–5	32.0	73.0	41.0	32.0	73.9	41.9
	Age 65–69					
ISCED 1–2	1.9	54.2	52.3	1.9	52.2	50.3
ISCED 3	1.1	58.6	57.5	1.1	60.2	59.1
ISCED 4–5	1.8	74.5	72.7	1.8	75.6	73.8
	Age 70–74					
ISCED 1–2	0.5	51.6	51.0	0.5	49.2	48.6
ISCED 3	2.7	57.6	55.0	2.7	58.0	55.4
ISCED 4–5	1.3	72.3	71.0	1.3	74.4	73.1

Notes: ISCED 1–2: low level of education; ISCED 3: medium level of education; and ISCED 4–5: high level of education.

what lower additional work capacity is estimated for men and a somewhat higher working capacity for women.

8.4.1   Sensitivity Analyses

As mentioned before, table 8.3A shows that it is mainly SAH that is associated with the employment probability. Several studies have argued that SAH is likely to suffer from various sources of bias. One often mentioned possibility is that nonworking individuals justify their nonemployment status by reporting worse than actual health (e.g., Bound 1991). To investigate the importance of possible biases in SAH, we also construct a health index excluding SAH. Table 8.7 presents the implications for the estimates of additional work capacity. The column headed "PVW health index" repeats the findings reported in table 8.4. The results in the next column, which is based on a health index excluding SAH, are rather similar to those in the previous column. It may also be argued that many of the other health variables such as ADLs suffer from measurement error (e.g., Flores and Kalwij 2013). Hence, we have also used a more restrictive set of health variables that are less likely to suffer from measurement error to construct the PVW health

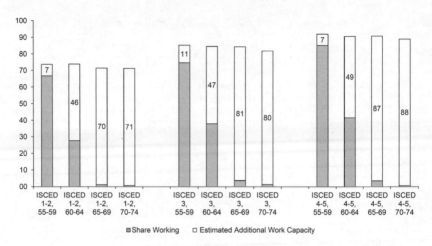

Fig. 8.9   Share of men working and additional work capacity by age and education

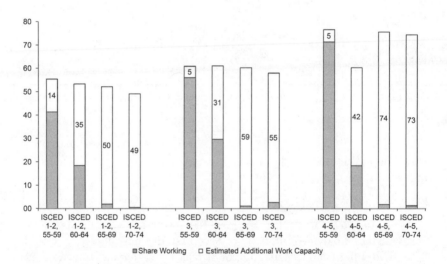

Fig. 8.10   Share of women working and additional work capacity by age and education

index. As it turns out, the results based on a health index that includes severe chronic conditions, BMI and grip strength, are again very close to those in the other two columns (not reported here).[6]

Finally, we construct an index obtained by regressing SAH on the objec-

6. Grip strength has not been used for the PVW health index. It is measured in the survey at most twice for each hand. Grip strength is defined as the maximum grip strength measurement. We also control for missing grip strength as these are mostly due to very frail people who are not capable, or very hesitant, of squeezing a grip-strength dynamometer.

Table 8.6A **Work capacity by education (single regression)**

	Men, all health variables model			Men, PVW health index model		
Education	Actual working (%)	Predicted working (%)	Estimated additional work capacity (%–points)	Actual working (%)	Predicted working (%)	Estimated additional work capacity (%–points)
	Age 55–59					
ISCED 1–2	66.8	74.1	7.3	66.8	74.8	8.1
ISCED 3	74.6	85.4	10.7	74.6	85.8	11.2
ISCED 4–5	85.1	91.7	6.6	85.1	90.1	5.0
	Age 60–64					
ISCED 1–2	27.6	74.8	47.2	27.6	75.1	47.5
ISCED 3	37.8	86.1	48.3	37.8	85.1	47.2
ISCED 4–5	41.6	89.0	47.4	41.6	87.3	45.7
	Age 65–69					
ISCED 1–2	3.7	76.3	72.6	3.7	75.3	71.6
ISCED 3	3.7	86.5	82.8	3.7	84.6	80.8
ISCED 4–5	3.6	89.1	85.5	3.6	87.1	83.4
	Age 70–74					
ISCED 1–2	1.1	73.3	72.1	1.1	73.7	72.6
ISCED 3	1.4	83.3	81.9	1.4	81.7	80.3
ISCED 4–5	0.7	87.6	86.9	0.7	85.8	85.1

Notes: ISCED 1–2: low level of education; ISCED 3: medium level of education; and ISCED 4–5: high level of education.

Table 8.6B **Work capacity by education (single regression)**

	Women, all health variables model			Women, PVW health index model		
Education	Actual working (%)	Predicted working (%)	Estimated additional work capacity (%–points)	Actual working (%)	Predicted working (%)	Estimated additional work capacity (%–points)
	Age 55–59					
ISCED 1–2	41.4	53.9	12.5	41.4	53.8	12.3
ISCED 3	56.0	61.9	5.8	56.0	62.6	6.5
ISCED 4–5	71.4	77.9	6.5	71.4	77.6	6.2
	Age 60–64					
ISCED 1–2	18.4	52.3	33.9	18.4	51.5	33.0
ISCED 3	29.7	62.1	32.4	29.7	62.3	32.6
ISCED 4–5	32.0	75.4	43.4	32.0	75.5	43.5
	Age 65–69					
ISCED 1–2	1.9	50.9	49.0	1.9	49.7	47.8
ISCED 3	1.1	61.7	60.6	1.1	61.0	59.9
ISCED 4–5	1.8	78.1	76.2	1.8	78.1	76.2
	Age 70–74					
ISCED 1–2	0.5	48.9	48.3	0.5	47.0	46.4
ISCED 3	2.7	61.0	58.4	2.7	59.6	56.9
ISCED 4–5	1.3	76.4	75.1	1.3	76.4	75.1

Notes: ISCED 1–2: low level of education; ISCED 3: medium level of education; and ISCED 4–5: high level of education.

Table 8.7   Work capacity using alternative health indices

		Additional work capacity		
	No. obs.	Actual working (%)	PVW health index (as in table 8.4) (%–points)	PVW health index, excluding SAH (%–points)	SAH-based health index (%–points)
		Men			
55–59	967	74.9	7.9	8.4	7.9
60–64	1,073	34.4	46.8	47.5	47.2
65–69	951	3.7	77.1	77.7	77.4
70–74	641	1.1	77.2	78.1	77.9
		Women			
55–59	1,219	52.2	9.5	9.8	9.9
60–64	1,266	23.4	35.2	35.4	34.5
65–69	969	1.8	54.8	55.2	53.5
70–74	742	0.9	51.1	50.5	—

Notes: SAH-based health index: based on predictions of an SAH-ordered probit model and includes severe conditions, BMI and grip strength variables as covariates. For this index, the predictions for working turned out to be negative for women age seventy to seventy-four and this result has been omitted.

tive health indicators (e.g., Bound et al. 1999). We estimate an ordered probit model in which the SAH categories are related to severe chronic conditions (BMI and grip strength). The SAH-based health index is next used to predict additional work capacity and these results are reported in the last column of table 8.7. Again, these results are rather close to those in the preceding two columns

These analyses show that the results are insensitive to the choice of health variables and to the way these are combined in indices for the explanation of employment. In all variants we obtain large estimates of additional work capacity. We will discuss this result further in section 8.6.

8.5   Work Capacity: A Combination of the Methods of Milligan and Wise, and Cutler, Meara, and Richards-Shubik

The additional work capacity based on the Cutler, Meara, and Richards-Shubik method (section 8.4) is about 50 percent higher than that based on the Milligan and Wise method (section 8.3). It is likely that this difference results from inherent differences between the two methods. For instance, the additional work capacity based on the Milligan and Wise method depends on the comparison year that ideally should be a year of full employment. For the Netherlands, the comparison year 1981 was a time of high unemployment and not of full employment. Hence, one may expect an underestimation of additional work capacity when using 1981 as a comparison year. The additional work capacity based on the Cutler, Meara, and Richards-Shubik method may be an overestimate under two scenarios: (a) if the health variables we choose do not vary with age (as is the case with SAH; figure 8.3B shows that SAH is essentially flat until age sixty-five and increases only slowly after that) or (b) if the health variables in our data set are noisy so that their influence on employment is attenuated. Clearly, if measured health does not vary with age then our estimates will imply that people at older ages will have the same work capacity as younger workers. If the included health variables only have a weak relation with employment, then their deterioration with age will have only a weak estimated effect on work capacity.

To obtain further insight into these issues we combine the two methods of Milligan and Wise, and Cutler, Meara, and Richards-Shubik and refer to it as the third method. The third method consists of adding age-year specific mortality rates to the employment models that we estimated when applying the Cutler, Meara, and Richards-Shubik method in section 8.4. The mortality rates are the same ones we used when applying the Milligan and Wise method of section 8.3. The main idea behind the third method is that it may take into account unobserved health limitations on an aggregate level that are not captured by the PVW health index or by the individual health indicators.

Table 8.8 shows that a higher mortality rate is associated with lower employment. The association is strong; a doubling of the mortality rate would result in about a 12-percentage-point lower employment rate for men and about a 23-percentage-point lower employment rate for women. Based on the results of table 8.8 we once again predict additional work capacity at ages fifty-five to seventy-four, and these results are reported in table 8.9. The results in the column headed "PVW health index" have been copied from table 8.4. In the next column we present results without including the PVW health index and only (log-) mortality in the employment equations. Such a model could be interpreted as a parametric version of the Milligan

Table 8.8	Employment regressions, PVW health index and mortality rate				
		Men 50–54		Women 50–54	
Variable	Coefficient	Std. error	Coefficient	Std. error
PVW health index (0–100)	0.0035	0.0005*	0.0049	0.0005*
Low educated (ISCED 1 and 2)	−0.0788	0.0296*	−0.0531	0.0323
High educated (ISCED 4 and 5)	0.0022	0.0306	0.1044	0.0362*
Born abroad	−0.0939	0.0287*	−0.0090	0.0311
Married	0.1945	0.0318*	−0.0625	0.0349
Occupational pension fund participant	0.1627	0.0267*	0.2880	0.0279*
log-mortality rate (age-year specific)	−0.1719	0.0716*	−0.3397	0.0854*
Constant	−0.5565	0.4062	−1.7148	0.5039*
No. obs.	708		982	

*Significant at the 5 percent level.

Table 8.9   Work capacity including mortality rates by year, age, and gender

	No. obs.	Actual working (%)	PVW health index (as in table 8.4) (% points)	Mortality as health indicator (% points)	PVW health index and mortality (% points)
			Men		
55–59	967	74.9	7.9	−1.1	−0.2
60–64	1073	34.4	46.8	29.7	31.0
65–69	951	3.7	77.1	50.8	53.0
70–74	641	1.1	77.2	41.3	43.7
			Women		
55–59	1219	52.2	9.5	−3.3	−3.6
60–64	1266	23.4	35.2	7.1	8.5
65–69	969	1.8	54.8	12.9	15.0
70–74	742	0.9	51.1	—	—

Notes: For women age seventy to seventy-four, the predictions for working sometimes turned out to be negative and these results have been omitted from the table.

and Wise method. Estimated additional work capacity is much lower than predicted in the preceding column and closer to those reported in table 8.1 (Milligan and Wise method). In the last column, additional work capacities are predicted based on the estimation results of table 8.8. They show that the additional work capacity for men age sixty-five to sixty-nine is about 53 percentage points. At these ages for women, additional work capacity is about 15 percentage points and is considerably lower than for men while they work less and are relatively healthier. This outcome is the direct result of the fact that in table 8.8 the effect of mortality on employment is much higher for women than for men. This higher coefficient implies that labor supply of women is much more elastic with respect to health than that of men. The results in the final two columns of table 8.9 are fairly similar. They both show that for men predicted additional work capacity declines with age after age sixty-five.

8.6   Conclusions

Both the results of the Milligan-Wise and the Cutler-Meara-Richards-Shubik approach to calculate additional work capacity at older age groups suggest that the potential employment rates of older workers in the Netherlands by far exceed the actual employment rates. The Milligan-Wise approach shows that, in comparison to 1981, considerably fewer persons with the same mortality rate were working in 2010. The Cutler-Meara-Richards-Shubik approach shows that, given their health, the employment rates of older persons could be much higher than is currently the case.

Our preferred set of results is based on a combination of the Milligan-Wise and Cutler, Meara, and Richards-Shubik approaches and consists of an extension of the latter approach with (aggregate) mortality as an additional health indicator. We find that for men, additional work capacity is about 31 percentage points at ages sixty to sixty-four, increases to 53 percentage points at ages sixty-five to sixty-nine, and is reduced to about 44 percentage points at ages seventy to seventy-four. For women, additional work capacities are much lower at all ages.

The interpretation of the results is not quite straightforward. The calculations ignore the potential effect of work on health. The literature on the effect of retirement on health is not clear cut, although in our reading of the literature retirement is probably beneficial for one's health (Kalwij, Knoef, and Alessie 2013; Coe and Zamarro 2011; Bloemen, Hochguertel, and Zweerink 2013; Kuhn, Wuellrich, and Zweimueller 2010; Hernaes et al. 2013). By the same token, this would suggest that (at least for some occupations) working longer may have a negative effect on health. This possibility has implications for both the Milligan-Wise and the Cutler-Meara-Richards-Shubik methods, and as well the third method that combines both approaches. To see why, consider both approaches one by one.

Assume for the sake of argument that retirement (or rather not working) is good for health. The Milligan-Wise approach is based on keeping health (or rather mortality) constant and then calculating how much one can work. Imagine as a counterfactual that individuals keep working and their health deteriorates as a result (possibly at an increasing rate when one gets older). By the logic of that approach, their work capacity will fall and hence the additional capacity will be less than forecast. One can also make the same point in a different way. Suppose that the decrease in mortality observed over the last couple of decades is largely the result of the fact that people have been able to work less. Then, inducing them to go back to work would increase mortality again. We do not consider the latter case likely, but it seems reasonable to assume that estimated additional work capacity is an upper bound of the real additional work capacity for the reasons given.

The argument with respect to the Cutler-Meara-Richards-Shubik approach is similar. This approach relates work at ages fifty to fifty-four to observed employment and then uses that to forecast employment based on observed health at later ages. If individuals would actually work at these later ages and their health were to deteriorate as a result, predicted additional work capacity would be less than predicted. Thus, also in this case, it may be safe to take the estimates as upper bounds on true additional work capacity.

As we have argued in section 8.5, even if work has no negative effect on health, the Cutler-Meara-Richards-Shubik approach is very likely a severe overestimation of additional work capacity. This comes about because some of the subjective variables hardly vary with age, so that the approach essentially assumes that people at all ages have the same work capacity. The more objective variables vary more with age, but their predictive value for work at

fifty to fifty-four is reduced due to measurement error and potential reporting bias (e.g., of ADLs). So if the latter variables deteriorate with age, their
predicted effect on employment is attenuated.

References

Bloemen, H., S. Hochguertel, and J. Zweerink. 2013. "The Causal Effect of Retire-
ment on Mortality: Evidence from Targeted Incentives to Retire Early." IZA Dis-
cussion Paper no. 7570, Institute for the Study of Labor.
Bound, J. 1991. "Self-Reported versus Objective Measures of Health in Retirement
Models." *Journal of Human Resources* 26:106–38.
Bound J., M. Schoenbaum, T. Stinebrickner, and T. Waidmann. 1999. "The Dynamic
Effects of Health on the Labor Force Transitions of Older Workers." *Labour
Economics* 6:179–202.
Centraal Bureau voor de Statistiek (CBS). 2009. *Documentatierapport Inkomenspanel
Onderzoek (IPO)*. Voorburg: Centrum voor Beleidsstatistiek.
Coe, N., and G. Zamarro. 2011. "Retirement Effects on Health in Europe." *Journal
of Health Economics* 30 (1): 77–86.
Cutler, D. M., E. Meara, and S. Richards-Shubik. 2012. "Health and Work Capacity
of Older Adults: Estimates and Implications for Social Security Policy." Unpub-
lished Manuscript. Available at SSRN: http://ssrn.com/abstract=2577858.
De Vos, K., A. Kapteyn, and A. Kalwij. 2012. "Disability Insurance and Labor
Market Exit Routes of Older Workers in The Netherlands." In *Social Security
Programs and Retirement around the World: Historical Trends in Mortality and
Health, Employment, and Disability Insurance Participation and Reforms,* edited
by David A. Wise, 419–47. Chicago: University of Chicago Press.
Euwals, R., R. de Mooij, and D. van Vuuren. 2009. "Rethinking Retirement; from
Participation to Allocation." CPB Special Publication no. 80, CPB Netherlands
Bureau for Economic Policy Analysis.
Flores, M., and A. Kalwij. 2013. "What Do Wages Add to the Health-Employment
Nexus? Evidence from Older European Workers." Netspar Discussion paper no.
03/2013–005, Network for Studies on Pension, Ageing and Retirement at Tilburg
University.
Gruber, J., and D. A. Wise, eds. 2004. *Social Security Programs and Retirement
around the World: Micro-Estimation.* Chicago: University of Chicago Press.
Hernaes, E., S. Markusen, J. Piggott, and O. L. Vestad. 2013. "Does Retirement Age
Impact Mortality?" *Journal of Health Economics* 32:586–98.
Kalwij, A., K. de Vos, and A. Kapteyn. 2015. "Health, Disability Insurance and
Labor Force Exit of Older Workers in the Netherlands." In *Social Security Pro-
grams and Retirement around the World: Disability Insurance Programs and Retire-
ment,* edited by David A. Wise. Chicago: University of Chicago Press.
Kalwij, A., M. Knoef, and R. Alessie. 2013. "Pathways to Retirement and Mortality
Risk in the Netherlands, 2013." *European Journal of Population* 29 (2): 221–38.
Kapteyn, A., and K. de Vos. 1999. "Social Security and Retirement in the Nether-
lands." In *Social Security and Retirement around the World,* edited by David A.
Wise, 269–304. Chicago: University of Chicago Press.
Kuhn, A., J. P. Wuellrich, and J. Zweimueller. 2010. "Fatal Attraction? Access to
Early Retirement and Mortality." IZA Discussion Paper no. 5160, Institute for
the Study of Labor.

Maestas, N. 2010. "Expectations and Realizations of Work after Retirement." *Journal of Human Resources* 45:718–48.

Maestas, N., and J. Zissimopoulos. 2010. "How Longer Work Lives Ease the Crunch of Population Aging." *Journal of Economic Perspectives* 24:139–60.

Mannheim Research Institute for the Economics of Aging (MEA). 2011. *Release Guide 2.5.0 Waves 1 & 2*. www. share-project.org.

Milligan, K. S., and D. Wise. 2012. "Health and Work at Older Ages: Using Mortality to Assess the Capacity to Work across Countries." NBER Working Paper no. 18229, Cambridge, MA.

OECD. 2015. http://stats.oecd.org/.

Poterba, J., S. Venti, and D. A. Wise. 2013. "Health, Education, and the Post-Retirement Evolution of Household Assets." *Journal of Human Capital* 7 (4): 297–339.

Wise, D. A., ed. 2012. *Social Security Programs and Retirement around the World: Historical Trends in Mortality and Health, Employment, and Disability Insurance Participation and Reforms*. Chicago: University of Chicago Press.

9

Health Capacity to Work at Older Ages
Evidence from Spain

Pilar García-Gómez, Sergi Jiménez-Martín,
and Judit Vall Castelló

9.1 Introduction

There are large concerns about the sustainability of social security systems due to population aging among developed countries, and Spain is not an exception. Spain has one of the lowest fertility rates in Europe (below 1.4, according to Eurostat [Lanzieri 2013]), while life expectancy at birth was the highest in 2012 at 82.5 years compared to an average EU-28 of 79.2 (OECD

Pilar García-Gómez is an associate professor at the Erasmus School of Economics, Erasmus University Rotterdam, and a research fellow at Tinbergen Institute. Sergi Jiménez-Martín is associate professor of economics at Universitat Pompeu Fabra, an affiliated professor at Barcelona GSE, and an associate researcher at FEDEA. Judit Vall Castelló is the research director at the Centre for Research in Health and Economics at Universitat Pompeu Fabra.

This chapter is part of the National Bureau of Economic Research's International Social Security (ISS) project, which is supported by the National Institute on Aging (grant P01 AG012810). Pilar García-Gómez also thanks the Netherlands Organization for Scientific Research under the Innovation Research Incentives Scheme (VENI) for financial support. Sergi Jiménez also thanks project ECO2014–52238-R for financial help. The authors are indebted to Arnau Juanmartí for expert research assistance. We also thank the members of the other country teams in the ISS project for comments that helped to shape this chapter. This chapter uses data from the Survey of Health, Ageing and Retirement in Europe (SHARE). The SHARE data collection has been primarily funded by the European Commission through the 5th Framework Program (project QLK6-CT-2001–00360 in the thematic program Quality of Life), through the 6th Framework Program (projects SHARE-I3, RII-CT-2006–062193, COMPARE, CIT5-CT-2005–028857, and SHARELIFE, CIT4-CT-2006–028812), and through the 7th Framework Program (SHARE-PREP, No. 211909, SHARE-LEAP, No. 227822 and SHARE M4, No. 261982). Additional funding is also gratefully acknowledged from the US National Institute on Aging (U01 AG09740–13S2, P01 AG005842, P01 AG08291, P30 AG12815, R21 AG025169, Y1-AG-4553–01, IAG BSR06–11, and OGHA 04–064) and the German Ministry of Education and Research, as well as from various national sources (see http://www.share-project.org/ for a full list of funding institutions). For acknowledgments, sources of research support, and disclosure of the authors' material financial relationships, if any, please see http://www.nber .org/chapters/c13746.ack.

2014). In a similar vein, life expectancy at age sixty-five has been improving over time; in 1960 men age sixty-five expected to live 13.1 more years, while the expectations were 18.7 in 2012 (García-Gómez, Jiménez-Martín, and Vall Castelló 2012; OECD 2014). This trend is expected to continue in the coming decades (European Commission 2012).

In parallel, there was a tendency in the 1980s and early 1990s toward reducing employment participation of older workers (Gruber and Wise 1999, 2004; Boldrin, Jiménez-Martín, and Peracchi 1999, 2004). The decreasing trends were reversed in the mid-1990s, but employment participation rates have remained considerably lower than the ones observed in the late 1970s (see, for example, García-Gómez, Jiménez-Martín, and Vall Castelló 2012). There is a large body of literature that shows that financial incentives have an effect on employment decisions (Gruber and Wise 2004), but bad health has also been found to hamper labor force participation of (older) workers (García-Gómez 2011; Cervini-Pla and Vall Castelló 2015). Therefore, it remains an extremely relevant policy question whether future social security reforms have room to increase the labor market involvement of older individuals, and whether there is latent work capacity among Spanish older workers.

In this chapter, we aim to provide a first set of estimates to whether there is health-related unused work capacity among Spanish older workers. We do so following two alternative methods and focusing on employment as our measure of work capacity. First, we use the method proposed by Milligan and Wise (2015) and estimate that in 2010 individuals age fifty-five to sixty-nine would have worked an additional 7.08 years if they would have worked as much as individuals with the same mortality rates in 1976. Second, we use individual-level data from the Survey of Health, Ageing and Retirement in Europe and the method suggested by Cutler, Meara, and Richards-Shubik (2012) to estimate that work capacity increases over 60 percent once the normal retirement age of sixty-five kicks in. We are nonetheless cautious with our conclusions as these results hinge upon somewhat strong assumptions.

The rest of the chapter is organized as follows. Section 9.2 illustrates trends in labor force participation and their relation with trends in subjective and objective health measures. Section 9.3 simulates gains of work capacity of older workers using the Milligan-Wise method, while estimates using the Cutler-Meara-Richards-Shubik method are presented in section 9.4. In section 9.5 we analyze the evolution over time of poor health by education quartiles. Finally, section 9.6 concludes.

9.2   Trends in Labor Force Participation and Health

As in many industrialized countries, labor force participation in Spain has changed substantially in the last decades. We use data from the Spanish Labor Force Survey (*Encuesta de Población Activa* [EPA]) to illustrate

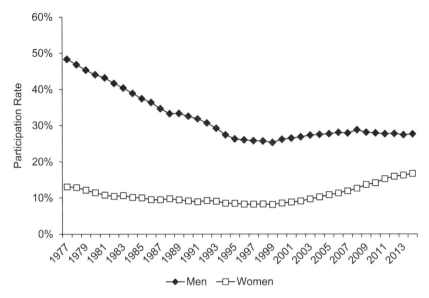

Fig. 9.1   Labor force participation by gender, ages fifty-five and older (1977–2014)
Source: Spanish Labor Force Survey.

trends in labor force participation since 1977. The EPA is a rotating quarterly survey carried out by the Spanish National Institute that contains detailed information on labor market behavior, education, and household characteristics of approximately 180,000 individuals every quarter. In particular, it asks every individual about her labor market status the week prior to the interview. We use this information to estimate average annual participation rates combining data from all quarters in a given year. Figure 9.1 plots the evolution of labor force participation for men and women at least fifty-five years of age in Spain since 1977 and figure 9.2 shows the evolution of labor force participation for men and women at least sixteen years of age in the same period. We can see in figure 9.1 that there was a steep decline in the labor force participation of men at least fifty-five years of age between 1977 and the mid-1990s; while 48 percent of men at least fifty-five years of age were in the labor force in 1977, only 25 percent stayed in the labor force during the 1990s. This declining trend was slightly reversed at the turn of the century. However, the participation rate was only 28 percent in 2014, which still represents a much lower value than in 1977. This decrease in labor market participation since the late 1970s is substantially explained by the incentives provided by social security institutions (Boldrin, Jiménez-Martín, and Peracchi 1999). In Spain, legislation promoting early retirement has had a large effect on the number of early retirees, particularly during the 1970s and 1980s (Boldrin, Jiménez-Martín, and Peracchi 2001). In addition, the

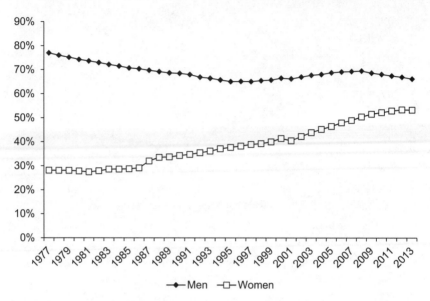

Fig. 9.2   Labor force participation by gender, ages sixteen and older (1977–2014)
Source: Spanish Labor Force Survey.

importance of other exit routes for individuals approaching retirement, such as unemployment or disability insurance, have also been documented in the literature, particularly for the group of individuals at least fifty-five years of age (Jiménez-Martín and Vall Castelló 2009; García-Gómez, Jiménez-Martín, and Vall Castelló 2012).

Several competing phenomena can be behind the reversal of this downward trend in male participation (and especially employment) since the late 1990s. Part of the reversal of this trend can be attributable to the effects of business cycle conditions, changes in the legislation, increasing levels of education, and the increase in the inflow of immigrants, which have, typically, higher participation rates than native Spanish people (Congregado, Golpe, and van Stel 2011; Aragón, de la Fuente, and Rocha 2009; Cuadrado et al. 2007).[1]

The evolution of labor market behavior of women is markedly different from that of men (see figures 9.1 and 9.2). First, labor market participation for women at least fifty-five years of age remained fairly constant between 1977 and 2001 at around 10 percent. Second, there is a remarkable increase in the participation rates in the last fifteen years, so participation is currently higher than it was during the late 1970s (figure 9.1). The steady increase in

---

1. Immigrants are typically younger than age fifty-five when they first arrive in the country. In any case, as the highest immigration inflow in Spain occurred in the late 1990s, some of those immigrants have already crossed the age fifty-five threshold.

the last fifteen years in labor force participation of older females relates to the overall trend in labor force participation of women (see figure 9.2). Similar to other developed countries, labor market participation of women has experienced a steady and continuous increase, from 28 percent in 1977 to 53 percent in 2014. We find that trends in labor market participation of men and women have been converging, although there is still a substantial gap in 2014: 53 percent of women participate in the labor market compared to 66 percent of men. This increase is concentrated among young women, mainly driven by a substitution of low-educated older women by more educated younger generations (Boldrin, Jiménez-Martín, and Peracchi 2001). As the increase in female participation rates are mainly driven by cultural changes regarding the role of women in society, and not by changes in the incentives provided by the social security schemes, we focus on males in the rest of the chapter.

9.2.1   Labor Force Participation and Health of Males

We now turn to revise the evolution of two health measures, mortality and self-assessed health, for Spanish males age fifty to seventy-five. Several factors have been identified as determinants of the evolution of population health such as the health care system, individual behavior, and social environment, among others. We use data from the Human Mortality Database (HMD) and the Spanish National Health Survey (ENS) to analyze the evolution of both mortality and self-reported health in the last thirty years. The Spanish National Health Survey (ENS) is a set of nationwide, cross-sectional surveys that collect information on health, health care use, lifestyles, and socioeconomic characteristics of the Spanish population. Figure 9.3 plots the age profile of self-assessed health and mortality for males in 1987, 1993, and 2006. Self-assessed health is obtained from ENS and shows the percentage that rate their general health as fair or poor, while mortality rates by age are obtained from HMD. Figure 9.3 shows that, as expected, health (measured both by self-assessed health and mortality) deteriorates with age. We also see that the large gains in mortality obtained during the last decades have been concentrated among the elderly. A reduction in mortality would translate in an increase in the population able to work if these changes go hand in hand with an improvement of the health of the population in the working age. The international evidence is inconclusive regarding whether changes in mortality are translated into a compression or expansion of morbidity (Klijs, Mackenbach, and Nusselder 2009). The evidence shown in figure 9.3 also points out that the self-reported health of the older Spanish has improved over time: in 1987, 51 percent of men age sixty-five reported having fair to poor health, while this proportion falls to 46 percent in 1993, and to 41 percent in 2006. This improvement in self-reported health over time is observed specially among men age fifty-eight to seventy.

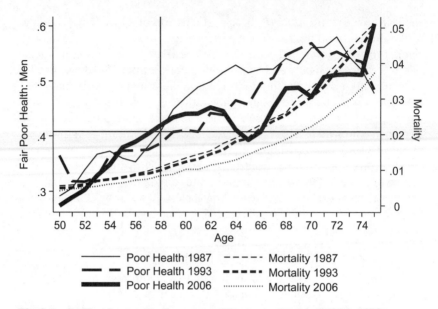

Fig. 9.3 SAH and mortality for men age fifty to seventy-five (1987 to 2006)
Source: Own elaboration from data from the Human Mortality Database and the Spanish National Health Survey.

Summing up, the last decades have witnessed a decrease in older mens' labor force participation and, at the same time, an improvement in the general health of men in their sixties. Thus, in what follows, we examine how much older Spanish men could work today if they experienced the relationship between health and employment of earlier years, that is, what is the unused health capacity to work.

9.3 Health Capacity to Work using the Milligan-Wise Method

We begin our analysis following the methodology first developed by Milligan and Wise (2015). The aim of this method is to get an estimate of the ability to work at older ages by comparing the relationship between mortality and employment in some previous period to the relationship between employment and mortality now. Thus, the idea is to get the potential employment possibilities of current cohorts if they worked as much as individuals that exhibited the same mortality rate almost thirty years ago. Once we get this potential employment (for a given mortality rate) estimate, its difference with respect to the current employment rate constitutes an estimate of the additional work capacity for current cohorts.

This method implicitly assumes that mortality is a good proxy for health and that the relationship between health and mortality has remained moderately stable during this thirty-year period. Despite the potential limitations behind these assumptions, we have chosen to use mortality as our proxy of health (rather than a measure more directly related to ability to work such as self-assessed health or prevalence of limiting health problems) for several reasons. First, the use of mortality data allows cross-country comparison of the estimates, while self-reported measures are subject to reporting bias across countries (Jürges 2007; Milligan and Wise 2012). Second, mortality data is available yearly for a long period of time, while self-assessed health is only available for the years 1987, 1993, 1995, 1997, 2001, 2003, and 2006 (in the National Health Survey, which, in turn, has a smaller number of observations if we want to have self-assessed health at each age). Last, although mortality represents a more extreme event in life than a change in self-assessed health, Milligan and Wise (2012) show that, within countries, improvements in self-assessed health show a very similar evolution than improvements in mortality.

We use data for mortality from the Human Mortality Database for years 1976 to 2010 and data for employment from the Labour Force Survey from the National Institute of Statistics in Spain also for the years 1976 to 2010. We consider only men in our analysis due to the late incorporation of Spanish women in the labor market, which would make our analysis much more difficult to interpret.

We plot the relationship between employment and mortality for Spanish men in two different periods: 1976–1980 and 1991–1995 in figure 9.4 and

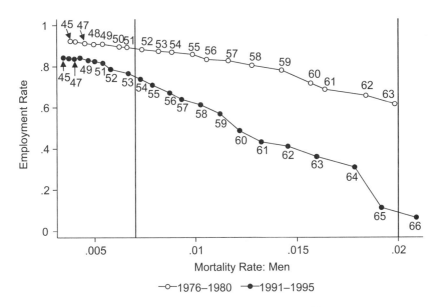

Fig. 9.4 **Employment versus mortality (1976–1980 versus 1991–1995)**

Source: Own elaboration from data from the Human Mortality Database and the Spanish Labor Force Survey.

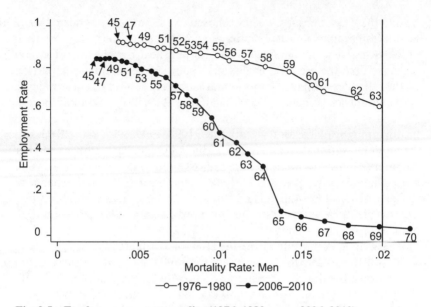

Fig. 9.5   Employment versus mortality (1976–1980 versus 2006–2010)
Source: Own elaboration from data from the Human Mortality Database and the Spanish Labor Force Survey.

1976–1980 and 2006–2010 in figure 9.5.[2] We can see that for a given mortality rate employment is lower in the two latter periods compared to the earlier one. For example, the employment rate at 0.7 percent mortality rate (first vertical line plotted in figures 9.4 and 9.5) is 89 percent in 1976–1980, 77 percent in 1991–1995, and 71 percent in 2006–2010. Similarly, at a 2 percent mortality rate (second vertical line plotted in figures 9.4 and 9.5), the employment rate in 1976–1980 was around 60 percent, in 1991–1995 around 10 percent, and in 2006–2010 around 3 percent. One of the reasons behind these large differences is that each of these mortality rates are also reached at later ages. For instance, the 2 percent mortality rate is reached at sixty-three years old in 1976–1980, but the same mortality rate is achieved at age sixty-five and a half in 1991–1995, and at age sixty-nine in 2006–2010. As mentioned before, this goes in line with observed increases in life expectancy.

Therefore, following the Milligan-Wise method, we estimate that, at a 2 percent mortality rate, if men in 2006–2010 would have worked as much as men in 1976–1980, the employment rate in 2006–2010 would have been 57 percentage points higher (observed employment rate is 3 percent, while the employment rate in 1976–1980 was 60 percent, that is, a difference of 57 percentage points). In other words, men in 2006–2010 age sixty-nine (with

2. We pool data for those five years for employment and mortality and calculate average employment and average mortality rate at each age.

a mortality rate of 2 percent) would have worked 57 percentage points more than men in 1976–1980 with the same mortality rate, which they achieved at age sixty-three.

We follow this same logic (but for single years and single ages) to estimate the additional employment capacity in 2010 using the relationship between employment and mortality from 1976. The results are shown in table 9.1 for men in each age from fifty-five to sixty-nine in 2010. In order to calculate the additional employment capacity, we proceed as follows. First, we take the mortality rate for men age fifty-five in 2010 and go back to the employment rate of men in 1976 that had the same mortality rate than the fifty-five-year-olds in 2010. Once we have this (equal-mortality) employment rate, we subtract it from the current employment rate for fifty-five years old in 2010 to estimate the additional work capacity for men age fifty-five in 2010. The third column of table 9.1 reports the employment rate in 2010, while the employment rate in 1976 at the same mortality rate can be found in the fourth column. Thus, as can be seen in the last column (first row) of table 9.1, men age fifty-five in 2010 could have worked an additional 18.8 percent, which is translated into 0.18 additional years of work on average. If we perform the same estimation for the older individuals included in our sample, we can see that men age sixty-nine in 2010 could have worked an additional 0.69 years of work.

If we repeat this calculation for each age from fifty-five to sixty-nine

Table 9.1   **Additional employment capacity in 2010 using 1976 employment-mortality relationship**

Age	Death rate in 2010 (%)	Employment rate in 2010 (%)	Employment rate in 1976 at same death rate (%)	Additional employment capacity (%)
55	0.58	73.6	92.4	18.8
56	0.65	71.7	91.1	19.4
57	0.71	67.7	90.3	22.6
58	0.75	62.9	89.9	27.0
59	0.84	61.8	89.4	27.6
60	0.87	52.2	89.4	37.2
61	0.93	44.7	89.1	44.4
62	1.07	40.6	86.3	45.7
63	1.11	34.7	84.5	49.8
64	1.22	29.4	84.3	54.9
65	1.32	9.2	82.8	73.6
66	1.44	7.9	81.6	73.7
67	1.57	5.1	79.0	74.0
68	1.63	4.6	74.6	70.0
69	1.79	3.7	72.8	69.2
Total years		5.7		7.08

and we sum up all the additional work capacity, we get a total additional employment capacity of 7.08 years of work (last column of table 9.1). We can compare this number with the average amount of employment of 5.7 years observed among Spanish males age fifty-five to sixty-nine in 2010 (see third column of table 9.1, last row). Thus, we can observe that, in Spain, the estimated additional capacity to work is much larger than the current average amount of employment for men age fifty-five to sixty-nine. However, notice that the legal normal retirement age in Spain is sixty-five years old and most Spanish men do actually retire at this age (or earlier). This is different in other countries, like the United States, where it is quite common to work after the normal retirement age. This fact implies that the estimated additional capacity to work increases by 20 percentage points from 54.9 percent at age sixty-four to 73.6 percent at sixty-five, as employment drops from almost 30 percent (at sixty-four) to 9.2 percent (at sixty-five) and the mortality rate in 2010 of individuals age sixty-five years old (1.32 percent) is reached at a much lower age in 1976 with an employment rate as high as 82.8 percent.

Labor market conditions have gone through important changes during the time period of analysis (from 1976 to 2010). Therefore, the estimated additional employment capacity depends to a great extent on the year that we choose as the baseline year. In the analysis shown in table 9.1, 1976 was the baseline year used to calculate the additional work capacity for individuals in 2010, but one could perform the same exercise choosing a different base year. We therefore repeat the exercise using all years from 1976 until 2009 as base year in order to provide a sensitivity measure of the robustness of our results to the specification chosen. Figure 9.6 plots the cumulate additional employment capacity for men age fifty-five to sixty-nine in 2010 compared to a baseline year that ranges from 1976 to 2009. We see that the largest estimated value corresponds to the value for the baseline year 1976 (7.08, as shown in table 9.1).

Using mortality as our health measure allows us to make use of very detailed information over a long time period as well as to compare the results across several countries. However, it also assumes that the additional years of life can be used to work, which may not be the case if individuals are not healthy enough to continue working. However, as figure 9.3 shows, self-assessed health has also improved during this period, especially among individuals age sixty or older. This result is similar to the evolution of self-assessed health reported for other countries in this volume.

The advantages of using mortality data are larger in countries like Spain in which longitudinal or large cross-sectional health surveys are not available. The sample size of the Spanish National Health Survey limits the analysis based on single ages, and changes in the questions asked prevent comparison based on other measures of health-like limitations in daily activities. Despite these limitations, we perform a similar analysis using two measures

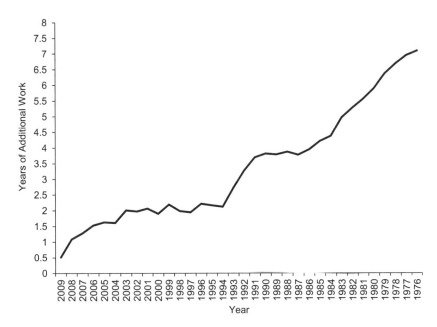

Fig. 9.6   Estimated additional employment capacity by year of comparison
Source: Own elaboration from data from the Human Mortality Database and the Spanish Labor Force Survey.

of subjective health to assess the robustness of the previous conclusions to measures that can better capture work limitations.

Figure 9.7 plots the relationship between self-assessed health and employment in 1987 and 2006 for individuals age forty-five to seventy years old, while figure 9.8 plots the relationship between work limitations[3] and employment for the same group of individuals and years. As before, employment is taken from the Spanish Labour Force Survey. As we need to calculate both employment rates as well as self-assessed health (and work limitations) at each age for the two survey years (1987 and 2006), the number of observations for the health variables at each age can be relatively small and, thus, the estimates are quite unstable[4]. For this reason, we apply a smooth transformation of the two health variables averaging the level of the current age with the level of the previous and next age.

3. More specifically, work limitations correspond to answering "yes" to at least one of the following two survey questions: (a) During the last twelve months, did you suffer a disease or illness that limited your principal activity (work, study, house work, etc.)?; and (b) During the last two weeks, did you have to reduce your principal activity for at least half a day for any of the symptoms or pains described before?

4. For example, the number of observations varies from 120 (minimum value) for age seventy to 289 (maximum value) for age forty-five in the survey of 1987, and from 113 (minimum value) for age sixty-eight to 235 (maximum value) at age forty-five for the survey of 2006.

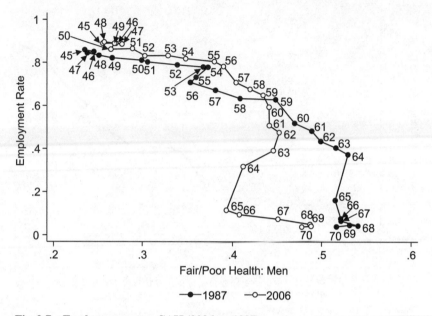

Fig. 9.7 Employment versus SAH (2006 vs. 1987)

Source: Own elaboration from data from the Spanish National Health Survey and the Spanish Labor Force Survey.

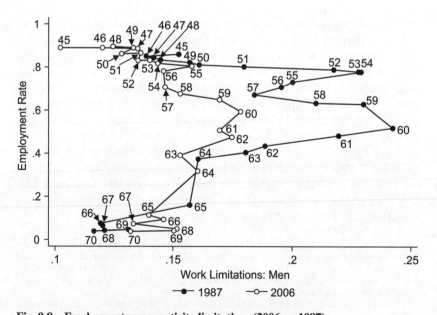

Fig. 9.8 Employment versus activity limitations (2006 vs. 1987)

Note: Own elaboration from data from the Spanish National Health Survey and the Spanish Labor Force Survey.

We see that the percentage of men that reports their health to be at best fair and the percentage that reports being limited for work does not change between 1987 and 2006 for those age forty-five to fifty-five (figures 9.7 and 9.8) However, both health measures improve in 2006 compared to 1987 for men at least fifty-five years of age. Figures 9.7 and 9.8 also illustrate that employment falls sharply at the normal retirement age of sixty-five.

To summarize, using the Milligan-Wise method we estimate an additional capacity to work of 7.08 years from ages fifty-five to sixty-nine in 2010 with respect to equal-mortality values in 1976. This value is larger than the observed employment capacity of 5.7 years for men age fifty-five to sixty-nine in 2010. The finding of a bigger estimated additional capacity to work than the current observed capacity to work is somewhat counterintuitive and unexpected. However, in the Spanish labor market context, this is mainly explained by the strong decrease in employment at the normal retirement age of sixty-five years old for Spanish men. For example, in 2010 employment is observed to decrease by 20 percentage points (from 29.4 percent to 9.2 percent) from age sixty-four to age sixty-five for men in Spain.

9.4 Health Capacity to Work using the Cutler, Meara, and Richards-Shubik Method

We also estimate the capacity to work using information from younger workers in the same year to estimate the relationship between health and employment as suggested by Cutler, Meara, and Richards-Shubik (2012). We first estimate a regression on employment decisions controlling for a large number of individual and health characteristics of individuals age fifty to fifty-four. Then, we use the estimated coefficients to predict the employment probabilities of older workers using their current explanatory variables (current health and individual characteristics). The novelty of this method is to use the estimates from individuals (baseline group) that are presumably not affected by social security benefits as they are years away from the normal and early retirement age.

We use individual data from the Survey on Health, Ageing and Retirement in Europe (SHARE) for wave 1 (2004–2005), wave 2 (2006–2007), wave 4 (2010–2011), and wave 5 (2013). SHARE is a multidisciplinary cross-national panel that contains detailed information on sociodemographic characteristics, health and labor status, among others, for a representative sample of the population age fifty and older in Europe. We pool information from the four waves mentioned above, and have a sample of 4,684 men and 5,466 women age fifty to seventy-four.

We estimate regressions of the following form:

(1) $\text{Employment} = \beta_0 + \beta_1 \text{health}_{it} + \beta_2 X_{it} + \varepsilon_{it}$,

where Employment is a dummy equal to 1 if the individual is employed and health is a comprehensive set of health measures: (a) dummy variables

Table 9.2A   Summary statistics, men

	Age group				
	50–54	55–59	60–64	65–69	70–74
Employed	0.74701	0.66869	0.41682	0.06256	0.00961
Health_exc	0.07910	0.06984	0.03676	0.04356	0.03088
Health_vgood	0.28060	0.22773	0.19133	0.14950	0.12247
Health_good	0.44627	0.45749	0.44581	0.44554	0.42812
Health_fair	0.12985	0.17915	0.23186	0.25941	0.31842
Health_poor	0.06418	0.06478	0.09425	0.10099	0.10011
Mobilit2	0.16269	0.22470	0.29689	0.37624	0.43497
ADLany	0.03731	0.04352	0.04995	0.07921	0.09808
IADLany	0.05821	0.04656	0.08577	0.11782	0.13220
Eurod	1.57187	1.73077	1.77843	1.81205	1.93069
Heartat	0.05357	0.06539	0.08937	0.13708	0.14665
Stroke	0.00446	0.01006	0.03010	0.03550	0.02763
Cholester	0.22917	0.24849	0.29069	0.29882	0.27418
Lungdis	0.03720	0.03924	0.06115	0.09172	0.09458
Cancer	0.00149	0.00604	0.00188	0.00690	0.01275
Highblpr	0.19048	0.24044	0.30386	0.38856	0.41233
Arthritis	0.19048	0.24044	0.30386	0.38856	0.41233
Diabetes	0.03869	0.06439	0.08278	0.12525	0.12327
Osteopor	0.00595	0.00905	0.00376	0.00394	0.00638
Alzheimer's	0.00149	0.00604	0.00188	0.00690	0.01275
Back	0.19494	0.21429	0.21919	0.24063	0.24973
Asthma	0.00744	0.00704	0.01223	0.00986	0.01169
Underweight	0.00448	0.00000	0.00192	0.00101	0.00323
Overweight	0.47982	0.50154	0.51631	0.51558	0.51832
Obese	0.18087	0.21392	0.18138	0.19900	0.19289
Smokerform	0.26339	0.30584	0.38852	0.41716	0.47078
Smokecurr	0.37463	0.32490	0.23113	0.19524	0.15672
Educ_lessthHS	0.64030	0.65231	0.72683	0.79715	0.85297
Educ_hs	0.17910	0.17026	0.11902	0.08359	0.05946
Educ_collegemore	0.17164	0.17231	0.15220	0.11417	0.08324
Married	0.79762	0.83702	0.85419	0.87870	0.86291
No. obs.	672	994	1,063	1,014	941

for different categories of self-assessed health (excellent, very good, good, fair, and poor); (b) mobility limitations (dummy variable if the individual has at least one arm function and fine motor limitations); (c) dummy variable if limited in any activity of daily living (ADLs); (d) dummy variable if limited in any instrumental activity of daily living (IADLs); (e) EUROD mental health index; (f) dummy variables for different health problems (AMI, stroke, cholesterol, lung disease, cancer, high blood pressure, arthritis, diabetes, osteoporosis, Alzheimer's, back pain, and asthma); (g) dummy variables that capture if the individual is underweight, overweight, or obese; and (h) smoking behavior (former or current smoker). Last, we control for

Table 9.2B   **Summary statistics, women**

	Age group				
	50–54	55–59	60–64	65–69	70–74
Employed	0.50921	0.40575	0.21891	0.03330	0.00720
Health_exc	0.07067	0.04710	0.02710	0.02511	0.01738
Health_vgood	0.25363	0.18671	0.15297	0.11839	0.07055
Health_good	0.41433	0.44155	0.41346	0.38475	0.34867
Health_fair	0.19458	0.25736	0.29983	0.33722	0.36810
Health_poor	0.06680	0.06728	0.10664	0.13453	0.19530
Mobilit2	0.31462	0.38015	0.50175	0.56822	0.70829
ADLany	0.03872	0.05299	0.07605	0.07361	0.14944
IADLany	0.06389	0.09588	0.14773	0.16338	0.30911
Eurod	2.71724	2.75576	3.01157	3.03137	3.65263
Heartat	0.01838	0.02860	0.06376	0.07239	0.11236
Stroke	0.00387	0.00336	0.01223	0.01519	0.03371
Cholester	0.15184	0.24222	0.28734	0.32082	0.32482
Lungdis	0.02805	0.02523	0.03319	0.03664	0.05312
Cancer	0.00193	0.00168	0.00437	0.00983	0.01328
Highblpr	0.16731	0.23970	0.32052	0.44504	0.52809
Arthritis	0.16731	0.23970	0.32052	0.44504	0.52809
Diabetes	0.11896	0.14718	0.22620	0.23056	0.30950
Osteopor	0.01741	0.03448	0.05328	0.05094	0.06742
Alzheimer's	0.00193	0.00168	0.00437	0.00983	0.01328
Back	0.31915	0.32044	0.34847	0.36282	0.41267
Asthma	0.01354	0.00925	0.01135	0.01340	0.01634
Underweight	0.01265	0.00853	0.00527	0.00091	0.00103
Overweight	0.29572	0.37255	0.38016	0.40018	0.39917
Obese	0.17607	0.19693	0.22300	0.23519	0.24716
Smokerform	0.15184	0.14718	0.11790	0.07596	0.05312
Smokecurr	0.25194	0.16835	0.08392	0.05211	0.01738
Educ_lessthHS	0.63770	0.71931	0.81311	0.88370	0.90729
Educ_hs	0.18945	0.14335	0.08415	0.05220	0.04375
Educ_collegemore	0.16797	0.13219	0.09920	0.06136	0.04271
Married	0.84623	0.83011	0.80961	0.79267	0.69969
No. obs.	1,034	1,189	1,145	1,119	979

educational attainment and marital status and estimate this equation using linear probability model. Tables 9.2A and 9.2B for men and women, respectively, provide descriptive statistics for all the relevant variables for the different age groups, along with sample sizes. Table 9.2C includes a description of the variables displayed in tables 9.2A and 9.2B.

Sample size for individuals age fifty to fifty-four (see tables 9.2A and 9.2B) may not be large enough to precisely estimate all the coefficients for the large set of health conditions. Therefore, we also perform an alternative version of this regression model in which we create a single health index that combines the information provided by a set of health variables. We

Table 9.2C   **Definition of variables in tables 9.2A and 9.2B**

Variable	Definition
Employed	Dummy equal to 1 if the individual is employed
Health_exc	Dummy equal to 1 if the individual states to be in excellent health
Health_vgood	Dummy equal to 1 if the individual states to be in very good health
Health_good	Dummy equal to 1 if the individual states to be in good health
Health_fair	Dummy equal to 1 if the individual states to be in fair health
Health_poor	Dummy equal to 1 if the individual states to be in poor health
Mobilit2	Dummy equal to 1 if the individual has at least one arm function and fine motor limitations
ADLany	Dummy equal to 1 if the individual has difficulty with an activity of daily living (ADL)
IADLany	Dummy equal to 1 if the individual has difficulty with an instrumental activity of daily living (IADL)
Eurod	EUROD mental health index
Heartat	Dummy equal to 1 if the individual ever experienced AMI
Stroke	Dummy equal to 1 if the individual ever experienced stroke
Cholester	Dummy equal to 1 if the individual ever experienced cholesterol
Lungdis	Dummy equal to 1 if the individual ever experienced lung disease
Cancer	Dummy equal to 1 if the individual ever experienced cancer
Highblpr	Dummy equal to 1 if the individual ever experienced high blood pressure
Arthritis	Dummy equal to 1 if the individual ever experienced arthritis
Diabetes	Dummy equal to 1 if the individual ever experienced diabetes
Osteopor	Dummy equal to 1 if the individual ever experienced osteoporosis
Alzheimer's	Dummy equal to 1 if the individual ever experienced Alzheimer's
Back	Dummy equal to 1 if the individual ever experienced back pain
Asthma	Dummy equal to 1 if the individual ever experienced asthma
Underweight	Dummy equal to 1 if the individual is underweight
Overweight	Dummy equal to 1 if the individual is overweight
Obese	Dummy equal to 1 if the individual is obese
Smokerform	Dummy equal to 1 if the individual is a former smoker
Smokecurr	Dummy equal to 1 if the individual is a current smoker
Educ_lessthHS	Dummy equal to 1 if the individual has less than high school education
Educ_hs	Dummy equal to 1 if the individual has high school education
Educ_collegemore	Dummy equal to 1 if the individual has college education or more
Married	Dummy equal to 1 if the individual is married

follow Poterba, Venti, and Wise (2013) and construct a health index based on twenty-four health questions, including self-reported health diagnoses, functional limitations, and other health indicators. To do so, we first obtain the first principal component of these twenty-four indicators, which is subsequently used to predict percentile scores for each individual. Thus, the index has to be interpreted as higher values implying better health. Poterba, Venti, and Wise (2013) show that the health index is strongly related to mortality and future health events such as stroke and diabetes onset, though not to new cancer diagnoses.

Table 9.3A   **Employment regressions, all health variables**

Variable	Men 50–54		Women 50–54	
	Coefficient	Std. error	Coefficient	Std. error
Health_exc	0.240**	0.101	0.215**	0.0921
Health_vgood	0.153*	0.0892	0.243***	0.0788
Health_good	0.213**	0.0838	0.227***	0.0738
Health_fair	0.0646	0.0817	0.167**	0.0713
Mobilit2	−0.194***	0.0504	−0.0388	0.0382
ADLany	0.104	0.0972	0.0474	0.0967
IADLany	−0.203**	0.0799	−0.142*	0.0777
Eurod	−0.0369***	0.00923	−0.0182***	0.00670
Heartat	−0.0289	0.0699	0.0176	0.112
Stroke	0.0711	0.216	0.405*	0.232
Cholester	0.0525	0.0364	0.0464	0.0424
Lungdis	−0.113	0.0815	0.192**	0.0930
Cancer	−0.0687	0.386	−0.639*	0.335
Highblpr	−0.0534	0.0401	−0.0109	0.0417
Diabetes	−0.131	0.0864	−0.0548	0.0527
Osteopor	0.0645	0.189	−0.117	0.114
Back	0.0590	0.0418	0.00664	0.0369
Asthma	0.296*	0.173	−0.0473	0.127
Underweight	−0.386*	0.219	−0.150	0.130
Overweight	−0.00716	0.0335	−0.0267	0.0341
Obese	0.0672	0.0449	−0.0756*	0.0426
Smokerform	0.0876**	0.0389	0.0207	0.0426
Smokecurr	−0.0583*	0.0351	0.0604*	0.0355
Educ_hs	0.0798**	0.0404	0.126***	0.0395
Educ_collegemore	0.148***	0.0416	0.362***	0.0408
Married	0.0806**	0.0376	−0.149***	0.0408
Constant	0.569***	0.100	0.417***	0.0885
No. obs.	645		1,005	
R-squared	0.294		0.189	

***Significant at the 1 percent level.
**Significant at the 5 percent level.
*Significant at the 10 percent level.

Tables 9.3A and 9.3B show the results of estimating equation (1) for individuals age fifty to fifty-four, including either a large number of health variables (9.3A) or the health index (9.3B). Table 9.3C shows the factor loadings of the first principal component. All loadings are positive so that larger values of the first principal component represent worse health. The results are shown separately for men and women due to the potentially differential effect of the explanatory variables on employment for men and women. Overall, we find the expected sign of the association between health

Table 9.3B   **Employment regressions, PVW health index**

Variable	Men 50–54		Women 50–54	
	Coefficient	Std. error	Coefficient	Std. error
Health index	0.00570***	0.000653	0.00373***	0.000535
Educ_hs	0.106**	0.0425	0.158***	0.0390
Educ_collegemore	0.187***	0.0430	0.390***	0.0404
Married	0.133***	0.0395	–0.136***	0.0410
Constant	0.193***	0.0561	0.308***	0.0504
No. obs.	630		970	
R-squared	0.169		0.157	

***Significant at the 1 percent level.
**Significant at the 5 percent level.
*Significant at the 10 percent level.

Table 9.3C   **First principal component index of health**

Health measure	Wave 1	Wave 2	Wave 4	Wave 5
Difficulty walking several blocks	0.2540	0.2601	0.2847	0.2832
Difficulty lifting/carrying	0.2962	0.2966	0.2961	0.3080
Difficulty pushing/pulling	0.2750	0.3048	0.2904	0.2978
Difficulty with an ADL	0.2431	0.2596	0.2687	0.2747
Difficulty climbing stairs	0.3086	0.3012	0.2895	0.2950
Difficulty stooping/kneeling/crouching	0.3072	0.3125	0.2977	0.3093
Difficulty getting up from chair	0.2895	0.2990	0.2868	0.3019
Self-reported health fair or poor	0.2827	0.2605	0.2423	0.2688
Difficulty reaching/extending arms up	0.2390	0.2422	0.2597	0.2622
Ever experience arthritis	0.1404	0.0983	0.1261	0.1071
Difficulty sitting two hours	0.1987	0.2333	0.2353	0.2293
Difficulty picking up a coin	0.1478	0.1501	0.1931	0.1785
Back problems	0.2268	0.1982	0.1851	0.1641
Ever experience heart problems	0.1286	0.1331	0.1292	0.1290
Hospital stay	0.1093	0.1273	0.1164	0.1363
Doctor visit	0.1014	0.0931	0.0813	0.0930
Ever experience psychological problem	0.2313	0.1980	0.2152	0.2220
Ever experience stroke	0.0808	0.0866	0.0816	0.0798
Ever experience high blood pressure	0.0406	0.0363	0.0285	0.0398
Ever experience lung disease	0.1000	0.1075	0.0770	0.0772
Ever experience diabetes	0.2269	0.1990	0.1967	
BMI at beginning of observation period	0.0841	0.0864	0.1001	0.0697
Nursing home stay	0.0347	0.0104	0.0315	0.0394
Ever experience cancer		0.0670	0.0700	0.0982
N	2,165	1,967	3,088	5,787

and education and the probability of working for both men and women: more educated individuals and those in better health are more likely to be employed. However, there are some differences in the magnitude of the estimates between men and women. For example, the decrease in the employment probability is larger for men with mobility problems or depression compared to women, while having a college degree increases the employment probability of women twice that of men. On the other hand, we find an opposite sign for marital status: being married is associated with a higher employment probability for men but lower for women. The estimates using the health index are similar to the ones using the large set of health variables.

We use the estimates presented in tables 9.3A and 9.3B to predict employment probabilities for four age groups (fifty-five to fifty-nine, sixty to sixty-four, sixty-five to sixty-nine, and seventy to seventy-four). Table 9.4 shows these predictions and actual employment rates. The difference between the predicted and the observed percentage of individuals working in each group represents the estimated work capacity, also shown in table 9.4. We find that predicted employment decreases with age, but the decrease is very modest compared to the actual decrease, and this is independent of how health is included in the model. In fact, even the magnitude of the estimated work capacity is extremely similar in both cases. Therefore, the rest of the analysis is only shown using the estimates from the model that controls for health using the health index.

Figures 9.9 and 9.10 plot the percentage of men and women working in each age group as well as the estimated additional capacity to work for each age group and gender. We first note that both the actual and predicted probabilities of working are lower for women than for men for all age groups. This is not surprising as we are analyzing individuals over the age of fifty in the first decade of the twenty-first century, which correspond to the cohorts of 1960 and before for which women showed very low labor market participation rates. Furthermore, the actual percentage of individuals working in the age groups fifty-five to fifty-nine and sixty to sixty-four remains relatively high (67.7 percent and 42.6 percent for men and 41.3 percent and 22.4 percent for women). However, when the normal retirement age kicks in at age sixty-five, the actual percentage of individuals working drops substantially to 6.3 percent and 0.8 percent for ages sixty-five to sixty-nine and seventy to seventy-four for men (3.6 percent and 0.5 percent for women). Obviously, there is no health-related shock that affects individuals at age sixty-five so that the predicted percentage of individuals working is reduced smoothly over the ages of sixty to sixty-four, sixty-five to sixty-nine, and seventy to seventy-four. Therefore, when individuals reach the normal retirement age their actual employment decreases sharply while the predicted employment probabilities decrease relatively slower and, thus, the estimated capacity to work increases substantially from age sixty-five. That is, the additional capacity to work is estimated to be 5.4 percent (6.6 percent) for men (women)

Table 9.4   Simulations of work capacity

Age group	Use all health variables				Use PVW health index			
	No. obs.	Actual % working	Predicted % working	Estimated work capacity (%)	No. obs.	Actual % working	Predicted % working	Estimated work capacity (%)
Men								
55–59	945	67.3	74.4	7.1	919	67.6	73.0	5.4
60–64	993	42.4	71.2	28.8	970	42.6	68.9	26.3
65–69	947	6.1	67.5	61.3	912	6.3	65.3	59.1
70–74	894	1.0	64.8	63.8	861	0.8	62.3	61.5
Women								
55–59	1,147	40.9	47.5	6.6	1,109	41.3	47.9	6.6
60–64	1,109	22.1	42.4	20.3	1,049	22.4	43.1	20.7
65–69	1,056	3.4	39.2	35.8	1,006	3.6	39.7	36.1
70–74	931	0.8	34.8	34.0	862	0.5	36.2	35.7

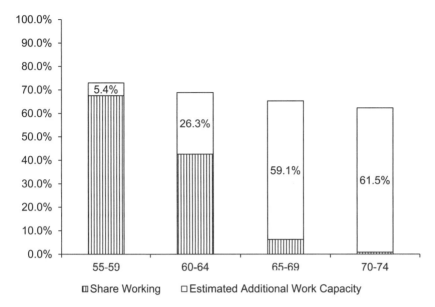

Fig. 9.9 Share of men working and additional work capacity by age
Source: Own elaboration from data from the Survey on Health, Ageing and Retirement in Europe.

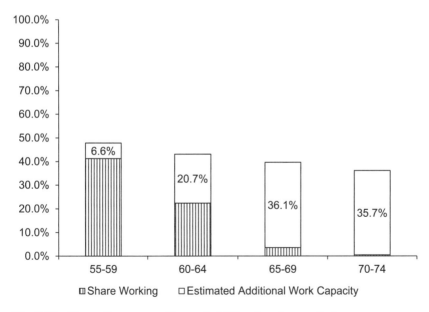

Fig. 9.10 Share of women working and additional work capacity by age
Source: Own elaboration from data from the Survey on Health, Ageing and Retirement in Europe.

ages fifty-five to fifty-nine, 26.3 percent (20.7 percent) for ages sixty to sixty-four, 59.1 percent (36.1 percent) for the age group sixty-five to sixty-nine, and 61.5 percent (35.7 percent) for ages seventy to seventy-four.

The work capacity is expected to be different for individuals with different educational attainment as labor opportunities may differ and a negative association between education and health has been found across the board. In addition, different health conditions may hinder employment opportunities differently depending on the educational attainment. Therefore, we provide estimates of the work capacity by education in two ways: (a) estimate separate regressions by education group to estimate work capacity for men and women (table 9.5A for men and 9.5B for women), and (b) use estimates shown in tables 9.3A and 9.3B to estimate work capacity for men and women (table 9.6A for men and 9.6B for women). We divide the sample in two groups based on educational attainment depending on whether they have or have not completed secondary education. In general, we see that higher-educated individuals show higher employment rates at each age group and gender but, at the same time, they also have higher estimated additional employment capacity as their health is better compared to low-educated individuals. However, there is an exception to this rule; lower-educated women age fifty-five to fifty-nine have a larger estimated additional capacity to work than high-educated women. This result is probably due to the fact that low-educated women at these ages show very low employment rates, although having a relatively good health status. Figures 9.11 and 9.12 plot the results of tables 9.5A and 9.5B for men and women, respectively, for the regressions using all health variables and a single regression for each educational group.

The Cutler, Meara, and Richards-Shubik method (Cutler, Meara, Richards-Shubik 2012) allows to estimate the health capacity to work using a group of contemporaneous individuals. Therefore we do not assume that labor market conditions are similar in different points in time as needed in the Milligan-Wise method (Milligan and Wise 2015). However, we still need to assume that individuals age fifty to fifty-four do not face any disincentive effects from the social security system to stop working. This seems a reasonable assumption for Spain as beneficial access to disability benefits kicks in at age fifty-five (in which benefits are increased from 55 to 75 percent of the regulatory base for partial disability) and early retirement schemes, which have been reformed over time, do not begin before age sixty. The only program that could pose a threat to this assumption is the unemployment benefit scheme, which includes an access to (permanent) unemployment subsidies for individuals age fifty-two or older until retirement (fifty-five after the last reform in 2013). However, this program gains in importance as the individual get closer to the early retirement age, especially after age fifty-five. Additionally, the Cutler et al. method also includes the implicit assumption that health affects employment decisions of individuals age fifty

Table 9.5A   Work capacity by education (regression by education group)

Education	No. obs.	Men, all health variables model			Men, PVW model		
		Actual % working	Predicted % working	Estimated work capacity (%)	Actual % working	Predicted % working	Estimated work capacity (%)
Age 55–59							
Low education	600	62.1	67.9	5.8	62.5	65.9	3.4
Medium edu.	329	75.7	85.1	9.4	76.0	85.9	9.9
Age 60–64							
Low education	715	38.6	64.9	26.3	38.7	62.8	24.1
Medium edu.	285	49.3	82.6	33.3	50.0	83.7	33.7
Age 65–69							
Low education	737	4.2	62.7	58.5	4.2	60.8	56.6
Medium edu.	209	12.3	80.4	68.1	12.4	81.6	69.2
Age 70–74							
Low education	736	0.3	61.6	61.3	0.1	58.6	58.5
Medium edu.	135	5.1	77.5	72.5	4.4	81.0	76.5

Table 9.5B Work capacity by education (regression by education group)

Education	No. obs.	Women, all health variables model			Women, PVW model		
		Actual % working	Predicted % working	Estimated work capacity (%)	Actual % working	Predicted % working	Estimated work Capacity (%)
Age 55–59							
Low education	799	32.4	39.2	6.8	32.8	39.1	6.4
Medium edu.	322	62.	67.6	5.6	62.1	69.6	7.4
Age 60–64							
Low education	856	17.9	36.6	18.7	18.2	36.8	18.6
Medium edu.	213	39.3	66.1	26.8	39.0	68.8	29.9
Age 65–69							
Low education	892	3.1	35.8	32.7	3.3	36.3	33.0
Medium edu.	132	5.1	62.3	57.2	5.3	66.4	61.1
Age 70–74							
Low education	785	0.7	33.1	32.4	0.4	34.0	33.6
Medium edu.	93	1.0	52.7	51.7	1.1	63.9	62.9

Table 9.6A Work capacity by education (single regression)

Education	No. obs.	Men, all health variables model			Men, PVW model		
		Actual % working	Predicted % working	Estimated work capacity (%)	Actual % working	Predicted % working	Estimated work capacity (%)
Age 55–59							
Low education	339	76.6	79.3	2.7	76.6	76.1	−0.5
Medium edu.	636	62.2	71.5	9.3	62.2	70.9	8.6
Age 60–64							
Low education	280	51.6	76.8	25.1	51.6	73.2	21.6
Medium edu.	745	38.5	69.9	31.4	38.5	67.8	29.3
Age 65–69							
Low education	199	14.1	75.7	61.5	14.1	70.2	56.1
Medium edu.	782	4.3	66.9	62.7	4.3	65.6	61.3
Age 70–74							
Low education	136	5.1	72.1	67.0	5.1	68.8	63.7
Medium edu.	789	0.3	65.8	65.6	0.3	63.5	63.3

Table 9.6B Work capacity by education (single regression)

Education	No. obs.	Women, all health variables model			Women, PVW model		
		Actual % working	Predicted % working	Estimated work capacity (%)	Actual % working	Predicted % working	Estimated work capacity (%)
				Age 55–59			
Low education	327	62.3	56.3	−6.0	62.3	54.2	−8.1
Medium edu.	838	32.4	45.5	13.1	32.4	47.9	15.5
				Age 60–64			
Low education	211	39.8	54.7	14.9	39.8	53.6	13.7
Medium edu.	918	17.9	41.9	24.0	17.9	44.9	27.0
				Age 65–69			
Low education	127	5.5	55.4	49.9	5.5	50.5	45.0
Medium edu.	965	3.1	40.8	37.7	3.1	44.0	40.9
				Age 70–74			
Low education	89	1.1	49.1	48.0	1.1	49.2	48.1
Medium edu.	871	0.7	36.8	36.1	0.7	40.8	40.1

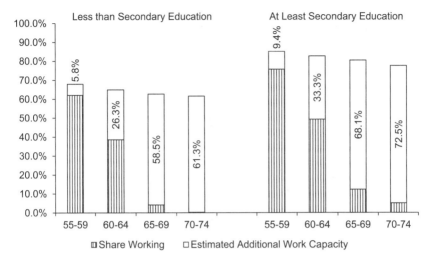

Fig. 9.11   Share of men working and additional work capacity by age and education

Source: Own elaboration from data from the Survey on Health, Ageing and Retirement in Europe.

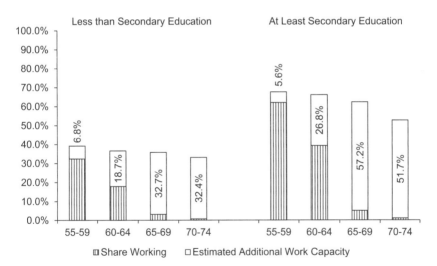

Fig. 9.12   Share of women working and additional work capacity by age and education

Source: Own elaboration from data from the Survey on Health, Ageing and Retirement in Europe.

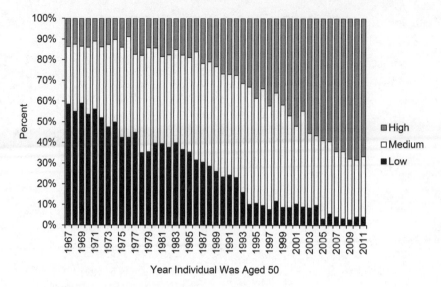

Year Individual Was Aged 50

Fig. 9.13   Distribution of years of education completed by cohort (by year cohort attained age fifty), men

Source: Own elaboration from the Spanish Labor Force Survey.

Note: Low education refers to individuals who did not complete primary education. Medium education refers to individuals who have primary education completed, while high education refers to individuals who have completed secondary education and above.

to fifty-four in a similar way than those older than fifty-five. If older individuals are systematically concentrated in certain type of jobs for which negative health shocks represent a stronger limitation to work than younger individuals, then our results would be biased.

9.5   Changes in Self-Assessed Health by Education Level over Time

It is well established that education is correlated with health and mortality across the board (Cutler and Lleras-Muney 2010). Therefore, trends in self-assessed health and mortality can be (partly) driven by changes in educational attainment. In addition, jobs opportunities for a given level of education may change over time. In this section, we first illustrate how the educational attainment of the Spanish population age fifty has changed over time, and later illustrate the evolution of self-assessed health using comparable groups of education.

Figures 9.13 and 9.14 show the distribution of education completed by cohort and gender.[5] They clearly show that education accumulation has

5. Low education refers to individuals who did not complete primary education. Medium education refers to individuals who have completed primary education, while high education refers to individuals who have completed secondary education and above.

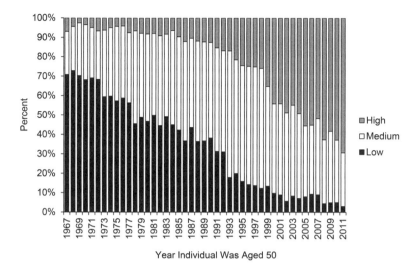

Fig. 9.14 Distribution of years of education completed by cohort (by year cohort attained age fifty), women

Source: Own elaboration from the Spanish Labor Force Survey.

Note: Low education refers to individuals who did not complete primary education. Medium education refers to individuals who have primary education completed, while high education refers to individuals who have completed secondary education and above.

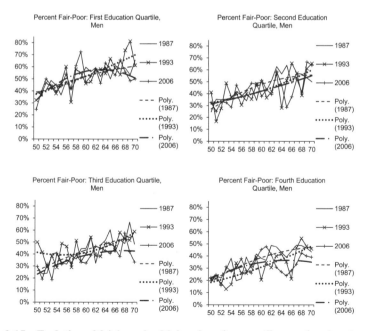

Fig. 9.15 Evolution of fair/poor health by education quartile over time (men)

Source: Own elaboration from data from the Spanish National Health Survey.

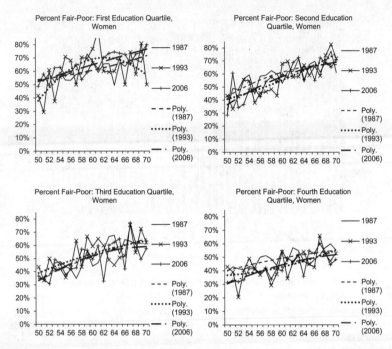

Fig. 9.16   Evolution of fair/poor health by education quartile over time (women)
Source: Own elaboration from data from the Spanish National Health Survey.

changed dramatically in the Spanish cohorts that turned age fifty between the late 1960s and the current years. While the older cohorts have very little education (a large majority, 60 and 70 percent for men and women, had only low education), the younger ones have much more education (60 percent of men and 70 percent of women that are age fifty in 2011 have high education).

Figures 9.15 and 9.16 present the evolution of the fraction having bad health by education quartile and gender in three periods of time (1987, 2003, and 2006). The fraction having bad health is defined as the fraction that declares having fair or poor self-assessed health. We find a clear decreasing gradient of the fraction having bad health by education quartile for both genders. Alternatively, the decreasing gradient over time is much less clear. Therefore, we find that the improvement in the health status of the population shown before seems to be driven by changes in the educational attainment of the Spanish population rather than by changes in the health status of individuals within a given education quartile.

9.6   Conclusion

One of the caveats behind any pension reform that extends the normal retirement age is whether workers are capable of working longer. In this chapter we have explored whether Spanish workers have the health capacity to work longer using two alternative methods. First, we have estimated what would be the current level of employment if individuals with a given mortality rate today worked as much as individuals with the same mortality rate in the past. Second, we have used a contemporaneous younger cohort to evaluate the work capacity assuming that the same health problem hampers employment in the same way for the two groups of individuals. The conclusions from both analyses are similar: there is a large employment potential among the population age fifty-five to sixty-nine. In particular, using the Milligan-Wise method (Milligan and Wise 2014), we estimate an additional capacity to work of 7.08 years from fifty-five to sixty-nine in 2010 with respect to equal-mortality values in 1976. Similarly, using the Cutler-Meara- Richards-Shubik method (Cutler, Meara, Richards-Shubik 2012), we detect substantial gains that increase both with age (between 20 and 26 percent for individuals age sixty to sixty-four and between 36 and 61 percent for individuals age seventy to seventy-four) and the level of education.

There are several strong assumptions behind the analysis done in this exercise. Therefore, the results should be taken as an indication that there is potential employment capacity among the population older than fifty-five in Spain rather than as a conclusive result for policy purposes. Further research using more detailed employment and health information is needed before one could drive large policy reforms to increase participation rates at older ages.

References

Aragón, J., J. Cruces, L. de la Fuente, and F. Rocha. 2009. "La Situación de las Personas de 55 a 64 Años en Relación al Mercado de Trabajo y sus Trayectorias Laborales." *Estudios de la Fundación 1º de Mayo*.

Boldrin, M., S. Jiménez-Martín, and F. Peracchi. 1999. "Social Security and Retirement in Spain." In *Social Security and Retirement around the World*, edited by J. Gruber and D. Wise. Chicago: University of Chicago Press.

———. 2001. "Sistema de Pensiones y Mercado de Trabajo en España." *Books, Fundacion BBVA / BBVA Foundation*, 1, (201120):355.

———. 2004. "Micro-Modeling of Retirement Behavior in Spain." In *Social Security Programs and Retirement around the World: Micro-Estimation*, edited by J. Gruber and D. Wise. Chicago: University of Chicago Press.

Cervini-Pla, M., and J. Vall Castelló. 2015. "The Earnings and Employment Losses before Entering the Disability System." IZA Working Paper no. 8913, Institute for the Study of Labor.

Congregado, E., A. A. Golpe, and A. van Stel. 2011. "Exploring the Big Jump in the Spanish Unemployment Rate: Evidence on an 'Added-Worker' Effect." *Economic Modelling* 28:1099–105.

Cuadrado, P., A. Lacuesta, J. M. Martínez, and E. Pérez. 2007. "El Futuro de la Tasa de Actividad Española: Un Enfoque Generacional." *Documentos de Trabajo, Banco de España* No. 0732.

Cutler, D. M., and A. Lleras-Muney. 2010. "Understanding Differences in Health Behavior by Education." *Journal of Health Economics* 29:1–28.

Cutler, D. M., E. Meara, and S. Richards-Shubik. 2012. "Health and Work Capacity of Older Adults: Estimates and Implications for Social Security Policy." Unpublished Manuscript. Available at SSRN: http://ssrn.com/abstract=2577858.

European Commission. 2012. *The 2012 Ageing Report: Economic and Budgetary Projections for the 27 EU Member States (2010–2060)*. Brussels: European Commission.

García-Gómez, P. 2011. "Institutions, Health Shocks and Labour Market Outcomes across Europe." *Journal of Health Economics* 30 (1): 200–13.

García-Gómez, P., S. Jiménez-Martín, and J. Vall Castelló. 2012. "Health, Disability, and Pathways to Retirement in Spain." In *Social Security Programs and Retirement around the World: Historical Trends in Mortality and Health, Employment, and Disability Insurance Participation and Reforms*, edited by D. Wise. Chicago: University of Chicago Press.

Gruber, J., and D. Wise, eds. 1999. *Social Security and Retirement around the World*. Chicago: University of Chicago Press.

———. 2004. *Social Security and Retirement around the World: Micro-Estimation*. Chicago: University of Chicago Press.

Jiménez-Martín, S., and J. Vall Castelló. 2009. "Business Cycle Effects on Labour Force Transitions for Older People in Spain." FEDEA Working Paper no. 2009–25, Fundación de Estudios de Economía Aplicada.

Jürges, H. 2007. "True Health vs Response Styles: Exploring Cross-Country Differences in Self-Reported Health." *Health Economics* 16 (2): 163–78.

Klijs, B., J. Mackenbach, and W. Nusselder. 2009. "Compression of Morbidity: A Promising Approach to Alleviate the Societal Consequences of Population Aging." Netspar Discussion Paper no. 12/2009–058, Network for Studies on Pensions, Aging and Retirement.

Lanzieri, G. 2013. "Towards a 'Baby Recession' in Europe? Differential Fertility Trends during the Economic Crisis." *Eurostat, Statistics in Focus*. http://ec.europa.eu/eurostat/documents/3433488/5585916/KS-SF-13-013-EN.PDF/a812b080-7ede-41a4-97ef-589ee767c581.

Milligan, K., and D. Wise. 2012. "Introduction and Summary." In *Social Security Programs and Retirement around the World: Historical Trends in Mortality and Health, Employment, and Disability Insurance Participation and Reforms*, edited by D. Wise. Chicago: University of Chicago Press.

———. 2015. "Health and Work at Older Ages: Using Mortality to Assess the Capacity to Work across Countries." *Journal of Population Aging* 8:27–50.

Organisation for Economic Co-operation and Development (OECD). 2014. "Health at a Glance: Europe 2014." OECD Publishing. http://dx.doi.org/10.1787/health_glance_eur-2014-en.

Poterba, J., S. Venti, and D. Wise. 2013. "Health, Education, and the Post-Retirement Evolution of Household Assets." NBER Working Paper no. 18693, Cambridge, MA.

10

Health, Work Capacity, and Retirement in Sweden

Per Johansson, Lisa Laun, and Mårten Palme

One of Sweden's former Prime Minister Fredrik Reinfeldt's most controversial statements during his time in office between 2006 and 2014 was that the sustainability of Sweden's welfare state depends on the ability of the workforce to prolong their active time in the labor market. He added that people in the future should prepare themselves to stay in the workforce until age seventy-five. This question was put high on the policy agenda, and a government committee was appointed to suggest measures to delay the labor market exit (see Statens Offentliga Utredningar 2013).

Policy initiatives to delay retirement have also been implemented. The minimum mandatory retirement age increased from age sixty-five to sixty-seven in 2001. In 2007, an additional earned income tax credit and a payroll tax reduction were introduced for workers older than age sixty-five, with the purpose of increasing labor supply at older ages. Laun (2012) shows that these reforms seem to have increased labor force participation past age sixty-five.

One of the main issues in the subsequent public policy debate was to what extent the health status of the population would allow a delayed retirement age. Although life expectancy has increased rapidly over the last couple of

Per Johansson is professor of statistics at Uppsala University, a researcher at IFAU, and a research fellow at IZA. Lisa Laun is a researcher at IFAU. Mårten Palme is professor of economics at Stockholm University.

This chapter is part of the National Bureau of Economic Research's International Social Security (ISS) project, which is supported by the National Institute on Aging (grant P01 AG012810). Lisa Laun gratefully acknowledges financial support from the Swedish Research Council for Health, Working Life and Welfare, FORTE (dnr 2013–0209). Per Johansson gratefully acknowledges the financial support from the Swedish Research Council for Health, Working Life and Welfare, FORTE (dnr 2013–2482). For acknowledgments, sources of research support, and disclosure of the authors' material financial relationships, if any, please see http://www.nber.org/chapters/c13747.ack.

decades, skeptics pointed out that the development of self-reported health is less unambiguous and that one can even see a slight deterioration in some health measures, such as the share of people with obesity (BMI > 29.9).[1]

This chapter investigates what available microdata can tell us about whether or not and to what extent older workers in Sweden have the health capacity to extend their work lives. To address this question, we use two different methods. The first one estimates how much people with a given mortality rate today would work if they were to work as much as people with the same mortality rate worked in the past. This approach builds on the work by Milligan and Wise (2012). The calculations we make are based on plots of the relationship between employment and mortality over time. We use employment data from the LOUISE data set, administered by Statistics Sweden, and mortality data from the Cause of Death Register, administered by the Swedish Board of Health and Welfare. We focus on men and women age fifty-five to sixty-nine in 2009 and compare them to their counterparts in terms of mortality during the period 1985–2008 in this analysis.

The second method uses a regression framework and estimates how much people with a given level of health could work if they were to work as much as their younger counterparts in similar health. This approach builds on the work by Cutler, Meara, and Richards-Shubik (2012). We use data from the Survey of Health, Ageing and Retirement (SHARE) to estimate the relationship between health and employment for younger workers age fifty to fifty-four, and use these estimates together with the characteristics of older workers age fifty-five to seventy-four to predict the older individuals' ability to work based on health.

Finally, we document potential heterogeneity in health capacity across education groups. We look at changes in the development of self-assessed health by age between 1991 and 2010. In particular, we study if there are different developments in different quartiles in the distribution of educational attainment measured as number of years of schooling.

The results show that the increase in employment between the years 1998 and 2009 among men has been very similar to the decrease in the mortality rate. However, since 1985, there has been a decrease in the employment rate among men in the age group fifty-five to sixty-nine corresponding to more than three years at a constant mortality rate. Among females there has been no change in the employment rate in the age group fifty-five to sixty-nine between 1985 and 2009 at a constant mortality rate, primarily due to the general increase in the female labor force participation rate. Our analysis of health and employment among older workers shows very large potentials for increased employment of older workers. Finally, our results show no empirical evidence for increased health inequality in Sweden since the early 1990s.

1. See Socialstyrelsen (2013) for an overview.

The chapter is organized as follows: We first document the recent development of labor force participation and health in Sweden. Section 10.2 presents the results from the Milligan-Wise method and section 10.3 those from the Cutler et al. method. Section 10.4 presents the results on heterogeneity in the development of health across education groups. Finally, section 10.5 concludes.

10.1   Trends in Labor Force Participation and Health in Sweden

Figure 10.1 presents the development of labor force participation rates for men between 1963 and 2014 in different age groups. The figure shows that the labor force participation rate has varied substantially over time and differently for different age groups. The most dramatic development has been in the age group sixty to sixty-four. For this group, participation fell from 85 percent in the early 1960s to 55 percent in the late 1990s. Since then, the labor force participation rate increased consistently to above 70 percent in 2014. The developments in the other age groups forty-five to fifty-four and fifty-five to fifty-nine have followed a similar pattern, but have been less dramatic.

For men older than age sixty-five, there was a marked decline in labor force participation rates until the mid-1970s. The decline in the age group sixty-five to sixty-nine can primarily be attributed to the change in the normal retirement age from sixty-seven to sixty-five. In recent years, since the mid-1990s, there has been a trend towards a higher labor force participation

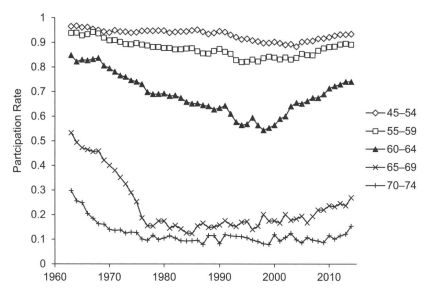

Fig. 10.1   Men's labor force participation by age group (1963–2014)
Source: Swedish Labor Force Survey, Statistics Sweden.

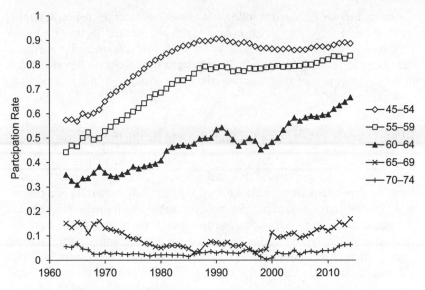

Fig. 10.2 Women's labor force participation by age group (1963–2014)
Source: Swedish Labor Force Survey, Statistics Sweden.

rate in the age group sixty-five to sixty-nine. In 2014 it was almost 27 percent, which is more than double compared to the rate in the mid-1980s.

Figure 10.2 shows the trends of labor force participation among women. Compared to men, there is a very different development. For the two youngest age groups, forty-five to fifty-four and fifty-five to fifty-nine, there was a dramatic increase in labor force participation from the early 1960s until the early 1990s. Since then the rates have been quite stable at 90 and 80 percent, respectively. For women age sixty to sixty-four, there has been a steady increase in labor force participation, except for a period in the 1990s. In 2014, participation in this age group was almost 67 percent. As for men, there is an increase in labor force participation rates for the age group sixty-five to sixty-nine, although on a slightly lower level.

Figure 10.3A presents the trends in mortality for men age fifty to seventy-four between 1985 and 2010. The mortality data comes from the Cause of Death Register administered by the National Board of Health and Welfare. There is a trend toward lower mortality rates over the entire period under study. In 1985, the mortality rate of men age fifty-five is about 0.8 percent. In 2009, that mortality rate is not reached until age sixty-one.

Figure 10.3B presents self-assessed health by age for men age fifty to seventy-four in 1991, 2000, and 2010, based on the Swedish Level of Living Survey (LNU). This survey is managed by the Stockholm Institute of Social Research (SOFI) at Stockholm University and contains data on socioeconomic characteristics and information on living conditions obtained through

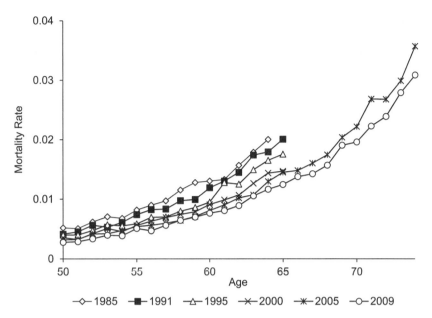

Fig. 10.3A   Mortality for men age fifty to seventy-four (1985–2010)
Source: Swedish Cause of Death Register.

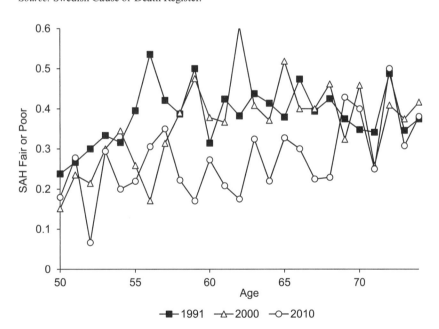

Fig. 10.3B   Self-assessed health fair or poor for men age fifty to seventy-four (1985–2010)
Source: Swedish Level of Living Survey (LNU).

interviews along with register data for individuals age sixteen to seventy-four and permanently living in Sweden. The sample size is about 6,000 individuals, about 0.1 percent of the Swedish population in the age interval under study.

The series show the fraction of the population reporting fair or poor health. There is an age gradient in self-assessed health, with an increasing share of individuals reporting fair or poor health as they age. The main message in figures 10.3A and 10.3B is that there is a trend toward improved self-assessed health. Between 1991 and 2000, there are improvements primarily in younger ages, below age fifty-eight. Between 2000 and 2010, on the other hand, the improvement in health primarily occurs in older ages, above age fifty-eight. The average share reporting fair or poor health declined from around 0.4 on average to around 0.25 above age sixty between 2000 and 2010, which is a quite substantial improvement over the last decade.

10.2 Estimating Health Capacity to Work Using the Milligan-Wise Method

Using a methodology suggested by Milligan and Wise (2012), we calculate how much people with a given mortality rate today would work if they were to work as much as people with the same mortality rate worked in the past. Advantages with using mortality data—rather than other measures of health that may be more related to an individual's work capacity—are that it can be very accurately measured and that it is available across countries, which facilitates comparisons.

The mortality data in this analysis comes from the Cause of Death Register administered by the National Board of Health and Welfare. Employment data is taken from the LOUISE (or SYS) register, administered by Statistics Sweden. An individual is defined as employed if, in a given year, he or she has labor income above one price base amount.

The period we consider is 1985 through 2009. The restriction in historic time is given by the availability of data on employment. The data covers individuals up to age sixty-four for the period 1985–1989, to age sixty-five for the period 1990–2000, and to age sixty-nine for the period 2001–2009. We calculate age-specific averages of the data on mortality and employment in three years: 1985, 1995, and 2009. The analysis displays the employment rate at each level of mortality for specific time periods and compares the curves across time.

Figures 10.4A and 10.4B present the results on the employment-mortality curves for men and women, respectively, in 1985 and 2009. Figure 10.4A shows that even though the employment rate, as we saw in figure 10.1, has increased slightly between 1985 and 2010, it has been far from enough to offset the rapid growth in life expectancy for men in order to maintain the relation between mortality and employment. For women, however, figure 10.4B shows that the employment growth actually has kept up with the reduced mortality rate since the two curves essentially coincide.

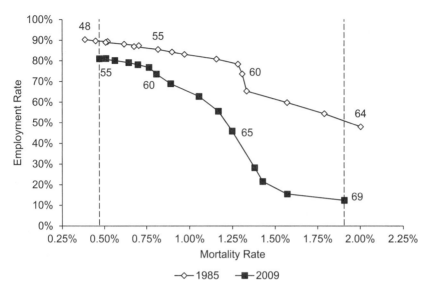

Fig. 10.4A   Mortality and employment in 1985 and 2009 (men)

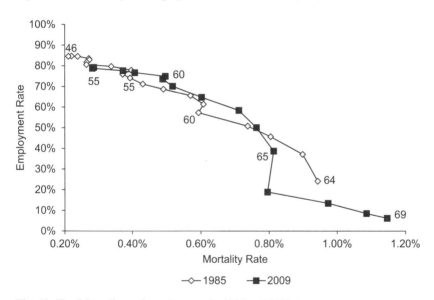

Fig. 10.4B   Mortality and employment in 1985 and 2009 (women)

Table 10.1A presents the results from asking how much more men age fifty-five to sixty-nine in 2009 could have worked if they had worked as much as men with the same mortality rate worked in 1985. Table 10.1B shows the corresponding estimates for women. An additional 7.86 percentage points of men could have worked at age fifty-five, which generates on

Table 10.1A   Additional employment capacity in 2009 using 1985 employment-
                     mortality relationship (percent, men)

Age	Mortality rate in 2009	Employment rate in 2009	Employment rate at same mortality rate	Additional employment capacity
55	0.51	81.11	88.97	7.86
56	0.47	80.99	89.62	8.63
57	0.56	80.12	88.56	8.44
58	0.65	79.11	87.92	8.81
59	0.70	78.11	86.76	8.65
60	0.77	76.80	86.11	9.31
61	0.81	73.58	85.68	12.10
62	0.89	68.91	84.43	15.52
63	1.06	62.79	82.08	19.29
64	1.17	55.64	80.60	24.96
65	1.25	45.91	79.05	33.14
66	1.38	28.22	64.25	36.03
67	1.43	21.58	63.14	41.56
68	1.57	15.45	59.77	44.32
69	1.91	12.40	50.93	38.53
Total years		8.61		3.17

average 0.0786 additional work years (one additional year for 7.86 percent of the fifty-five-year-olds). Similarly, an additional 8.63 percentage points of men at age fifty-six could have worked for one more year.

If we repeat this analysis for each age through age sixty-nine and cumulate the amounts, we get a total potential additional employment capacity of 3.17 years for men. This is equivalent to integrating between the two curves from one vertical line, indicating the starting age, to the next vertical line, indicating the last age group included in figure 10.4A. The average amount of employment between ages fifty-five and sixty-nine in 2009 is 8.61 years. This implies that an additional 3.17 years would represent an almost 37 percent increase over the ages fifty-five to sixty-nine.

Table 10.1B shows the results from a corresponding exercise on data for females. Due to the age restrictions described earlier, the estimates can only be obtained for women between ages fifty-five and sixty-six in 2009. The mortality counterpart in 1985 for women ages sixty-seven to sixty-nine was older than age sixty-four, and therefore not included in our data. For men, the mortality gain was large enough between 1985 and 2009 for the mortality counterpart to be age sixty-four or younger in 1985, which is covered by the data and enables us to compare all ages.

As is evident from the estimates in table 10.1B, there is a much more modest predicted gain in labor force participation for women compared to men: only a 0.02 years gain corresponding to 0.3 percent of the employment rate in the age interval. Some of the gender difference can be attributed to the

Table 10.1B   **Additional employment capacity in 2009 using 1985 employment-mortality relationship (percent, women)**

Age	Mortality rate in 2009	Employment rate in 2009	Employment rate at same mortality rate	Additional employment capacity
55	0.29	79.25	80.33	1.08
56	0.28	78.79	80.38	1.59
57	0.37	77.63	75.84	-1.79
58	0.41	76.67	73.01	-3.66
59	0.50	74.92	68.45	-6.47
60	0.49	73.55	68.76	-4.79
61	0.52	70.09	67.59	-2.50
62	0.60	64.66	56.83	-7.83
63	0.71	58.33	51.89	-6.44
64	0.76	50.01	48.79	-1.22
65	0.81	38.68	44.84	6.16
66	0.80	18.82	46.33	27.51
67	0.97	13.40		
68	1.09	8.46		
69	1.15	6.17		
Total years		7.89		0.02

fact that we were unable to include the age group sixty-seven to sixty-nine. However, the main background to this difference is the exceptional increase in female labor force participation rates that happened in the 1970s and 1980s and affected the birth cohorts that now are in the age groups fifty-five to sixty-nine. Since our focus in this study is to assess the potentials for prolonged work lives, the historical increase in the female labor force participation disturbs the comparison, making our method less suitable for the female subsample.

The Milligan-Wise method implicitly assumes that all gains in decreased mortality can be translated into additional work capacity. This is a strong assumption. It can be the case that decreased mortality is achieved through prolonged life, but with lost work capacity. A simple way to take this possibility into consideration is to assume that, say, two-thirds of the gain in decreased mortality is translated into prolonged work capacity by simply multiplying the figure above by two-thirds and arriving at an estimate of 2.11 years rather than 3.17 years for men.

Another question is which years to choose for comparison. As can be seen in figure 10.1, the break in the trend toward decreased labor force participation among older men since the early 1960s happened in the mid-1990s. In figures 10.5A and 10.5B, we replicate the analysis from figure 10.4A and 10.4B but use data from 1995, when the labor force participation started to increase, instead of 1985.

From the data shown above we know that the mortality rate was lower in

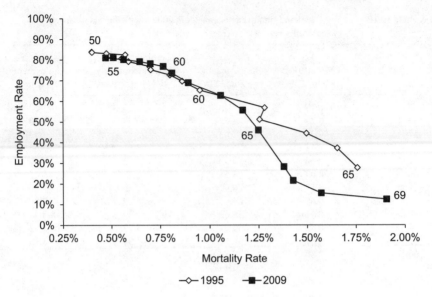

Fig. 10.5A   Mortality and employment in 1995 and 2009 (men)

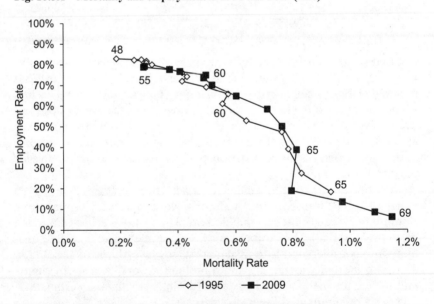

Fig. 10.5B   Mortality and employment in 1995 and 2009 (Women)

2009 than in 1995 at all ages and the employment rate was higher in 2009 than in 1995. The fact that the curves for the two periods in figure 10.5A lie very close to each other suggest that the employment increase for men is large enough to keep up with the decreased mortality. For men in the very oldest ages, however, with the highest mortality rates and the lowest employment rates, there is a slight divergence between the curves. For women, figure 10.5B shows that the curves again lie very close to each other, implying that the increase in employment was proportional to the mortality gains between the two years.

Figure 10.6 presents the estimated additional employment capacity in 2009 as a function of the comparison year used, for males and females, respectively. Because of the age restriction described above, it is not always possible to obtain a comparable employment estimate for all ages up to age sixty-nine in 2009. This will slightly affect the comparison over time, but the patterns should still be informative.

For males, the estimated additional employment capacity is small compared to all years in the period between 1998 and 2009, since the mortality decrease is accompanied with an employment increase during this era. However, compared to years in the 1985–1990 period, the estimated additional capacity is substantial. As noted above, the situation for females is very different because there is an effect across cohorts toward a higher labor force participation rate.

We also use data on self-assessed health (SAH) and activity limitation (cannot run 100 meters) from the Swedish Level of Living Survey (LNU) to measure subjective health in 1991, 2001, and 2010, respectively. The total sample size is 0.1 percent of the Swedish population ages sixteen to seventy-five, that is, about 6,000 individuals. This means that we have around thirty-five to sixty men for each one-year birth cohort in ages fifty-five to seventy-five. Figures 10.7 and 10.8 present the results from the approach

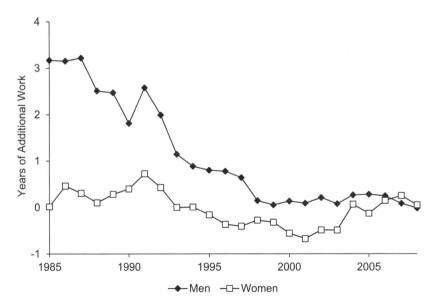

Fig. 10.6   Estimated additional employment capacity in 2009 by year of comparison for men and women

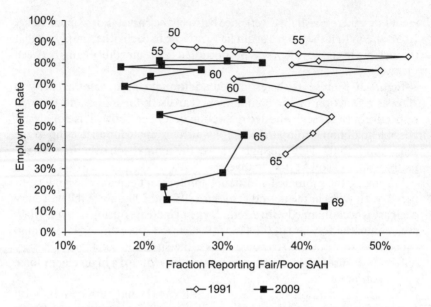

Fig. 10.7A Self-assessed health (share reporting fair or poor) and employment in 1991 and 2009 (men)

Source: Statistics Sweden and the Level of Living Survey. SAH for year 2009 is in fact from year 2010.

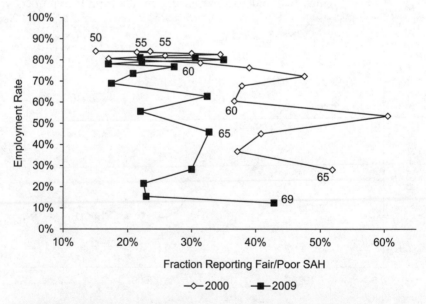

Fig. 10.7B Self-assessed health (share reporting fair or poor) and employment in 2000 and 2009 (men)

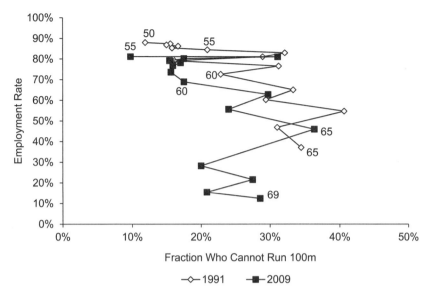

Fig. 10.8A   Activity limitation (share who cannot run 100m) and employment in 1991 and 2009 (men)

Source: Statistics Sweden and the Level of Living Survey. Activity limitation for year 2009 is in fact from year 2010.

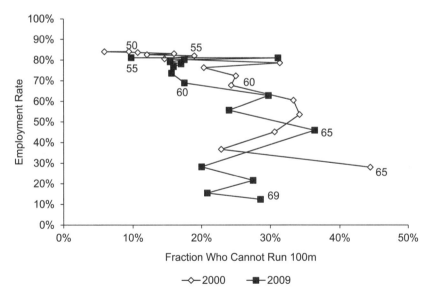

Fig. 10.8B   Activity limitation (share who cannot run 100m) and employment in 2000 and 2009 (men)

Source: Statistics Sweden and the Level of Living Survey. Activity limitation for year 2009 is in fact from year 2010.

used in figures 10.4A and 10.4B with SAH and activity limitation in place of mortality. Whereas the employment data is for 2009, the subjective health data is from 2010. The horizontal axis shows the share of individuals who report themselves to be in fair or poor health (figure 10.7) and the share who report that they cannot run 100 meters (figure 10.8).

As the sample size for each age is small, the graphs are quite noisy. However, the same pattern of health improvement over time is seen as shown for mortality in figures 10.4A and 10.4B. For example, in 1991, 40 percent of fifty-five-year-olds were in fair or poor health, as compared to 22 percent of fifty-five-year-olds in 2009. The equivalent figures for activity limitations are 21 percent in 1991 and 10 percent in 2009.

In short, estimates based on the Milligan-Wise method suggest a significant amount of additional work capacity for men. We estimate that the additional capacity from ages fifty-five to sixty-nine is 3.17 years using the 1985 employment-mortality curve as a comparison, or 0.8 years compared to 1995. For women, however, this method suggests that the additional work capacity is limited when using previous cohorts as a benchmark. The results also suggest that the largest potential for additional employment capacity can be found among the oldest, primarily older than age sixty-five. This is due to the large drop in employment after age sixty-five that cannot be related to a sudden change in health status of older individuals.

10.3   Estimating Health Capacity to Work Using the Cutler et al. Method

In this section we investigate the work capacity of older workers by asking how much they would work if they work as much as their younger counterparts in similar health. The method we use was originally suggested by Cutler, Meara, and Richards-Shubik (2012). The analysis is done in two steps. First, we estimate the relationship between health and employment for a sample of workers whose decision to exit from the labor market is driven by health considerations rather than preferences for leisure. We use the age group fifty to fifty-four, since previous research (see, e.g., Johansson, Laun, and Palme 2016) has shown that workers in this age group almost exclusively use the disability insurance program or sickness insurance for their labor market exit. This age group is also far from being able to claim benefits from the public old age pension program at age sixty-one. Second, we use the coefficients from the estimated regressions and the actual characteristics of individuals age fifty-five to seventy-four to predict the older individuals' ability to work based on health.

The data used in the analysis is taken from the Survey of Health, Ageing and Retirement in Europe (SHARE). We use wave 1, wave 2, wave 4, and wave 5, conducted in 2004, 2007, 2011, and 2014, respectively. The numbers of observations are 2,997; 2,711; 1,945; and 4,531. The SHARE survey collects rich data on health, as well as data on employment and demographics and is therefore well suited for this analysis.

We estimate the following linear probability model:

$$\text{Employment} = \beta_0 + \beta_1 \text{health}_i + \beta_2 X_i + \varepsilon_i,$$

where Employment is a dummy equal to 1 if the individual is employed; health is a vector of health measures that we describe in detail below; and X is a vector of nonhealth personal characteristics, such as educational attainment and marital status. We estimate this equation using ordinary least squares (OLS).

In an alternative specification the health vector is summarized and replaced by a single index value. We follow the method suggested by and described in Poterba, Venti, and Wise (2013). They use the first principal component of twenty-seven questions in the US Health and Retirement Survey (HRS), including self-reported health diagnoses, functional limitations, medical care usage, and other health indicators. Not all of these questions are included in the SHARE survey. For the sake of comparability we use the set of twenty-four variables that is also used in the chapter 12 of this volume. Each individual's index value is transformed to a percentile score. This means that the coefficient for the index value can be interpreted as the effect of moving 1 percentage point in the health distribution on employment probability.

Our analysis relies on three key assumptions:

1. Health is exhaustively measured by our health measure, that is, there are no unmeasured or omitted dimensions of health. An important implication of this assumption is that the health measures should be consistent across ages. That is, for example, the SAH measures should not be given an interpretation relative to a peer group of similar age as the respondent.

2. The health-employment relationship is independent of age, that is, the relation estimated for the younger individuals (age fifty to fifty-four) applies for the older ones (age fifty-five to seventy-four).

3. Exit from the labor market is determined by health reasons only. Nonhealth-related retirement among our sample of younger individuals would cause a downward bias in the estimate of health on retirement. The choice of a relatively young age group helps with avoiding this problem.

Tables 10.2A and 10.2B present summary statistics for the male and female samples, respectively. The employment rate of men falls from 89 percent at ages fifty to fifty-four to 84 percent at ages fifty-five to fifty-nine, 70 percent at ages sixty to sixty-four, 13 percent at ages sixty-five to sixty-nine, and 4 percent at ages seventy to seventy-four. Employment rates for women are slightly lower in each age group: 84 percent at ages fifty to fifty-four, 80 percent at ages fifty-five to fifty-nine, 60 percent at ages sixty to sixty-four, 8 percent at ages sixty-five to sixty-nine, and 1 percent at ages seventy to seventy-four. As expected, health measures decline with age. The share of men in poor or fair health rises from 8 percent at ages fifty to fifty-four to 24 percent at ages seventy to seventy-four. As in most surveys, women report

Table 10.2A   Summary statistics, pooled SHARE samples (men)

	Age group				
	50–54	55–59	60–64	65–69	70–74
Employed	0.89	0.84	0.70	0.13	0.04
Health, poor	0.02	0.04	0.04	0.04	0.06
Health, fair	0.06	0.12	0.14	0.14	0.18
Health, good	0.30	0.28	0.33	0.34	0.34
Health, very good	0.32	0.29	0.28	0.28	0.22
Health, excellent	0.29	0.28	0.20	0.20	0.20
Physical limitations (= 1)	0.09	0.11	0.12	0.18	0.17
Physical limitations (> 1)	0.06	0.11	0.15	0.15	0.20
ADL any	0.04	0.03	0.06	0.06	0.08
IADL any	0.01	0.01	0.02	0.02	0.04
CESD (depression index)	0.01	0.04	0.02	0.04	0.03
Heart	0.04	0.08	0.11	0.16	0.19
Stroke	0.01	0.03	0.03	0.04	0.06
Psychological problems	0.13	0.02	0.08	0.02	0.14
Lung diseases	0.02	0.02	0.05	0.07	0.09
Cancer	0.01	0.04	0.02	0.04	0.03
High blood pressure	0.15	0.23	0.34	0.42	0.42
Arthritis	0.03	0.04	0.05	0.05	0.04
Diabetes	0.04	0.06	0.12	0.15	0.14
Back pain	0.40	0.41	0.37	0.36	0.35
Weight, under	0.00	0.00	0.00	0.00	0.00
Weight, over	0.47	0.31	0.34	0.32	0.28
Weight, obese	0.24	0.43	0.44	0.43	0.44
Smoker, former	0.43	0.52	0.64	0.67	0.72
Smoker, current	0.51	0.63	0.70	0.70	0.73
Education, HS grad	0.21	0.15	0.10	0.09	0.07
Education, some college	0.25	0.15	0.13	0.12	0.13
Education, college	0.34	0.23	0.15	0.09	0.07
Married	0.68	0.56	0.43	0.45	0.41
N	394	719	823	850	706

worse SAH, despite having lower mortality rates: 14 percent report fair or poor health in the age group fifty to fifty-four and 27 percent at ages seventy to seventy-four.

As for the SAH measures, several indicators for functional limitation and diagnoses reflect health deterioration by age. The share of men with more than one limitation on their physical activity increases from 6 percent at ages fifty to fifty-four to 20 percent at ages seventy to seventy-four. The corresponding values for women are 16 and 32 percent. The share with limitations in instrumental activities of daily living (IADLs) shows a similar trend, although on a much lower level, rising from 1 to 4 percent for men. The corresponding shares for women are 3 and 4 percent. Diagnoses such

Table 10.2B   **Summary statistics, pooled SHARE samples (women)**

	Age group				
	50–54	55–59	60–64	65–69	70–74
Employed	0.84	0.80	0.60	0.08	0.01
Health, poor	0.03	0.05	0.05	0.04	0.06
Health, fair	0.11	0.14	0.16	0.16	0.21
Health, good	0.30	0.30	0.31	0.33	0.37
Health, very good	0.31	0.26	0.26	0.26	0.24
Health, excellent	0.25	0.24	0.22	0.20	0.12
Physical limitations (= 1)	0.15	0.18	0.16	0.19	0.22
Physical limitations (> 1)	0.16	0.22	0.25	0.26	0.32
ADL any	0.04	0.05	0.07	0.07	0.09
IADL any	0.03	0.03	0.03	0.02	0.04
CESD (depression index)	0.02	0.03	0.03	0.05	0.05
Heart	0.03	0.05	0.06	0.10	0.13
Stroke	0.00	0.02	0.03	0.02	0.04
Psychological problems	0.30	0.26	0.11	0.02	0.06
Lung diseases	0.02	0.05	0.05	0.07	0.08
Cancer	0.02	0.03	0.03	0.05	0.05
High blood pressure	0.19	0.26	0.29	0.37	0.45
Arthritis	0.04	0.09	0.11	0.11	0.11
Diabetes	0.05	0.05	0.06	0.07	0.09
Back pain	0.45	0.46	0.49	0.42	0.45
Weight, under	0.01	0.01	0.01	0.01	0.02
Weight, over	0.23	0.23	0.23	0.26	0.26
Weight, obese	0.31	0.45	0.47	0.45	0.44
Smoker, former	0.38	0.50	0.57	0.60	0.62
Smoker, current	0.56	0.62	0.75	0.77	0.79
Education, HS grad	0.19	0.14	0.12	0.10	0.08
Education, some college	0.21	0.14	0.12	0.14	0.13
Education, college	0.34	0.27	0.15	0.10	0.07
Married	0.62	0.51	0.40	0.36	0.32
N	565	954	959	1,010	719

as the share with high blood pressure rises from 15 percent at age fifty to fifty-four to 42 at age seventy to seventy-four for men.

Tables 10.3A and 10.3B show the results from our regressions. Table 10.3A shows the results from the specification where we have included all health indicators separately in the regression models and table 10.3B shows the results where we have summarized the health indicators in health indices. The estimates show highly significant effects of the subjective health indicators on the probability of being employed, in particular, for males. Men in fair (poor) health are 18 (57) percentage points less likely to be employed than those reporting excellent health. The corresponding estimates for women are 27 and 28. Having IADL limitations lowers men's (women's)

Table 10.3A   **Employment regressions, all health variables**

	Men 50–54		Women 50–54	
Variable	Coefficient	Std. err.	Coefficient	Std. err.
Health, very good	0.02	0.04	−0.01	0.04
Health, good	−0.04	0.04	−0.10	0.04***
Health, fair	−0.18	0.07***	−0.27	0.06***
Health, poor	−0.57	0.11***	−0.28	0.10***
Physical limitations (= 1)	−0.10	0.05*	0.01	0.04
Physical limitations (> 1)	−0.02	0.07	−0.11	0.05**
ADL any	−0.10	0.08	−0.22	0.08***
IADL any	−0.44	0.18***	−0.33	0.09***
CESD (depression index)	0.08	0.17	−0.13	0.09
Heart	0.06	0.07	−0.08	0.09
Lung disease	0.06	0.20	0.36	0.19*
Stroke	−0.04	0.01***	0.00	0.01
High blood pressure	0.04	0.04	0.03	0.04
Arthritis	0.09	0.09	0.06	0.07
Diabetes	−0.02	0.07	0.02	0.07
Back pain	0.01	0.03	0.04	0.03
Weight, over	0.00	0.03	−0.04	0.04
Weight, obese	0.07	0.05	0.01	0.04
Smoker, former	0.08	0.04**	0.07	0.04*
Smoker, current	0.10	0.04***	0.03	0.04
Education, mandatory	0.01	0.05	0.02	0.05
Education, some college	0.02	0.05	−0.03	0.05
Education, college/univ.	0.05	0.05	0.05	0.05
Married	0.08	0.03**	0.04	0.03
N	393		564	

Note: "Health, excellent" excluded category.
***Significant at the 1 percent level.
**Significant at the 5 percent level.
*Significant at the 10 percent level.

Table 10.3B   **Employment regressions, PVW health index**

	Men 50–54		Women 50–54	
Variable	Coefficient	Std. err.	Coefficient	Std. err.
PVW index	0.003	0.001***	0.004	0.001***
Education, mandatory	0.046	0.057	0.042	0.061
Education, some college	0.066	0.056	−0.016	0.060
Education, college grad	0.101	0.055*	0.079	0.057
Married	0.113	0.037***	0.022	0.038
N	333		457	

***Significant at the 1 percent level.
**Significant at the 5 percent level.
*Significant at the 10 percent level.

employment by 44 (33) percentage points. Having activities of daily living (ADL) limitations limits women's activity with 22 percentage points.

The results shown in table 10.3B are obtained from the index version of the model. The results show that the Poterba, Venti, and Wise (PVW) index works very well for summarizing the health information in the data, since the coefficient for the index is estimated with high precision. A 10-percentage-point increase in the index (e.g., being at the 60th rather than 50th percentile of health) raises the probability of employment by 3 percentage points for men and 4 percentage points for women.

Table 10.4 reports the results from a simulation where we have used the two versions of our model to predict employment for five-year age groups in the age interval fifty-five to seventy-five for males and females, respectively. To facilitate interpretation of the results we report key outcomes in figures 10.9 and 10.10. Since the estimation of the model using the PVW index turned out so well, and predictions from a parsimonious specification is preferred, we present the predictions from the model using the PVW index in figures 10.9 and 10.10.

The health index model predicts the share of men (women) employed to be 88 (82) percent at ages fifty-five to fifty-nine, 84 (80) percent at ages sixty to sixty-four, 83 (80) percent at ages sixty-five to sixty-nine, and 81 (76) percent at ages seventy to seventy-four. This decline can, of course, be attributed to the deterioration of health by age. The share of men (women) that is actually working declines more rapidly with age than do our predictions, from 83 (81) percent at ages fifty-five to fifty-nine to 70 (62) percent, 15 (8) percent, and 4 (1) percent in the older age groups. For the males (females) the capacity is 4.95 (1.22) percent at ages fifty-five to fifty-nine, 13.59 (18.08) percent at ages sixty to sixty-four, 68.05 (71.37) percent at ages sixty-five to sixty-nine, and 76.74 (75.20) percent at ages seventy to seventy-four.

A concern often heard in the public policy debate is that low-educated blue-collar workers with physically demanding jobs are less able to postpone their exit from the labor market for health reasons. To examine this argument more closely, we will look at heterogeneous effects by dividing the sample into two groups: those with a high school (HS) education or more and those without a high school education (< HS).

Our simulations of work capacity by education group and gender are shown in tables 10.5A and 10.5B and in figures 10.11 and 10.12. The results show very small differences in both actual and predicted share working for both males and females between the two groups with high and low educational attainments, respectively.

10.4   Changes in Self-Assessed Health by Education Level over Time

In this section we investigate the changes in self-assessed health (SAH). We use data from the Swedish Level of Living Survey (LNU), briefly described

Table 10.4   **Simulation of work capacity**

Age group	Use all health variables				Use PVW health index			
	N	Actual % working	Predicted % working	Estimated work capacity (%)	N	Actual % working	Predicted % working	Estimated work capacity (%)
				Men				
55–59	719	83.87	90.38	6.40	542	83.03	87.98	4.95
60–64	823	69.50	89.08	19.58	617	70.34	83.93	13.59
65–69	849	12.94	89.49	76.54	662	14.50	82.56	68.05
70–74	703	4.11	88.08	83.95	540	4.26	81.00	76.74
				Women				
55–59	953	80.19	83.56	3.29	712	80.76	81.98	1.22
60–64	959	60.38	83.56	23.18	695	62.30	80.38	18.08
65–69	1,010	7.52	83.53	76.00	764	8.25	79.62	71.37
70–74	719	0.97	80.41	79.43	569	0.86	76.06	75.20

Note: Actual working in all health and **PVW** models vary due to differences in sample sizes.

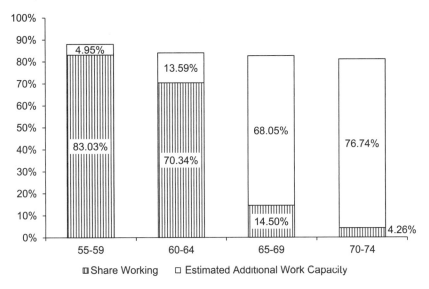

Fig. 10.9   Share of SHARE men working and additional work capacity by age

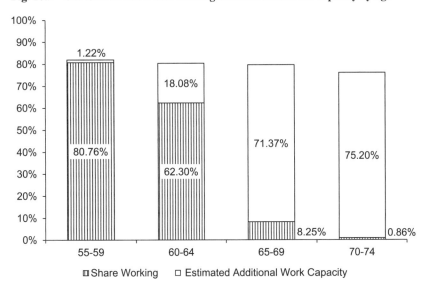

Fig. 10.10   Share of SHARE women working and additional work capacity by age

in section 10.1. In addition to the overall development we will look at the development by educational group separately, considering the fact that in Sweden, like in most other developed countries, there has been a substantial increase in the average educational attainment across birth cohorts. This implies that the selection into educational levels may have changed.

Table 10.5A   **Work capacity by education (single regression, men)**

	All health variables			PVW model		
Education	Actual % working	Predicted % working	Estimated % WC	Actual % working	Predicted % working	Estimated % WC
		Age 55–59				
< High school	81.88	88.41	6.53	79.14	82.96	3.82
HS or college/univ.	87.13	93.64	6.18	87.12	93.26	6.14
		Age 60–64				
< High school	69.98	88.67	18.69	71.76	80.01	8.25
HS or college/univ.	68.26	90.15	21.89	67.86	90.83	22.97
		Age 65–69				
< High school	13.17	88.87	75.68	15.29	79.44	64.15
HS or college/univ.	12.09	91.77	79.68	12.36	91.04	78.68
		Age 70–74				
< High school	4.81	87.85	83.02	5.22	78.35	73.13
HS or college/univ.	1.38	88.93	87.54	1.45	88.71	87.26

Note: Actual percent working in all health and PVW models vary due to differences in sample size.

Table 10.5B   **Work capacity by education (single regression, women)**

	All health variables			PVW model		
Education	Actual % working	Predicted % working	Estimated % WC	Actual % working	Predicted % working	Estimated % WC
		Age 55–59				
< High school	77.02	82.88	5.72	76.28	79.01	2.73
HS or college/univ.	84.90	84.58	−0.31	84.70	84.58	−0.11
		Age 60–64				
< High school	59.40	83.82	24.42	61.37	78.90	17.53
HS or college/univ.	63.04	82.84	19.80	64.05	83.16	19.11
		Age 65–69				
< High school	7.78	83.30	75.52	9.14	78.16	69.01
HS or college/univ.	6.69	84.27	77.57	6.14	83.05	76.91
		Age 70–74				
< High school	0.69	80.71	80.01	0.45	75.67	75.22
HS or college/univ.	2.10	79.18	77.07	2.17	77.32	75.15

Note: Actual percent working in all health and PVW models vary due to differences in sample size.

Figure 10.13 shows the development of the average number of years of schooling along with the first and third quartiles by birth cohort groups for those born by the end of the nineteenth century to those born in 1980. There is a steady increase, with an accelerating path for at least the average, starting with those born in the early 1940s. Over the entire period shown in the graph, the average number of years of schooling increases from about 6.5 to 15 years.

Figure 10.14A shows self-assessed health by age between ages fifty and seventy-five for the survey years 1991, 2000, and 2010. The sample size for

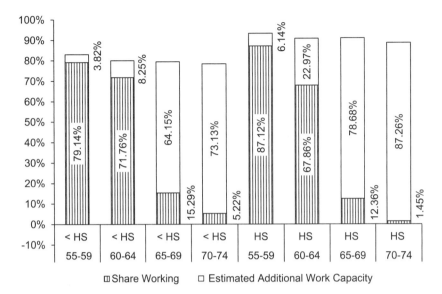

Fig. 10.11 Share of SHARE men working and additional work capacity by age and education

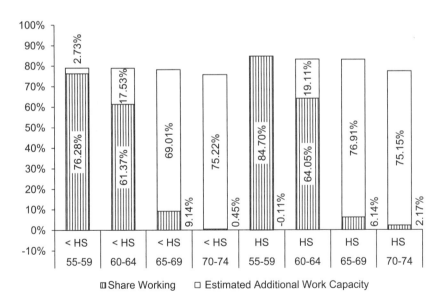

Fig. 10.12 Share of SHARE women working and additional work capacity by age and education

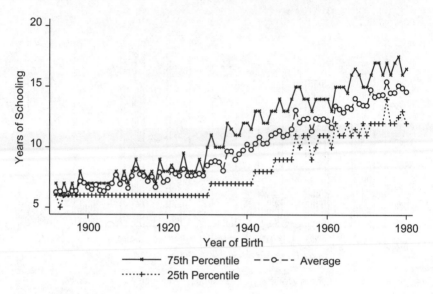

Figure 10.13   **The development of average number of years of schooling along with the first and the third quartiles by year of birth**
Source: Swedish Level of Living Survey.

each one-year age group is quite limited (between fifty and one hundred). The graphs are therefore noisy, and we have added smoothed graphs to ease comparisons. The upper panel shows the results for both gender groups combined and the lower ones for males and females separately.

As expected, figure 10.14A shows a decline in SAH with age. For the 2010 sample, around 25 percent of the fifty-year-olds reported poor or fair health compared to above 40 percent of the seventy-five-year-olds. More interestingly, figure 10.14A also shows a marked improvement in SAH primarily between 2000 and 2010. When splitting up the graphs in separate ones for males and females in the lower panel of figure 10.14A, it can be seen that the improvement is primarily attributed to males in the age group sixty to seventy.

In figure 10.14B we break up the data by quartile of number of years of schooling. Since the sample sizes are smaller in each education quartile than for the overall sample, we only present the smoothed graphs. The graphs show that the development is very similar within each education group: the 1991 and 2000 graphs are very similar, but there is a marked improvement reflected in the 2010 graphs. That is, the improvements in SAH seem to be equally shared between the four education groups and we find no evidence of increased health inequality in that dimension.

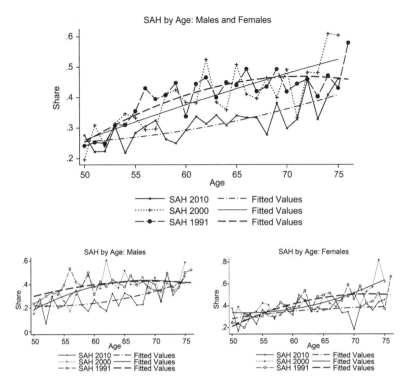

Fig. 10.14A   Share reporting fair or poor health by age in 1991, 2000, and 2010 (overall and by gender groups, respectively)

Source: Swedish Level of Living Survey.

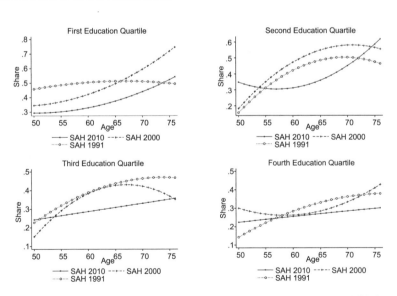

Fig. 10.14B   Share reporting fair or poor health by age in 1991, 2000, and 2010 (each panel reports separate results for quartiles by years of schooling)

Source: Swedish Level of Living Survey.

10.5   Discussion and Conclusion

The Swedish history of labor force participation since the early 1960s shows big changes and great differences between the gender groups. For men there was a large decline in labor force participation rates until the late 1990s and since then a sharp increase in labor force participation rates. The development in the age group between sixty and sixty-four has been most pronounced. In this group the LFP rates decreased from about 85 percent to 55 percent in the mid-1990s and have since then increased to almost 75 percent. For females the development has been dominated by the great increase in female labor force participation that took place between the mid-1960s and 1980. However, the labor force participation in the age group sixty to sixty-four has continued to increase since then, and is now on a level of above 65 percent.

The research question for this chapter is to investigate whether or not there are potentials, with respect to health and work capacity of the population, for extending this trend toward delayed retirement further. We use two different methods. First, a method originally suggested by Milligan and Wise (2012), which calculates how much people would participate in the labor force today compared to a particular point back in time at a constant mortality rate, considering the fact of a continuously decreasing mortality rate. Second, the Cutler, Meara, and Richards-Shubik (2012) method, which asks how much people would participate in the labor force if they would work as much as the age group fifty to fifty-four at a particular level of health.

Given the methodological differences, the results obtained from using the two methods, respectively, are not really comparable. They should be viewed as complements rather than substitutes. The Cutler et al. method suggests a potential increase of labor force for men (women) in the age group sixty to sixty-four of 19.6 (23.2) percent, using the specification when all health indicators are included, and on 13.6 (18.1), using the PVW index specification. The Milligan-Wise method suggests that the labor force participation rate for men could increase in the age group sixty to sixty-four by on average 16.2 percent if the labor force participation rate in 2014 would have been the same as in 1985 at a constant mortality rate. For females, given the great increase in female labor force participation across cohorts, the increased labor force participation rate has kept pace, and even increased slightly more, than the corresponding decrease in the mortality rate over this era in the age group sixty to sixty-four.

Finally, section 10.5 shows that the trend toward improved population health reflected in lower mortality rates also applies to self-assessed health between the years 2000 and 2014. We did not find any evidence suggesting that there is an increase in health inequality measured as differences in self-assessed health between different quartiles in the distribution of educational attainments.

References

Cutler, D. M., E. Meara, and S. Richards-Shubik. 2012. "Health and Work Capacity of Older Adults: Estimates and Implications for Social Security Policy." Unpublished Manuscript. Available at SSRN: http://ssrn.com/abstract=2577858.

Johansson, P., L. Laun, and M. Palme. 2016. "Pathways to Retirement and the Role of Financial Incentives in Sweden." In *Social Security Programs and Retirement around the World: Disability Insurance Programs and Retirement*, edited by D. Wise. Chicago: University of Chicago Press.

Laun, L. 2012. "The Effect of Age-Targeted Tax Credits on Retirement Behavior." IFAU Working Paper no. 2012:18, Institute for Evaluation of Labour Market and Education Policy.

Milligan, K. S., and D. A. Wise. 2012. "Health and Work at Older Ages: Using Mortality to Assess the Capacity to Work across Countries." NBER Working Paper no. 18229, Cambridge, MA.

Poterba, J., S. Venti, and D. A. Wise. 2013. "Health, Education, and the Post-Retirement Evolution of Household Assets." NBER Working Paper no. 18695, Cambridge, MA.

Socialstyrelsen. 2013. "Folkhälsan I Sverige. Årsrapport 2013." http://www.socialstyrelsen.se/Lists/Artikelkatalog/Attachments/19032/2013-3-26.pdf.

Statens Offentliga Utredningar. 2013. *Åtgärder för ett Längre Arbetsliv. Slutbetänkande från Pensionsåldersutredningen*. Stockholm: Fritzes.

Health Capacity to Work at Older Ages
Evidence from the United Kingdom

James Banks, Carl Emmerson, and Gemma Tetlow

11.1 Introduction

Over recent years there has been growing enthusiasm among policy-makers to increase employment rates of older people in the United Kingdom. This has been driven by concerns about the financial sustainability of publicly funded support for older people and the adequacy of private pension saving.[1] A number of policies have been implemented with the explicit intention of enabling or encouraging people to work for longer—such as increasing the state pension age, increasing normal pension ages in public

James Banks is professor of economics at the University of Manchester and deputy research director of the Institute for Fiscal Studies. Carl Emmerson is deputy director of the Institute for Fiscal Studies. Gemma Tetlow is a former program director at the Institute for Fiscal Studies and is currently an economics correspondent for the *Financial Times*.

This chapter is part of the National Bureau of Economic Research's International Social Security (ISS) project, which is supported by the National Institute on Aging (grant P01 AG012810). The authors are grateful to Richard Blundell and to the other participants of that project for useful comments and advice. We are grateful to the ESRC-funded Centre for the Microeconomic Analysis of Public Policy at IFS (grant no. RES-544–28–5001) for providing funding for this project. We are also grateful to Rowena Crawford, Richard Disney, and George Stoye for useful comments. Data from the Labour Force Survey (LFS) and the English Longitudinal Study of Ageing (ELSA) were made available by the UK Data Archive, while data on mortality probabilities were made available by the Office for National Statistics. ELSA was developed by a team of researchers based at the National Centre for Social Research, University College London, and the Institute for Fiscal Studies. The data were collected by the National Centre for Social Research. The funding is provided by the National Institute of Aging in the United States, and a consortium of UK government departments coordinated by the Office for National Statistics. Responsibility for interpretation of the data, as well as for any errors, is the authors' alone. For acknowledgments, sources of research support, and disclosure of the authors' material financial relationships, if any, please see http://www.nber.org/chapters/c13748.ack.

1. See, for example, Pensions Commission (2005).

sector occupational pension schemes, and abolishing mandatory retirement ages. The government has also now committed to holding regular reviews of the state pension age, with future increases in the state pension age being "based on the principle that people should spend a given proportion of their lives receiving a State Pension" (DWP 2015). However, one concern that is often raised about such policies is that there are some people who are unable to work because of their health.[2]

In this chapter we present two approaches to try to understand whether and how many older people in England have sufficiently good health to be able to work, and thus whether there appears to be potential (on the grounds of health alone) to increase employment rates among this group. Each approach endeavours to estimate a counterfactual employment rate for current older people based on employment rates seen among a similarly healthy group of people—either in earlier years or at a younger age. We are interested in understanding how health affects the ability to work, and thus how we might expect employment rates to change over time as the health of successive cohorts changes, under the maintained assumption that health is the only factor determining employment.

Clearly, health is not the only factor that determines whether or not people actually do work. Some people may not work for other reasons. For example, some may be unable to work because of other calls on their time, such as caring responsibilities. Some may want to work but be unable to find suitable employment, either because of a general lack of labor demand or because of specific discrimination against older workers. By focussing here on health, our objective is not to diminish the importance of these other factors, nor to draw firm conclusions about how much people *should* work, but rather to suggest how much they *could* work *given their health*. In other words, the aim is to help policymakers understand how much health constrains the ability of (different groups of) older people to work. If it does, policymakers interested in increasing employment rates may need to devote time and energy to understanding and (possibly) addressing this constraint. If it does not, then it suggests that other factors should perhaps instead be focused on.

We present results from two alternative approaches. Both approaches aim to estimate how much current older people could work, given their health, by finding another group of people who have very similar health, and looking at how many of them work. In other words, we attempt to construct a counterfactual employment rate. The first approach uses data from earlier years to compare employment rates of current older people to the employment rates of people with the same level of health in an earlier year—if the former is lower than the latter, we conclude that there is "additional work capacity" among the current older population. The second approach uses data on younger individuals at the same point in time. In this case, spare

2. See, for example, Department for Work and Pensions (2010).

work capacity is measured as the difference between the employment rate of older people and the employment rate of similarly healthy younger people. The other chapters in this volume present similar analysis for other countries. Results from the different countries can, therefore, be compared to construct a third type of counterfactual—using similarly healthy individuals in different countries to estimate how much older people in the United Kingdom could work if they had the same health-specific employment rate as people in another country.

Health is a complex concept with many different facets. It is difficult to measure health comprehensively and it is hard to find consistent measures of health over time and/or across countries. A further difficulty arises in understanding how health (and different aspects of it) affects ability to work. These issues make the current endeavor challenging and explain why we take two alternative approaches to addressing the question, each of which has its own strengths and weaknesses.

Our first approach takes a simple measure of health, but one that is—without any doubt—defined in the same way over time and across countries. This is the one-year death rate of people of a specific age. We examine how the employment rates of men and women with a given probability of death have changed over long periods of time. This is an approach presented by Banks et al. (2012) and also by Milligan and Wise (2012). The strength of this method is that we can be confident that this measure of health—which is readily available for long time periods—is defined in the same way in each year. The weakness is that this measure of "health" may not be a particularly relevant one for determining whether or not someone is able to work: there are many conditions that may not affect one's immediate survival probability very much, but heavily impact one's ability to work, and vice versa.

The second approach—based on a method proposed by Cutler, Meara, and Richards-Shubik (2012)—uses a much more comprehensive set of measures of individuals' health from the English Longitudinal Study of Ageing (ELSA) and examines how these are related to employment rates. The strength of this approach is that we are able to include a much richer set of indicators of health that may impact on work capacity. The weakness of this approach is that it relies on the assumption that the impact of health on work capacity does not vary by age. We are also limited in the application of this approach because the data required are only available for England from 2002 onward, meaning that we cannot look at a very long time period.

Both the methods we use rely on finding a comparison group for whom health is the only reason for not working. This assumption is more problematic for women, especially when using the Milligan-Wise method, since the tendency for women to be out of the labor market for reasons not related to their health was particularly large in the past. Therefore, for women we present two alternative sets of results for each method. First, we present results by comparing women to other women with the same observed health (i.e., analogous to the approach we use for men). Second, we compare women to men with the same observed health.

We present results separately for men and women and for those with different skill levels in order to highlight heterogeneity in currently underutilised work capacity. We focus on those between fifty-five and seventy-four years of age. We use a measure of "skills" that is not defined on the basis of the job that an individual is currently doing because we want to be able to compare similar individuals who are and are not in work. Therefore, we split people into skill groups based on the age that they left full-time education. However, this poses a challenge when looking over long periods of time because average levels of education have risen significantly over time—suggesting that those leaving education at very young ages become an increasingly selected group of (very low skilled) people in later cohorts. This point was noted for the United States by Bound et al. (2014) and is also apparent for the United Kingdom in figure 11.1, which shows the age of leaving full-time education for people reaching age fifty in each year from 1975 to 2015. Figure 11.1 shows clearly two significant reforms to the compulsory school-leaving age that affected people who have reached age fifty over the last forty years. The school-leaving age was first raised from age fourteen to age fifteen (in April 1947, affecting those reaching age fifty from 1983 onward), and then raised from age fifteen to age sixteen (in September 1972, affecting those reaching age fifty from 2008 onward). Therefore, in order to compare similar groups of people across time, we define "education quartiles" within year of birth—that is, grouping together the "highest skilled" quarter of the population born in a given year, and so on.[3] We define these quartiles separately for men and women to allow for time-varying differences in the education opportunities afforded to men and women, although this actually has relatively little effect on the grouping of individuals for the cohorts we examine here.

Throughout this chapter we will abstract from the possibility that work and/or retirement may have a direct causal effect on individuals' health. This is a potentially important concern and our results should be interpreted with this caveat in mind. A multitude of theoretical reasons have been postulated for why work, and hence exits from work, might directly affect physical and/or mental health and well-being. These theoretical reasons, which are reviewed in more detail by Banks, Chandola, and Matthews (2015), suggest that there may be substantial heterogeneity in how work (and exits from work) affect health, with work potentially having positive effects in some instances and negative in other. Empirical evidence on the effect of retirement on health is mixed. A number of studies have shown strong

3. From figure 11.1 it is clear that some of the quartile splits fall in the middle of a group. In these cases we randomly assign people within that group to one or other of the quartiles in question in order to achieve four equally sized groups.

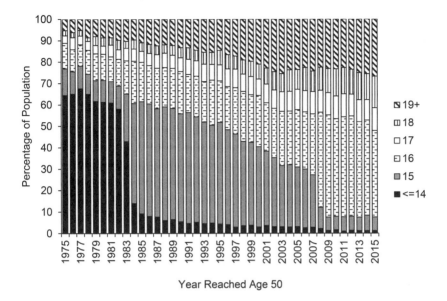

Fig. 11.1   Distribution of age of leaving full-time education by cohort

Source: Based on sample of all individuals born between 1925 and 1960 observed in the Health Survey for England (1991–2012).

correlations between exits from work and health, but there is heterogeneity in whether retiring from work is found to be associated with better or worse health. More robust causal analyses are rarer in the literature and find weaker effects (particularly for physical health) and mixed results.

Both the methods we use suggest that there is currently significant additional health capacity to work at older ages among both men and women in the United Kingdom. Looking at individuals in the past who had similar levels of health, and also looking at currently younger individuals with similar health, it seems that—for the majority of people—health is not a significant factor limiting capacity to extend working lives. However, our estimates also suggest that capacity to work is not 100 percent among those age fifty-five to seventy-four, and so there is a significant minority of this group for whom our results suggest health does limit their capacity to work.

Exactly how much additional capacity to work there is found to be depends on the counterfactual used. In particular, using the Milligan-Wise method, additional work capacity is found to be larger the further back in time one looks to construct the counterfactual. In this chapter we have gone back as far as 1977. Comparing to 1977, we find that men had 9.2 years of additional work capacity between the ages of fifty-five and seventy-four in 2013, compared to 2.0 years when we instead compare 2013 to 1995. Were we to go back further than 1977, we would be very likely to conclude that there was even more capacity to work among current older people. What is clear, however, is that there is additional work capacity. The method proposed by Cutler, Meara, and Richards-Shubik (2012) also confirms this. Using this method, we find that there is little heterogeneity in additional work capacity by skill level among men, but that there appears to be significantly more spare work capacity among high-skilled women than among low-skilled women.

The Milligan-Wise method also suggests that the increases in employment rates seen among older women since the mid-1990s are entirely in line with the estimated growth in work capacity over the same period. In other words, growth in employment has not led to a change in the estimated amount of additional work capacity.

The remainder of this chapter is structured as follows: section 11.2 briefly describes how employment rates and health have evolved in the United Kingdom over the last few decades. Section 11.3 describes the method and presents the results for the first empirical approach we have used. Section 11.4 describes the second empirical approach. Section 11.5 concludes.

11.2   Changes in Health and Employment Rates over Time

Advances in medicine, improvements in living conditions, and greater understanding of the adverse effects of behaviors such as smoking, have led to rapid improvements in life expectancy and many objective measures of health across virtually all developed economies, including the United Kingdom, over the last half a century. For example, as figures 11.2 and 11.3 show, the chance of dying at any given age has fallen steadily over time, with the reductions in mortality being particularly large at older ages. Figure 11.2 shows, for example, that men age sixty in 1970 had a 2.1 percent chance of dying in the next year, while in 2015 this mortality chance was not reached until about age seventy-one. The improvements in mortality have been slightly smaller for women (shown in figure 11.3): women age sixty in 1970 had a 1.1 percent chance of dying in the next year, which is a mortality probability not reached until age sixty-nine in 2015.

However, other measures of health that have been collected over long time periods and which may be more closely related than mortality to capacity to work tend not to show this same sort of improvement. Figure 11.4 shows that the fraction of people at any age reporting that they were in "poor" health changed little between the period 1991–1999 and 2004–2012, even though there were significant reductions in mortality over this period. Figure 11.5 confirms that this lack of time variation is also present among individual education groups (where the education quartiles are defined in the way described above). Banks et al. (2012) document that this is also the case in the United Kingdom over longer time periods and using various other measures of health, such as reporting having a limiting long-standing illness.

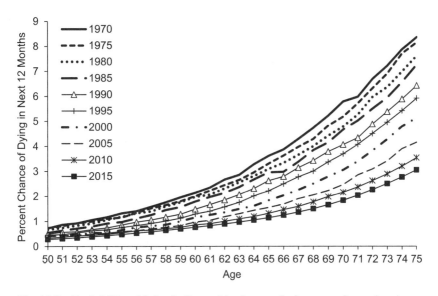

Fig. 11.2   Probability of dying in the next twelve months by age and year (men)
Source: Office for National Statistics.

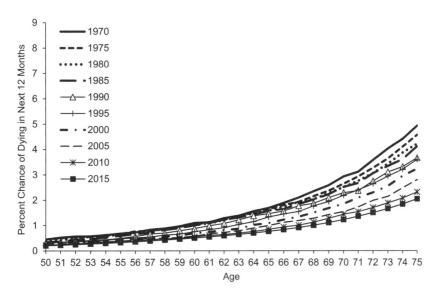

Fig. 11.3   Probability of dying in the next twelve months by age and year (women)
Source: Office for National Statistics.

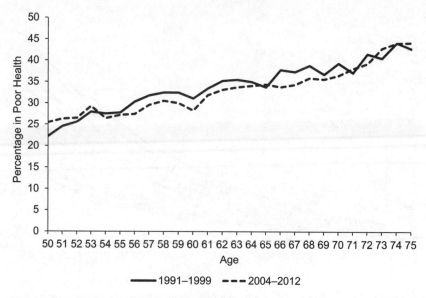

Fig. 11.4   Changes in self-assessed health over time
Source: Health Survey for England, 1991–2012.
Notes: "Poor" health includes anyone reporting fair, bad, or very bad self-assessed general health.

This lack of time trend is in spite of the fact that all of these measures show systematic variation by age and education level in cross-section. For example, figure 11.6 shows that—pooling years of data together—there is a systematic relationship between age and ill health and between education and ill health. Within each education group, older individuals are more likely to report being in poor health. Furthermore, at a given age, those with higher levels of education report being in better health than those with lower levels of education. The latter fact is consistent with the extensive literature that has documented—but not universally agreed on the causes of—the relationship between socioeconomic status and health.[4]

The discrepancy between lack of improvement over time in self-assessed measures of health but improvements in mortality could be for at least two reasons. First, there are many facets of ill health that might not increase mortality, but nonetheless would impact on self-assessed health—in other words, it may be true that some measures of health (including, perhaps, those that are relevant for capacity to work) have not been improving over time in the same way as mortality. Second, self-assessed health could be affected by reporting biases—that is, people's true health has been improving but this is not reflected in the way they answer questions about their health. To help

4. For a review of the literature, see Cutler and Lleras-Muney (2006).

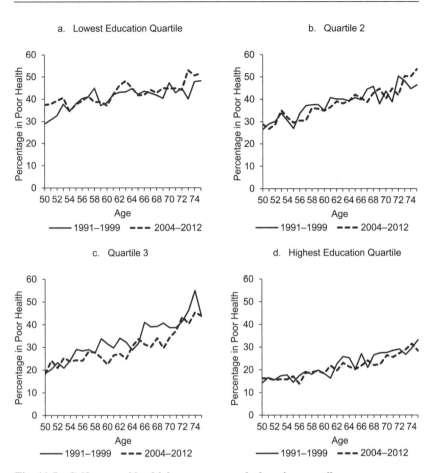

Fig. 11.5   Self-assessed health by age, year, and education quartile

Source: Health Survey for England, 1991–2012.

Notes: "Poor" health includes anyone reporting fair, bad, or very bad self-assessed general health.

to disentangle this we would ideally like to examine a wider range of more objective measures of people's health over the same time periods. However, such data have only been collected on a systematic and consistent basis in England in recent years—for example, in ELSA. Therefore, such data cannot be used to look at developments in the twentieth century. There is some evidence, though, that reporting bias is important to some extent. Disney and Webb (1991) found that self-reported disability was related to labor market conditions. Banks et al. (2009) find that differences in reporting styles can account for large differences across countries in reported problems with pain (a leading cause of work disability) despite limited differences in the prevalence of conditions that cause pain and limited differences in the use of

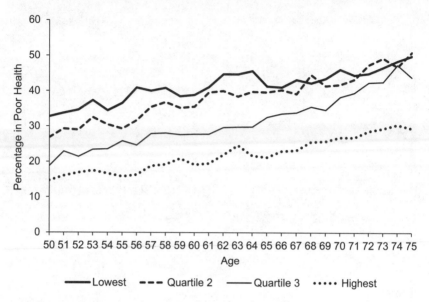

Fig. 11.6 Self-assessed health by age and education level
Source: Health Survey for England, 1991–2012.
Notes: "Poor" health includes anyone reporting fair, bad, or very bad self-assessed general health.

medication and technologies to reduce pain. Kapteyn, Smith, and van Soest (2007) also find that differences in reporting styles can explain a significant part of differences in reported prevalence of work disability between the United States and the Netherlands.

Changes in employment rates among older people have diverged from trends in health (when measured using either mortality rates or self-reported health). As figure 11.7 shows, employment rates of older men fell sharply between the 1970s and mid-1990s, before rising steadily over the last twenty years. Employment rates of older women also declined somewhat between the 1970s and mid-1980s before rising steadily thereafter (figure 11.8). In other words, while health appears to have steadily increased over time (at least when measured using mortality data, and still not have to have fallen when measured using self-reported health), employment rates initially fell (suggesting that health capacity to work of those out of work probably grew) and then started to rise again (suggesting that more recently employment rates may have kept pace with, or possibly outstripped, growing health capacity to work).

Earlier research highlighted the importance of financial incentives from public- and employer-sponsored pension schemes in incentivising early retirement in the United Kingdom and elsewhere (Gruber and Wise 1999, 2004). Others have also demonstrated the importance of disability benefits in facilitating exit from the labor market, particularly during periods of

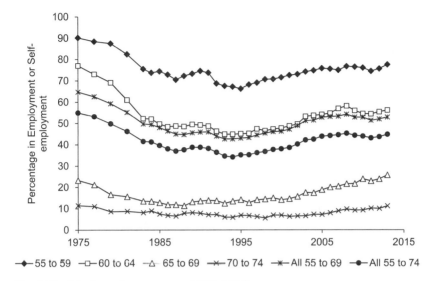

Fig. 11.7   Men's employment rates (1975–2014)
Source: Labour Force Survey.

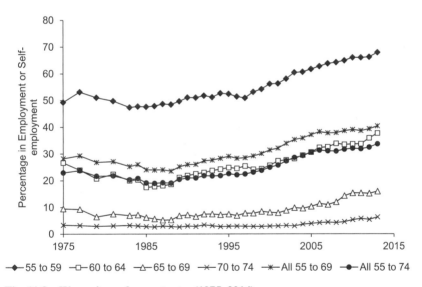

Fig. 11.8   Women's employment rates (1975–2014)
Source: Labour Force Survey.

weak economic activity (Benítez-Silva, Disney, and Jiménez-Martín 2010). The increases in employment rates in the United Kingdom since the mid-1990s likely reflect a reversal of some of these factors. For example, early retirement options in employer-provided pension schemes have become less easily available, the state pension has been reformed (including removing the earnings test on pension receipt) to reduce incentives to leave work, and there have been substantial reforms aimed at reducing on-flow to, and increasing off-flow from, disability benefits. However, empirical evidence on some of these factors is limited—for example, Chandler and Tetlow (2014) provide a description of these changes in employment rates, while Banks, Blundell, and Emmerson (2015) provide an initial descriptive evaluation of the effect of disability benefit reforms on employment rates.

This section has shown that—on some measures at least—health improved significantly between the 1970s and 2010s, and yet employment rates of older people have perhaps not kept pace. This appears to be particularly true among men, for whom employment rates are now around the same level as they were in the late 1970s, despite large improvements in many dimensions of health. It is also clear that employment rates drop sharply between those in their late fifties and those in their late sixties, even though there does not appear to be a similar steep decline in health. Both these facts suggest that there may be unused potential for older people to work. In the next two sections we present two approaches to quantifying this extra potential. Both approaches attempt to identify how health affects the capacity to work by finding a group whose actual employment is assumed to be *only* affected by their health and then using this information to predict work capacity for other groups. The first method (which was proposed by Milligan and Wise 2012) does this by looking back in time. The second method (which adapts the approach taken by Cutler, Meara, and Richards-Shubik 2012) looks to a younger age group at the same point in time.

11.3 Using Mortality as an Indicator of Health (The Milligan-Wise Approach)

The probability that someone of a given age and sex dies within the next year is an indicator of the average health of that particular group, which can be measured accurately and consistently across time and across countries. Milligan and Wise (2012) therefore suggest using this measure of health to examine how the relationship between health and the probability of being in paid work has changed over time.

To do this for the United Kingdom, we use two data sources. Mortality probabilities are taken from official life tables from the Office for National Statistics (ONS). These are calculated based on official death records and are available by sex and single year of age for every calendar year since 1951. Employment rates are taken from the Labour Force Survey (LFS), which was collected in 1975, 1977, 1981, annually from 1983 to 1991, and quarterly since 1992. These data allow us to calculate employment rates by sex and single year of age in each year for which there are data. On average, among individuals age fifty-five to seventy-four we have around 2,000 individuals of each age/sex combination in each year; the sample size increases over time

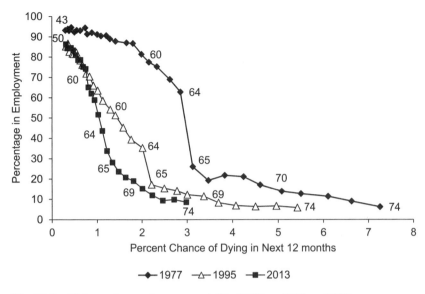

Fig. 11.9   Male employment versus mortality (2013 vs. 1995 vs. 1977)
Source: Labour Force Survey and Office for National Statistics.

(in particular, it is smaller before 1992 and larger after). We define as being "in employment" those who are in paid employment either as an employee or through self-employment.

The basic idea of the Milligan-Wise approach is to compare employment rates of groups of individuals in different years who had the same mortality rate as one another. So, for example, in order to estimate "work capacity" for men in 2013 (our most recent year of data) on the basis of the behavior of men in 1995, we do the following. First, we take men of a given age (*a*) in 2013 and find their one-year mortality probability from the ONS data (which we will denote $m(a,2013)$). We then estimate what age group (*a'*) in 1995 had that same one-year mortality probability. As an example, figure 11.9 shows that men age sixty-four in 2013 had a 1.1 percent chance of dying in the next year, which was very similar to the mortality probability of men age fifty-nine in 1995. We then compare the employment rates of these two groups and estimate additional work capacity as the gap between them—as shown in equation (1) below. In the case of the example just set out, men age sixty-four in 2013 had an employment rate of 44 percent, compared to 58 percent among men age fifty-nine in 1995: suggesting (perhaps) additional work capacity of 15 percentage points in 2013.[5] Figure 11.10 shows the share of men employed in 2013, the predicted share employed (shown by the full

5. In the majority of cases where there is not a group with exactly the same mortality probability in the two years, we use a linear interpolation between two adjacent age groups.

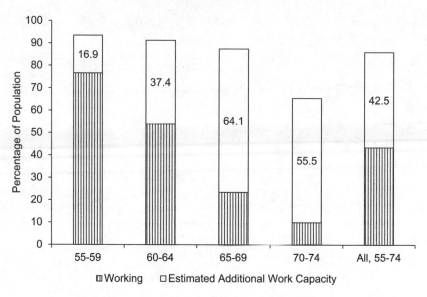

Fig. 11.10   **Share of men working and additional work capacity comparing men in 2013 to men in 1977 by age (Milligan-Wise approach)**

Source: Authors' calculations using the Labour Force Survey and mortality data from the Office for National Statistics.

height of the stacked bars) based on men with a similar mortality probability in 1977, and the difference between these, which we term the estimated additional work capacity. The figure splits the results by age group. This suggests that there are particularly large amounts of additional work capacity among men just over the state pension age, which is consistent with the large drop in employment observed at the state pension age being due to factors other than deteriorating health.

(1) $SC_{a,t} = \Pr(w_{a',t} = 1) - \Pr(w_{a,2013} = 1)$ where $m(a',t) = m(a, 2013)$.

We conduct the equivalent exercise for women. However, since employment rates of earlier cohorts of women were lower for reasons that are not related to their health, we also conduct a second simulation for women. That is, we simulate work capacity of women using the observed historical employment rates of men with similar mortality probabilities. So, for example, we compare sixty-nine-year-old women in 2013 to women age sixty-two in 1977 (as shown in figure 11.11). Among this group the employment rate was 22.7 percent. The actual employment rate among sixty-nine-year-old women in 2010 was 11.5 percent, implying additional work capacity of 11.2 percentage points. However, comparing to men with similar mortality probabilities in 1977 suggests much higher spare work capacity among sixty-nine-year-old women, at 79.1 percentage points. The estimated variation in additional work capacity among women in different age groups is shown in figure 11.12 (from comparing the employment rates of women in 2013 to those of women in 1977 who are similar in terms of their mortality probability) and in figure 11.13 (from comparing the employment rates of women in 2013 to those of similar men in 1977).The procedure outlined in equation (1) provides an estimate of the percentage of individuals of a given

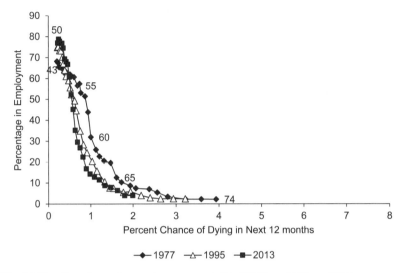

Fig. 11.11   Female employment versus mortality (2013 vs. 1995 vs. 1977)
Source: Labour Force Survey and Office for National Statistics.

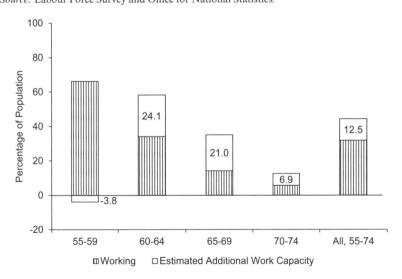

Fig. 11.12   Share of women working and additional work capacity comparing women in 2013 to women in 1977 by age (Milligan-Wise approach)
Source: Authors' calculations using the Labour Force Survey and mortality data from the Office for National Statistics.

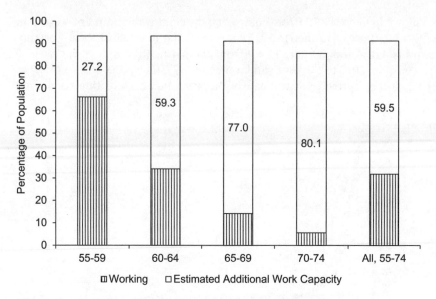

Fig. 11.13   Share of women working and additional work capacity comparing women in 2013 to men in 1977 by age (Milligan-Wise approach)
Source: Authors' calculations using the Labour Force Survey and mortality data from the Office for National Statistics.

age (a) in 2013 who could have worked (but did not), under the assumption that they could work as much as those with the same mortality probability in year t ($S_{a,t}$). We then estimate the average years of spare work capacity between ages fifty-five and seventy-five by summing these percentages over $a \in [55,74]$, as shown in equation (2). The results are summarised in figure 11.14 (with the results of an equivalent exercise, but instead looking at ages fifty-five to sixty-nine, shown in figure 11.15).[6] For men, these results are particularly sensitive to the choice of base year: comparing current employment rates by mortality to those in the recent past suggests some (but relatively little) spare work capacity. In other words, recent increases in employment rates among older men by age are almost sufficient to match the improvements in one-year mortality rates at those ages over the same period. But, if we go further back, this is no longer the case: employment rates by a given level of one-year mortality probability have fallen significantly since the late 1970s. For example in 2013, compared to 1977, there is an average of 8.6 years of spare work capacity between the ages of fifty-five and seventy-four.

(2) $SC_t = \sum_{a=55}^{74} SC_{a,t}.$

6. We also present alternative results summing over ages fifty-five to sixty-nine, for comparison with results from other countries presented in this volume.

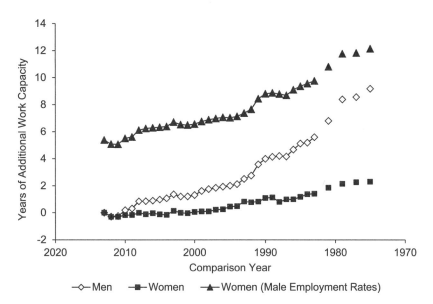

Fig. 11.14   **Estimated additional employment capacity by year of comparison by sex, fifty-five to seventy-four-year-olds (Milligan-Wise approach)**

Source: Authors' calculations using the Labour Force Survey and mortality data from the Office for National Statistics.

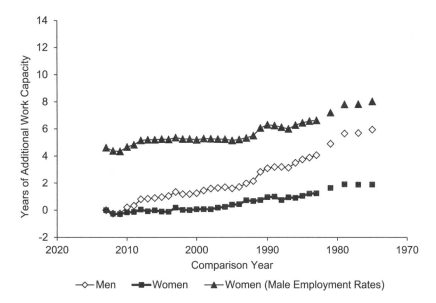

Fig. 11.15   **Estimated additional employment capacity by year of comparison by sex, fifty-five to sixty-nine-year-olds (Milligan-Wise approach)**

Source: Authors' calculations using the Labour Force Survey and mortality data from the Office for National Statistics.

For women, the results are sensitive to whether women are compared to the employment rates of women with similar mortality probabilities in the past or to the employment rates of men with similar mortality probabilities in the past. Women's employment rates are now rather similar to those for men. However, this was not the case in the past, as figures 11.7 and 11.8 show. These differences in employment rates between men and women in the past are unlikely to be due differences in health between men and women. Rather, it seems more likely that there were other factors that led to fewer women than men working in the past, some of which have changed over recent decades, leading to a rapid increase in women's employment rates. Therefore, it is interesting to compare currently older women's employment rates not only to the employment rate of similarly healthy women in the past, but also to that of similarly healthy men in the past. Comparing to women with similar mortality probabilities in the past, we find that there is relatively little spare work capacity among current older women (a little over two years when comparing 2013 to 1977). However, when we compare to similarly healthy men in the past, the estimates suggest considerable spare work capacity—for example, as much as 11.8 years when older women in 2013 are compared to men in 1977. In both cases, however, the results suggest that spare capacity among women has not been changing over the last fifteen years—suggesting that increases in female employment rates over this period have been sufficient to keep pace with declines in mortality.

11.4   Using a Comprehensive Set of Health Indicators (The Cutler-Meara-Richards-Shubik Approach)

A drawback of the approach adopted in section 11.3 is that mortality is a crude indicator of the health conditions that are likely to be important for determining someone's ability to work. An alternative approach, therefore, is to make use of more detailed information on the health of older workers and nonworkers. This is possible in more recent years using data from ELSA. Since 2002–03, ELSA has (biennially) collected data on the health, economic behavior, and a range of other circumstances of a representative sample of the household population age fifty and older in England. This allows us to look more closely at how a wide variety of health conditions and limitations have been related to employment of older people over the last decade and produce an alternative estimate of spare work capacity.

A second advantage of using these data to explore this question, rather than the approach used in section 11.3, is that we can examine whether there is heterogeneity within age/sex groups—in particular, across education groups. This was not possible using the approach adopted in section 11.3 because detailed data are not available in the United Kingdom on how mortality varies across education groups over time.

Following an approach originally suggested by Cutler, Meara, and

Richards-Shubik (2012), in this section we estimate the potential work capacity of those age fifty-five to seventy-four on the basis of the relationship between health and employment observed among those age fifty to fifty-four. Under the (potentially strong) assumptions that: (a) health is the only factor that prevents anyone age fifty to fifty-four from working, and (b) a given health condition constrains older people's capacity to work in the same way as it does younger people's capacity, we can use the relationship between health and employment among those age fifty to fifty-four to estimate capacity to work among those age fifty-five to seventy-four, based on their observed health.

To do this we estimate regressions of the form shown in equation (3) for the subsample of ELSA respondents who were between ages fifty and fifty-four in any of the first six waves of ELSA (from 2002–03 to 2012–13). We then use the coefficients from this regression, combined with the observed health of the older group, to predict work capacity for those age fifty-five to seventy-four.

$$(3) \qquad W_i = \gamma H_i + X_i'\beta + \varepsilon_i,$$

where W_i is an indicator equal to 1 if someone is engaged in paid employment or self-employment and 0 otherwise, H_i is a set of indicators of an individual's health, and X_i are other characteristics (including a time dummy). We estimate regressions separately for men and women as linear probability models. To estimate these regressions we pool data from the first six waves of ELSA; this provides approximately 3,000 male and 4,300 female person-year observations for use in the regression. As each individual may be included in the data more than once, we cluster the standard errors at the individual level.

The indicator of health that we use is based on the first principal component of twenty-three health indicators from the ELSA data. This is a summary measure of health that was first suggested by Poterba, Venti, and Wise (2011, 2013; henceforth PVW); the twenty-three indicators we include are those that most closely approximate the measures used by PVW. We have also estimated equation (3) including each health indicator separately, rather than using the index. We find that estimated work capacity is virtually identical following both approaches and so do not report results from the latter approach here.[7]

Deciding which variables to include in X_i is complicated and ultimately a matter of judgment on the basis of untestable assumptions. Since the ultimate objective is to use the coefficients from these regressions to predict work capacity out of sample, we would ideally like to ensure that all relevant measures of health (and how health constrains employment) are included but that we are not including any other factors that determine employment

---

7. Results are available from the authors on request.

but are not health related. For example, we definitely would not want to include in X_i whether or not an individual is eligible for pension income, since this is not health related but is likely to be strongly predictive of work. However, while there are some indicators that clearly do not capture health and some that clearly do, there is also a gray area of characteristics that may reflect additional information on health (i.e., information that is not already controlled for in the PVW index) but may equally well capture other non-health-related factors. On the one hand, omitting such factors risks biasing the coefficient on the health measure. On the other hand, including such measures if they are not in fact related to health runs the risk that the predictions of work capacity will pick up not only health capacity but also other factors.

Bearing in mind this trade-off, we include in our regressions indicators for being nonwhite, and for having a partner. Both of these have been shown to be related to differences in health outcomes, even after controlling for quite detailed measures of observed health status. We also control for education level. This is because the way that health constrains work capacity may depend on the type of work that someone has the skills to do, which we proxy by their education level.[8]

Tables 11.1A and 11.1B present summary statistics on the health and employment of men and women (respectively) age fifty to seventy-four in the first six waves of ELSA. These show that—in many dimensions—health deteriorates with age. The second row of the table summarises the PVW health index. This measure of health is expressed as a percentile ranking of individuals—with 100 being the healthiest person and 0 being the least healthy person—where individuals are ranked among all those age fifty to seventy-four. Table 11.1A suggests that, among men, those age fifty to fifty-four are on average at the 66th percentile of the health distribution, while men age seventy to seventy-four are on average at the 49th percentile; this suggests that health does decline quite significantly on average between age fifty to fifty-four and seventy to seventy-four. Women's health is slightly worse on average than men's at all ages: women age fifty to fifty-four are on average at the 61st percentile, while women age seventy to seventy-four are on average at the 41st percentile.

The rest of tables 11.1A and 11.1B show how specific measures of health differ across the age groups. For example, 23 percent of men and 22 percent of women age fifty to fifty-four report that they are in excellent health, while this is true of only 12 percent of men and women age seventy to seventy-four. The fraction of men (women) with at least one physical limitation rises from

---

8. We also estimated separate regressions for each education group to allow for the fact that the effect of the health measure on employment may be different for each education group. However, since the results were quantitatively and qualitatively similar to those obtained from simply including a dummy indicator for education level, we only present the latter results here. Results of the fully interacted model are available from the authors on request.

Table 11.1A   Summary statistics, men

Percent (unless otherwise stated)	50–54	55–59	60–64	65–69	70–74	All, 50–74
In paid work	84.9	76.2	55.6	22.0	10.7	50.1
PVW index (mean percentile)	65.9	60.1	56.3	53.5	49.2	56.8
Self-reported health						
Excellent	22.8	17.6	16.3	13.6	11.5	16.1
Very good	35.3	34.3	32.7	30.5	30.0	32.6
Good	26.3	27.7	29.4	32.3	31.9	29.6
Fair	10.7	13.9	15.4	17.0	18.6	15.2
Poor	4.9	6.5	6.2	6.6	8.0	6.5
Limitations in activity and function						
1 physical limitation	13.6	14.7	14.9	16.3	18.0	15.5
> 1 physical limitation	17.9	24.4	29.0	32.8	40.0	29.0
Any ADL limitation	11.7	14.7	17.4	18.6	24.4	17.4
Any IADL limitation	4.8	5.8	6.3	6.0	7.6	6.1
Depressed (CES-D > 3)	10.1	9.8	8.1	7.7	8.4	8.8
Diagnoses						
Heart disease	9.9	14.6	18.0	24.7	30.5	19.6
Stroke	1.1	1.9	3.0	4.4	6.5	3.4
Psychiatric disorder	10.1	11.0	10.6	8.1	6.1	9.3
Lung disease	2.3	4.2	5.7	8.0	9.3	5.9
Cancer	2.4	3.0	5.2	8.4	11.2	6.0
Hypertension	29.0	36.6	41.8	45.9	49.8	40.9
Arthritis	16.0	23.0	29.3	32.2	36.1	27.6
Diabetes	6.5	8.5	10.2	12.6	15.7	10.7
Back pain	14.6	16.5	17.1	17.3	17.6	16.7
Risk factors						
BMI missing	4.6	3.6	3.0	3.2	2.8	3.4
Underweight	1.3	1.2	1.2	1.6	2.1	1.5
Normal weight	22.4	21.0	20.3	19.8	18.9	20.4
Overweight	43.9	45.7	46.7	48.8	51.0	47.2
Obese	27.8	28.4	28.8	26.6	25.1	27.5
Current smoker	22.4	19.2	16.3	14.0	11.8	16.6
Former regular smoker	28.6	36.3	43.7	46.8	51.5	41.7
Former occasional smoker	4.2	4.8	5.1	5.0	4.6	4.8
Former smoker, DK frequency	6.3	5.5	5.8	6.0	5.5	5.8
Nonsmoker	38.4	34.1	28.9	28.2	26.3	30.9
Smoking status missing	0.1	0.1	0.1	0.0	0.2	0.1
Education						
Lowest quartile	23.6	23.5	23.5	23.8	24.1	23.7
Quartile 2	25.3	24.1	23.7	23.6	24.0	24.0
Quartile 3	25.6	25.3	25.6	26.1	25.7	25.6
Highest quartile	25.5	27.2	27.2	26.6	26.3	26.7
Ethnicity—white	95.6	95.8	97.1	97.0	97.3	96.6
Married	73.0	74.6	78.7	76.7	75.6	75.9
Sample size	2,948	5,118	4,889	4,235	3,632	20,822

Source: Authors' calculations using the English Longitudinal Study of Ageing (2002–03 to 2012–13).

Table 11.1B   **Summary statistics, women**

Percent *(unless otherwise stated)*	50–54	55–59	60–64	65–69	70–74	All, 50–74
In paid work	77.9	67.0	35.5	14.2	5.4	41.6
PVW index (mean percentile)	60.8	54.8	50.4	46.1	41.4	61.0
Self-reported health						
Excellent	21.5	17.2	16.5	14.0	11.5	16.2
Very good	34.6	34.6	33.6	31.5	29.6	33.0
Good	27.4	28.6	29.8	31.7	32.4	29.9
Fair	12.3	14.1	15.5	17.2	19.2	15.5
Poor	4.2	5.6	4.5	5.6	7.3	5.4
Limitations in activity and function						
1 physical limitation	15.3	15.7	17.7	17.0	15.2	16.3
> 1 physical limitation	29.6	35.9	40.3	48.3	57.0	41.6
Any ADL limitation	12.4	16.6	17.1	21.4	27.6	18.8
Any IADL limitation	6.6	8.0	8.3	9.2	12.0	8.7
Depressed (CES-D > 3)	14.5	14.1	11.7	12.6	13.6	13.3
Diagnoses						
Heart disease	8.8	11.3	14.7	18.4	23.7	15.1
Stroke	0.9	1.2	2.2	3.9	5.4	2.6
Psychiatric disorder	13.6	16.8	16.2	13.4	9.6	14.3
Lung disease	2.6	4.3	5.4	7.3	7.8	5.4
Cancer	4.2	7.2	8.9	11.1	10.2	8.3
Hypertension	24.3	30.6	38.9	43.8	51.6	37.4
Arthritis	22.8	33.0	41.4	48.2	52.2	39.2
Diabetes	3.8	4.9	7.1	8.3	10.3	6.7
Back pain	18.1	20.9	22.3	23.9	26.8	22.3
Risk factors						
BMI missing	5.5	3.1	2.1	1.9	2.6	3.0
Underweight	3.2	3.1	2.5	2.8	3.4	3.0
Normal weight	32.4	29.1	27.6	25.5	23.9	27.8
Overweight	30.8	33.3	35.4	37.8	37.5	34.9
Obese	28.0	31.3	32.3	32.0	32.5	31.3
Current smoker	22.1	19.9	16.3	12.6	11.7	16.7
Former regular smoker	21.1	28.2	31.9	32.9	31.3	29.2
Former occasional smoker	5.2	5.6	6.3	6.8	7.8	6.3
Former smoker, DK frequency	5.1	3.7	3.7	3.1	3.6	3.8
Nonsmoker	46.5	42.6	41.7	44.4	45.4	43.9
Smoking status missing	0.1	0.0	0.1	0.2	0.2	0.1
Education						
Lowest quartile	24.7	24.3	23.7	23.8	23.8	24.0
Quartile 2	25.2	24.2	23.6	24.3	24.1	24.2
Quartile 3	25.6	25.6	25.7	25.3	25.0	25.5
Highest quartile	24.6	26.0	27.1	26.6	27.1	26.3
Ethnicity—white	94.9	96.5	97.5	97.8	97.8	96.9
Married	73.2	70.2	69.1	64.6	54.3	66.7
Sample size	4,316	6,205	5,596	4,751	4,182	25,050

Source: Authors' calculations using the English Longitudinal Study of Ageing (2002–03 to 2012–13).

32 percent (45 percent) among those age fifty to fifty-four to 58 percent (72 percent) among those age seventy to seventy-four.

The fraction of men who have never smoked is highest among the youngest age group (38 percent of men age fifty to fifty-four, compared to 26 percent of men age seventy to seventy-four), while for women the peak in smoking prevalence seems to have happened somewhat later—with 47 percent of those age fifty to fifty-four being nonsmokers compared to 42 percent of those age sixty to sixty-four and 45 percent of those age seventy to seventy-four.

Overall, tables 11.1A and 11.1B suggest that health does deteriorate on average with age. This suggests that there will be less capacity to work among older people than there is among younger people. Our simulation results— presented below—quantify the scale of this.

The results from our regressions are shown in table 11.2. These show that there is a large and statistically significant association between health (as measured by the PVW index) and employment for both men and women. The coefficients shown in table 11.2 suggest that a 10-percentage-point increase in the index (for example, being at the 60th percentile of health, rather than at the median) would be associated with a 6-percentage-point increase in employment rates among men and a 5-percentage-point increase

Table 11.2   **Employment regressions**

	Men, 50–54	Women, 50–54
PVW index	0.006***	0.005***
	(0.000)	(0.000)
Education level (rel. to lowest quartile):		
Second quartile	0.016	0.028
	(0.021)	(0.022)
Third quartile	−0.015	0.046**
	(0.021)	(0.021)
Most educated	0.014	0.074***
	(0.020)	(0.021)
Married	0.131***	0.002
	(0.018)	(0.016)
Nonwhite	−0.043	−0.162***
	(0.037)	(0.041)
Constant	0.381***	0.458***
	(0.031)	(0.025)
Sample size	2,948	4,316

Notes: Estimated using ordinary least squares (OLS). Standard errors are shown in parentheses and are clustered at the individual level. Using data from waves 1–6 of ELSA.

***Significant at the 1 percent level.

**Significant at the 5 percent level.

*Significant at the 10 percent level.

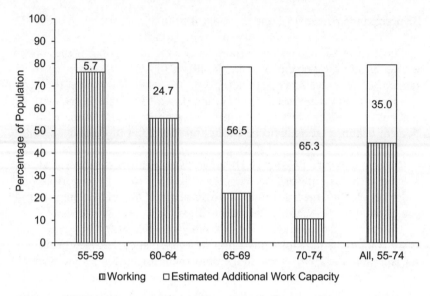

Fig. 11.16   Share of men working and additional work capacity by age (Cutler-Meara-Richards-Shubik approach)

Source: Authors' calculations using the English Longitudinal Study of Ageing (2002–03 to 2012–13).

among women. The results also show that, conditional on other measures of health, more highly educated women are more likely to be in work, as are married men and white women.

Figures 11.16 and 11.17 show the results of our simulation exercise for men and women age fifty-five to seventy-four. These figures show the share employed, the predicted share employed (shown by the full height of the stacked bars), and the difference between these, which we term the estimated additional work capacity. Based on their health status, we estimate that 80 percent of men age sixty to sixty-four have the capacity to work, while 56 percent of them are actually working—suggesting that there is additional work capacity of 25 percent of men in this age group. This compares to spare work capacity of 37 percent estimated for sixty- to sixty-four-year-old men in 2013 using the Milligan-Wise approach and comparing to behavior in 1977 (as shown in figure 11.10), or 10 percent when comparing to 1995 (not shown).

Predicted work capacity declines somewhat with age for both men and women. Predicted work capacity declines from 82 percent among fifty-five- to fifty-nine-year-old men to 76 percent among seventy- to seventy-four-year-old men—a drop of 6 percentage points. Among women the decline is from 75 percent to 69 percent—also a drop of 6 percentage points. However, actual employment rates decline much more sharply across these age groups.

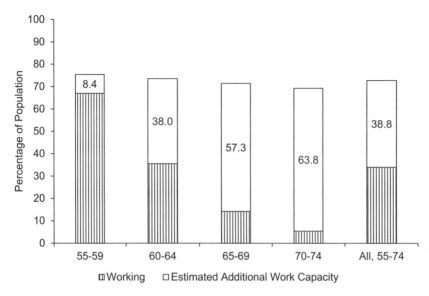

Fig. 11.17   Share of women working and additional work capacity by age, using female regression coefficients (Cutler-Meara-Richards-Shubik approach)
Source: Authors' calculations using the English Longitudinal Study of Ageing (2002–03 to 2012–13).

For men, employment rates drop from 76 percent at ages fifty-five to fifty-nine to 11 percent at ages seventy to seventy-four—a decline of 66 percentage points. For women, employment rates drop by 62 percentage points (from 67 percent to 5 percent). Consequently, additional work capacity rises sharply with age—for example, from 6 percent among men age fifty-five to fifty-nine to 65 percent among men age seventy to seventy-four.

Figure 11.18 shows an alternative set of results for women—using the coefficients from the male regression, coupled with women's observed health, to predict additional work capacity among women. These results are very similar (particularly for the sixty-five and older age group) to the results shown in figure 11.17. This similarity suggests that, since 2002, the relationship between health and employment is similar among men and women in their early fifties. This is in contrast to the results from the Milligan-Wise method, which suggested that the relationship between mortality and employment had been very different for men and women in earlier decades.

Figures 11.19 and 11.20 show how additional work capacity differs across education groups. The first thing to note is that—as has been documented elsewhere (for example, Chandler and Tetlow 2014)—more highly educated people are more likely to be in employment at ages fifty-five to seventy-four than less highly educated people. However, these figures also show that predicted work capacity is lower among less educated groups: this reflects the

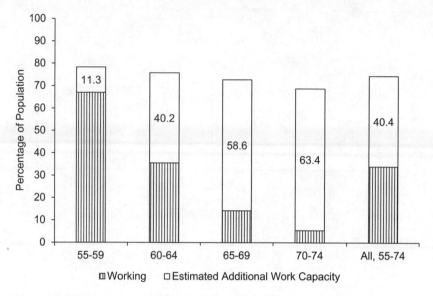

Fig. 11.18   Share of women working and additional work capacity by age, using male regression coefficients (Cutler-Meara-Richards-Shubik approach)
Source: Authors' calculations using the English Longitudinal Study of Ageing (2002–03 to 2012–13).

fact that they are in poorer health on average than more highly educated people.[9] As a result, predicted additional work capacity is actually similar across all education groups for men. For example, among men age sixty-five to sixty-nine, additional work capacity is estimated to be 56 percent for the most educated quartile and 55 percent for the least educated quartile. Among women, the more highly educated are estimated to have greater additional work capacity than the less highly educated—suggesting that the difference in employment rates seen between the high and low educated are not as large as the better health of the more educated group would imply. For example, among women age sixty-five to sixty-nine, additional work capacity is estimated to be 61 percent for the most educated quartile, compared to 53 percent for the least educated quartile.

11.5   Conclusions

This chapter has presented two alternative methods for estimating how much current older people could work, given their health. The idea behind both methods is to find a comparison group, whose employment rate is

9. For example, among men age fifty to fifty-four, those in the highest education quartile are on average at the 73rd percentile of the health distribution, while those in the lowest education quartile are on average at the 58th percentile.

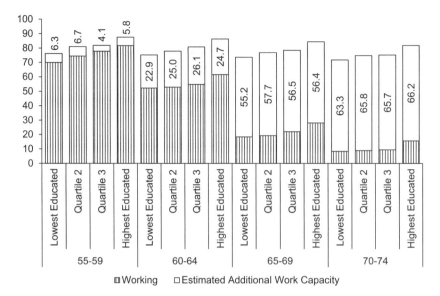

Fig. 11.19 Share of men working and additional work capacity by age and education (Cutler-Meara-Richards-Shubik approach)

Source: Authors' calculations using the English Longitudinal Study of Ageing (2002–03 to 2012–13).

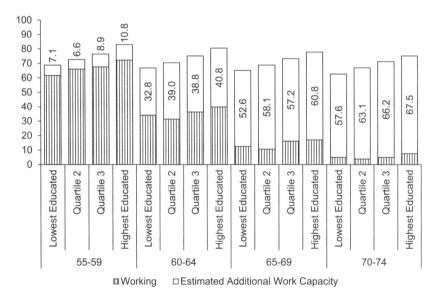

Fig. 11.20 Share of women working and additional work capacity by age and education, using female regression coefficients (Cutler-Meara-Richards-Shubik approach)

Source: Authors' calculations using the English Longitudinal Study of Ageing (2002–03 to 2012–13).

constrained only by their health, and use this group to construct an estimate of "work capacity" for current older people. The first method we have presented (the Milligan-Wise method) uses data on employment rates of men and women in earlier years to estimate what fraction of those with a particular one-year mortality probability could work. The second method (the Cutler-Meara-Richards-Shubik approach) instead uses data on employment rates of younger people at the same point in time.

Exactly how much additional work capacity there is thought to be among current older people depends on which group we compare them to, and which measure of health we use. However, all the various comparisons presented in this chapter suggest that older people do, on average, have capacity to work more than they currently do, given their health. Estimated spare work capacity is particularly large if we compare the behavior of current older men and women to that of similarly healthy older men in the late 1970s. Were we to extend our analysis even further back in time, we would likely conclude that there was even more spare capacity.

Among men, the amount of spare work capacity is found to be similar across those with different skill levels. However, among women, we find that there is significant heterogeneity in spare capacity across the skill distribution. High-skilled women have greater spare work capacity than low-skilled women.

References

Banks, J., R. Blundell, A. Bozio, and C. Emmerson. 2012. "Disability, Health, and Retirement in the United Kingdom." In *Social Security Programs and Retirement around the World: Historical Trends in Mortality and Health, Employment, and Disability Insurance Participation and Reforms*, edited by D. A. Wise. Chicago: University of Chicago Press.

Banks, J., R. Blundell, and C. Emmerson. 2015. "Disability Benefit Receipt and Reform: Reconciling Trends in the United Kingdom." *Journal of Economic Perspectives* 29 (2): 173–90.

Banks, J., T. Chandola, and K. Matthews. 2015. "Retirement and Health." In *International Encyclopedia of the Social & Behavioral Sciences*, 2nd ed., edited by James D. Wright, 598–601. Oxford: Elsevier.

Banks, J., A. Kapteyn, J. Smith, and A. van Soest. 2009. "Work Disability is a Pain in the ****, Especially in England, the Netherlands, and the United States." In *Health at Older Ages: The Causes and Consequences of Declining Disability among the Elderly*, edited by D. M. Cutler and D. A. Wise. Chicago: University of Chicago Press.

Benítez-Silva, H., R. Disney, and S. Jiménez-Martín. 2010. "Disability, Capacity for Work and the Business Cycle: An International Perspective." *Economic Policy* 63:483–536.

Bound, John, Arline Geronimus, Javier Rodriguez, and Timothy A. Waidmann. 2014. "The Implications of Differential Trends in Mortality for Social Security

Policy." MRRC Working Paper no. 2014–314, Michigan Center for Retirement Research, University of Michigan.

Chandler, D., and G. Tetlow. 2014. "Retirement in the 21st Century." IFS Report no. R98, Institute for Fiscal Studies. http://www.ifs.org.uk/publications/7384.

Cutler, David M., and Adriana Lleras-Muney. 2006. "Education and Health: Evaluating Theories and Evidence." NBER Working Paper no. 12352, Cambridge, MA.

Cutler, David M., Ellen Meara, and Seth Richards-Shubik. 2012. "Health and Work Capacity of Older Adults: Estimates and Implications for Social Security Policy." Unpublished Manuscript. Available at SSRN: http://ssrn.com/abstract=2577858.

Department for Work and Pensions (DWP). 2010. *When Should the State Pension Age Increase to 66?* https://www.gov.uk/government/uploads/system/uploads/attachment_data/file/184776/spa-inc-to-66-call-for-evidence.pdf.

———. 2015. "2010 to 2015 Government Policy: State Pension Age." Policy Paper. https://www.gov.uk/government/publications/2010-to-2015-government-policy-state-pension-age/2010-to-2015-government-policy-state-pension-age.

Disney, R., and S. Webb. 1991. "Why Are There So Many Long-Term Sick in Britain?" *Economic Journal* 101 (405): 252–62.

Gruber, J., and D. Wise, eds. 1999. *Social Security Programs and Retirement around the World*. Chicago: University of Chicago Press.

———. 2004. *Social Security Programs and Retirement around the World: Microestimation*. Chicago: University of Chicago Press.

Kapteyn, Arie, James P. Smith, and Arthur van Soest. 2007. "Vignettes and Self-Reports of Work-Disability in the United States and the Netherlands." *American Economic Review* 97 (1): 461–73.

Milligan, Kevin S., and David A. Wise. 2012. "Health and Work at Older Ages: Using Mortality to Assess the Capacity to Work across Countries." NBER Working Paper no. 18229, Cambridge, MA.

Pensions Commission. 2005. *A New Pension Settlement for the Twenty-First Century: The Second Report of the Pensions Commission*. http://webarchive.nationalarchives.gov.uk/+/http:/www.dwp.gov.uk/publications/dwp/2005/pensionscommreport/main-report.pdf.

Poterba, J. M., S. F. Venti, and D. A. Wise. 2011. "Family Status Transitions, Latent Health, and the Post-Retirement Evolution of Assets." In *Explorations in the Economics of Aging*, edited by D. A. Wise, 23–69. Chicago: University of Chicago Press.

———. 2013. "Health, Education, and the Post-Retirement Evolution of Household Assets." NBER Working Paper no. 18695, Cambridge, MA.

Health Capacity to Work at Older Ages
Evidence from the United States

Courtney Coile, Kevin Milligan, and David A. Wise

The Social Security and Medicare programs face large projected deficits in the decades to come. Many of the reforms that have been suggested to put these programs on firmer financial footing include the expectation that individuals will have longer working lives. For example, the recent National Commission on Fiscal Responsibility and Reform (NCFRR 2010) called for the Social Security full retirement age (FRA) to be indexed to life expectancy, rising by eight months for each additional year of life expectancy so as to keep the relative share of life spent in work and retirement roughly constant. A recent study of Social Security reform options by the Congressional Budget Office (2010) explored raising the FRA from age sixty to age sixty-eight or seventy and raising the number of years of earnings used in the Social Security benefit formula from thirty-five to thirty-eight.

A critical question raised by such proposals is whether older workers have the ability to work longer. There are numerous potential impediments to

Courtney Coile is professor of economics at Wellesley College. She is a research associate of the National Bureau of Economic Research, and an associate director of the NBER's Retirement Research Center. Kevin Milligan is professor of economics in the Vancouver School of Economics, University of British Columbia, and a research associate of the National Bureau of Economic Research. David A. Wise is the John F. Stambaugh Professor of Political Economy at the Kennedy School of Government at Harvard University. He is the area director of Health and Retirement Programs and director of the Program on the Economics of Aging at the National Bureau of Economic Research.

This chapter is part of the National Bureau of Economic Research's International Social Security (ISS) project, which is supported by the National Institute on Aging (grant P01 AG012810). The authors are indebted to Maurice Dalton for expert research assistance. We also thank the members of the other country teams in the ISS project for comments that helped to shape this chapter, as well as seminar participants at Wellesley College and the Center for Retirement Research at Boston College. For acknowledgments, sources of research support, and disclosure of the authors' material financial relationships, if any, please see http://www.nber.org/chapters/c13749.ack.

longer work lives. Labor demand is one concern. If older workers are paid more than younger workers but are not more productive, as Hellerstein, Neumark, and Troske (1999) suggest, then employers may be reluctant for older workers to extend their work lives. Lahey (2008) and Neumark, Burn, and Button (2015) find evidence of age discrimination in hiring against older women, which may make it more difficult for older workers to find new work following a job loss or to change jobs. Health is another major area of concern, since most measures of health decline with age. Put simply, are older workers healthy enough to work longer?

This chapter explores whether older Americans have the health capacity to extend their work lives. We use two methods to assess capacity to work at older ages. The first effectively asks: If people with a given mortality rate today were to work as much as people with the same mortality rate worked in the past, how much could they work? We make calculations based on plots of the relationship between employment and mortality over time, using data from Current Population Survey and the Human Mortality Database from 1977 to 2010, building on earlier work by Milligan and Wise (2012a). For this analysis we focus on men, as sharply increasing rates of women's labor force participation over time make it difficult to interpret the results for women.

The second method asks: If people with a given level of health were to work as much as their younger counterparts in similar health, how much could they work? This approach builds on the work of Cutler, Meara, and Richards-Shubik (2012), who use this method to explore the ability of workers just beyond the Social Security early eligibility age (EEA) of sixty-two to work, based on the relationship between health and retirement or disability status for slightly younger workers, those age fifty-seven to sixty-one. We similarly use data from the Health and Retirement Study (HRS) to estimate the relationship between health and employment for a sample of younger males and females, age fifty-one to fifty-four, and use these estimates along with the actual characteristics of older individuals, age fifty-five to seventy-four, to project the latter's capacity to work based on health.

We also explore whether health capacity to work varies by education group, as averages for the population as a whole may mask substantial heterogeneity in workers' ability to extend their work lives. We do this first by conducting the Cutler et al. analysis separately by education group. Second, we explore how self-assessed health (SAH), a broad summary measure of health, has evolved over time by education group. As we discuss in more detail below, one challenge with such an analysis is that average levels of education are rising over time. As Bound et al. (2014) note, relying on fixed education categories such as high school dropout may be problematic when the share of the population in this category is changing substantially. Like Bound et al., we overcome this challenge by creating education quartiles and exploring how health by education quartile has changed over time.

Our central finding is that both methods suggest significant additional health capacity to work at older ages. For the Milligan-Wise method, we estimate that men would work an average of 4.2 additional years between the ages of fifty-five and sixty-nine if the employment-mortality relationship that existed in 1977 were in effect today. This is an increase of over 50 percent relative to the average 7.9 years currently worked in this age range. This estimate reflects substantially higher employment—16 percentage points higher at ages fifty-five to fifty-nine, 27 points at ages sixty to sixty-four, and 42 points at ages sixty-five to sixty-nine—relative to actual 2010 employment rates. Results using this method depend on the base year used for comparison, as both employment and mortality are changing over time—for example, estimated additional work capacity is 1.8 years when using 1995 (roughly the trough of employment in recent years) as the base year. In interpreting these results, we caution that this method implicitly assumes that all gains in life expectancy can translate into longer work lives. If one instead uses the NCFRR's logic that a year of additional life expectancy might translate into eight additional months of work and four additional months of retirement, for example, these values could be multiplied by two-thirds.

Using the Cutler et al. method, we also project that men's employment rates would be higher—4 percentage points higher at ages fifty-five to fifty-nine, 17 points at ages sixty to sixty-four, and 31 points at ages sixty-five to sixty-nine—than they are now, based on the relationship between employment and health for younger individuals and the actual health of older individuals. Results for women are very similar. These higher employment rates translate into an additional 2.5 to 2.8 years of work between the ages of fifty-five and sixty-nine, estimates of roughly the same magnitude as those generated by the Milligan-Wise method. When we conduct this analysis by education group, we find that estimates of additional work capacity are quite similar across education groups for men, while work capacity rises with education for women. Finally, in our analysis of the evolution of self-assessed health by education quartile, we find that while all groups have experiences health gains over time, workers in the top quartile of education have the largest gains in percentage terms.

In the sections that follow, we first provide some brief background on trends in labor force participation and health in the United States. Next, we outline our methodology and present the results we obtain using our two main methods, and also report the results of our exploration of changes in health over time by education group. We conclude with a discussion of the implications of our findings.

12.1   Trends in Labor Force Participation and Health

The labor force participation rate for US men and women has varied substantially during the period since World War II, as evident from figures 12.1 and 12.2. For men age fifty-five to sixty-four, participation fell from 90 percent in 1948 to a low of 66 percent in 1994 before rising again and reaching 70 percent by 2013. For men age sixty-five and older, trends were

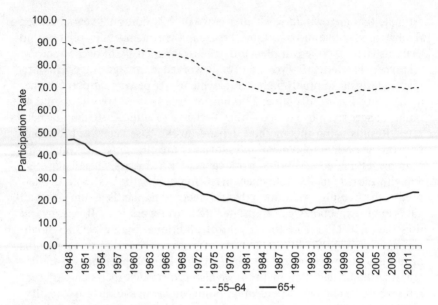

Fig. 12.1 Men's labor force participation, ages fifty-five to sixty-four and sixty-five and older (1948–2013)

Source: Bureau of Labor Statistics (series LNU01300190 and LNY01300199).

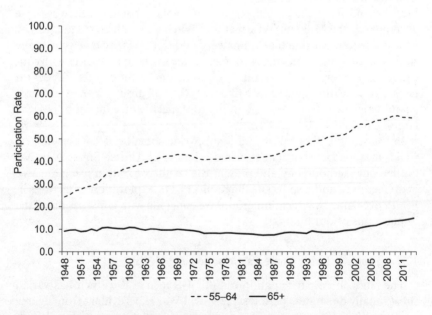

Fig. 12.2 Women's labor force participation, ages fifty-five to sixty-four and sixty-five and older (1948–2013)

Source: Bureau of Labor Statistics (series LNU01300347 and LNU01300354).

similar, with labor force participation falling from 47 percent in 1948 to a low of 16 percent in 1993 and then rising to 24 percent in 2013, a 50 percent increase over the lowest value.

The decline in men's participation over much of the second half of the twentieth century spawned a large literature on retirement. Much of the early literature focused on the effect of Social Security and employer-provided pensions on retirement, as Social Security and pensions became more ubiquitous and more generous in real terms over this period. These public and private retirement benefit programs made earlier retirement possible, and also sometimes provided strong incentives to exit the labor force at particular ages, as in the case of many defined-benefit (DB) pensions.

More recently, Munnell (2015) discussed the factors that might be responsible for the turnaround in older men's labor force participation over the past two decades. These include: program changes to Social Security (raising the FRA from sixty-five to sixty-seven over time, removing the earnings test for those below the FRA, and raising the actual adjustment for delayed claiming beyond the FRA); a shift from DB to defined-contribution-style (DC) pensions, which lack incentives to retire at particular ages; a decline in employer-sponsored retirement health insurance, which may necessitate staying on the job until reaching Medicare eligibility at age sixty-five; increases in workers' level of education and a shift away from physically demanding jobs; and joint decision making with (often younger) wives. Munnell also cites improved health and longevity as a contributing factor.

Labor force participation trends for women look very different than those for men because of the large increases over time in participation by women of all ages, including older women. For women age fifty-five to sixty-four, participation rose steadily from 24 percent in 1948 to 59 percent in 2013. Participation among women age sixty-five and older rose as well, from 9 percent in 1948 to 15 percent in 2013.

Trends in mortality and health are also of interest and are displayed in figure 12.3 for men ages fifty to seventy-five over the past four decades, based on authors' calculations from the National Health Interview Survey (NHIS) and Human Mortality Database. The well-known age gradient in mortality is evident in this figure, as is the trend over time toward lower mortality rates. Whereas in 1970–74, men age fifty-five experienced an annual mortality rate of 1 percent, in the 2005–09 period, that mortality rate is not reached until age sixty-one. Similarly, men age sixty-three in 1970–74 had a mortality rate of 2 percent, a rate that applied to men age seventy in 2005–09. Improvements in self-assessed health are also evident from the figure, although the data is noisier (due to smaller sample sizes) and the age gradient is less pronounced over the ages sixty to seventy. Roughly 20 percent of men age fifty-two report themselves to be in fair or poor health in 1972–74; in 2005–09 and 2010–13, it is not until men reach ages sixty to sixty-two that 20 percent are in fair/poor health; and at age fifty-two, only 14 percent are in fair/poor health in these later periods.

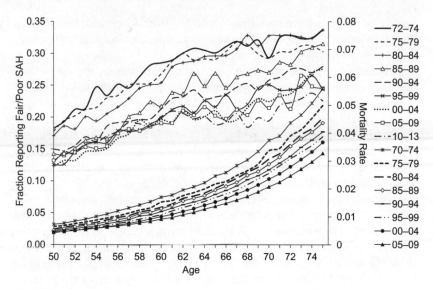

Fig. 12.3   SAH and mortality for men age fifty to seventy-five (1972 to 2013)

In sum, figure 12.3 makes evident that health deteriorates with age and that health at any given age has improved over time, while figure 12.1 shows that older men's labor force participation fell until the mid-1990s and has been rising in the period since. In the analysis that follows, we effectively bring together these trends in labor force participation and health as we explore how much individuals today could work based on the employment-mortality relationship of the past.

12.2   Estimating Health Capacity to Work Using the Milligan-Wise Method

For the first part of our analysis, which relies on the methodology developed in Milligan and Wise (2012a), we use the relationship between mortality and employment that existed at an earlier point in time along with current mortality data to generate an estimate of individuals' ability to work at older ages. Effectively, this method asks: If people today were to work as much as people with the same mortality rate worked in the past, how much would they work?

One natural question is why we choose to focus on mortality rather than on another measure of health that might be more closely related to the individual's ability to work, such as whether they are in poor health or have any limitations in their activities of daily living. One answer is that mortality is defined consistently across countries, which is important because this analysis is part of a larger international project. Data on mortality is also available over a long period of time, often for the entire population as part of the government's collection of data on vital events including births, deaths, and marriages, allowing precise estimates of mortality rates at single ages for single years. As one additional source of support for this choice, Milligan and Wise (2012b) show that while there are differences across countries in the level of SAH, there is "a fairly tight *within-country* relationship between improvements in mortality and improvements in self-assessed health," suggesting that there is a strong relationship between the two measures.

The mortality data used for this analysis come from the Human Mortality Database, which combines data from the National Center for Health Statistics and the US census. The employment data is from the March Current Population Survey. The period we consider is 1977 through 2010, with the start year chosen to correspond to that used in Milligan and Wise (2012a). The analysis is quite straightforward, as it requires mapping an employment-mortality curve, which displays the employment rate at each level of mortality for a given year, then repeating this for other years and making some calculations based on comparisons of the different curves. As noted earlier, we conduct this exercise for men only, as the large increases in women's labor force participation over time make it difficult to interpret the results for women.

Our approach is illustrated in figure 12.4, which plots the employment-

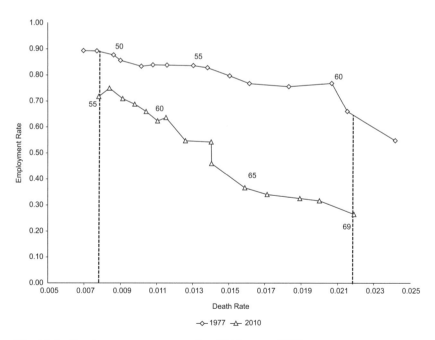

Fig. 12.4   Employment versus mortality (2010 versus 1977)

Table 12.1   Additional employment capacity in 2010 using 1977 employment-mortality relationship

Age	Death rate in 2010 (%)	Employment rate in 2010 (%)	Employment rate in 1977 at same death rate (%)	Additional employment capacity (%)
55	0.78	71.8	89.1	17.3
56	0.84	75.0	88.1	13.1
57	0.91	70.9	85.4	14.4
58	0.98	68.8	84.1	15.3
59	1.04	65.9	83.6	17.6
60	1.11	62.3	83.9	21.5
61	1.15	63.6	83.8	20.2
62	1.26	54.7	83.7	28.9
63	1.40	54.3	82.3	28.0
64	1.40	46.0	82.2	36.2
65	1.59	36.6	77.4	40.8
66	1.71	34.1	76.2	42.1
67	1.89	32.6	75.9	43.4
68	2.00	31.7	76.5	44.8
69	2.19	26.5	64.4	37.9
Total years		7.9		4.2
Average: 55–59	0.9	70.5	86.0	15.6
Average: 60–64	1.3	56.2	83.2	27.0
Average: 65–69	1.9	32.3	74.1	41.8

mortality curve for men in 2010 and in 1977. In 2010, the one-year mortality rate for fifty-five-year-old men was about 0.8 percent, and the employment rate at this age was 72 percent. In 1977, forty-nine-year-old men had a mortality rate of 0.8 percent, while the mortality rate for fifty-five-year-olds was 1.3 percent. This reflects the mortality improvements over time discussed in the previous section. In 1977, the labor force participation for forty-nine-year-olds was 89 percent. Thus, if men in 2010 had the same employment rate as did men in 1977 with the same mortality rate, the employment rate of fifty-five-year-olds would have been 17 percentage points higher, 89 percent instead of 72 percent.

In table 12.1, we extend this exercise through age sixty-nine, asking how much more men in 2010 could have worked over the age range fifty-five to sixty-nine if they had worked as much as men with the same mortality rate worked in 1977. At age fifty-five, an additional 17 percent of men could have worked, which generates an average 0.17 additional work years (one additional year for 17 percent of fifty-five-year-olds). At age fifty-six, an additional 13 percent of men could have worked for an additional 0.13 work years. Repeating this analysis at each subsequent age through age sixty-nine and cumulating the amounts, we arrive at a total potential additional employment capacity of 4.2 years. This is equivalent on the graph to integrating between the two curves from one vertical line to the next. As the average amount of employment between ages fifty-five and sixty-nine in 2010 is 7.9 years, an additional 4.2 years would represent a 53 percent increase over the baseline years of work.

It is worth noting that this method implicitly assumes that all mortality gains can translate into additional work capacity. This may not be the case if workers are living longer but are not in good health in those additional years of life. The relationship between mortality and morbidity changes over time has been the subject of a number of recent studies. Cutler, Ghosh, and Landrum (2014) argue that functional measures of health are improving, providing strong evidence for compression of morbidity based on measured disability, though disease rates have remained relatively constant so there is less evidence of compression based on disease-free survival rates. Others (such as Crimmins et al. 2009; Crimmins and Beltrán-Sánchez 2010) believe that the period of disabled life is expanding or that evidence is more mixed. As noted above in figure 12.3, we find that the share of individuals reporting themselves to be in fair or poor health at a given age has been dropping over time.

A second concern is that it may not be reasonable to expect that an additional year of life would translate into a full additional year of work. The NCFRR, for example, suggests that changes in the Social Security FRA be made so as to keep the share of life spent in work and retirement constant, at two-thirds and one-third, respectively. Using this benchmark, one could multiply the figure above by two-thirds, arriving at an estimate of 2.8 years rather than 4.2 years (for simplicity, we do not make this conversion for the numbers reported below).

Another issue that arises in implementing this method is the choice of year to use for comparison to the present. In figure 12.5, we replicate the analysis from figure 12.4 but use 1995 as a comparison year rather than 1977. This year was chosen because it is roughly the trough of labor force participation in the postwar period, as discussed above. At every age, the mortality rate is lower in 2010 than in 1995, consistent with earlier discussions. However, employment rates are higher in 2010 than in 1995—at age sixty-two, for example, the employment rate was 55 percent in 2010 versus 43 percent in 1995. Although employment at a given age has increased over time, it has not increased by enough to keep up with mortality increases, and for that reason the 1995 employment-mortality curve still lies above that for 2010, although the gap between the two curves is less than that between the 2010 and 1977 curves. Using 1995 as the comparison year, the estimated additional employment capacity from ages fifty-five to sixty-nine is 1.8 years, which is substantially smaller than the estimate of 4.2 years that we obtain when we use 1977 as the comparison year.

In figure 12.6, we show the estimated additional employment capacity as

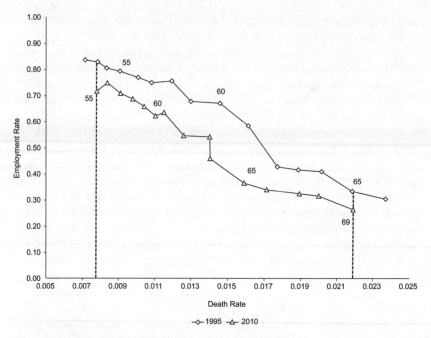

Fig. 12.5   Employment versus mortality (2010 versus 1995)

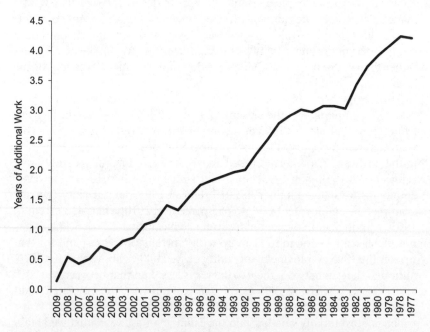

Fig. 12.6   Estimated additional employment capacity by year of comparison

a function of the base year used. For base years close to 2010, the estimated additional employment capacity is small, as we are essentially asking if men with a given mortality rate in 2010 worked as much as men with the same mortality rate did in, say, 2008, and how much would they work; the resulting value is small because neither mortality nor employment changes much over a short period of time. But as shown in the 1995 and 1977 examples, when we look back over a longer period of time, the estimated additional capacity is much larger. This is both because mortality has improved over time, as the 1995 example illustrates, and because employment rates today are lower than they were in the late 1970s and early 1980s (though higher than in the mid-1990s), as seen in the 1977 example.

While we have argued above that it is appealing to use mortality to assess work capacity, it is also valuable to estimate work capacity using other measures of health if appropriate data exists. In the United States, the existence of the long-running National Health Interview Survey (NHIS) makes this possible. In figures 12.7 and 12.8, we replicate the approach used in figure 12.4 with self-assessed health and activity limitation in place of mortality. In these figures, the horizontal axis reflects the share of individuals who report themselves to be in fair or poor health (figure 12.7) or the share reporting

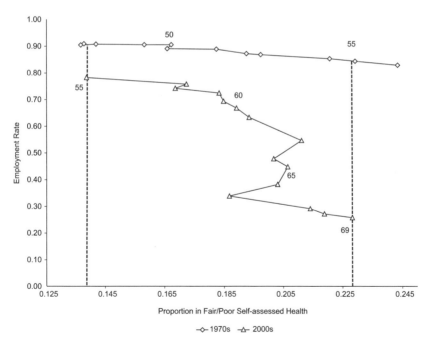

Fig. 12.7   Employment versus SAH health, 1970s versus the first decade of the twenty-first century

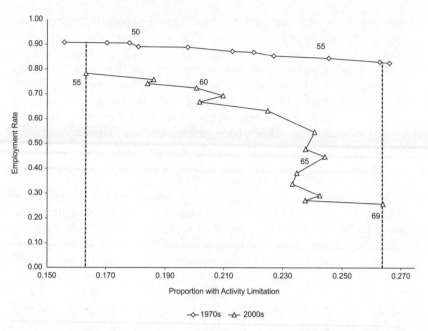

Fig. 12.8   Employment versus activity limitation, 1970s versus the first decade of the twenty-first century

that they have any activity limitations (figure 12.8).[1] We now average data over the 1970s and the first decade of the twenty-first century rather than use a single year of data to obtain greater precision, since the sample available through the NHIS is much smaller than the universe of death records used for the mortality analysis.

These figures show the same pattern of health improvement over time that was seen for mortality in figure 12.4. For example, in the 1970s, 23 percent of fifty-five-year-olds were in fair or poor health, as compared to 14 percent of fifty-five-year-olds in the first decade of the twenty-first century; for activity limitations, the equivalent figures are 25 percent for the 1970s and 16 percent for the first decade of the twenty-first century. When we use the employment-health curves from the 1970s and early twentieth century to generate an estimate of work capacity using the method shown in table 12.1, we find that the additional capacity between ages fifty-five and sixty-nine is 5.1 years using self-assessed health and 4.9 years using activity limitations. These values are slightly larger than the 4.2 years we found using mortality as our measure of health between 1977 and 2010. In the remaining discussion, we focus on our mortality estimates.

1. We code respondents as activity-limited if they report not being able to perform major activity, are limited in amount/kind of major activity, or are limited in other activities or limited in any way.

In short, estimates based on the Milligan-Wise method suggest a significant amount of additional work capacity. We estimate that the additional capacity from ages fifty-five to sixty-nine is 4.2 years using the 1977 employment-mortality curve as a point of comparison, or 1.8 years using 1995 as the base year. To change the assumption that an additional year of life expectancy translates into an additional year of work capacity, one can apply a fractional factor to these estimates—using the logic of the NFCRR that the share of life spent in work and retirement should remain roughly constant, for example, might suggest multiplying these values by two-thirds.

Another point of interest is what this method suggests about the ability of older individuals to work at specific ages. This can be inferred from the bottom of table 12.1, using 1977 as the comparison year. This analysis suggests that at ages fifty-five to fifty-nine, an additional 16 percent of men could be employed (averaging additional employment capacity values for ages fifty-five to fifty-nine); at ages sixty to sixty-four and sixty-five to sixty-nine, this figure rises to 27 percent and 42 percent, respectively. These estimates can be compared to the results we generate using the next method.

12.3   Estimating Health Capacity to Work Using the Cutler et al. Method

We now turn to our second method of estimating health capacity to work, employing the approach developed in Cutler, Meara, and Richards-Shubik (2012). In this method, we essentially ask: If older individuals in a given state of health worked as much as their younger counterparts, how much would they work? Implementing this method involves a two-step process. First, we run regressions to estimate the relationship between health and employment, using a sample of individuals young enough that their employment decisions should not be affected by the availability of Social Security benefits. We choose to focus on those age fifty-one to fifty-four, who are still many years away from the Social Security EEA, with the age fifty-four cutoff chosen largely for ease of comparison with the other studies in this volume. For the second step, we combine the regression coefficients from step one along with the actual characteristics of individuals age fifty-five to seventy-four to predict the older individuals' ability to work based on health.

The data used in the analysis is the Health and Retirement Study (HRS). The HRS began in 1992 as a longitudinal study of individuals then age fifty-one to sixty-one and their spouses, with biannual interviews; in the years since, the study has been refreshed with younger cohorts in order to provide a representative survey of individuals older than age fifty. Currently, data through 2012 (wave 11) is available; we use data from waves 2–11 in the analysis, starting with wave 2 because some of the health variables we use are not available in wave 1. The HRS is ideally suited for a study such as this one because of the rich data on health, as well as data on employment and demographics. In our regressions, we start at age fifty-one since the

HRS is a representative sample for this group. We have a sample of roughly 5,700 male and 9,900 female person-year observations for the regressions; a further 52,000 male and 64,000 female person-year observations are used in our simulations of work capacity.

We estimate regressions of the following form:

$$\text{Employment} = \beta_0 + \beta_1 \text{health}_i + \beta_2 X_i + \varepsilon_{it},$$

where Employment is a dummy equal to 1 if the individual is employed and health is a comprehensive set of health measures, including dummy variables for self-reported health status, limitations on physical activity, limitations on activities of daily living (ADLs) and instrumental activities of daily living (IADLs), individual health conditions, being over- or underweight, and being a current or former smoker. We also include variables for educational attainment, race, marital status, occupation, health insurance, and pension coverage, as well as wave fixed effects to capture any time trends in employment. We estimate this equation as a linear probability model.

We estimate an alternative version of this regression model where the full set of health variables is replaced by a single health index value, developed using the approach described in Poterba, Venti, and Wise (2013). The idea is to construct a health index based on twenty-seven questions, including self-reported health diagnoses, functional limitations, medical care usage, and other health indicators. To do so, one first obtains the first principal component of these indicators, which is the weighted average of indicators where the weights are chosen to maximize the proportion of the variance of the individual health indicators that can be explained by this weighted average. The estimated coefficients from the analysis are then used to predict a percentile score for each respondent, referred to as the health index. An individual's health index value typically will vary by HRS survey wave, as updated health information is incorporated. As Poterba, Venti, and Wise (2013) demonstrate, the health index is strongly related to mortality and future health events such as stroke and diabetes onset, though not to future new cancer diagnoses.

It is worth noting some of the key assumptions underlying our analysis. First, we assume that there are no unmeasured or omitted dimensions of health. If there were, health might be declining more rapidly with age than reflected in the health variables we have, and our estimates of ability to work at older ages could be overstated. We aim to minimize this concern by including a comprehensive set of health variables, as well as by using a health index that is likely a good reflection of overall health. Second, our approach implicitly assumes that the health-employment relationship that exists for younger individuals (age fifty-one to fifty-four) is the same as that for older individuals (age fifty-five to seventy-four). For example, if younger workers were concentrated in white-collar jobs and older workers in blue-collar jobs, then it might be easier for a younger worker with a health problem to continue working than it would be for an older worker with the same health issue; if an issue like this were present, it would lead us to overstate the ability of older individuals to work. Finally, it will pose something of a problem if there is a large amount of "discretionary" (non-health-related) retirement among our sample of younger individuals, as this will cause us to estimate a lower health capacity to work than what might actually exist. We have chosen a relatively young sample for the estimation to try to avoid this problem.[2]

Summary statistics for the male and female samples are shown in tables 12.2A and 12.2B. The share of employed men falls from 79 percent at ages fifty-one to fifty-four to 75 percent at ages fifty-five to fifty-nine, 59 percent at ages sixty to sixty-four, 39 percent at ages sixty-five to sixty-nine, and 27 percent at ages seventy to seventy-four. Employment rates for women are roughly 10 percentage points lower in each age group. The health measures show a decline in health with age. The share of men in fair or poor health rises from 22 percent at ages fifty-one to fifty-four to 27 percent at ages seventy to seventy-four. Values for women are similar but slightly higher, 24 percent at ages fifty-one to fifty-four. This reflects the known result that women live longer but report themselves to be in worse health.

Continuing to some of the other health measures, the share of men with more than one limit on their physical activity rises from 33 percent at ages fifty-one to fifty-four to 48 percent at ages seventy to seventy-four, while values for women are substantially higher, 46 percent at ages fifty-one to fifty-four, but show a somewhat flatter age gradient.[3] The share of individuals with limitations in ADLs rises from 10 percent to 12 percent for men across the five age categories, and from 10 to 15 percent for women; the share with limitations in IADLs are fairly flat with respect to age for men but rise from 6 to 10 percent for women.[4] Finally, the share of individuals with diagnosed medical conditions also rises with age. Arthritis and high

---

2. We also acknowledge that health may be endogenous in the regressions we run, if employment status has a causal effect on health. Whether this is the case, and what the sign of the effect is, is a subject of debate in the literature. Charles (2004) and Johnston and Lee (2009) find positive effects of retirement on mental health, while Bound and Waidmann (2007) find some evidence of a positive effect on physical health for men. By contrast, in their study of the mortality effects of reduced Social Security payments to the "notch" generation, Snyder and Evans (2006) note that younger cohorts responded to the benefit cut by increasing their post-retirement work effort with positive effects on mortality, suggesting that moderate work at older ages may be beneficial for health. Unfortunately, without more clarity from the literature it is difficult to sign the potential bias from ignoring this potential endogeneity. Estimating the causal effect of retirement on health is a fruitful area for future work.

3. The full set of activities includes: walking one block, walking several blocks, jogging for one mile, sitting for two or more hours, climbing stairs, stooping/kneeling/crouching, carrying weights over ten pounds, and picking up a dime. Individuals may be coded as having difficulty with one or more than one of these activities. The relatively large share of the sample with at least one limit on physical activity may be due in part to the inclusion of jogging one mile, which is a particularly difficult task for many older individuals.

4. The ADLs include: dressing, walking across the room, bathing, eating, and getting in/out of bed; IADLs include managing meals, groceries, and medication.

Table 12.2A   Summary statistics, men

	Age group				
	51–54	55–59	60–64	65–69	70–74
Employed	0.7907	0.7455	0.5870	0.3895	0.2694
Health: Excellent	0.1755	0.1647	0.1412	0.1236	0.1101
Health: Very good	0.3162	0.3117	0.3102	0.3019	0.2893
Health: Good	0.2886	0.2964	0.3048	0.3240	0.3317
Health: Fair	0.1569	0.1561	0.1746	0.1853	0.1966
Health: Poor	0.0629	0.0711	0.0692	0.0652	0.0723
Physicial limits: One	0.2376	0.2709	0.2692	0.2761	0.2346
Phyisical limits: Many	0.3324	0.3753	0.4280	0.4685	0.4800
ADL: Any	0.0955	0.0983	0.1063	0.1010	0.1224
IADL: Any	0.0508	0.0460	0.0448	0.0431	0.0550
CESD score (0–8)	1.4267	1.3385	1.2165	1.0849	1.1031
Heart disease	0.1050	0.1449	0.1930	0.2542	0.3178
Stroke	0.0370	0.0477	0.0654	0.0868	0.1079
Psychiatric condition	0.0279	0.0395	0.0533	0.0678	0.0893
Lung disease	0.1067	0.1044	0.1012	0.0883	0.0826
Cancer	0.0300	0.0463	0.0772	0.1213	0.1741
High blood pressure	0.3754	0.4235	0.4811	0.5302	0.5632
Arthritis	0.2639	0.3419	0.4309	0.5097	0.5202
Diabetes	0.1261	0.1520	0.1841	0.2086	0.2270
Weight: Under	0.0026	0.0046	0.0054	0.0050	0.0053
Weight: Over	0.4543	0.4591	0.4507	0.4671	0.4626
Weight: Obese	0.3354	0.3184	0.3067	0.2902	0.2639
Smoker: Former	0.3757	0.4339	0.4971	0.5519	0.6031
Smoker: Current	0.2742	0.2433	0.2073	0.1635	0.1170
Education: HS dropout	0.1516	0.1644	0.1938	0.2193	0.2464
Education: HS graduate	0.3090	0.3137	0.3259	0.3417	0.3354
Education: Some college	0.2706	0.2517	0.2220	0.1935	0.1825
Education: College grad	0.2688	0.2700	0.2580	0.2450	0.2354
Race: Hispanic	0.1404	0.1166	0.0946	0.0851	0.0755
Race: Black	0.1722	0.1562	0.1485	0.1267	0.1180
Race: Other	0.0407	0.0281	0.0251	0.0200	0.0187
Married	0.7872	0.7960	0.8128	0.8338	0.8108
Occupation: Blue collar	0.2676	0.3520	0.4089	0.4348	0.3943
Occupation: Low skill	0.0477	0.0560	0.0593	0.0601	0.0551
Health insurance: Own	0.5521	0.5690	0.5480	0.3583	0.2712
Health insurance: Spouse	0.1368	0.1365	0.1378	0.0975	0.0509
Pension coverage	0.5050	0.5220	0.5162	0.4925	0.4422
No. obs.	5,725	12,405	12,300	10,727	10,372

blood pressure are the most common issues, rising for men from 27 and 38 percent at age fifty-one to fifty-four to 52 and 56 percent at age seventy to seventy-four. Potentially more serious health conditions such as cancer and stroke also rise dramatically with age. The relevance of these statistics for our analysis is that they show that health deteriorates with age, so if our regres-

Table 12.2B   Summary statistics, women

	Age group				
	51–54	55–59	60–64	65–69	70–74
Employed	0.6932	0.6257	0.4642	0.2766	0.1686
Health: Excellent	0.1663	0.1531	0.1298	0.1097	0.0967
Health: Very good	0.3087	0.3027	0.3026	0.3044	0.2968
Health: Good	0.2900	0.2806	0.3016	0.3178	0.3266
Health: Fair	0.1657	0.1874	0.1862	0.1891	0.2011
Health: Poor	0.0694	0.0762	0.0798	0.0789	0.0789
Physical limits: One	0.2336	0.2296	0.2154	0.1915	0.1651
Physical limits: Many	0.4560	0.4979	0.5306	0.5509	0.5223
ADL: Any	0.1030	0.1226	0.1363	0.1365	0.1463
IADL: Any	0.0637	0.0783	0.0843	0.0815	0.0967
CESD score (0–8)	1.6920	1.7094	1.6183	1.5505	1.5310
Heart disease	0.0868	0.1090	0.1366	0.1855	0.2229
Stroke	0.0553	0.0670	0.0847	0.0990	0.1012
Psychiatric condition	0.0246	0.0332	0.0451	0.0572	0.0715
Lung disease	0.1696	0.1791	0.1741	0.1679	0.1452
Cancer	0.0688	0.0827	0.1026	0.1300	0.1447
High blood pressure	0.3550	0.4129	0.4823	0.5576	0.5895
Arthritis	0.3697	0.4763	0.5763	0.6502	0.6515
Diabetes	0.1108	0.1399	0.1621	0.1943	0.1942
Weight: Under	0.0115	0.0128	0.0140	0.0150	0.0190
Weight: Over	0.2987	0.3164	0.3315	0.3387	0.3430
Weight: Obese	0.3807	0.3662	0.3542	0.3342	0.2946
Smoker: Former	0.2943	0.3080	0.3415	0.3797	0.3800
Smoker: Current	0.2298	0.2093	0.1785	0.1414	0.1085
Education: HS dropout	0.1575	0.1908	0.2220	0.2386	0.2536
Education: HS graduate	0.3491	0.3580	0.3834	0.3963	0.4075
Education: Some college	0.2752	0.2488	0.2218	0.2091	0.1981
Education: College grad	0.2181	0.2022	0.1725	0.1559	0.1409
Race: Hispanic	0.1278	0.1182	0.1035	0.0880	0.0778
Race: Black	0.1952	0.1975	0.1864	0.1645	0.1433
Race: Other	0.0331	0.0276	0.0220	0.0195	0.0170
Married	0.7486	0.6745	0.6442	0.6254	0.5584
Occupation: Blue collar	0.0903	0.1065	0.1220	0.1234	0.1027
Occupation: Low skill	0.1295	0.1546	0.1728	0.1762	0.1490
Health insurance: Own	0.4200	0.4164	0.3705	0.2041	0.1451
Health insurance: Spouse	0.2899	0.2692	0.2496	0.1682	0.1438
Pension coverage	0.4134	0.4018	0.3591	0.3215	0.2935
No. obs.	9,936	17,366	17,158	13,998	14,295

sions suggest a strong relationship between health and employment, then the predicted share of individuals that is employed (estimated in the second step of our analysis) will decrease with age, as health declines.

The results of estimating our regression model are shown in tables 12.3A and 12.3B for the all health variables and health index versions of our model,

Table 12.3A   Employment regressions, all health variables

	Men 51–54		Women 51–54	
Variable	Coefficient	Std. error	Coefficient	Std. error
Health: Very good	−0.0137	0.0129	−0.0009	0.0114
Health: Good	−0.0233*	0.0140	−0.0033	0.0124
Health: Fair	−0.0904**	0.0175	−0.0707**	0.0153
Health: Poor	−0.2046**	0.0247	−0.1835**	0.0211
Physical limits: One	0.0054	0.0111	0.0141	0.0103
Physical limits: Many	−0.0118	0.0110	0.0063	0.0091
ADL: Any	−0.2004**	0.0180	−0.1282**	0.0152
IADL: Any	−0.1448**	0.0228	−0.1259**	0.0180
CESD score (0–8)	−0.0047*	0.0027	−0.0090**	0.0020
Heart disease	−0.0319**	0.0147	−0.0358**	0.0138
Stroke	−0.0327	0.0234	−0.0578**	0.0171
Psychiatric condition	−0.1060**	0.0268	−0.0362	0.0245
Lung disease	−0.0993**	0.0153	−0.0749**	0.0108
Cancer	−0.0423*	0.0250	−0.0250*	0.0146
High blood pressure	−0.0189**	0.0096	−0.0041	0.0086
Arthritis	−0.0094	0.0105	−0.0021	0.0084
Diabetes	−0.0539**	0.0137	−0.0237*	0.0126
Weight: Under	−0.0726	0.0835	−0.0655*	0.0350
Weight: Over	−0.0011	0.0115	−0.0015	0.0097
Weight: Obese	0.0068	0.0126	−0.0135	0.0100
Smoker: Former	−0.0161	0.0102	0.0195**	0.0087
Smoker: Current	−0.0232**	0.0118	−0.0045	0.0098
Education: HS dropout	−0.0038	0.0142	−0.0462**	0.0122
Education: Some college	0.0045	0.0113	0.0237**	0.0095
Education: College grad	0.0028	0.0126	0.0178*	0.0108
Race: Hispanic	0.0365**	0.0141	0.0288**	0.0128
Race: Black	−0.0356**	0.0123	−0.0431**	0.0105
Race: Other	0.0016	0.0219	−0.0027	0.0209
Married	0.0748**	0.0112	−0.0156*	0.0094
Occupation: Blue collar	−0.0155	0.0119	0.0736**	0.0137
Occupation: Low skill	−0.0301	0.0212	0.1294**	0.0118
Health insurance: Own	0.1651**	0.0122	0.1979**	0.0106
Health insurance: Spouse	0.0832**	0.0142	0.0236**	0.0102
Pension coverage	0.1602**	0.0111	0.2886**	0.0095
No. obs.	5,725		9,936	

**Significant at the 5 percent level.
*Significant at the 10 percent level.

respectively. Table 12.3A shows that there are large and statistically significant effects of many of the health variables on employment. For example,
relative to men in excellent health, men in poor (fair) health are 20 (9) percentage points less likely to be employed; for women, these values are 18
and 7 points. Having ADL or IADL limitations lowers men's employment
by 20 and 14 points, respectively, and lowers women's employment by 13
points. Having limits on physical activity has no significant effect on employ-

Table 12.3B   Employment regressions, PVW health index

Variable	Men 51–54		Women 51–54	
	Coefficient	Std. error	Coefficient	Std. error
PVW index	0.0048**	0.0002**	0.0034**	0.0001
Education: HS dropout	–0.0123	0.0145	–0.0700**	0.0124
Education: Some college	0.0078	0.0116	0.0220**	0.0097
Education: College grad	–0.0071	0.0126	0.0131	0.0108
Race: Hispanic	0.0236*	0.0141*	0.0323**	0.0127
Race: Black	–0.0478**	0.0124**	–0.0350**	0.0103
Race: Other	–0.0137	0.0223	–0.0138	0.0213
Married	0.0898**	0.0112**	–0.0026	0.0095
Occupation: Blue collar	–0.0100	0.0122	0.0749**	0.0140
Occupation: Low skill	–0.0344	0.0218	0.1376**	0.0121
Health Insurance: Own	0.1869**	0.0124**	0.2294**	0.0108
Health Insurance: Spouse	0.1046**	0.0144**	0.0487**	0.0104
Pension coverage	0.1714**	0.0113**	0.3001**	0.0097
No. obs.	5,662		9,842	

Note: Sample size is slightly smaller than in models on table 12.3A due to missing observations for PVW index for some observations.
**Significant at the 5 percent level.
*Significant at the 10 percent level.

ment, perhaps because these issues are more widespread and consequently less severe. Some of the individual health conditions are associated with statistically significant decreases in the probability of employment of up to 10 percentage points, such as having experienced a stroke, psychiatric condition, or diabetes.

In the version of the model with the health index, table 12.3B, the index is strongly associated with employment. A 10-percentage-point increase in the index (e.g., being at the 60th rather than 50th percentile of health) raises the probability of employment by 4.8 percentage points for men and by 3.4 percentage points for women. We believe that this suggests that the index functions well as a summary statistic for health. This is reassuring, because in some cases—for example, in a number of the other countries participating in the larger project of which this chapter is part—there is insufficient data to estimate models like those shown in table 12.3A. We focus on the results from table 12.3B in the discussion below.

In table 12.4, we report the results of our simulation exercise. This table shows, for men and women in five-year age groups from age fifty-five to seventy-four, the share employed, the predicted share employed (calculated as described above by combining the coefficients from the regression analysis and the actual characteristics of these individuals), and the difference between these, which we term the estimated additional work capacity. For ease of exposition, key values are also reported in figures 12.9 and 12.10.

Table 12.4   Simulations of work capacity

Age group	Use all health variables				Use PVW health index			
	No. obs.	Actual % working	Predicted % working	Estimated work capacity (%)	No. obs.	Actual % working	Predicted % working	Estimated work capacity (%)
Men								
55–59	12,405	74.6	78.5	3.9	12,331	74.6	78.2	3.6
60–64	12,300	58.7	76.8	18.1	12,229	58.7	75.6	16.9
65–69	10,727	38.9	73.2	34.2	10,626	39.0	70.4	31.4
70–74	10,372	26.9	68.5	41.6	9,581	27.2	66.2	39.0
Women								
55–59	17,366	62.6	67.6	5.0	17,255	62.6	67.1	4.5
60–64	17,158	46.4	64.9	18.5	16,969	46.5	63.2	16.7
65–69	13,998	27.7	60.4	32.8	13,585	27.7	57.0	29.3
70–74	13,681	16.9	57.6	40.7	12,576	16.8	54.2	37.4

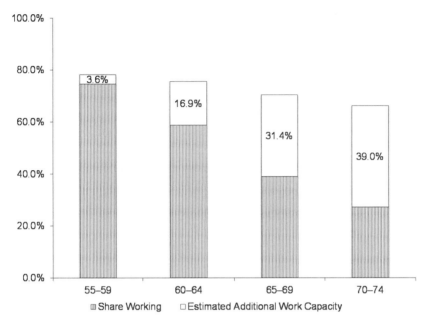

Fig. 12.9   Share of HRS men working and additional work capacity by age

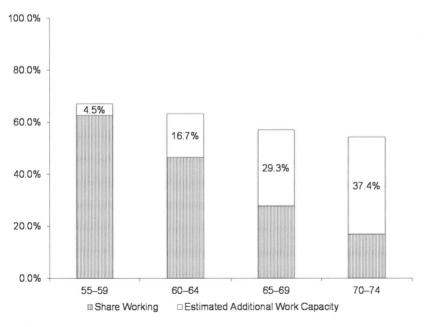

Fig. 12.10   Share of HRS women working and additional work capacity by age

Focusing on the health index results, we predict the share of men employed to be 78 percent at ages fifty-five to fifty-nine, 76 percent at ages sixty to sixty-four, 70 percent at ages sixty-five to sixty-nine, and 66 percent at ages seventy to seventy-four. These projections decline with age because health declines with age and our regression coefficients reflect a strong association between health and employment. However, the share of men that is actually working declines more quickly with age than do our predictions, from 75 percent at ages fifty-five to fifty-nine to 59 percent, 39 percent, and 27 percent in the older age groups. As a result, we estimate that additional capacity to work is substantial and rising sharply with age, from 4 percent at ages fifty-five to fifty-nine to 17 percent at ages sixty to sixty-four, 31 percent at ages sixty-five to sixty-nine, and 39 percent at ages seventy to seventy-four. Results using the model including individual health variables are quite similar. In terms of the results for women, while both the predicted and actual share working are somewhat lower than those for men, the estimated work capacity numbers are very similar, at 5 percent, 17 percent, 29 percent, and 37 percent across the four age groups.

How do these results compare to those obtained using the Milligan-Wise method? As noted earlier, that analysis (done for men only) suggested that employment would be 16 percentage points higher at ages fifty-five to fifty-nine, 27 points higher at ages sixty to sixty-four, and 42 percentage points higher at ages sixty-five to sixty-nine if people today worked as much as people with the same mortality rate worked in 1977. These values are 10–12 percentage points higher than the numbers found here. We can also compare the implied total additional years of work between ages fifty-five and sixty-nine. Using the Milligan-Wise approach, we obtained a value of 4.2 years, using 1977 as the base year. Here, assuming additional employment of 4/17/31 percent at ages fifty-five to fifty-nine/sixty to sixty-four/sixty-five to sixty-nine, we estimate that men would work an additional 2.6 years on average. As noted above, however, the numbers from the Milligan-Wise method would be smaller if one used a more recent year for comparison or assumed that only some share of the gains in mortality would translate into increases in employment, so making either or both of these adjustments would make the two sets of numbers more similar. Given how different the two methods employed in this chapter are, it is striking and perhaps somewhat reassuring that they generate results of roughly similar magnitude.

One potential concern with the analysis to date is that our estimates reflect population averages, which may mask substantial heterogeneity in the ability to work longer. In particular, less educated and lower-income individuals may have less potential to extend their work lives because they are in worse health or have jobs where employment is more sensitive to health status. In the case of the Milligan-Wise analysis, it was unfortunately not possible to explore how the employment-mortality relationship has changed over time by education group or income group because US mortality records do not include that information.[5]

For the present analysis, however, it is possible to augment our basic results with an analysis that estimates work capacity separately by education. We reestimate the regression model separately by education group, which allows the relationship between employment and health to differ by education group—as might be the case, for example, if workers with less education are concentrated in blue-collar jobs where it is more difficult to continue working once one experiences a health problem than it would be in the white-collar jobs held by more highly educated workers.[6]

Our simulations of work capacity by education group are shown in tables 12.5A and 12.5B (and in tables 12.6A and 12.6B, using regression coefficients estimated jointly for all education groups) and in figures 12.11 and 12.12. Although the actual and predicted share working varies substantially by education group—for example, the actual and predicted share working among men ages fifty-five to fifty-nine are 85 and 89 percent for college graduates versus 61 and 63 percent for high school dropouts—the estimates of additional work capacity are fairly similar across education groups for men. Specifically, estimated additional work capacity for men at ages fifty-five to fifty-nine is in the range of 2–6 percent for all education groups, and similarly is 15–21 percent at ages sixty to sixty-four, 28–35 percent for ages sixty-five to sixty-nine, and 35–42 percent at ages seventy to seventy-four, using the health index model estimates. We report the implied total additional years of work between ages fifty-five and sixty-nine in table 12.7, and show that the value for high school dropouts (2.3 years) is similar to that for college graduates (2.5 years), though high school graduates have a somewhat larger capacity (3.1 years). Thus, there is no clear pattern in estimated additional work capacity with respect to education for men. In table 12.5B, we find that less educated women consistently have lower estimated additional work capacity—for example, among those ages sixty-five to sixty-nine, additional work capacity is 24 percent for high school dropouts versus 36 percent for college graduates. As shown in table 12.7, the additional years of work capacity is 2.1 for female high school dropouts, 2.5 for high school graduates, and 3.1 for college graduates. Thus, overall, the evidence is somewhat mixed,

5. Brown, Liebman, and Pollet (2002) show that mortality rates are higher for less educated groups, based on an analysis of data from the National Longitudinal Mortality Study. Unfortunately, this data set does not have sufficient sample size and years of coverage to be used for our analysis.

6. We also generate results by education in a simpler way, continuing to use a common set of regression coefficients for all education groups but reporting the actual share working, predicted share working, and estimated additional work capacity separately by education group. The results of this exercise, which are shown in tables 12.6A and 12.6B, are qualitatively similar to those in tables 12.5A and 12.5B, though differences across education groups for women are only about two-thirds as large.

Table 12.5A   Work capacity by education (regression by education group)

	Men, all health variables model				Men, PVW model			
Education	Obs.	Actual % working	Predicted % working	Estimated work capacity (%)	Obs.	Actual % working	Predicted % working	Estimated work capacity (%)
Age 55–59								
< High school	2,039	60.4	63.8	3.4	2,019	60.6	63.4	2.7
High school	3,891	71.9	78.2	6.3	3,864	71.9	77.5	5.6
Some college	3,122	75.9	77.8	1.8	3,104	75.9	78.2	2.3
College grad	3,349	84.9	89.2	4.3	3,344	84.9	88.5	3.6
Age 60–64								
< High school	2,384	46.6	64.3	17.6	2,367	46.8	62.2	15.4
High school	4,009	54.8	77.4	22.6	3,980	54.6	75.2	20.6
Some college	2,731	61.0	76.1	15.2	2,711	61.0	76.3	15.2
College grad	3,174	70.7	87.7	17.0	3,169	70.7	86.8	16.0
Age 65–69								
< High school	2,352	30.6	62.7	32.1	2,318	30.7	58.5	27.8
High school	3,665	35.0	73.5	38.5	3,631	34.8	69.8	35.0
Some college	2,076	38.6	73.1	34.5	2,059	38.9	72.3	33.4
College grad	2,628	52.1	84.0	31.9	2,612	52.1	82.3	30.2
Age 70–74								
< High school	2,556	19.9	58.3	38.4	2,302	20.1	55.2	35.1
High school	3,479	24.3	69.9	45.7	3,221	24.1	66.4	42.3
Some college	1,893	26.9	68.7	41.8	1,756	27.7	67.8	40.1
College grad	2,442	38.1	80.2	42.1	2,300	38.2	79.0	40.8

Note: Actual percent working in all health and PVW models may differ due to differences in sample size.

Table 12.5B Work capacity by education (regression by education group)

Education	Women, all health variables model				Women, PVW model			
	Obs.	Actual % working	Predicted % working	Estimated work capacity (%)	Obs.	Actual % working	Predicted % working	Estimated work capacity (%)
Age 55–59								
< High school	3,314	41.2	46.6	5.4	3,296	41.2	46.1	4.9
High school	6,217	62.6	66.9	4.3	6,178	62.5	66.4	3.9
Some college	4,320	68.1	73.0	4.9	4,285	68.3	72.5	4.1
College grad	3,512	75.9	81.4	5.5	3,493	75.9	81.3	5.4
Age 60–64								
< High school	3,809	30.8	45.6	14.8	3,768	30.8	44.3	13.4
High school	6,579	45.9	64.3	18.4	6,515	45.9	62.6	16.7
Some college	3,805	53.2	72.1	19.0	3,749	53.4	69.9	16.5
College grad	2,960	58.9	80.5	21.6	2,932	58.9	79.6	20.7
Age 65–69								
< High school	3,340	18.2	44.1	25.9	3,232	18.3	41.9	23.6
High school	5,548	27.3	59.7	32.4	5,392	27.3	56.5	29.3
Some college	2,927	32.0	69.0	36.9	2,837	32.0	63.7	31.7
College grad	2,182	37.3	74.6	37.3	2,123	37.6	73.4	35.8
Age 70–74								
< High school	3,469	12.3	42.8	30.5	3,151	12.3	41.4	29.1
High school	5,575	15.9	57.0	41.1	5,131	15.8	53.8	38.0
Some college	2,710	20.7	66.5	45.8	2,494	20.4	60.8	40.4
College grad	1,927	22.3	70.4	48.0	1,800	22.8	70.4	47.7

Note: Actual percent working in all health and PVW models may differ due to differences in sample size.

Table 12.6A   Work capacity by education (single regression)

Education	Men, all health variables model				Men, PVW model			
	Obs.	Actual % working	Predicted % working	Estimated work capacity (%)	Obs.	Actual % working	Predicted % working	Estimated work capacity (%)
Age 55–59								
< High school	2,039	60.4	63.6	3.2	2,019	60.6	63.6	3.0
High school	3,891	71.9	76.8	4.9	3,864	71.9	76.3	4.4
Some college	3,122	75.9	79.1	3.2	3,104	75.9	79.0	3.1
College grad	3,349	84.9	88.9	4.0	3,344	84.9	88.4	3.5
Age 60–64								
< High school	2,384	46.6	63.6	17.0	2,367	46.8	62.7	16.0
High school	4,009	54.8	76.6	21.8	3,980	54.6	74.9	20.2
Some college	2,731	61.0	77.4	16.4	2,711	61.0	76.7	15.7
College grad	3,174	70.7	86.5	15.8	3,169	70.7	85.2	14.4
Age 65–69								
< High school	2,352	30.6	63.0	32.4	2,318	30.7	60.1	29.4
High school	3,665	35.0	73.4	38.3	3,631	34.8	70.2	35.4
Some college	2,076	38.6	73.5	34.9	2,059	38.9	71.5	32.7
College grad	2,628	52.1	81.7	29.5	2,612	52.1	79.0	26.9
Age 70–74								
< High school	2,556	19.9	59.2	39.2	2,302	20.1	57.4	37.2
High school	3,479	24.3	69.0	44.7	3,221	24.1	66.4	42.3
Some college	1,893	26.9	69.1	42.2	1,756	27.7	67.0	39.3
College grad	2,442	38.1	77.3	39.2	2,300	38.2	74.2	36.0

Note: Actual percent working in all health and PVW models may differ due to differences in sample size.

Table 12.6B   Work capacity by education (single regression)

Education	Women, all health variables model				Women, PVW model			
	Obs.	Actual % working	Predicted % working	Estimated work capacity (%)	Obs.	Actual % working	Predicted % working	Estimated work capacity (%)
Age 55–59								
< High school	3,314	41.2	47.0	5.8	3,296	41.2	46.8	5.6
High school	6,217	62.6	67.4	4.8	6,178	62.5	66.9	4.3
Some college	4,320	68.1	72.3	4.2	4,285	68.3	71.9	3.6
College grad	3,512	75.9	81.4	5.5	3,493	75.9	80.7	4.8
Age 60–64								
< High school	3,809	30.8	46.3	15.5	3,768	30.8	45.5	14.7
High school	6,579	45.9	65.2	19.3	6,515	45.9	63.4	17.5
Some college	3,805	53.2	70.8	17.6	3,749	53.4	69.0	15.6
College grad	2,960	58.9	80.5	21.6	2,932	58.9	78.1	19.2
Age 65–69								
< High school	3,340	18.2	45.7	27.4	3,232	18.3	43.4	25.1
High school	5,548	27.3	61.4	34.1	5,392	27.3	57.8	30.6
Some college	2,927	32.0	66.0	34.0	2,837	32.0	62.0	30.0
College grad	2,182	37.3	73.2	35.9	2,123	37.6	69.2	31.6
Age 70–74								
< High school	3,469	12.3	44.6	32.3	3,151	12.3	42.5	30.2
High school	5,575	15.9	58.8	42.9	5,131	15.8	55.3	39.5
Some college	2,710	20.7	63.5	42.8	2,494	20.4	59.0	38.6
College grad	1,927	22.3	69.2	46.9	1,800	22.8	65.2	42.4

Note: Actual percent working in all health and PVW models may differ due to differences in sample size.

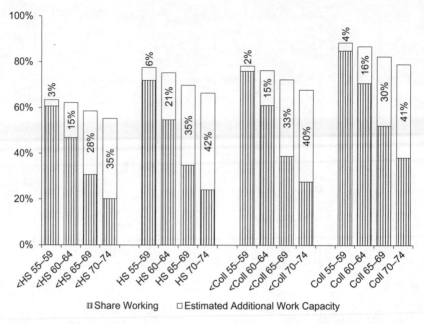

Fig. 12.11 Share of HRS men working and additional work capacity by age and education

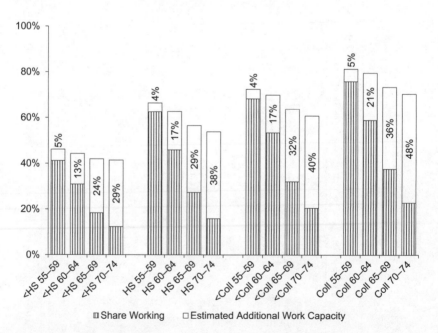

Fig. 12.12 Share of HRS women working and additional work capacity by age and education

Table 12.7   **Years of additional employment capacity, ages fifty-five to sixty-nine**

	Men		Women	
	All health variable model	PVW index model	All health variable model	PVW index model
All	2.8	2.6	2.8	2.5
By education (separate regressions)				
< High school	2.7	2.3	2.3	2.1
High school	3.4	3.1	2.8	2.5
Some college	2.6	2.5	3.0	2.6
College grad	2.7	2.5	3.2	3.1
By education (single regression)				
< High school	2.6	2.4	2.4	2.3
High school	3.3	3.0	2.9	2.6
Some college	2.7	2.6	2.8	2.5
College grad	2.5	2.2	3.1	2.8

Note: Calculated using estimated work capacity by age (at ages fifty-five to fifty-nine, sixty to sixty-four, and sixty-five to sixty-nine) from tables 12.4, 12.5A, 12.5B, 12.6A, and 12.6B.

with no differences in estimated work capacity by level of education for men but greater estimated capacity to work among more educated women.

12.4   Changes in Self-Assessed Health by Education Level over Time

We undertake one final analysis to explore potential heterogeneity in health capacity. Several recent studies, including Waldron (2007), Bosworth and Burke (2014), and National Academies of Sciences (2015), find that life expectancy has been growing more rapidly over time for high-income groups than for low-income groups. Is the same true for other key health measures such as self-assessed health (SAH)? In this section of the chapter, we aim to explore how SAH has evolved over time for those with different levels of socioeconomic status (SES).

To explore such a question, one first needs a measure of SES that can be found in a data set with information on health over a long period of time. In theory, lifetime income (used by Waldron [2007] and others in studies of mortality) is an attractive measure, but most health data sets will at best have current income, which may be only loosely related to lifetime income, especially for older individuals, many of whom have retired. Education thus may be preferred as a measure that is both widely available and highly correlated with lifetime income. However, using education introduces its own set of problems, as pointed out by Bound et al. (2014). Responding to Olshansky et al. (2012), who estimate that white male high school dropouts experienced sharply decreasing life expectancy over the period 1990 to 2008, Bound et al. counter that this finding can arise from ignoring rising levels of education

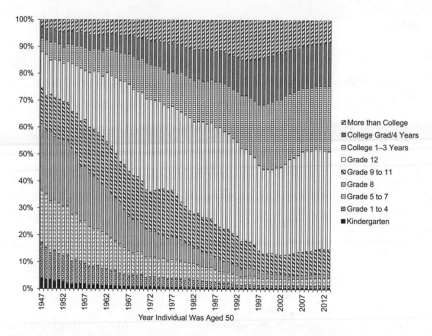

Fig. 12.13   Distribution of educational attainment by cohort for men (by year cohort attained age fifty)

over time. As more recent cohorts have far fewer high school dropouts than past cohorts, individuals in recent cohorts who are high school dropouts may be more negatively selected relative to high school dropouts in earlier cohorts. Failing to account for this can generate misleading results. Bound et al. suggest correcting for this by using education quartiles, which provide consistent groups to analyze over time (as the lowest quartile of education is always the lowest quartile, whether dominated by those with an 8th grade education or high school graduates).

We implement this suggestion and estimate trends in SAH by education quartile. Figure 12.13 shows the distribution of educational attainment for men by birth cohort. For cohorts reaching age fifty in 1950 (born in 1900), the median individual had an 8th grade education and about 70 percent of individuals had less than a high school education. Thereafter, educational attainment rises rapidly. By 1965, the median fifty-year-old is a high school graduate, and by 1996, the median fifty-year-old has some college. Since the late 1990s, however, there is some evidence of a reversal in this trend.

Figure 13 may be used to illustrate how the education quartiles are defined. For the 1950 cohort of fifty-year-olds, for example, the lowest quartile includes all of those with a kindergarten to grade 4 education. The group with grade 5 to 7 education extends beyond the first quartile, so we randomly sample from among this group to fully populate the lowest quartile. The next quartile includes the rest of the grade 5 to 7 group and most of the grade 8 group, again using random sampling to determine which will be allocated to the 2nd education quartile and which to the 3rd. The 3rd quartile largely consists of the rest of the grade 8 group, all those with grade 9 to 11 education, and about half of the high school graduates, while the top quartile includes the rest of the high school graduates and everyone with some college or more education. In the 2000 cohort of fifty-year-olds, the lowest quartile includes some high school graduates and everyone with less than high school, while the top quartile includes most of the college graduates and everyone with graduate education. The key point is that the educational composition of the population changes substantially over time, so we focus on education quartiles to have a consistent measure of the less and more educated. The trends for women, shown in figure 12.14, are fairly similar, with women having somewhat more high school graduates in the early years and a leveling off rather than retrenchment in educational attainment in recent years.

In figure 12.15, we plot the share of men who report themselves to be in fair or poor health by age for three different time periods, 1972–85, 1986–95, and 1996–2013, reporting results separately by education quartile. The data for these figures comes from the National Health Interview Survey, and data is aggregated over many years for greater precision. The familiar negative relationship between age and health is evident from the figures, as is the fact that health is better among the higher education quartiles. What

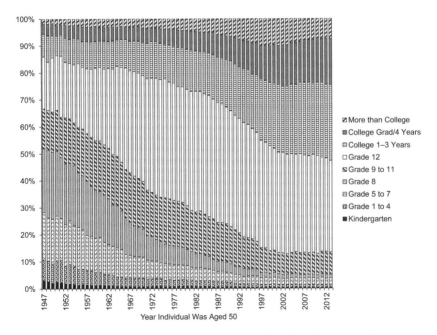

Fig. 12.14   Distribution of educational attainment by cohort for women (by year cohort attained age fifty)

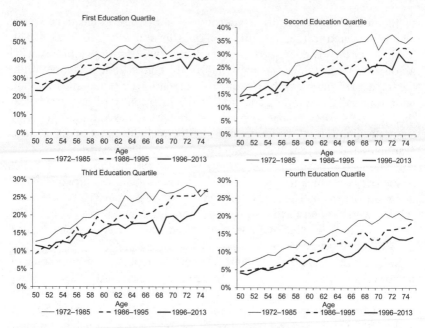

Fig. 12.15   Evolution of SAH by education quartile for men

interests us particularly is the evolution of SAH over time across education quartiles. We find that all quartiles experience improvements in health over time. However, as a percentage change from the 1972–85 values, the highest education group experiences the largest improvements in health over time, as reported in table 12.8. Averaging across ages fifty to seventy-five, the share of men in fair/poor health in the highest education quartile drops by 39 percent between the earliest and latest period, versus by 24 percent for the 3rd quartile, 23 percent for the 2nd quartile, and 19 percent for the 1st quartile. The pattern for women, shown in figure 12.16 and summarized in table 12.8, is similar—they experience a 34 percent average improvement in the top education quartile and a 15 percent improvement in the bottom quartile.

In sum, as other studies have found for life expectancy, gains in SAH appear to be accruing disproportionately to high SES individuals. Although there is no direct link to employment in this section of our analysis, these findings suggests that over time, it may be becoming easier for higher SES individuals to extend their work lives because their health is improving more rapidly than that of lower SES individuals.

12.5   Discussion and Conclusion

Possible future changes to Social Security and other programs that benefit the elderly are likely to include the expectation that people will work longer. Do older individuals have the health capacity to do so? In this chapter we

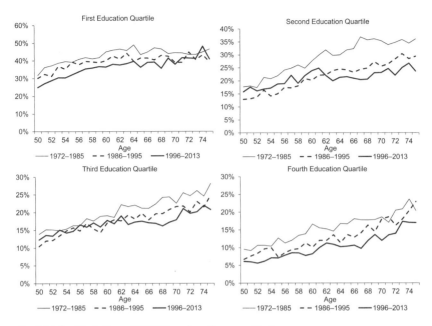

Fig. 12.16   Evolution of SAH by education quartile for women

Table 12.8   Average improvement in SAH at ages fifty to seventy-five by education quartile

	1st (%)	2nd (%)	3rd (%)	4th (%)
Men	19	23	24	39
Women	15	25	15	34

have explored this question using two methods. We first ask, if people with a given mortality rate today worked as much as those with the same mortality rate in the past, how much could they work? Next we ask, if older individuals with a given health status worked as much as their younger counterparts, how much could they work? Both methods suggest that there is substantial additional work capacity. Evaluating work capacity purely on the basis of health, our analysis suggests that the share of older men working at ages sixty to sixty-four could be 17–27 percentage points higher than it is today, while the share working at ages sixty-five to sixty-nine could be 31–42 percentage points higher; estimates for women are similar. Our analysis also implies that the average number of years worked between ages fifty-five and sixty-nine, currently 7.9, could rise by at least 2.5 years, even allowing for a portion of recent life expectancy increases to be channeled into leisure.

We find mixed evidence regarding the heterogeneity of work capacity, with greater work capacity among more educated women as compared to less educated women, but no such finding for men. We further find that gains in SAH over time, measured in percentage terms, have been concentrated among high-education groups. Although this finding is not linked directly to employment in our analysis, it suggests that more highly educated individuals may be finding it easier to extend their work lives.

As noted throughout the chapter, there are many assumptions and caveats that apply to our analysis, such as the concern that mortality may not be perfectly correlated with work ability or that we do not directly address the possible endogeneity of health. Nonetheless, our basic conclusion that most people are healthy enough to work longer than they do now seems likely to be sound. As illustrated in figure 12.1, although older men are working more than they used to, labor force participation rates today are still well below pre-1980 levels for fifty-five- to sixty-four-year-olds (and below pre-1970 levels for those sixty-five and above). This fact, along with the declines in mortality and poor health over time seen in figure 12.3, suggests that many people can work longer. The Milligan-Wise approach offers one way to quantify the additional work capacity that is suggested by these coincident trends in employment and health. Similarly, the summary statistics in table 8.2 show that employment declines rapidly as workers reach their sixties, while health declines steadily but quite gradually with age. The fact that health does not plummet along with employment suggests that there are reasons other than health for the employment decline, such as the availability of Social Security. The Cutler et al. approach offers a means to estimate how much of a decline in employment with age we might expect based solely on declining health. The exact values we estimate for potential increases in employment rates or years of work are less important than the overall conclusion that, using two very different approaches, we consistently find that individuals are healthy enough to work longer.

It is important to recall that our analysis does not address other factors that may affect workers' ability to work longer, such as cyclicality in labor demand or age discrimination, to the extent that these factors matter more for today's older workers than they did for workers with the same mortality rate in the past (Milligan-Wise method) or for younger workers (Cutler et al. method). It is also useful to recall that our work addresses the work capacity of the population overall, not that of any given individual. Even when the health of the population is improving, there will always be individuals that are too sick to work. It is important for policymakers to consider the needs of such individuals when making policy decisions—for example, by providing a well-designed disability insurance program. Finally, it is critical to reiterate that our estimates should not be taken as a reflection of how much older workers "should" work. As noted above, the Milligan-Wise method implicitly assumes that all life expectancy gains can be translated into additional years of work. This may not be the case, and even if it is possible it may not be a socially desirable outcome, since leisure time has value as well.

We intend for our analysis to contribute to the discussion about relatively modest changes to Social Security and related policies. Are older workers healthy enough to work another year or two if they must? We believe that for a majority of older workers our results suggest that the answer is yes.

References

Bosworth, B. P., and K. Burke. 2014. "Differential Mortality and Retirement Benefits in the Health and Retirement Study." Brookings Institution Working Paper. https://www.brookings.edu/research/differential-mortality-and-retirement -benefits-in-the-health-and-retirement-study/.

Bound, John, Arline Geronimus, Javier Rodriguez, and Timothy A. Waidmann. 2014. "The Implications of Differential Trends in Mortality for Social Security Policy." MCRR Working Paper no. 2014–314, Michigan Center for Retirement Research, University of Michigan.

Bound, John, and Timothy Waidmann. 2007. "Estimating the Health Effects of Retirement." MCRR Working Paper no. 2007–168, Michigan Retirement Research Center, University of Michigan.

Brown, Jeffrey R., Jeffrey B. Liebman, and Joshua Pollet. 2002. "Appendix: Estimating Life Tables That Reflect Socioeconomic Differences in Mortality." In *The Distributional Aspects of Social Security and Social Security Reform*, edited by Martin Feldstein and Jeffrey B. Liebman, 447–57. Chicago: University of Chicago Press.

Charles, Kerwin. 2004. "Is Retirement Depressing? Labor Force Inactivity and Psychological Well-Being in Later Life." *Research in Labor Economics* 23:269–99.

Congressional Budget Office. 2010. *Social Security Policy Options.* Washington, DC: Congressional Budget Office.

Crimmins, Eileen M., and Hiram Beltrán-Sánchez. 2010. "Mortality and Morbidity Trends: Is There Compression of Morbidity?" *Journal of Gerontology: Social Sciences* 66B (1): 75–86.

Crimmins, Eileen M., Mark D. Hayward, Aaron Hagedorn, Yasuhiko Saito, and Nicolas Brouard. 2009. "Changes in Disability-Free Life Expectancy for Americans 70 Years Old and Older." *Demography* 46 (3): 627–46.

Cutler, David M., Kaushik Ghosh, and Mary Beth Landrum. 2014. "Evidence for Significant Compression of Morbidity in the Elderly US Population." In *Discoveries in the Economics of Aging*, edited by David A. Wise. Chicago: University of Chicago Press.

Cutler, David M., Ellen Meara, and Seth Richards-Shubik. 2012. "Health and Work Capacity of Older Adults: Estimates and Implications for Social Security Policy." Unpublished Manuscript. Available at SSRN: http://ssrn.com/abstract=2577858.

Hellerstein, Judith K., David Neumark, and Kenneth R. Troske. 1999. "Wages, Productivity, and Worker Characteristics: Evidence from Plant-Level Production Functions and Wage Equations." *Journal of Labor Economics* 17 (3): 409–46.

Johnston, David W., and Wang-Sheng Lee. 2009. "Retiring to the Good Life? The Short-Term Effects of Retirement on Health." *Economic Letters* 103 (1): 8–11.

Lahey, Joanna N. 2008. "Age, Women, and Hiring: An Experimental Study." *Journal of Human Resources* 43 (1): 30–56.

Milligan, Kevin S., and David A. Wise. 2012a. "Health and Work at Older Ages: Using Mortality to Assess the Capacity to Work across Countries." NBER Working Paper no. 18229, Cambridge, MA.

———. 2012b. "Introduction and Summary." In *Social Security Programs and Retirement around the World: Historical Trends in Mortality and Health, Employment, and Disability Insurance Participation and Reforms*, edited by David A Wise. Chicago: University of Chicago Press.

Munnell, Alicia H. 2015. "The Average Retirement Age—An Update." Issue Brief no. 15-4, Center for Retirement Research at Boston College, March.

National Academies of Sciences, Engineering, and Medicine. 2015. *The Growing Gap in Life Expectancy by Income: Implications for Federal Programs and Policy Responses.* Report of the Committee on the Long-Run Macroeconomic Effects of the Aging US Population-Phase II. Washington, DC: The National Academies Press.

National Commission on Fiscal Responsibility and Reform. 2010. *The Moment of Truth: Report of the National Commission on Fiscal Responsibility and Reform.* Washington, DC: White House.

Neumark, David, Ian Burn, and Patrick Button. 2015. "Is It Harder for Older Workers to Find Jobs? New and Improved Evidence from a Field Experiment." NBER Working Paper no. 21669, Cambridge, MA.

Olshansky, S. Jay, Toni Antonucci, Lisa Berkman, Robert H. Binstock, Axel Börsch-Supan, John T. Cacioppo, Bruce A. Carnes, et al. 2012. "Differences in Life Expectancy Due to Race and Educational Differences are Widening and Many May Not Catch Up." *Health Affairs* 31 (8): 1803–13.

Poterba, James, Steve Venti, and David A. Wise. 2013. "Health, Education, and the Post-Retirement Evolution of Household Assets." NBER Working Paper no. 18695, Cambridge, MA.

Snyder, Stephen E., and William N. Evans. 2006. "The Effect of Income on Mortality: Evidence from the Social Security Notch." *Review of Economics and Statistics* 88 (3): 482–95.

Waldron, Hilary. 2007. "Trends in Mortality Differentials and Life Expectancy for Male Social Security-Covered Workers, by Socioeconomic Status." *Social Security Bulletin* 67 (3). https://www.ssa.gov/policy/docs/ssb/v67n3/v67n3p1.html.

Contributors

James Banks
Arthur Lewis Building-3.020
School of Social Sciences
The University of Manchester
Manchester M13 9PL
United Kingdom

Paul Bingley
SFI-The Danish National Centre for
    Social Research
Herluf Trolles Gade 11
1052 Copenhagen K
Denmark

Didier Blanchet
INSEE
15 Blvd Gabriel Peri BP 100
92244 Malakoff Cedex, France

Axel Börsch-Supan
Munich Center for the Economics of
    Aging
Max Planck Institute for Social Law
    and Social Policy
Amalienstrasse 33
80799 Munich
Germany

Agar Brugiavini
Dipartimento di Scienze Economiche
Universita' "Ca' Foscari" Venezia
Cannaregio, 873
30121 Venezia
Italy

Eve Caroli
PSL, University Paris Dauphine,
    LEDa-LEGOS,
Paris School of Economics and IZA
Place du Maréchal de Lattre de
    Tassigny
75775 Paris Cedex 16
France

Courtney Coile
Department of Economics
Wellesley College
106 Central Street
Wellesley, MA 02481

Klaas de Vos
CentERdata
Tilburg University
Warandelaan 2
5037 AB Tilburg
The Netherlands

Carl Emmerson
Institute for Fiscal Studies
7 Ridgmount Street
London WC1E 7AE
United Kingdom

Pilar García-Gómez
Erasmus School of Economics
Erasmus University Rotterdam
P.O. Box 1738
3000 DR Rotterdam
The Netherlands

Nabanita Datta Gupta
Department of Economics and
    Business Economics
Aarhus University
Fuglesangs Allé 4
8210 Aarhus V
Denmark

Sergi Jiménez-Martín
Universitat Pompeu Fabra
Ramon Trias Fargas 25–27
08005 Barcelona
Spain

Per Johansson
Department of Statistics
Uppsala University
Box 513
SE-751 20 Uppsala
Sweden

Alain Jousten
University of Liège
Law Faculty, Tax Institute and HEC-
    Liège
Place des Orateurs 3
Bât. B31
4000 Liège 1
Belgium

Hendrik Jürges
University of Wuppertal
Schumpeter School of Business and
    Economics
Rainer-Gruenter-Str. 21 [FN.01]
42119 Wuppertal
Germany

Adriaan Kalwij
Department of Economics
Utrecht University
Kriekenpitplein 21–22
3584 EC Utrecht
The Netherlands

Arie Kapteyn
Center for Economic and Social
    Research
University of Southern California
635 Downey Way
Los Angeles, CA 90089–3332

Lisa Laun
Institute for Evaluation of Labour
    Market and Education Policy
    (IFAU)
Box 513
SE-751 20 Uppsala
Sweden

Mathieu Lefebvre
Bureau d'Economie Théorique et
    Appliquée (BETA)
University of Strasbourg
UMR 7522 du CNRS
61, avenue de la Forêt Noire
67085 Strasbourg
France

Kevin Milligan
Vancouver School of Economics
University of British Columbia
6000 Iona Drive
Vancouver, British Columbia
V6T 1L4 Canada

Takashi Oshio
Institute of Economic Research
Hitotsubashi University
2–1 Naka, Kunitachi
Tokyo 186–8603 Japan

Mårten Palme
Department of Economics
Stockholm University
SE-106 91 Stockholm
Sweden

Giacomo Pasini
Dipartimento di Scienze Economiche
Universita' "Ca' Foscari" Venezia
Cannaregio, 873
30121 Venezia
Italy

Peder J. Pedersen
Department of Economics and
    Business Economics
Aarhus University
Fuglesangs Allé 4
8210 Aarhus V
Denmark

Corinne Prost
INSEE- CREST
15 Blvd. Gabriel Péri BP 100
92214 Malakoff Cedex
France

Muriel Roger
CES Université Paris 1 Panthéon-
    Sorbonne
106 Blvd de l'Hôpital75013
Paris, France

Tammy Schirle
Department of Economics
Wilfrid Laurier University
75 University Avenue West
Waterloo, Ontario
N2L 3C5 Canada

Satoshi Shimizutani
Ricoh Institute of Sustainability and
    Business
Ricoh Company, Ltd.
Marunouchi Kitaguchi Bldg 20th fl.
    1–6-5
Marunouchi, Chiyoda-ku
Tokyo 100–0005 Japan

Gemma Tetlow
Institute for Fiscal Studies
7 Ridgmount Street
WC1E 7AE London
United Kingdom

Lars Thiel
University of Wuppertal
Rainer-Gruenter-Str. 21
(FN) 42119 Wuppertal
Germany

Emiko Usui
Institute of Economic Research
Hitotsubashi University
Kunitachi
Tokyo 186–8603 Japan

Judit Vall Castelló
Centre for Research in Health and
    Economics
Universitat Pompeu Fabra
Ramon Trias Fargas 25–27
08005 Barcelona
Spain

Guglielmo Weber
University of Padua
Dipartimento di Scienze Economiche
Via del Santo 33
35123 Padova
Italy

David A. Wise
NBER
1050 Massachusetts Avenue
Cambridge, MA 02138

Author Index

Note: Page numbers followed by "f" refer to figures.

Alessie, R., 265
Aliaj, A., 52
Alt, B., 150
Aragón, J., 272
Au, D. W. H., 62
Aubert, P., 139

Bago d'Uva, T., 125
Banks, J., 331, 332, 334, 337, 340
Bassanini, A., 137
Behaghel, L., 131
Beltrán-Sánchez, H., 367
Benítez-Silva, H., 339
Bingley, P., 86
Blanchflower, D. G., 164
Bloemen, H., 265
Blundell, R., 340
Bohacek, R., 201
Boldrin, M., 270, 271, 272
Börsch-Supan, A., 101, 150, 158, 162
Bosworth, B. P., 79, 387
Bound, J., 26, 60, 79, 166, 171, 259, 262, 332, 360, 373n2, 387
Brønnum-Hansen, H., 96
Brown, J. R., 381n5
Brugiavini, A., 181, 182
Bucher-Koenen, T., 150
Burke, K., 79, 387
Burn, I., 31, 360
Button, P., 31, 360

Cambois, E., 130
Caroli, E., 137, 139
Carriere, Y., 79
Case, A., 132
Cervini-Pla, M., 270
Chandler, D., 340, 353
Chandola, T., 332
Charles, K., 373n2
Christensen, K., 95
Coe, N., 265
Coile, C. C., 32, 69
Congregado, E., 272
Coppola, M., 150
Crimmins, E. M., 367
Crossley, T. F., 62
Cuadrado, P., 272
Cutler, D. M., 6, 42, 55, 60, 69, 87, 101, 113, 117, 130, 134, 138, 161, 182, 191, 201, 236, 244, 270, 281, 290, 296, 299, 302, 314, 326, 331, 334, 336n4, 340, 346, 360, 367, 371

Datta Gupta, N., 86
De la Fuente, L., 272
Dellis, A., 35
Desmet, R., 35
Desmette, D., 36
De Vos, K., 243
Disney, R., 337, 339

Emmerson, C., 340
Etilé, F., 125
Euwals, R., 243
Evans, W. N., 373n2

Flores, M., 259
Frey, C. B., 139

Galarneau, D., 79
García-Gómez, P., 270, 272
Ghosh, K., 367
Goldman, D. P., 170
Golpe, A. A., 272
Groot, W., 166
Gruber, J., 1, 2, 4, 20, 243, 270, 337, 338

Hansen, G., 97, 97f
Hellerstein, J. K., 360
Hochguertel, S., 265

Jiménez-Martin, S., 270, 271, 272, 339
Johansson, P., 314
Johnston, D., 125
Jousten, A., 35, 36, 36n1, 54
Jürges, H., 64, 153, 155, 158, 167, 171, 275

Kalwij, A., 243, 259, 265
Kapteyn, A., 243, 338
Kemptner, D., 153
Klijs, B., 273
Knoef, M., 265
Kuhn, A., 265

Lahey, J. N., 31, 360
Landrum, M. B., 367
Lanzieri, G., 269
Larsen, M., 89
Laun, L., 301, 314
Lefebvre, M., 35, 36
Levine, P. B., 32
Liebman, J. B., 381n5
Lindebloom, M., 125
Lleras-Muney, A., 296, 336n4
Lochner, L., 170

Mackenbach, J. P., 170, 273
Maestas, N., 246
Mathers, C. D., 95
Matthews, K., 332
Meara, E., 6, 42, 55, 60, 69, 87, 101, 113, 117, 130, 134, 161, 182, 191, 201, 244, 270, 281, 290, 299, 302, 314, 326, 331, 334, 340, 346, 360, 371
Milan, A., 63
Milcent, C., 125
Milligan, K. S., 6, 13, 24, 38, 39, 54, 59n1, 63, 69, 87, 90, 155, 158, 182, 186, 201, 244, 270, 274, 275, 290, 299, 302, 306, 326, 331, 340, 360, 364, 365
Munnell, A. H., 363

Neumark, D., 31, 360
Nusselder, W., 273

Oishi, A. S., 220, 222
Olsen, H., 97, 97f
Olshansky, S. J., 387
Osborne, M. A., 139
Oshio, T., 220, 222, 240
Oswald, A. J., 164

Palme, M., 314
Paxson, C., 132
Pedersen, P. J., 86, 89
Peracchi, F., 181, 182, 270, 271, 272
Perelman, S., 35
Pollet, J., 381n5
Poterba, J., 14, 43, 46, 69, 102, 131, 164, 192, 229, 253, 284, 315, 347, 372
Propper, C., 125

Rausch, J., 150
Reinhold, S., 153, 171
Richards-Shubik, S., 6, 42, 43, 55, 60, 69, 87, 101, 113, 117, 130, 134, 161, 182, 191, 201, 244, 270, 281, 290, 299, 302, 314, 326, 331, 334, 340, 347, 360, 371
Robine, J. M., 130
Rocha, F., 272
Roger, M., 139

Salanauskaite, L., 36n1, 54
Salm, M., 171
Schellhorn, M., 62
Schirle, T., 59n1, 61, 62, 64
Schreurs, B., 36
Shields, M., 125
Shimizutani, S., 220, 222, 240
Siegel, M., 171
Sieurin, A., 130
Smith, J. P., 170, 338
Snyder, S. E., 373n2

Sullivan, D. F., 95, 96
Sundmacher, L., 171

Tetlow, G., 340, 353
Troske, K. R., 360
Tubeuf, S., 125

Usui, E., 240

Vall Castelló, J., 270, 272
Van Doorslaer, E., 125
Van Looy, D., 36
Van Soest, A., 338
Van Stel, A., 272
Vendramin, P., 36
Venti, S., 14, 43, 46, 69, 102, 131, 164, 192, 229, 253, 284, 315, 347, 372
Vézina, M., 63
Vogt, V., 171

Waidmann, T., 373n2
Waldron, H., 23, 79, 387
Webb, S., 337
Whitehouse, E. R., 86
Wise, D. A., 1, 2, 4, 6, 14, 20, 24, 38, 39, 46, 54, 63, 69, 86, 87, 90, 102, 113, 131, 155, 158, 164, 182, 186, 192, 201, 229, 243, 244, 253, 270, 274, 275, 284, 290, 299, 302, 306, 315, 326, 331, 338, 340, 347, 360, 364, 365, 372
Wolfson, M., 79
Wong, I., 63
Wuellrich, J. P., 265

Zamarro, G., 265
Zissimopoulos, J., 246
Zweerink, J., 265
Zweimueller, J., 265

Subject Index

Note: Page numbers followed by "f" or "t" refer to figures or tables, respectively.

Ability to work, 36–38, 54
ADLs (activities of daily living), 373–77, 373n4
Age, school-leaving, 332, 333f
"Arduous jobs" discussion, 36

Belgium: CMR method for, 42–54; debate over work-capacity issues in, 36; employment regressions for, 46–47, 46t; employment vs. mortality rates for men, 39–40, 39f, 42f; literature on link between health and work capacity, 36; men's employment rate in, 37f; MW method for, 38–42, 54–55; PVW index for, 46–47; SAH and mortality for men by age group in, 38f; summary statistics using SHARE data, 44t, 45t; women's employment rate in, 37f

Canada: changes in self-assessed health by education level over time for, 79–81; employment regressions by health variables for, 73–74, 73t; employment regressions by PVW health index, 73t, 74; estimating health capacity to work using Cutler et al. method, 69–78; estimating health capacity to work using MW method, 63–69; health and longevity in, introduction to, 59–61; labor force participation and health trends in, 61–62; men's labor force participation (ages fifty-five to sixty-five) in, 61f; summary statistics for, 71–72, 71t, 72t; women's labor force participation (ages fifty-five to sixty-five) in, 62f

Canadian Community Health Survey (CCHS), 70, 70n8, 70n9

Capacity to work: estimated additional, for men, by country, 18–21, 19–20f; estimated additional, for women, by country, 21–22f, 21–23; estimates of additional, 15–23. *See also* Health capacity to work

CCHS (Canadian Community Health Survey), 70, 70n8, 70n9

CMR method. *See* Cutler et al. (CMR) method

Cutler, Meara, and Richards-Shubik method. *See* Cutler et al. (CMR) method

Cutler et al. (CMR) method, 7; estimating health capacity to work using, for Belgium, 42–54, 55; estimating health capacity to work using, for Canada, 69–78; estimating health capacity to work using, for Denmark, 87; estimating health capacity to work using, for Italy, 191–205; estimating health capacity to work using, for Japan, 220–21, 228–39; estimating health capacity to

Cutler et al. (CMR) method (*continued*)
work using, for Spain, 281–96; estimating health capacity to work using,
for Sweden, 302, 314–19; estimating
health capacity to work using, for the
Netherlands, 244, 251–62; estimating health capacity to work using, for
United Kingdom, 331–32, 334, 346–54;
estimating health capacity to work
using, for United States, 371–87; predicting capacity to work using, 15–23,
16t; steps involved in, 14–15. *See also*
Health capacity to work; Milligan-Wise
(MW) method

Denmark: labor force participation and
health trends in, 88–90, 88f, 89f; life expectancies after pensionable age in, 86;
old age pension system in, 86; SAH and
employment by age over time for, 96–
101; using Cutler et al. method for, 87;
using MW method for, 87; work capacity estimates based on historical mortality for, 90–96; work capacity estimates based on self-assessed health for,
101–8

Education: changes in SAH and, for
Canada, 79–81; changes in SAH and,
for United States, 387–90; changes in
SAH by, for men in United Kingdom,
28, 29f; changes in SAH by, over time
for Italy, 205–7; changes in SAH by,
over time for Spain, 296–98; changes in
SAH by, over time for Sweden, 319–25;
changes in self-reported morbidity by,
over time for Germany, 171–73; distribution of, for men in United States, 26,
26f; evolution of SAH by, for men in
France, 27–28, 28f; evolution of SAH
by, for men in Germany, 28–29, 30f;
health capacity to work and, for United
States, 360, 381–87, 382–85t, 386f;
SAH by, for France, 125–27
ELSA (English Longitudinal Study of Ageing), 15, 346–47
Employment of men ages sixty to sixty-four,
4–6, 5t, 6f
Employment rates, in ISS countries, 4
English Longitudinal Study of Ageing
(ELSA), 15, 346–47
Estimates of additional capacity to work,
15–23

France: Cutler et al. method for, 113–14,
130–36, 130–37; employment rates
since 1975 in, 111–13, 112f; employment vs. mortality over time in, 114–15,
115f; evolution of SAH by education
for men in, 27–28, 28f; heterogeneity in
mortality-based work capacity, managers and professionals vs. blue collars,
118–21, 119f, 120f; issues raised by
Cutler et al. approach for, 136–37;
labor force attachment of older workers in, 111–13; measuring mortality-
based work capacity for, 115–16, 116f;
MW method based on SAH for, 127–
30; MW method for, 113–22; SAH
trends by education in, 125–27; SAH
trends over time in, 122–25

Germany: at beginning of 1972 reform of
pension system, 154; changes in self-
reported morbidity by education level
over time for, 171–73; estimating work
capacity using health changes across
age groups for, 161–71; estimating
work capacity using long-term changes
in morbidity for, 160–61; estimating
work capacity using long-term changes
in mortality for, 155–60; evolution of
SAH by education for men in, 28–29,
30f; health capacity to work in, introduction to, 149–51; labor force participation trends in, 151, 152–55; mortality
rates in, 152–54, 152f, 153f; PVW index
for, 165–68; SHARE summary statistics for, 162–65, 163t, 164t, 165t; trends
in mortality, morbidity, and labor force
participation at older ages in, 152–55

Health: estimated relationship between employment and, 15, 16–17t; facets of
measuring, 331–32; using mortality as
indicator of, 340–46
Health and Retirement Study (HRS), 14–15.
See also Self-assessed health (SAH)
Health capacity to work, 3–4; approaches
for evaluating, 6–7; estimating, for
Germany, 155–71; estimating, using
Cutler et al. method, for Canada,
69–78; estimating, using Cutler et al.
method, for Sweden, 314–19; estimating, using MW method, for Canada,
63–69; estimating, using MW method,
for Italy, 186–90; estimating, using MW

method, for Sweden, 306–14; in Germany, 149–51; prediction of, 15–23; in United Kingdom, 333–34; using Cutler et al. method, for Italy, 191–205; using Cutler et al. method, for Japan, 228–29; using MW method, for Italy, 186–90; using MW method, for Japan, 223–28. *See also* Capacity to work; Cutler et al. (CMR) method; Milligan-Wise (MW) method

Health index. *See* PVW (Poterba, Venti, and Wise) index

Health indicator data sets, using, for health capacity to work, 346–54

HRS (Health and Retirement Study), 14–15

IADLs (instrumental activities of daily living), 373–77, 373n4

International Social Security (ISS) project, 1; findings of prior phases of, 1–2; researchers participating in, 2–3. *See also* Seventh phase of ISS project

ISS project. *See* International Social Security (ISS) project

Italy: changes in SAH by education level over time for, 205–7; employment regression estimates for, 195–201, 196t, 197t; estimating health capacity to work using Cutler et al. method, 191–205; estimating health capacity to work using MW method, 186–90; health capacity of older workers in, 182–83; obstacles to longer working lives in, 182; population aging in, 181–82; summary statistics for, 192–95, 193t, 194t; trends in labor force participation and health in, 183–86; trends in SAH for men age fifty to seventy-five, 185–86, 185f

Japan: debate on pensionable age in, 219–20; estimating health capacity to work using Cutler et al. method, 228–39; estimating health capacity to work using MW method, 223–28; estimating work capacity of older workers in, 220–21; labor force participation and health trends for, 221–23

Labor force participation trends: for Canada, 61–62, 61f, 62f; for Denmark, 88–90, 88f, 89f; in Germany, 151; for Italy, 183–86, 184f; for Japan, 221–23;

for the Netherlands, 245–48; for Spain, 270–74; for United States, 361–64

Milligan-Wise (MW) method, 7–14, 13t; assumptions about morality and, 309; based on SAH, 127–30; for employment vs. mortality of men in eleven countries, 9, 10–12f; estimating health capacity to work using, for Belgium, 38–42, 54–55; estimating health capacity to work using, for Canada, 63–69; estimating health capacity to work using, for Denmark, 87; estimating health capacity to work using, for Italy, 186–90; estimating health capacity to work using, for Japan, 220–21, 223–28; estimating health capacity to work using, for United States, 7–9, 8f, 9f, 364–71; estimating health capacity to work using, in Spain, 274–81; estimating health capacity to work using, in Sweden, 302, 306–14; estimating health capacity to work using, in the Netherlands, 244, 248–51; estimating health capacity to work using, in United Kingdom, 333–34, 340–46; limitations of, 116–17; years of additional work capacity for men at ages fifty-five to sixty-nine with, 9. *See also* Cutler et al. (CMR) method; Health capacity to work

Morbidity: changes in self-reported, by education level over time for Germany, 171–73; estimating work capacity for Germany using long-term changes in, 160–61

Mortality: assumptions about, and MW method, 309; estimating work capacity for Germany using long-term changes in, 155–60; as indicator of health, in United Kingdom, 340–46; reasons for using, for ability to work, 364–65; work capacity estimates based on historical, for Denmark, 90–96

MW method. *See* Milligan-Wise (MW) method

Netherlands, the: combination of methods for examining work capacity in, 262–64; Cutler et al. method for examining work capacity in, 251–62; data used for work capacity at older ages for, 244–45; estimating work capacity using Cutler

Netherlands, the (*continued*)
    et al. method for, 244; estimating work
    capacity using MW method for, 244;
    historical trends in employment and
    health for, 245–48; MW method for ex-
    amining work capacity in, 248–51;
    older male employment rates in, 243;
    pension policy reforms in, 243–44

PVW (Poterba, Venti, and Wise) index, 14,
    16–17t, 43–47, 46t, 192, 319, 372; for
    Germany, 165–68

SAH. *See* Self-assessed health (SAH)
School-leaving age, 332, 333f
Self-assessed health (SAH): changes in,
    by education level and time, in Spain,
    296–98; changes in, by education level
    and time, in Sweden, 319–25; changes
    in, by education level over time, in Italy,
    205–7; changes in, by education level
    over time, in United States, 387–90;
    and employment by age over time, for
    Denmark, 96–101; introduction to, 7,
    23–29; and mortality by age for men
    in United States, 23–24, 23f; trends
    in, for France, 122–30; trends in, for
    Japan, 222–23; work capacity estimates
    based on, for Denmark, 101–8. *See also*
    Health
Seventh phase of ISS project: introduction
    to, 3–7; researchers participating in,
    2–3. *See also* International Social Secu-
    rity (ISS) project
SHARE. *See* Survey of Health and Retire-
    ment in Europe (SHARE)
SLID (Survey of Labour and Income
    Dynamics), 79, 79n11
Spain: changes in self-assessed health by
    education level over time in, 296–98;
    demographic trends in, 269–70; esti-
    mating health capacity to work using
    Cutler et al. method, 281–96; estimat-
    ing health capacity to work using MW
    method for, 274–81; trends in labor
    force participation and health, 270–74
Survey of Health and Retirement in Europe
    (SHARE), 14, 43; Italy, 191; the
    Netherlands, 251; summary statistics,
    44–45t
Survey of Labour and Income Dynamics
    (SLID), 79, 79n11
Sweden: changes in self-assessed health by

education level over time in, 319–25;
    estimating health capacity to work
    using Cutler et al. method, 302, 314–
    19; estimating health capacity to work
    using MW method, 302, 306–14; retire-
    ment policy initiatives in, 301–2; trends
    in labor force participation and health
    in, 303–6
Swedish Level of Living Survey (LNU),
    304–6

United Kingdom: additional work capacity
    in, 333–34; change in SAH vs. change
    in mortality in, 24, 25f; changes in
    health and employment rates over time
    in, 334–40; Cutler et al. method for ex-
    amining work capacity in, 331–32, 334,
    346–54; evolution of SAH by educa-
    tion for men in, 28, 29f; MW method
    for examining work capacity in, 331–
    34, 340–46; policy debates on increas-
    ing employment rates of older people
    in, 329–30
United States: changes in self-assessed
    health by education level over time in,
    387–90; Cutler et al. method for study
    of health capacity to work, 360–61,
    371–87; distribution of education for
    men in, 26, 26f; estimated additional
    work capacity for men in, by age, 15–
    18, 18f; evolution of SAH by education
    for men in, 26–27, 27f; findings on
    health capacity to work at older ages
    for, 360–61, 371; healthy capacity to
    extend working lives of Americans,
    introduction to, 359–60; MW method
    for study of health capacity to work,
    360–61, 364–71; SAH and mortality by
    age for men in, 23–24, 23f; SAH by age
    for men in, 24–26, 25f; trends in labor
    force participation and health in, 361–
    64; trends in mortality and health for,
    363–64, 364f; using MW method for,
    7–9; work capacity by education group
    for, 381–87, 382–85t, 386f

Work: ability to, 36–38, 54; determinants of
    being able to, 330. *See also* Capacity to
    work; Health capacity to work
Work capacity. *See* Capacity to work;
    Health capacity to work
Working lives, impediments to longer, 359–
    60. *See also* Health capacity to work